Advanced Sciences and Technologies for Security Applications

Series Editor

Anthony J. Masys, Associate Professor, Director of Global Disaster Management, Humanitarian Assistance and Homeland Security, University of South Florida, Tampa, USA

Advisory Editors

Gisela Bichler, California State University, San Bernardino, CA, USA

Thirimachos Bourlai, Lane Department of Computer Science and Electrical Engineering, Multispectral Imagery Lab (MILab), West Virginia University, Morgantown, WV, USA

Chris Johnson, University of Glasgow, Glasgow, UK

Panagiotis Karampelas, Hellenic Air Force Academy, Attica, Greece

Christian Leuprecht, Royal Military College of Canada, Kingston, ON, Canada

Edward C. Morse, University of California, Berkeley, CA, USA

David Skillicorn, Queen's University, Kingston, ON, Canada

Yoshiki Yamagata, National Institute for Environmental Studies, Tsukuba, Ibaraki, Japan

Indexed by SCOPUS

The series Advanced Sciences and Technologies for Security Applications comprises interdisciplinary research covering the theory, foundations and domain-specific topics pertaining to security. Publications within the series are peer-reviewed monographs and edited works in the areas of:

- biological and chemical threat recognition and detection (e.g., biosensors, aerosols, forensics)
- crisis and disaster management
- terrorism
- cyber security and secure information systems (e.g., encryption, optical and photonic systems)
- traditional and non-traditional security
- energy, food and resource security
- economic security and securitization (including associated infrastructures)
- transnational crime
- human security and health security
- social, political and psychological aspects of security
- recognition and identification (e.g., optical imaging, biometrics, authentication and verification)
- smart surveillance systems
- applications of theoretical frameworks and methodologies (e.g., grounded theory, complexity, network sciences, modelling and simulation)

Together, the high-quality contributions to this series provide a cross-disciplinary overview of forefront research endeavours aiming to make the world a safer place.

The editors encourage prospective authors to correspond with them in advance of submitting a manuscript. Submission of manuscripts should be made to the Editor-in-Chief or one of the Editors.

More information about this series at http://www.springer.com/series/5540

Margaret E. Kosal
Editor

Proliferation of Weapons- and Dual-Use Technologies

Diplomatic, Information, Military, and Economic Approaches

Editor
Margaret E. Kosal
Sam Nunn School of International Affairs
Georgia Institute of Technology
Atlanta, GA, USA

ISSN 1613-5113 ISSN 2363-9466 (electronic)
Advanced Sciences and Technologies for Security Applications
ISBN 978-3-030-73654-5 ISBN 978-3-030-73655-2 (eBook)
https://doi.org/10.1007/978-3-030-73655-2

© The Editor(s) (if applicable) and The Author(s), under exclusive license to Springer Nature Switzerland AG 2021
This work is subject to copyright. All rights are solely and exclusively licensed by the Publisher, whether the whole or part of the material is concerned, specifically the rights of translation, reprinting, reuse of illustrations, recitation, broadcasting, reproduction on microfilms or in any other physical way, and transmission or information storage and retrieval, electronic adaptation, computer software, or by similar or dissimilar methodology now known or hereafter developed.
The use of general descriptive names, registered names, trademarks, service marks, etc. in this publication does not imply, even in the absence of a specific statement, that such names are exempt from the relevant protective laws and regulations and therefore free for general use.
The publisher, the authors and the editors are safe to assume that the advice and information in this book are believed to be true and accurate at the date of publication. Neither the publisher nor the authors or the editors give a warranty, expressed or implied, with respect to the material contained herein or for any errors or omissions that may have been made. The publisher remains neutral with regard to jurisdictional claims in published maps and institutional affiliations.

This Springer imprint is published by the registered company Springer Nature Switzerland AG
The registered company address is: Gewerbestrasse 11, 6330 Cham, Switzerland

Contents

Introduction 1
Margaret E. Kosal

The Potential Impact of Video Manipulation and Fraudulent Simulation Technology on Political Stability 3
Shane Jacobeen

Artificial Intelligence: Unpacking Political, Rhetorical, and Security Factors 17
Margaret E. Kosal

The Impacts of Proliferation and Autonomy of Small Unmanned Aircraft Systems on Security 33
Tejas G. Puranik

Development and Proliferation of Flexible and Wearable Electronics: Opportunities and Challenges for National Security 53
Federico Pulvirenti

Assessment of Potential Security Threats from Advances in Neurotechnology 77
Sathya Balachander

The Future of Chemical Warfare: How Urbanization and Proliferation of Delivery Mechanisms Create the Need for In-Situ Defense 93
Colton M. Moran

Dragonflies in the African Bush: Security Ramifications of Low-Cost Light Attack/Air Reconnaissance Aircraft Proliferation and the Chinese Aviation Industry 111
Christopher Long

Exploring the Spread of Offensive Cyber Operations Campaigns 133
Holly M. Dragoo

The Interplay Between Frugal Science and Chemical and Biological Weapons: Investigating the Proliferation Risks of Technology Intended for Humanitarian, Disaster Response, and International Development Efforts 153
Michael Tennenbaum and Margaret E. Kosal

Military Aid and Innovation 205
Rana O. Shabb

The Impact of Displaced Persons on National Security 231
Alaina Totten

Data Driven Review of Health Security Adoption in 95 Countries 253
Judy Kruger

Analyzing the Threat, Vulnerability, and Consequences of Agroterrorism 279
Olufunke Adebola

Contributors

Olufunke Adebola Georgia Institute of Technology, Atlanta, GA, USA

Sathya Balachander UAB, Birmingham, USA

Holly M. Dragoo Georgia Institute of Technology, Atlanta, Georgia

Shane Jacobeen Atlanta, Georgia

Margaret E. Kosal Georgia Institute of Technology, Atlanta, Georgia

Judy Kruger Atlanta, GA, USA

Christopher Long Georgia Institute of Technology, Atlanta, GA, USA

Colton M. Moran Georgia Institute of Technology, Atlanta, GA, US

Federico Pulvirenti Georgia Institute of Technology, Atlanta, Georgia

Tejas G. Puranik Georgia Institute of Technology, Atlanta, GA, USA

Rana O. Shabb Georgia Institute of Technology, Atlanta, Georgia

Michael Tennenbaum Georgia Institute of Technology, Atlanta, Georgia

Alaina Totten Georgia Institute of Technology, Atlanta, Georgia

Introduction

Margaret E. Kosal

The rapid pace of technological evolution in diplomatic, information, military, and economic sectors has contributed to a dynamic international policy environment. Global political stability is greatly influenced by innovations originating from numerous sources, including university labs, the technology sector, and military research. Collectively, these innovations guide the movement of people, ideas and technology that in turn affect the international balance of power. The objective of this volume is to develop new insights into how the proliferation of innovative ideas, low-cost weapons, and dual-use technologies will impact the changing global security landscape.

Innovative and dual-use technologies are often appropriated or employed for nefarious purposes by hostile military powers and non-state actors alike. Such actions threaten global security and stability, and may compromise the comparative technological advantage enjoyed by some states. As the complexity of technological innovations continues to increase, existing control mechanisms such as international regulations and security arrangements may be insufficient to stem the tide of proliferation over time. As such, this volumes seeks to explore factors affecting and to propose policy solutions to curtail the threat to global stability posed by the inevitable proliferation of weapons and dual-use technology.

Future trend analysis is a tricky task. Colin Gray said, "Trend spotting is easy. It is the guessing as to the probable meaning and especially the consequences of trends that is the real challenge [1]." How, when, where, and in what form the shifting nature of technological progress may bring enhanced or entirely new capabilities, many of which are no longer the exclusive domain of the United States, is contested and requires better analytical tools to enable assessment. Contemporary analyses of these emerging technologies often expose the tenuous links or disconnections among

M. E. Kosal (✉)
Georgia Institute of Technology, Atlanta, Georgia
e-mail: margaret.kosal@inta.gatech.edu

© The Author(s), under exclusive license to Springer Nature Switzerland AG 2021
M. E. Kosal (ed.), *Proliferation of Weapons- and Dual-Use Technologies*,
Advanced Sciences and Technologies for Security Applications,
https://doi.org/10.1007/978-3-030-73655-2_1

the scientific and technical realities and mainstream scholarship on national and international security, especially with regard to potential to have impact on strategic and policy. The research in this volume is advancing the strategic understanding of these game-changing technologies and the development of meaningful and testable metrics and models to help reduce that surprise.

This volume examines emerging dual use technologies and considers potential security implications through a framework of diplomatic, information, military, and economic factors. The tools that can be used to assert national power and influence have often been summarized by the acronym DIME—Diplomatic, Informational, Military, and Economic [2]. Conceptually, a state that can exercise all of the elements of national pawer across the DIME spectrum will have advantages in pursuing its interests. This framework helps explain the impacts of multiple centers of weapons innovation across the globe; the sufficiency of international agreements to control them; areas at highest risk of instability due to proliferation; potential changes to the defense industrial base; and strategies to adapt to weapons innovation.

References

1. Gray C (2007) Another bloody century: future warfare. London, UK, Phoenix, p 38
2. US DoD Joint Chiefs of Staff, Strategy, Joint Doctrine Note 1–18, 25 Apr 2018, p II-5. https://www.jcs.mil/Portals/36/Documents/Doctrine/jdn_jg/jdn1_18.pdf

The Potential Impact of Video Manipulation and Fraudulent Simulation Technology on Political Stability

Shane Jacobeen

Abstract Video manipulation and fraudulent simulation technology combines facial recognition with a neural network to allow its users to create fake impersonations of public figures. As this technology proliferates, it has the political to intensify political instability around the globe. By increasing the impact of misleading content, 'video spoofing' could lead to a rise in incidents stemming from fake news, imitation of authority, and plausible deniability. As each of these scenarios threatens key tenants of political stability—especially in states with weak or compromised political structures—it is within US national security interests to prepare for—and counter—the threat posed by this emerging technology.

1 Introduction

Technological innovation and proliferation continue to have a profound influence on nearly every aspect of day-to-day life in the developed world. Our devices—from phones to refrigerators—continue to become 'smarter' and more connected; we now share the road with fully autonomous vehicles, and AI systems are automating an ever-broadening range of increasingly complex tasks. Yet along with the innovations that benefit humanity have come threats; in fact, the proliferation of weapons and dual-use technology are among the greatest challenges to national security facing the US in the modern era [46]. This threat has not gone unnoticed, a recent DARPA project resulted in the creation of industry—leading deepfake detection algorithm [32, 53]. Yet an aspect of fake video that has been largely unexplored is the potential role of deepfakes on political stability around the world. In this report, I explore the implications for US national security of the proliferation of dual-use video manipulation and fraudulent simulation technology.

S. Jacobeen (✉)
Atlanta, Georgia

2 Background

International political stability continues to be to be a priority of US national security and foreign policy [39]. Many definitions of political stability have been proposed over the years. Though varied, themes including the absence of violence, state functionality, and stability are common. For this work, I will consider the elegant and comprehensive definition proposed by J. Eli Margolis that defines political stability as "the health of authority, resilience, legitimacy, and replacement in a political object". Note that in this report, the 'political object' I will consider is the state [38].

Centralized political authority is a cornerstone of political stability [27]. A 2009 report for the CIA-funded Political Instability Task Force found that the nature of a state's regime type is the most important indicator of political instability. Unsurprisingly, the more factions vying for power in a state, the more internal conflict exists, and hence there is a higher chance for political instability [4]. Such instability occurred in Columbia in the 1980s, when traditional authority ceded influence to individual-led organizations, resulting in a violent and unstable state [6].

Historically, video recordings have played a significant role in maintaining the authority and legitimacy of states. From increasing the visibility of individuals in positions of power to providing evidence against criminals [40], video recordings have played an important role in establishing, maintaining, and challenging political stability around the world. This is because an unaltered video provides an incontrovertible evidence of events, making it one of the most reliable forms of evidence [14]. And with the recent proliferation of recording devices (CCTV systems, cell phones, etc.), video recordings are captured and distributed at an increasing rate. While concerns about treating video evidence as unassailable fact have been raised due to issues with authentication [10] and context [24, 28], the recording itself is often assumed to be an accurate depiction of events that transpired. Now, however, emerging technology is challenging video's role as the 'ultimate evidence'—with potentially serious implications for political stability around the world [15].

3 Relevance and Importance

Facial recognition technologies are quickly becoming more accurate and prevalent [23]. A paper published in the proceedings of the 2016 IEEE Conference on Computer Vision and Pattern Recognition describes how 'Face2Face' technology combines facial recognition technology with a neural network trained on real video to map a user's facial expressions to any target face in real time [59]. More recent approaches include analysis and manipulation of the speaker's surroundings to create more a realistic context for the speaker, making fake content even harder to detect [50]. Combined with technology like Adobe's VoCo or Lyrebird that can create a digital voice profile from a recorded sample as small as one minute in length [36], this technology can be used to create highly realistic video of anyone saying anything the creator desires.

One of the first widely-distributed examples of this came from the production team of WNYC's podcast 'Radiolab' and researchers at the University of Southern California, in which they created a highly-realistic video of former US President Barak Obama saying that the most important thing he can do post-presidency is play golf [61]. More sinister applications of this technology have also emerged, pornographic videos featuring celebrities and public figures—called 'deepfakes'— continue to proliferate [12, 54]. While early deepfakes contained anomalies that were readily apparent, continuous improvement of the technology has made it nearly impossible to identify fake videos without the use of sophisticated digital forensic tools.

Misinformation as a means of deception is nothing new. However, video as a medium for the distribution of fraudulent information is particular concerning because people tend to be more readily persuaded by video content than by static media [43]. Media richness theory (MRT), or information richness theory, is an extension of information processing theory that is used to asses and describe a communication medium's effectiveness [16]. MRT suggests that in general, the richer a medium is, the more effective it is at transmitting a message from the sender to a receiver. Here, 'richness' is assessed by a mediums ability to handle multiple information clues simultaneously, facilitate rapid feedback, establish a personal focus, and to utilize natural language. And while media richness theory has its critics and limitations, the persuasive superiority of video/audio to written/static media has been well documented [5, 57]. Much of the fake news circulated during the 2016 US presidential election was static content. Images and text, ranging from misleading to blatantly inaccurate, circulated social media networks with alarming speed [1]. By increasing the richness of the exploitable medium, the proliferation of video manipulation technology has the potential to substantially augment the effectiveness of false information.

Unsurprisingly, video manipulation and fraudulent simulation technology is beginning to elicit concern from government officials and industry professionals alike. Several Congressional lawmakers have expressed their concern for the potential use of fake video in the manipulation of the public and the resulting erosion of trust, including trust in government [25]. These concerns have been echoed by Tim Hwang, director of ethics and governance at the AI Initiative [41]. Concerned groups have recently begun exploring solutions to this problem, for example "Synthetic media, where AI is used to fake footage or audio clips of someone speaking" was one of the topics of interest at the AI's largest and most influential conference, Neural Information Processing Systems (NIPS), on December 8th, 2017. These concerns are well-founded; in 2020, Facebook removed accounts that spread content containing AI-generated faces that were in violation of its policy against "foreign or government interference" [29, 26].

Misinformation can arise from a plethora of sources, but when it is disseminated with the intention of disrupting the operations of a state or its citizens, it may be classified as *information warfare*. Generally defined as 'the collection of information and distribution of information to gain a competitive advantage over an adversary', information warfare is closely related to psychological warfare, which includes any attempts to make an adversary become less confident or feel hopeless or afraid [62]. Fake videos could be deployed for information warfare purposes in a plethora of ways, from slandering political opponents to misleading subordinates or followers. Perhaps most important is the potential erosion of the validity of video evidence: if fake video becomes commonplace, it may push us toward a scenario in which everyone has plausible deniability in the face of any type of recorded media.

In this report, I will examine the implications for national security of the proliferation of video manipulation technology by assessing its potential for political destabilization—events or movements perpetrated or amplified by video manipulation that demonstrably decrease a state's authority, resilience, legitimacy, or replacement capability. Specifically, I will consider three scenarios for the application of this technology—fake news, imitation of authority, and plausible deniability—to investigate its potential impact on social stability. These three scenarios were inspired by discussions with colleagues and experts. While this is not an exhaustive catalogue of the nefarious applications of fraudulent simulation and video manipulation, this initial investigation will provide an initial assessment that may be expanded to include additional applications as in the future.

4 Fake News

Hypothesis: Video manipulation and fraudulent simulation technology will exacerbate the impact of fake news.

As the distribution of news media continues to shift from classic sources (such as newspaper, television, and radio) to decentralized social media platforms, the distribution of ideas unverified and/or false content has become increasingly prevalent. In fact, a 2017 study found that 62% of American adults get news from social media [1]. This has facilitated the recent rise of 'fake news', during the 2016 election, the average American was exposed to at least one fake news story, and over half of those exposed perceived the stories as real [1]. While fake news is not new—fake images of destruction from hurricane Sandy in 2012 were shared online thousands of times [28]—increasingly connected social media networks are making it ever easier to disseminate misinformation [11].

Software robots, or 'bots', also play a large role in the spread of fake news. By creating false interest in specific content so that it gains popularity with relevance-based recommendation algorithms, bots can be used to increase the spread of targeted content among human users [56]. Fake stories are designed to feel real, and have strong personal and emotional resonance with the reader, in the hopes that the reader will then share it [8]. The more a piece is shared—by humans, algorithms, or robots—it gains strength not only be reaching new audiences, but also through repetition, the more times a user sees a viewpoint repeated, the more likely they are to perceive it as reality [9, 48]. Additionally, as the human mind ages, it becomes more susceptible to interpreting misinformation as valid [3]. Compounding the problem is the fact that once people come to believe something, they are often reluctant to change their beliefs, even in the face of incontrovertible evidence to the contrary [18, 20].

Whether it is spread maliciously or not, fake news can have dangerous ramifications. For example, in the 2016 'pizzagate' incident, an armed man arrived at a D.C. area pizzeria with the intention of freeing children that were reportedly being held hostage [31]. Furthermore, false media reports have played a role in numerous incidents of violent unrest around the world. In India in September 2013, a video of two men being beaten to death, with the false claim that the victims where Hindu and the mob was Muslim, stoked the fires of an ongoing feud to the point that 13,000 Indian troops were required to quell the resulting riots [37]. And in Iraq in 2006, a US Special Forces battalion was temporarily decommissioned during an investigation into images that appeared to show that they had murdered civilians in prayer in a mosque, when in fact the bodies had been rearranged to appear as such after a raid on a military facility [17]. While these incidents were all had relatively short-lived consequences, misinformation can have enduring consequences as well, such as the belief that vaccines cause autism in children.

4.1 Case Study: Vaccines and Autism

In 1998, a study was published that claimed to demonstrate a causal link between vaccines in children and the onset of autism. The public reaction was immediate and strong; many were dismayed that they had been egregiously misled. However, the study included only 12 cases and was poorly controlled, so the scientific community was skeptical. In the following decades, dozens of properly-controlled experiments involving thousands of participants were conducted, and no evidence for a causal link between vaccines and autism could be detected [49]. Furthermore, 10 of the 12 authors of the original 1998 paper redacted, saying that they didn't believe in a causal link. Furthermore, it came to light that the primary author, Dr. Andrew Wakefield, had been funded by lawyers engaged in lawsuits against vaccine-producing pharmaceutical companies [58].

Yet despite this overwhelming evidence to the contrary, a nontrivial percentage of the population still believes that vaccines can or do cause autism [21]. This belief has harmful and potentially deadly ramifications, low rates of vaccination is thought to be at least partly responsible for an outbreak of measles in Minnesota in 2017 that included 79 confirmed cases [35]. While this example of the repercussions of fake news is neither intentionally malicious or the consequence of video content, it is an illustration of the harmful potential of fake news.

Considering such examples of the role of misleading media in past dangerous and violent incidents, it is easily conceivable that an increase in the proliferation and persuasive power of fake news could increase the severity and frequency of such social instability. Previous research on persuasive media suggests that by opening the door to alteration of media-rich video [16], video manipulation fraudulent and simulation technology is poised to give fake news just such an increase in power. This in turn would increase fake news' threat to state's 'replacement' (elections) and 'authority' (CDC on vaccines) heath—key tenants of political stability. Though it is yet to be seen how the proliferation of such video spoofing technology will impact fake news, it is well within US national security interests to be aware of the possibilities and to explore countermeasures.

5 Imitation of Authority

Hypothesis: Video manipulation and fraudulent simulation technology could be used to direct the actions of subordinates or followers within an organization.

I now consider the possibility of fraudulent calls to action by impersonation of an authority figure. To consider this scenario, which will refer to as "imitation of authority', I consider two cases: formal and informal. The formal cases is that in which subordinates are legally or contractually obligated to obey their superiors, such as members of a military or cooperation. In the informal case, subordinates are members of the organization voluntarily, and thus have no legal incentive to follow the wishes of their superiors, though they may be ethically, emotionally, spiritually, or financially motivated to do so.

5.1 Imitation of Formal Authority

Because formal institutions (states, NGOs, large corporations) with well-defined chains of command typically have official channels for communication, the use of fraudulent simulation to engage in imitation of a formal authority is likely to involve technical challenges. In direct contrast to the case of fake news—where the distribution of misleading content requires no sophisticated technology or expertise—to imitate a formal authority, a perpetrator would also need to infiltrate the organization's communication channels. Organizations in which an instance of imitation of authority would cause significant harm (militaries, large corporations, etc.) are likely to have secure networks, in which case the distribution of misinformation along official channels would be difficult. Furthermore, it is not clear that video manipulation and fraudulent simulation would impact the severity of the outcome of such an incursion; it is plausible that in the case of direct orders from a superior via a channel that is perceived as secure, written content may well be just as effective. Nonetheless, the ability to disrupt communication in such an organization could have disastrous results, as effective, strategic communication is critical to the successful operation of large organizations such as the US military [19]. Thus, while its consequences would likely be among the most severe, imitation of formal authority appears an unlikely application of video manipulation and fraudulent simulation technology due to its technical difficulty and questionable feasibility.

5.2 Imitation of Informal Authority

In contrast, using video manipulation and fraudulent simulation technology to imitate leaders and authority figures via unofficial channels would be considerably easier. To consider the ease of content distribution and scale of response, consider the following case study.

5.2.1 Case Study: "I Can See Russia from My Porch"

In 2008, vice-presidential candidate Sarah Palin alluded in an interview to Alaska's proximity to Russia as evidence for her foreign policy experience. Shortly thereafter, while impersonating Palin on Saturday Night Live, actor/comedian Tina Fey delivered the now-(in)famous line "I can see Russia from my house". Yet according to a 2015 survey, seven out of ten Americans incorrectly attributed those words to Palin herself [55]. This is an example of how influential video content can be, even when the comedic intent of its creator is obvious: it is not hard to imagine that video that is *intended* to be misleading could have an even more profound effect. The ability to create misrepresentations of political leaders could seriously undermine their legitimacy and authority, hence threatening the stability of the institution they represent.

It is worth noting a few of the likely limitations of imitation of an informal authority. First, the scope of the content that can be successfully transmitted is fairly limited, as it would have to be at least reasonably in line with the fundamental values of the target audience; surely there would be an inverse relationship between acceptance of a message and its deviation from the receiver's core belief system. For example, to using video manipulation or fraudulent simulation for character assassination will likely do more to bolster the opinions of opponents than convert the target's followers, because people will often readily believe the worst of their adversaries [63].

Second, any political instability caused by imitation of an informal authority would likely be short lived. If such an event were to occur, it is reasonable to predict that within a relatively short timeframe, the fraudulent content would be identified, and knowledge of its inaccuracy would spread. On the other hand, if such impersonation events become commonplace, the volume of misinformation could overwhelm the legitimate authority's ability to effectively combat it. If were to escalates to the point that it became impossible to distinguish between real and fabricated content, a new scenario may begin to unfold: that of universal plausible deniability.

6 Plausible Deniability

Hypothesis: By eroding our ability to establish accountability through video evidence, video manipulation and fraudulent simulation technology could embolden individuals and groups around the world to increase malicious activity due to a lack of repercussions.

The establishment of a sort of 'plausible deniability', or a scenario in which actors make decisions with a deteriorated sense of accountability, is perhaps the most disturbing possibility for the proliferation of video manipulation and fraudulent simulation technology. I do not suggest that video spoofing, even if implemented perfectly, could ever result in *complete* plausible deniability. However, it may be able to tip the needle towards such a scenario by decreasing the validity, and therefore usefulness, of recorded media evidence. To explore the implications of such a scenario, consider the following case study from 2014.

6.1 Case Study: Malaysian Airlines Flight 17

On July 17th, 2014, passenger flight MH17 from Amsterdam to Kuala Lumpur was shot down over eastern Ukraine by a missile launched from a Buk surface-to-air missile system. While the perpetrators of this heinous attack that killed 298 passengers and crew may never be definitively identified, it is widely believed to have been the work of pro-Russian Ukrainian separatists [7]. Naturally, Russia's level of involvement in this incident was a topic of global interest. While Russia denies involvement, various points of evidence say otherwise; analysis of public video and images from open sources such as social media suggest that the Buk system used to down MH17 was previously part of the Russian Ground Forces 53rd Anti-Aircraft Rocket Brigade [2].

Even though this evidence has done little to bring the perpetrators to justice—Russia vetoed a proposal for an international tribunal in 2015—it nonetheless had consequences in the form of E.U. and U.S. sanctions [42]. However, in a future where rampant video manipulation and fraudulent simulation have eroded the credence of such evidence, such events may be entirely unaccompanied by retribution of any kind. And without evidence to prove responsibility, malicious actors may become emboldened by the reduced chance of international repercussions [45].

The threat to political stability of plausible deniability is not limited to large, international events. In fact, it is likely that large events—which are often recorded from multiple angles and complimented by other types of evidence—will have be associated with the highest levels of accountability. In contrast, personal accountability of public figures is more likely to become compromised, resulting in a loss of trust not only in the individuals themselves, but also in the roles that they hold. If this loss of trust were to spread to the public sphere, it could significantly jeopardize political stability at all levels [30, 44, 51].

7 Discussion

As previously discussed, political stability is most vulnerable in states with weak, ineffective, or contested governments [4, 6, 27]. Therefore, it is reasonable to expect the greatest threat to political stability of fake video in states and regions characterized by low governmental fidelity. According to the World Bank's Worldwide Governance Indicators, the most vulnerable regions are the Middle East, South Asia, and Africa (The World Bank Group, 2018. Additionally, governmental fidelity is correlated with GDP, poorer countries tend to be less stable.

Video manipulation technology has matured significantly over the past few years; as such, the potential risk to political stability has increased. While it is possible that the threat will recede as countermeasures are developed and deployed, this is far from a given—as we have already seen, nefarious actors are constantly finding new means of distributing misinformation. The asymmetric impact of the proliferation of video spoofing technology and its subsequent reduction in potency is displayed in Fig. 1.

The proliferation of fake video technology is also likely to vary in the severity of its impact is across environments. Contributing factors are likely to include population density, freedom information access, and governmental quality. Figure 2 is a summary of the threat assessment for different adversary types.

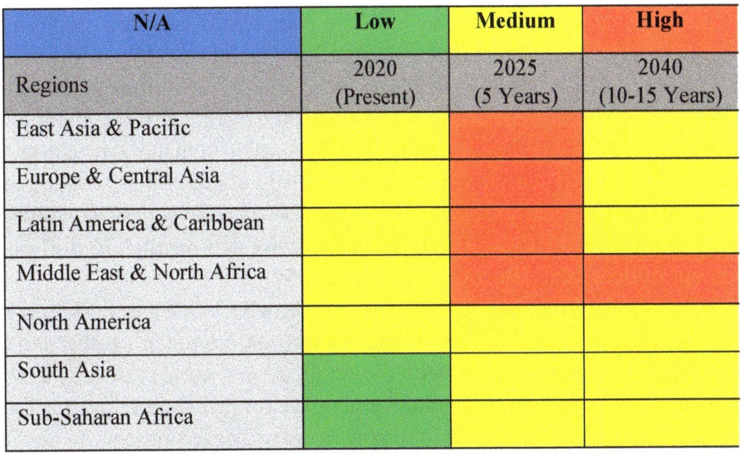

N/A	Low	Medium	High
Regions	2020 (Present)	2025 (5 Years)	2040 (10-15 Years)
East Asia & Pacific	yellow	red	yellow
Europe & Central Asia	yellow	red	yellow
Latin America & Caribbean	yellow	red	yellow
Middle East & North Africa	yellow	red	red
North America	yellow	red	yellow
South Asia	green	yellow	yellow
Sub-Saharan Africa	green	yellow	yellow

Fig. 1 Threat assessment of video spoofing technology in different parts of the world, now and in the future

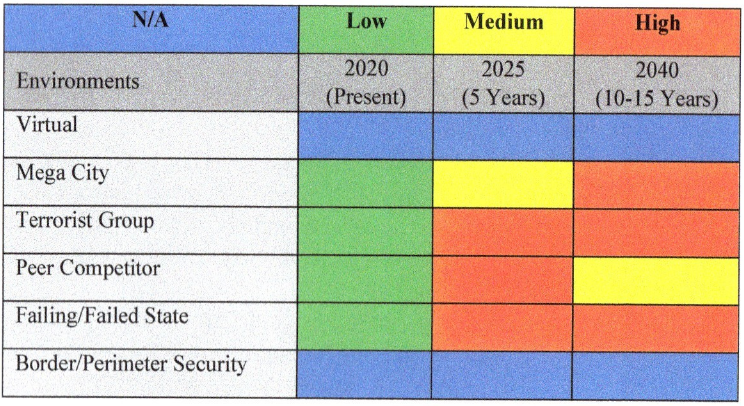

N/A	Low	Medium	High
Environments	2020 (Present)	2025 (5 Years)	2040 (10-15 Years)
Virtual			
Mega City	🟢	🟡	🟠
Terrorist Group	🟢	🟠	🟠
Peer Competitor	🟢	🟠	🟡
Failing/Failed State	🟢	🟠	🟠
Border/Perimeter Security			

Fig. 2 Threat assessment of video spoofing by different adversary types

8 Conclusions

By increasing the potential for political instability in state and regions around the world, the proliferation of video spoofing technology has potentially serious implications for US national security [13, 47]. Thankfully, several technologies that could be employed to combat the effectiveness of video manipulation already exist. These technologies use various methods to verify the authenticity of video recordings. For example, there exist numerous video watermarking techniques that allow authors to embed signatures of authenticity in the video itself [33]. Similarly, file validation techniques such as checksum hashing can be used to validate the authenticity of a file of any type. More sophisticated approaches employ steganalysis and statistical methods can be used to search video for digital irregularities that are indicators of post-creation modification [22, 52]. The need for such detection capabilities has not gone unnoticed; DARPA's 'MediFor' project invested nearly $70 million in the development of deepfake detection algorithms [15].

Each of these methods has its benefits and drawbacks. Watermarking requires effort by the creator to add a watermark, as well as diligence on the part of the viewer to verify it. Likewise, checksum file verification requires effort by the creator and diligence by the consumer. Digital forensic techniques the unique advantage of requiring no effort on the part of the creator. However, development of such tools is time-intensive, costly, and their effectiveness is not guaranteed.

Given that fake news spreads via exposure and repetition preferentially among those who are not diligent about the veracity of the media they consume [34], effective countermeasures will likely be those that require little to no effort on the part of the consumer. This is the main difficulty with the current available media verification methods; they all require nontrivial effort on the part of the consumer. And while this suggests that some form of automatic screening for veracity may be the most effective, such screening immediately raises fundamental questions about censorship: who gets to decide what media is 'valid'? These issues have repeatedly come to the forefront in the context of the US 2020 presidential election, as social media platforms have implemented various methods to combat the spread of misinformation. While the role of private companies in limiting the spread of misinformation is beyond the scope of the present study, it certainly merits an exploration in the context of the proliferation of video spoofing technology.

Though the proliferation of video manipulation and fraudulent simulation technology appears likely, it is encouraging that technological countermeasures already exist. The remaining challenge is to ensure that these methods are effectively employed. Unfortunately, current verification methods require a level of vigilance on the part of the consumer that is unreasonable to expect. However, authenticity verification would be much more effective if it were integrated in the channels through which content is distributed. Interest in limiting fake news already exists among the giants of social media; social media platforms like Facebook and Twitter experimented with various ways of combat the spread of fake news for some time [60]. Therefore, maintaining a healthy relationship with Silicon Valley to facilitate investigate the such verification methods should be a critical aspect of countermeasures considered against the deleterious influence of video spoofing technology [34]. Additionally, any educational measure that raises awareness of the existence of video manipulation and fraudulent simulation technology should be viewed as a positive step toward the promotion of healthy skepticism with respect to video recordings.

References

1. Allcott H, Gentzkow M (2017) Social media and fake news in the 2016 election. J Econ Perspect 31(2):211–235
2. Allen T, Haggard A, Higgins E, Kivimaki V-P, Ostanin I, Toler A (2014) MH17: source of the separatists' Buk. Investigation, bellingcat
3. Anderson ND, Craik FIM (2017) 50 years of cognitive aging theory. J Gerontol Ser B 72(1):1–6
4. Annett A (2001) Social fractionalization, political instability, and the size of government. IMF Econ Rev (IMF Econ Rev) 48(3):561–592
5. Appiah O (2006) Rich media, poor media: the impact of audio/video vs. text/picture testimonial ads on browsers' evaluations of commercial web sites and online products. J Curr Issues Res Advertising 28(1):73–86
6. Archer RP (1990) The transition from traditional to broker clientism in Columbia: political stability and social unrest. The Helen Kellogg Institute for International Studies, Research, South Bend, Indiana
7. BBC (2015) MH17 report: five key findings from the dutch safety board. BBC World, Oct 13
8. Bakir V, McStay A (2017) Fake news and the economy of emotions. Digit J 6(2):154–175
9. Balmas M (2012) When fake news becomes real. Commun Res 41(3):430–454
10. Beser ND, Duerr TE, Staisiunas GP (2003) Authentication of digital video evidence. In: Optical science and technology, SPIE's 48th annual meeting. SPIE
11. Boulianne S (2015) Social media use and participation: a meta-analysis of current research. Inf Commun Soc 18(5):524–538
12. Brandon J (2018) 'Deepfake' AI-generated videos threaten to wreak political havoc. New York Post, Mar 13

13. Chesney R, Citron D (2019) Deepfamkes and the new disinformation war. Foreign Affairs 147–155
14. Cohen G, Conway MA (2008) Memory in the real world. In: Cohen G, Conway M (eds). Psychology Press, New York, NY
15. DARPA (2018) DARPA research. Accessed October 1, 2020. https://www.darpa.mil/program/media-forensics
16. Daft RL, Lengel RH (1986) Organizational information requirements, media richness and structural design. Manage Sci (INFORMS) 32(5):554–571
17. Dauber CE (2009) The truth is out there: responding to insurgent disinformation and deception operations. Mil Rev 89(1):13
18. De keersmaecker J, Roets A (2017) 'Fake news': incorrect, but hard to correct. The role of cognitive ability on the impact of false information on social impressions. Intelligence 65:107–110
19. Defense Science Board (2008) Strategic communication. Department of Defense, Washington, DC, 158
20. Fazio LK, Brashier NM, Keith Payne B, Marsh EJ (2015) Knowledge does not protect against illusory truth. J Exp Psychol Gen 144(5):993–1002
21. Freed GL, Clark SJ, Butchart AT, Singer DC, Davis MM (2010) Parental vaccine safety concerns in 2009. Pediatrics 125(4):654–659
22. Fridrich J (ed) (2004) Information hiding. 6th International Workshop, Information Hiding 2004, Toronto, Canada, May 23–25, 2004, Revised Selected Papers. Springer
23. Gates KA (2011) Our biometric future: Facial recognition technology and the culture of surveillance. NYU Press, New York
24. Gates K (2013) The cultural labor of surveillance: video forensics, computational objectivity, and the production of visual evidence. Soc Semiot (Routledge) 23(2):242–260
25. Gershgorn D (2017) AI researchers are trying to combat how AI can be used to lie and deceive. Quartz, Dec 8
26. Gleicher N (2020) Removing coordinated inauthentic behavior. Facebook. September 22. Accessed October 18, 2020. https://about.fb.com/news/2020/09/removing-coordinated-inauthentic-behavior-china-philippines/
27. Goldstone JA, Bates RH, Epstein DL, Gurr TR, Lustik MB, Marshall MG, Ulfelder J, Woodward M (2010) A global model for forecasting political instability. Am J Polit Sci 54(1):190–208
28. Gupta A, Lamba H, Kumaraguru P, Joshi A (2013) Faking Sandy: characterizing and identifying fake images on Twitter during Hurricane Sandy. In: Proceedings of the 22nd international conference on the world wide web. International World Wide Web Conferences Steering Committee, pp 729–736
29. Hatmaker T (2020) Chinese propaganda network on Facebook used AI-generated faces. TechCrunch. September 22. Accessed October 18, 2020. https://techcrunch.com/2020/09/22/facebook-gans-takes-down-networks-of-fake-accounts-originating-in-china-and-the-philippines/?guccounter=1&guce_referrer=aHR0cHM6Ly93d3cuZ29vZ2xlLmNvbS8S&guce_referrer_sig=AQAAALNJb_hiNPSqZjSZecvWiGCY8tpXN7NHM_CV0izgsu0iCdk
30. Hetherington MJ (1998) The political relevance of political trust. Am Polit Sci Rev 92(4):791–808
31. Kang C, Goldman A (2016) In Washington pizzeria attack, fake news brought real guns. The New York Times
32. Knight W (2018) MIT technology review. August 7. Accessed October 1, 2020. https://www.technologyreview.com/2018/08/07/66640/the-defensedepartment-has-produced-the-first-tools-for-catching-deepfakes/
33. Langelaar GC, Setyawan I, Lagendijk RL (2000) Watermarking digital image and video data. A state-of-the-art overview. IEEE Signal Process Mag 17(5):20–46
34. Lazer DMJ, Baum MA, Benkler Y, Berinsky AJ, Greenhill KM, Menczer F, Metzger MJ et al (2018) The science of fake news. Science 359(6380):1094–1096

35. Leslie TF, Delamater PL, Tony Yang Y (2018) It could have been much worse: the Minnesota measles outbreak of 2017. Vaccine 36(14):1808–1810
36. Lyrebird.ai (2017) Lyrebird. Accessed on 24 Nov 2017. https://lyrebird.ai/
37. Magnier M (2013) "Hindu girl's complaint mushrooms into deadly Indian Riots. Los Angles Times, Sept 9
38. Margolis JE (2010) Understanding political stability and instability. Civ Wars 12(3):326–345
39. Mattis J (2018) Summary of the national defence strategy of the United States of America. The White House, Washington DC
40. May R (1995) Criminal evidence, 3rd edn. Sweet and Maxwell, London
41. Metz C, Collins K (2018) How an A.I. 'cat-and-mouse game' generates believable fake photos. The New York Times, Jan 2
42. Miller N (2016) "Malaysia Airlines flight MH17 was shot down from pro-Russian rebel controlled territory, investigation finds. The Sydney Morning Herald, Sept 29
43. Nash RA, Wade KA (2009) Innocent but proven guilty: eliciting internalized false confessions using doctored-video evidence. Appl Cogn Psychol 23(5):624–637
44. Newton K (2001) Trust, social capital, civil society, and democracy. Int Polit Sci Rev 22(2):201–214
45. Nieto M (1997) Public video surveillance: is it an effective crime prevention tool? California Research Bureau, Investigation, Sacramento, CA, p 41
46. Obama B (2015) National security strategy. The White House, Washington DC, p 29
47. Pantserev KA (2020) The malicious use of AI-based deepfake technology as the new threat to psychological security and political stability. In: Jahankhani H, Kendzierskyj S, Chelvachandran N, Iberra J (eds) Cyber defence in the age of AI, smart societies, and augmented humanity, pp 37–55. Springer, Cham
48. Pennycook G, Cannon TD, Rand DG (2017) Implausibility and illusory truth: prior exposure increases perceived accuracy of fake news but has no effect on entirely implausible statements. Social Science Research Network 57
49. Plotkin S, Gerber JS, Offit PA (2009) Vaccines and autism: a tale of shifting hypotheses. Clin Infect Dis 48(4):456–461
50. Prajwal KR, Mukhopadhyay R, Namboodiri V, Jawahar CV (2020) A lip sync expert is all you need for speech to lip generation in the wild. arxiv.org 9. https://doi.org/10.1145/3394171.3413532
51. Putnam R (1993) The prosperous community: social capital and public life. Am Prospect 13(1995):65–78
52. Richard GG, Roussev V (2006) Next-generation digital forensics. Commun ACM 49(2):67–80
53. Robitzsi D (2018) Futurism. November 19. Accessed October 1, 2020. https://futurism.com/darpa-68-million-technology-deepfakes
54. Roose K (2018) Here come the fake videos, too. The New York Times, Mar 4
55. Scheufele D (2015) (New) political interfaces in the life sciences. In: 33rd annual meeting of the association for politics and the life sciences. University of Wisconsin, Madison, Wisconson
56. Shao C, Ciampaglia GL, Varol O, Flammini A, Menczer F (2017) The spread of fake news by social bots. arXiv 16
57. Shen F, Sheer VC, Li R (2015) Impact of narratives on persuasion in health communication: a meta-analysis. J Advertising 44(2):105–113
58. The College of Physicians of Philadelphia (n.d.) The history of vaccines. Accessed on 16 Mar 2018. https://www.historyofvaccines.org/content/articles/do-vaccines-cause-autism
59. Thies J, Zollhofer M, Stamminger M, Theobalt C, Niessner M (2016) Face2Face: real-time face capture and reenactment of RGB videos. In: The IEEE conference on computer vision and pattern recognition (CVPR). IEEE, Honolulu, pp 2387–2395
60. Tiku N (2018) Facebook's latest fix for fake news: ask users what they trust. Wired, January 19
61. WNYC (2017) Future of Fake News. Accessed on Sept 2017. https://futureoffakenews.com/
62. Waltzman R (2017) The weaponization of information. Rand Coorperation, Testimony, Rand Coorperation, Santa Monica, p 10

63. Westen D, Blagov PS, Harenski K, Kilts C, Hamann S (2006) Neural bases of motivated reasoning: an fMRI study of emotional constraints on partisan political judgment in the 2004 U.S. presidential election. J Cogn Neurosci 18(11):1947–1958

Artificial Intelligence: Unpacking Political, Rhetorical, and Security Factors

Margaret E. Kosal

Abstract Artificial Intelligence (AI)-enabled capabilities have advanced considerably in the last decade and are expected to see increased employment by states and potentially by non-state actors in the ensuing years. This chapter explores how political, rhetorical, and security factors surrounding the research and development of AI-enabled capabilities interact and considers the implications for geopolitics. The widespread emphasis on the importance of AI globally, especially in the context of military capabilities and balance of power, is uncontested politically, and concurrently, it is also an area in need of more investigation by scholars.

1 Introduction

While the suggestion that emerging technologies will enable a new class of weapons that will alter the geopolitical landscape remains to be realized, a number of unresolved security puzzles underlying the emergence of potentially disruptive technologies have implications for international security, defense policy, governance, and arms control regimes. The extent to which emerging technologies may exacerbate or mitigate the global security and governance challenges that states will pose in the future to global security interests will remain an integral question as policy-makers and leaders navigate the complex global environment.

Among the technologies cited as being disruptive or game-changing, artificial intelligence (AI) is one of the most frequently mentioned, having been the focus of high-level strategic documents across US Presidential administrations [1]; cited specifically in Congressional funding legislation, i.e., 2019 National Defense Authorization Act [2]; and the subject of strategies across US Executive Branch Departments, including the Department of Defense [3].

Artificial Intelligence (AI) is cited as a revolutionary emerging technology key to the future of international security that is being pursued globally [4]. In the forward to

---

M. E. Kosal (✉)
Georgia Institute of Technology, Atlanta, Georgia
e-mail: margaret.kosal@inta.gatech.edu

© The Author(s), under exclusive license to Springer Nature Switzerland AG 2021
M. E. Kosal (ed.), *Proliferation of Weapons- and Dual-Use Technologies*,
Advanced Sciences and Technologies for Security Applications,
https://doi.org/10.1007/978-3-030-73655-2_3

a recent AI policy recommendation paper, former US Deputy Secretary of Defense Robert Work notes, "China, Russia, members of the European Union, Japan, and South Korea all are increasing AI research, development, and training. China, in particular, sees advances in AI as a key means to surpass the United States in both economic and military power. China has stated its intent to be the world leader in AI by 2030 and is making major investments to achieve that goal [5]."

How, to what extent, and in what ways Artificial Intelligence (AI) may affect conflict, cooperation, and international security is speculative ... and occasionally extremely speculative. Nonetheless thinking through geopolitically and technically-robust aspects of this emerging technology and how it is being conceptualized is useful generally in order to increase understanding and specifically to reduce the risks of misunderstanding. The concepts and applications below are grounded in geopolitical and technical robustness, nonetheless they are intended to be illustrative rather than predictive.

To start, one needs to attempt to define AI. A more precise statement might be 'to scope' rather try to define, as there is no single agreed upon definition domestically or internationally. The 2019 National Artificial Intelligence R&D Strategic Plan Update states that "Artificial intelligence enables computers and other automated systems to perform tasks that have historically required human cognition and what we typically consider human decision-making abilities [6]." The 2019 US National Defense Authorization Act uses the following points as a working definition:

(1) Any artificial system that performs tasks under varying and unpredictable circumstances without significant human oversight, or that can learn from experience and improve performance when exposed to data sets.
(2) An artificial system developed in computer software, physical hardware, or other context that solves tasks requiring human-like perception, cognition, planning, learning, communication, or physical action.
(3) An artificial system designed to think or act like a human, including cognitive architectures and neural networks.
(4) A set of techniques, including machine learning, that is designed to approximate a cognitive task.
(5) An artificial system designed to act rationally, including an intelligent software agent or embodied robot that achieves goals using perception, planning, reasoning, learning, communicating, decision making, and acting [7].

This description is a useful place to start; however, further distinctions are worth noting. The first is the difference between General AI and Narrow AI, sometimes referred to as strong and weak AI respectively. General AI describes a non-human cognitive capability that surpasses human intelligence across the breadth of human capability, including complex decision-making and critical thinking [8]. While general AI is often the image that comes to mind when describing AI, most experts agree that it is still several decades in the future, if it is even possible [8, 9]. All current AI effects fall into the category of narrow AI, where programs are designed to solve a specific problem. This includes everything from navigation, to image recognition, language translation, game playing, and self-driving cars [8].

Under the umbrella of narrow AI, there are multiple approaches and techniques with names often used interchangeably with AI that further cloud the issue. These techniques can include everything from Deep Neural Nets and Machine Learning (ML) to big data analytics and autonomy [10]. It is essential to understand that all of these additional terms more often describe the underlying "how" of narrow AI or a specific application. For example, a common application of narrow AI is a sophisticated algorithm and learning data set that utilizes multiple neural nets to accomplish image recognition [10]. Even the idea of narrow AI is challenging to define as it seems to change continuously. Each time scientists and engineers overcome previous technical hurdles, what was before unachievable then seems commonplace, and therefore no longer worthy of bearing the "AI" moniker. This increasing capability subsequently creates a new concept of AI [11]. Thus, in a very real way, the accepted definition of AI is continually changing, presenting an even more difficult task of clarifying the idea and what it means for international security and geopolitics.

2 Military Applications

Attempting to exhaustively catalog the potential military applications and uses of AI or those that may have national security significance is an ever-changing and expanding endeavor. Any glimpse will have some level of limitation due to temporality at the time of writing. This section outlines five example applications or capabilities that AI may prove significant operationally or strategic.

2.1 Situational Awareness

As the limits of human capacity to process large streams of data, especially in time-sensitive environments, the risk of "data overload" increases. While this has implications across military operations, it is often most visible in context of intelligence, surveillance, and reconnaissance (ISR) capabilities and subsequently generating usable analysis from ISR data to aid decision-makers, leaders, planning, and operations. AI, particularly in the context of machine learning, is seen as valuable for data fusion from heterogeneous streams originating in large number of sensors, communications networks, and other electronic devices.

The US DoD's Project Maven/Algorithmic Cross-Functional Team is a first attempt at a large scale employment of AI by the US military, which has been directed to identify and locate Daesh/ISIL fighters [12]. Its focus is on developing and deploying capabilities for "computer vision—an aspect of machine learning and deep learning—that autonomously extracts objects of interest from moving or still imagery" from to "massive amounts of moving or still imagery [13]."

2.2 Command and Control (C^2)

Beyond situational awareness, another potential application of AI is to increase command decision-making capacities. For example, the USAF Multi-domain Command and Control (MDC^2) system is meant to coordinate and potentially assign tasks for air, space, and cyber forces [14]. The goal is for the system to be able to "seamlessly analyse, fuse, and share what was once domain-centric information into a single C2 system that supports all domains and all levels of war" and is seen as critical for the maintaining asymmetric advantage in increasingly contested, electronically conjected, and complex spaces [15].

Another example under development is the Defence Advanced Research Project Agency's (DARPA) Artificial Intelligence Exploration (AIE) project [16]. Part of broader DARPA efforts to develop "a large, diverse portfolio of fundamental and applied R&D AI programs aimed at shaping a future for AI technology where machines may serve as trusted and collaborative partners in solving problems of importance to national security [17]," the AIE is a research program intended to jump-start new AI capabilities including generating, testing, and refining hypotheses to assist human decision-making [18]. It is important to note that DARPA is a research agency; the military services acquire and field systems. Additionally, when it comes to nuclear weapons, research and development is through the Department of Energy.

2.3 Cyber

The potential impacts of AI with respect to cyber capabilities, especially defense, are more complicated and multi-faceted. AI has the potential to reduce uncertainty by helping make cyber networks more secure through detection of anomalies, identification of vulnerabilities, and potentially to implement protective action (patch, isolate, self-heal, etc.) Examples include the DARPA 2016 Cyber Grand Challenge [19], which reduced process to seconds from previous metric of days to detect cyber intrusions [20], and the NSA's Sharkseer program, which monitors incoming email traffic to DoD servers for malware and other offensive cyber activities [21]. The program was transferred from the NSA to the Defense Information Systems Agency (DISA) after it was made public in Defense Authorization legislation. Machine learning is also likely to be used for software verification and validation. Even narrow AI is likely to enable better cyber defenses, thereby reducing vulnerability of networks and thereby increasing stability.

With respect to offensive cyber operations, AI may create vulnerabilities through introduction of incorrect training data as part of machine learning data sets. If an adversary can 'infect' or alter the training data that an algorithm employed for situational awareness or to assist in decision-making, it may alter the calculus and judgement of military or civilian decision makers. Another, complication is that something similar could hypothetically be pursued by a third party, i.e., spoofing, to mis-direct, analysts and decision-makers. This illustrates the need for security of training data and multi-level authentication.

Unexpected catastrophic failures or "flash crashes" are another concern with increasing incorporation of AI into complex, interconnected systems. Use of "spoofing" algorithms and other computational approaches have been implicated in multiple flash crashes that have caused large drops in the New York Stock Exchange and the value of the British currency in seconds [22]. Conceptually applying this to nuclear weapons and strategic stability [23] could be done through the lens of "Normal Accidents" theory, originally proposed by Charles Perrow and applied to nuclear weapons by Scott Sagan [24]. As nuclear command, control, and communications (NC3) systems are more closely inter-connected, the concern is that an error—completely accidental or introduced by an adversary—might cause a cascade that impacts the NC3 system. Such an event could reduce or undermine confidence.

2.4 Autonomy

While much attention in popular press and at the international level has been given to autonomous systems, i.e., unmanned aerial vehicles, aka 'drones,' and lethality, the direction of the vector regarding increasing or decreasing stability is not resolved. Currently all US operational systems require "human in the loop" or are below level 7 in terms of autonomy taxonomy [25]. These systems are restricted in scope and nature, i.e., fixed anti-missile capabilities on ships rather than general lethality. As systems are developed and deployed with higher levels of autonomy, broader scope, and the ability to move independently, the calculus will change.

One area of particular concern is swarms, i.e., multiple independent autonomous systems that can synchronize and coordinate collective offensive and/or defensive maneuvers [26]. Frequently these have been envisioned as large (n > 10) formations of low-cost UAVs that might be used to overwhelm ground or ship-based defensive systems or troops [27]. The underlying science and engineering to enable swarm technology is a vibrant and active technical field [28]. Realization of some of the hypothesized operational capabilities will require advances in engineering as well as AI, for the scenarios to be realized [29].

Regardless of the level of actual underlying technology, the idea of lethal autonomous systems utilizing AI has entered into geopolitics, as can be seen through accounts and reporting on the targeted assassination of a senior official in the Iranian nuclear program, Mohsen Fakhrizadeh, in November 2020 [30]. A senior Iranian military official "Gen [Ali] Fadavi, the deputy commander of the Revolutionary Guards, told a ceremony in Tehran on Sunday that a machine-gun mounted on the Nissan pick-up was 'equipped with an intelligent satellite system which zoomed in on martyr Fakhrizadeh' and 'was using artificial intelligence [31].' That description suggests use of a facial recognition algorithm being employed as part of the system. Fakhrizadeh, a nuclear physicist by training, was credited as being crucial to the Iranian nuclear program's activities in the early 2000s and was believed to continue to play a leadership role, even being compared with American Robert Oppenheimer [32]. While the specific details of how Fakhrizadeh was killed are unclear and precise technical detail is unlikely to ever be verified, the idea that AI-assisted autonomy was enabling capability is part of the geopolitical rhetoric.

2.5 Nuclear Weapons

The specific applications of AI to nuclear weapons directly often can take on a 'Dr. Strangelove"-esque motif, i.e., reminiscent of the 1964 dark comedy directed by Stanley Kubrick. With respect to nuclear weapons, it becomes even more important to disambiguate AI hype from the possible.

As far as implications for strategic stability, the application of AI that most often is mentioned is incorporation into launch on warning systems [33]. This could result in a decreased decision-time by another nuclear state. Typical scenarios start with AI applied to machine vision and signal processing, which is then combined with autonomy and/or sensor fusion, to enable asymmetric capabilities for ISR, automatic target recognition (ATR), and technical guidance capabilities. Such capabilities could increase the likelihood that survivable forces (e.g., submarine-launched ballistic missiles (SLBMs) and mobile missile launchers) could be targeted and even potentially destroyed, thereby also leading to increased plausibility of first strike [34]. It has been noted that such systems may undermine strategic stability even if state possessing such capabilities has no intention to use them [35], as an adversary cannot be sure and may hedge.

3 Rhetoric and Ideational Factors

The rhetoric surrounding AI today can cloud the discussion to the point where meaningful conversations can be lost before they even begin. On the most capable side of AI many people immediately start thinking in terms of Hollywood portrayed science fiction like Skynet from *The Terminator,* the machines from *The Matrix,* or Matthew Broderick almost starting World War III in the now-classic *WarGames*. On the other hand, AI is being used as part of advertising for automated cat litter-boxes, which, while perhaps novel, is not a strategic application [36]. The latter does illustrate succinctly how "AI" can become part of a marketing strategy to indicate prestige and technical sophistication. Geopolitically, claims of AI-enabled capabilities may seem more like science fiction than reality.

In geopolitics, rhetoric matters. It's not the only thing that matters nor often the most important, but it does matter. And therefore, one must be cognizant of hype. What kind of rhetorical invocation of AI-prestige might intentionally be evoked is worth considering.

While there is a great deal of uncertainty about defining what AI is and how will be develop, its potential to be revolutionary is frequently cited by policy-makers, pundits, technologists, and others [37]. In September 2017, Vladimir Putin declared Russia's AI intentions asserting:

> Artificial intelligence is the future, not only for Russia, but for all humankind. It comes with colossal opportunities, but also threats that are difficult to predict. Whoever becomes the leader in this sphere will become the ruler of the world. [38]

His statement connected achieving AI capabilities directly with geopolitical dominance, including an implicit causal relationship. It is explicitly called out as a marker of technologic superiority. It's also notable that the way AI is described almost suggests it's a discrete homogenous thing, like a nuclear weapon, which it isn't. It's not even a range of possible weapons, like chemical or biological weapons. It's enabling capabilities, more akin to materials science or nanotechnology [39], that often will not be separate or severable from other capabilities or systems.

The setting and audience to whom Putin made his address is also notable: it was an annual speech in celebration of the start of the new school year. The speech was reportedly broadcast to over 16,000 schools in Russia and seen by over one million people [38]. His words had multiple audiences. First, to the children listening representing a domestic audience, along with others who read or heard about it in Russian newspapers and other media outlets, notably *Rossiyskaya Gazeta*, the official newspaper of the Russian government, which other outlets cite. Putin's speech was also intended for international audiences, including technological competitors, the US and People's Republic of China (PRC).

Also in 2017, the PRC released a strategy document with a stated goal to attain the global AI lead by 2030 [40]. The document begins noting that "AI has become a new focus of international competition. AI is a strategic technology that will lead in the future; the world's major developed countries are taking the development of AI as a major strategy to enhance national competitiveness and protect national security [41]." Again, advanced capabilities in AI are linked directly to prestige and prominence of *developed* nations. The Chinese plan is explicitly more comprehensive, emphasizing economic and social aspects, which is characteristic of high-level Chinese strategy documents. That "national security" is mentioned overtly is notable, as most Chinese documents are more ambiguous.

While the PRC national-level document was released before any official national-level US AI strategy, whether that is significant or not needs more examination. Large scale strategic identification of AI had previously been identified by the National Academy of Science [42], the Defense Science Board [43], the now-discontinued Congressional Office of Technology Assessment (OTA) [44], and others. It is not unlikely that this can be attributed to the distributed and often independent nature of departments and agencies within and across the US Government. The US National Science Foundation (NSF), DoD, and other parts of the US government have been supporting AI research since the 1950s. By the 1960s, ARPA (the initial incarnation of what is now the DoD's Defense Advanced Research Projects Agency [DARPA]) sponsored research into AI targets specific areas, such as intelligent computing, neural nets, and the underlying basic science and mathematics needed for machine translation [45]. A December 1984 Defense Science Board report noted that the "Task Force was chartered to develop 'a candidate list of high priority defense applications, particularly artificial (also called machine) intelligence applications," and to identify "the potential impact of future supercomputer systems on military mission areas [46]." AI has been part of sustained investment in mathematics, computer science, and contributing fields in the ensuing decades.

The US issued an Executive Order on the American position in AI in 2019 asserting that "continued American leadership in AI is of paramount importance to maintaining the economic and national security of the United States and to shaping the global evolution of AI in a manner consistent with our Nation's values, policies, and priorities [47]." Like many other areas, there is a much greater level of transparency—in both quantity and substantive content—of US documents, strategies, and postures compared to the Russia Federation or the PRC.

Rhetoric has also been used by civil society groups concerned about the potential deleterious impact of AI. A prime example of this is the "Slaughterbots" video, which was produced by an NGO seeking an international treaty to ban lethal autonomous systems [48]. The video presents a fictional scenario in which an unspecified terrorist group exploits multiple technologies, including narrow AI for facial recognition, to wreak havoc and undermine confidence in a government, including an attack on the US Capitol and on an unspecified university in the UK. The video begins in the style of the highly popular TED talks and continues in the tone of a documentary. The technical veracity of many of the claims are disputed [49].

The "Slaughterbots" video has frequently become part of public and academic discourse surrounding AI and robotics ethics and development, which is what the creators wanted [50]. The video ends with a call for political action for a multilateral arms control effort to ban lethal autonomous systems employing AI capabilities. In many ways, the makers of the "Slaughterbots" video, the Future of Life Institute, and other supporting civil society groups are the most direct in who their message is intended to influence; they want the UN and its member states to draft and implement international law restricting or prohibiting certain types of robotics.

While the capabilities portrayed in the video are speculative, the PRC has been implicated in sales of unmanned aerial vehicles with some level of lethal capability to Pakistan, Saudi Arabia, and other states [51]. This shows that the concerns regarding advanced LAWs are not unfounded even if some of the depictions used to advocate for arms control and other governance measures are more speculative or sensationalized.

That need to differentiate rhetoric from significant intellectual and policy-relevant discourse was illustrated in the responses to a security-related blog post from summer 2019. A retired Air Force Colonel and a former Navy officer penned a piece on how AI might affect nuclear weapons strategy [52]. In particular they focused on how an adversary's use of AI might necessitate responses by the US. They focus on the possibility that AI may decrease or "compress" the time between when a nuclear weapon is launched and when the US detects such a launch, which creates less time for information to be gathered and shared with decision-makers and for a response. AI is not the only technology potentially creating such a dilemma, e.g., that is one part of the concern surrounding hypersonic missiles. The compression of detection and implications for decision time is not a new phenomenon [53], and it is a real one. Admittedly, the piece may be seen as characterized as containing nuclear policy wonk jargon; the authors were writing about the need to escape the political dilemma created when that decision-making time is compressed *and* possible political responses in the context of increasing AI capabilities: "There are three primary options we see for escaping the dilemma presented." Only the fourth option they present, i.e., not one of the three primary ones, includes any AI, whereas the first three deal with resiliency, survivability, deterrence, and second-strike capability. The writers of the initial piece were driving a conversation about hard choices that may need to be addressed through strategic analysis and presentation of situations that technology may enable.

Subsequently, a highly regarded policy-relevant outlet published a critical response focusing on that fourth option as if it was something that was being recommended [54]. It then received more attention when it was picked up and amplified in a popular online publication [55]. It is important that such discussions can be had in public rather than restricted to purely classified venues with small sets of people. One may certainly speculate that the piece received additional attention because of the authors' current and former affiliations.

3.1 Will AI Replicate Human Biases, Stereotypes, and Prejudices?

As machine learning applications such as facial recognition are increasingly employed, study of how the training data may replicate existing human biases has been well-documented [56]. A 2018 study demonstrated how racism can influence how people interact with robots [57]. The study conducted in New Zealand adapted the classic "shooter bias" test to robots, which studied implicit racial bias based on the speed with which white subjects identified a black person as a potential threat, the team was able to examine the reactions to "racialized" robots. The study's PI professor Christoph Bartneck, College of Engineering, University of Canterbury (NZ) noted that "We project our prejudices onto robots [58]."

Importantly, it's not just topics like racism in which the training set may be influenced by human biases: algorithms for finding chemical reaction conditions have been found to be influenced by the chemists that program them: "Anthropogenic biases in both the reagent choices and reaction conditions of chemical reaction datasets using a combination of data mining and experiments [59]." This is a particularly fascinating example because few of us would associate things like inorganic chemistry synthesis with cognitive bias. And to be explicit, it's not biases in the reactions, that's kinetics and thermodynamics; it's bias in the humans designing the reactions, to be specific. Chemistry professor Joshua Schrier from Fordham University summarized it well: "Considering machine learning's promise, it's a shame to make an algorithm that's just as stupid as humans because of the way it's trained [60]."

If human biases can impact machine learning outcomes for designing inorganic reactions, it's something to be cognizant of for other—potentially more consequential—decision-making assisted by AI. Beyond ethical concerns about racial, sexist, or other biases, on the operational and strategic levels, this is why ensuring training data sets are as free of bias as possible is critically important. From a security perspective there is a need to be vigilant in looking for bias, not only for ethical reasons, but because failure to recognize cases where it's metaphorically 'baked' into the mix through AI training sets or a machine learning algorithm may have real-world operational implications.

3.2 Who's Got the AI Advantage… or Creative Countermeasures

In their 2017 monograph, *Artificial Intelligence and National Security,* [which overall is excellent] authors Greg Allen and Taniel Chan, identify what they call "Potential Transformative Scenarios [61]." The first of these scenarios is titled "Supercharged surveillance brings about the end of guerilla warfare." Use of machine learning by the Chinese state has documented in context of oppression of the Uyghurs [62], for general surveillance, and as part of social capital efforts [63]. Other examples include Russia's extensive deployment of CCTV cameras and use of facial recognition in public areas [64] and plans to install such in schools [65]. Concerns have arisen over the potential for such to be used against protesters and dissidents [66]. It's not just authoritarian states, a 2019 analysis found that "[a]t least seventy-five out of 176 countries globally are actively using AI technologies for surveillance purposes [67]." The expansion of AI-assisted surveillance into the civilian realm is occurring globally.

While states clearly are pursuing development and deployment of surveillance technology, it's not clear how well they are addressing human creativity for countermeasures and whether the technology favors the dominant power, usually a state, or favors the challenger.

During the summer of 2019, democracy protesters in Hong Kong were innovating and using simple countermeasures to avoid surveillance and identification, such as physical barriers (masks), commercially-available laser pointers to dazzle the facial recognition cameras, and wrapping themselves in Mylar emergency blankets to minimize heat (IR, infrared) signatures. Thermal surveillance is thought to be employed within Hong Kong since at least 2004 when it may have been used to detect passengers infected with SARS. These efforts by protestors have been called "[a] war against Chinese artificial intelligence [68]." It suggests that states should not forget about human creativity, adaption of consumer products, and what are perceived as common or 'lower end' technologies. Thinking about the nature and how adversaries might employ simple, innovative countermeasures is understudied, if noticed at all. As was witnessed during Operation Iraqi Freedom (OIF) through the deadly use of improvised explosive devices, co-option of low-tech civilian infrastructure by insurgents asymmetrically is a real challenge.

4 Conclusions

This chapter surveyed anticipated military applications of artificial intelligence (AI) in the context of how security implications intersect with political and rhetorical factors. The widespread emphasis on the importance of AI globally, especially in the context military and security balance of power, is uncontested politically, and at the same time, it is also an area in need of more investigation by scholars. This can be seen in the rhetoric of political leaders, in civil society efforts to advocate for limiting threat of emerging technology that employs AI through legal governance, and in scholarly-level discourse, which can bleed into popular publications. This chapter also looked at areas that get highlighted in broader ethics debates or in context of domestic law enforcement, such as the problem of addressing and overcoming bias in training data sets used for machine learning applications, but that are often not considered with the same level of concern in security context where human cognitive biases may be different from racial, gender, or normative biases.

How and to which audiences—domestic, international, allies, and/or competitors—messages about AI are constructed and employed is another area in need of additional study and understanding. And all of that needs to be assessed in context of technical and operational robustness.

Broadly and underlying AI and almost all emerging technologies, the dual use conundrum has become a greater concern due to other characteristics of the changing strategic environment. The term "dual-use" technology has evolved to have multiple meanings. While in much of the nuclear security world, it refers to a demarcation between civilian and military uses. In the realm of emerging technologies, dual use more often refers to the fact that many applications of machine learning and artificial intelligence (as well as other emerging technologies) have legitimate uses in a wide range of scientific research and industrial activity, including defensive military uses, as well as could be potential misused for deleterious or nefarious purposes. The underlying conundrum is that intent can be hard to determine before use and impossible to predict if one is looking at the basic science and research.

Addressing some of the security challenges of AI-enabled systems, including reducing the risk from misuse of such technology will mean consideration of the highly transnational nature of technology, the people enabling it, and the materials and tacit knowledge required to use (or mis-use) it. Traditional and innovative new approaches to reducing risks from the emergence of new technology like AI are important policy elements in reducing the risk of malfeasant applications of technology.

Included in those choices are flexible approaches to coordination and reducing the risk of malfeasant use, which are important policy elements in reducing the potential risks posed by emerging technologies, like robotics, nanotechnology, the cognitive neurosciences, and synthetic genomics. Past methods for other technologies that don't consider the international nature of the science and technology industry are not adequate. Any international approaches must be interdisciplinary in focus, cognizant of the multi-polar post-Cold War—and increasingly post-9–11—world, and appreciate the role of private funders, commercial development, and transnational corporations.

References

1. White House Office of Science and Technology Policy (2016) Preparing for the future of artificial intelligence, Oct 2016; White House, Presidential Executive Order 13859 on Maintaining American Leadership in Artificial Intelligence, 11 Feb 2019, Federal Registrar 84(31). https://www.govinfo.gov/content/pkg/DCPD-201900073/pdf/DCPD-201900073.pdf
2. John S. McCain National Defense Authorization Act for Fiscal Year 2019, Public Law 115–232. U.S. Statutes at Large 132 (2018)
3. Department of Defense, Summary of the 2018 Department of Defense Artificial Intelligence Strategy: Harnessing AI to Advance Our Security and Prosperity, Washington, D.C., 2019. https://media.defense.gov/2019/Feb/12/2002088963/-1/-1/1/SUMMARY-OF-DOD-AI-STRATEGY.PDF
4. Allen G, Chan T (2017) Artificial intelligence and national security. Harvard Belfer Center
5. Rasser M, Lamberth M, Riikonen A, Guo C, Horowitz M, Scharre P (2019) The American AI century: a blueprint for action. Center for a New American Security, Washington, 2. https://www.cnas.org/publications/reports/the-american-ai-century-a-blueprint-for-action
6. Executive Office of the President, National Science and Technology Council, Select Committee on Artificial Intelligence (2019) The National Artificial Intelligence Research and Development Strategic Plan: 2019 Update, Washington, D.C., 2019, 1. https://www.nitrd.gov/pubs/National-AI-RD-Strategy-2019.pdf
7. John S. McCain National Defense Authorization Act for Fiscal Year 2019, Public Law 115–232. U.S. Statutes at Large 132 (2018):1697–1698
8. U.S. Library of Congress, Congressional Research Service (2019) Artificial Intelligence and National Security, by Kelley Sayler, R45178, 2. https://crsreports.congress.gov/product/pdf/R/R45178/5
9. Grace K, Salvatier J, Dafoe A, Zhang B, Evans O (2018) When will AI exceed human performance? Evidence from AI experts. J Artif Intell Res 62:731
10. Executive Office of the President, National Science and Technology Council, Select Committee on Artificial Intelligence (2019) The National Artificial Intelligence Research and Development Strategic Plan: 2019 Update, Washington D.C., 54. https://www.nitrd.gov/pubs/National-AI-RD-Strategy-2019.pdf
11. Executive Office of the President, National Science and Technology Council, Committee on Technology National Science Technology Council, Subcommittee on Machine Learning Artificial Intelligence. Preparing for the Future of Artificial Intelligence, Washington, D.C., 2016, 7. https://obamawhitehouse.archives.gov/sites/default/files/whitehouse_files/microsites/ostp/NSTC/preparing_for_the_future_of_ai.pdf
12. Allen GC (2017) Project Maven brings AI to the fight against ISIS. Bull At Sci, Dec 21, 2017. https://thebulletin.org/2017/12/project-maven-brings-ai-to-the-fight-against-isis/

13. Pellerin C (2017) Project Maven to deploy computer algorithms to war zone by Year's End. DoD News, July 21, 2017. https://www.defense.gov/Explore/News/Article/Article/1254719/project-maven-to-deploy-computer-algorithms-to-war-zone-by-years-end/
14. Lingel S et al (2020) Joint all-domain command and control for modern warfare: an analytic framework for identifying and developing artificial intelligence applications. RAND Corporation. https://www.rand.org/pubs/research_reports/RR4408z1.html
15. Zadalis T (2018) Multi-domain command and control: maintaining our asymmetric advantage. J Joint Air Power Competence Centre 26:10–15. Spring/Summer 2018. https://www.japcc.org/multi-domain-command-and-control/
16. DARPA (2018) Accelerating the exploration of promising artificial intelligence concepts. July 20, 2018. https://www.darpa.mil/news-events/2018-07-20a
17. DARPA (n.d.) AI Next Campaign. https://www.darpa.mil/work-with-us/ai-next-campaign
18. Department of Defense, Fiscal Year (FY) 2020 Budget estimates, defense advanced research projects agency defense-wide justification book volume 1 of 5 research, development, test & evaluation, defense-wide, p 18, Mar 2019. https://www.darpa.mil/attachments/DARPA_FY20_Presidents_Budget_Request.pdf
19. Fraze D (n.d.) DARPA Cyber Grand Challenge (CGC). https://www.darpa.mil/program/cyber-grand-challenge
20. Bing C (2017) The tech behind the DARPA grand challenge winner will now be used by the Pentagon. CyberScoop, Aug 17, 2017. https://www.cyberscoop.com/mayhem-darpa-cyber-grand-challenge-dod-voltron/
21. Lynch J (2018) The AI that protects DoD networks from zero-day exploits. Defense News, July 27, 2018. https://www.c4isrnet.com/dod/2018/07/27/the-ai-that-protects-dod-networks-from-zero-day-exploits/
22. Brush S, Schoenberg T, Ring S (2015) How a mystery trader with an algorithm may have caused the flash crash. Bloomberg News, Apr 21, 2015. https://www.bloomberg.com/news/articles/2015-04-22/mystery-trader-armed-with-algorithms-rewrites-flash-crash-story; Condliffe J (2016) Algorithms probably caused a flash crash of the British pound. Tech Review, Oct 7, 2016. https://www.technologyreview.com/2016/10/07/244656/algorithms-probably-caused-a-flash-crash-of-the-british-pound/
23. Maas MM (2018) Regulating for 'normal AI accidents': operational lessons for the responsible governance of artificial intelligence deployment. In: AIES'18: proceedings of the 2018 AAAI/ACM conference on AI, ethics, and society, Dec 2018, pp 223–228. https://doi.org/10.1145/3278721.3278766
24. Perrow C (1984) Normal accidents: living with high risk technologies. Princeton University Press; Sagan S (1995) The limits of safety: organizations, accidents, and nuclear weapons. Princeton University Press
25. Department of Defense Directive 3000.09. Autonomy in Weapon Systems. Updated May 8, 2017. https://www.esd.whs.mil/portals/54/documents/dd/issuances/dodd/300009p.pdf
26. Arquilla J, Ronfeldt DF (2000) Swarming and the future of conflict. RAND Corporation, Santa Monica; Johnson J Artificial intelligence, drone swarming and escalation risks in future warfare. RUSI J 165(2):26–36; Verbruggen M (2021) Drone swarms: coming (sometime) to a war near you. Bull At Sci Feb 3, 2021. https://thebulletin.org/2021/02/drone-swarms-coming-sometime-to-a-war-near-you-just-not-today/
27. Guitton MJ (2021) Fighting the locusts: implementing military countermeasures against drones and drone swarms. Scandinavian J Military Stud 4(1):26–36; Hammers TX (2016) Cheap technology will challenge U.S. Tactical Dominance. Joint Force Q 81:79–86
28. Brambilla M, Ferrante E, Birattari M, Dorigo M (2013) Swarm robotics: A review from the swarm engineering perspective. Swarm Intell 7(1):1–41; Garattoni L, Birattari M (2018) Autonomous task sequencing in a robot swarm. Sci Robot 3(20):eaat0430; Tsykunov E, Agishev R, Ibrahimov R, Labazanova L, Tleugazy A, Tsetserukou D (2019) SwarmTouch: guiding a swarm of micro-quadrotors with impedance control using a wearable tactile interface. IEEE Trans Haptics 12(3):363–374

29. Keerthi KS, Mahapatra B, Menon VG (2020) Into the world of underwater swarm robotics: architecture, communication, applications and challenges. Recent Adv Comput Sci Commun 13(2):110–119; Ilachinski A (2017) AI, robots, and swarms: issues, questions, and recommended studies, Center for Naval Analysis, Jan 2017. https://www.cna.org/cna_files/pdf/DRM-2017-U-014796-Final-SUMMARY.pdf
30. Wintour P (2020) Iran says AI and 'satellite-controlled' gun used to kill nuclear scientist. The Guardian (UK), Dec 7, 2020. https://www.theguardian.com/world/2020/dec/07/mohsen-fakhri zadeh-iran-says-ai-and-satellite-controlled-gun-used-to-kill-nuclear-scientist
31. Mohsen Fakhrizadeh: 'Machine-gun with AI' used to kill Iran scientist. BBC News, Dec 7, 2020. https://www.bbc.com/news/world-middle-east-55214359
32. Solomon J (2012) Iran's nuclear-arms guru resurfaces. The Wall Street Journal, Aug 30, 2012. https://www.wsj.com/articles/SB10000872396390444230504577615971688458892
33. Payne K (2018) Artificial intelligence: a revolution in strategic affairs? Survival 60(5):7–32; Johnson J (2019) The AI-cyber nexus: implications for military escalation, deterrence and strategic stability. J Cyber Policy, 4(3):442–460; 7(2); Fitzpatrick M (2019) Artificial intelligence and nuclear command and control. Survival 61(3):81–92; Shah SSH (2019) The perils of AI for nuclear deterrence. CISS Insights J Strategic Stud (Pakistan), Winter 2019 7(2). https://journal.ciss.org.pk/index.php/ciss-insight/article/view/10
34. Geist E, Lohn AJ (2018) How might artificial intelligence affect the risk of nuclear war? RAND
35. Davis ZS (2019) Artificial intelligence on the battlefield, Center for Global Security Research, Lawrence Livermore National Laboratory, March 2019
36. Lyons K (2020) This AI kitty litter box will analyze your cat's poops for some reason. The Verge, Vox Media, 7 Jan 2020. https://www.theverge.com/2020/1/7/21054690/ai-smart-kitty-litter-box-cats-poop-pee-ces-health
37. Sayler K (2019) Artificial intelligence and national security, by Congressional Research Service, R45178 (2019). https://crsreports.congress.gov/product/pdf/R/R45178/5
38. 'Whoever leads in AI will rule the world': Putin to Russian children on Knowledge Day. Russia Today (Moscow), Sept 1, 2017. https://www.rt.com/news/401731-ai-rule-world-putin/
39. Kosal ME (2015) Military applications of nanotechnology: implications for strategic security I," final report to the Project on Advanced Systems and Concepts for Countering Weapons of Mass Destruction (PASCC), Center on Contemporary Conflict, Naval Postgraduate School, under Grant No. N00244–12–1–0050, Jan 2015
40. New Generation Artificial Intelligence Development Plan (AIDP). An English translation is available by Graham Webster, Rogier Creemers, Paul Triolo, and Elsa Kania (translators), Full Translation: China's 'New Generation Artificial Intelligence Development Plan,' New America, Aug 1, 2017. https://www.newamerica.org/cybersecurity-initiative/digichina/blog/full-transl ation-chinas-new-generation-artificial-intelligence-development-plan-2017/; also see Next Generation Artificial Intelligence Development Plan Issued by State Council, China Science and Technology Journal, Department of International Cooperation Ministry of Science and Technology (MOST), P.R.China, #17, Sept 15, 2017. https://fi.china-embassy.org/eng/kxjs/P020171025789108009001.pdf
41. Allen GC (2019) Understanding China's AI strategy, CNAS report, Washington, D.C., Feb 6, 2019. https://www.cnas.org/publications/reports/understanding-chinas-ai-strategy
42. National Research Council (1997) Computer Science and Artificial Intelligence. The National Academies Press, Washington, DC. https://doi.org/10.17226/5812
43. Report of the Defense Science Board Task Force on University Responsiveness to National Security Requirements, Washington, D.C., Jan 1982, #ADA112070, https://apps.dtic.mil/dtic/tr/fulltext/u2/a112070.pdf; Report of the Defense Science Board, Autonomy, Washington, D.C., June 2016, #AD1017790, https://dsb.cto.mil/reports/2010s/DSBSS15.pdf
44. Information Technology and R&D: Critical Trends and Issues, U.S. Congress, Office of Technology Assessment, OTA-CIT-268, Washington, D.C., Feb 1985. https://hdl.handle.net/10822/708535
45. Guice J (1998) Controversy and the state: lord ARPA and intelligent computing. Soc Stud Sci 28(1):103–138. JSTOR. www.jstor.org/stable/285752

46. Defense Science Board, Military Applications of New-Generation Computing Technologies, Washington, D.C., Dec 1984, Report #ADA152154. https://apps.dtic.mil/dtic/tr/fulltext/u2/a152154.pdf
47. Executive Order 13859 of February 11, 2019, Maintaining American Leadership in Artificial Intelligence. Federal Registrar 84(31):1. https://www.govinfo.gov/content/pkg/DCPD-201900073/pdf/DCPD-201900073.pdf
48. "Slaughterbots" video, Stop Autonomous Weapons (Future of Life Institute, 2017) https://www.youtube.com/watch?v=HipTO_7mUOw; Cussins J (2017) AI Researchers Create Video to Call for Autonomous Weapons Ban at UN. The Future of Life Institute, Nov 14, 2017. https://futureoflife.org/2017/11/14/ai-researchers-create-video-call-autonomous-weapons-ban-un/
49. Scharre P (2017) Why you shouldn't fear Slaughterbots. IEEE Spectrum: Technology, Engineering, and Science News, 22 Dec 2017. https://spectrum.ieee.org/automaton/robotics/military-robots/why-you-shouldnt-fear-slaughterbots
50. Turchin A, Could slaughterbots wipe out humanity? Assessment of the global catastrophic risk posed by autonomous weapons. https://philpapers.org/rec/TURCSW; Oberhaus D (2017) Watch 'Slaughterbots,' A Warning About the Future of Killer Bots. Vice Dec17, 2017, https://motherboard.vice.com/en_us/article/9kqmy5/slaughterbots-autonomous-weapons-future-of-life; Tegmark M, Russel S, Conn A, Aguirre A (2018) Why You Should Fear 'Slaughterbots'—A Response IEEE Spectrum: Technology, Engineering, and Science News. https://spectrum.ieee.org/automaton/robotics/artificial-intelligence/why-you-should-fear-slaughterbots-a-response; Weaver N (2017) 'Slaughterbots' and other (anticipated) autonomous weapons problems. Lawfare Nov 28, 2017. https://www.lawfareblog.com/slaughterbots-and-other-anticipated-autonomous-weapons-problems; Jensen BM, Whyte C, Cuomo S (2020) Algorithms at war: the promise, peril, and limits of artificial intelligence. Int Stud Rev 22(3):526–550
51. Bocchi A (2019) China is selling autonomous weaponized drones to Saudi Arabia and Pakistan. Al Bawaba, Nov 18, 2019. https://www.albawaba.com/news/china-selling-autonomous-weaponized-drones-saudi-arabia-and-pakistan-1321951; Turner P (2019) SecDef: China is exporting killer robots to the Mideast. Defense One, Nov 5, 2019. https://www.defenseone.com/technology/2019/11/secdef-china-exporting-killer-robots-mideast/161100/
52. Lowther A, McGiffin C (2019) America needs a 'dead hand,'. War on the Rocks, Aug 16, 2019. https://warontherocks.com/2019/08/america-needs-a-dead-hand/.
53. Nichols DH (1988) Looking beyond the strategic defense initiative, Army War College, Mar 1988, Report No AD-A195 079. https://apps.dtic.mil/sti/citations/ADA195079
54. Field M (2019) Strangelove redux: US experts propose having AI control nuclear weapons. Bull At Sci, Aug 30, 2019. https://thebulletin.org/2019/08/strangelove-redux-us-experts-propose-having-ai-control-nuclear-weapons/
55. Gault M (2019) Experts want to give control of America's nuclear missiles to AI. Vice, Sept 3, 2019. https://www.vice.com/en/article/59n3y5/experts-want-to-give-control-of-americas-nuclear-missiles-to-ai
56. Chouldechova A, Putnam-Hornstein E, Benavides-Prado D, Fialko O, Vaithianathan R (2018) In: Proceedings of machine learning research 81:134–148; Bolukbasi T, Chang K-W, Zou J, Saligrama V, Kalai A (2016) Adv Neural Inf Proc Syst 4349–4357; Garg N, Schiebinger L, Jurafsky D, Zou J (2018) Word embeddings quantify 100 years of gender and ethnic stereotypes. PNAS 115:3635–E3644
57. American Society of Mechanical Engineers (ASME). https://www.asme.org/topics-resources/content/racism-runs-deep-even-against-robots
58. Bartneck C et al (2018) Robots and Racism. Association for Computing Machinery (ACM), HRI
59. Jia X et al (2019) Anthropogenic biases in chemical reaction data hinder exploratory inorganic synthesis. Nature 573:251–255. https://www.nature.com/articles/s41586-019-1540-5
60. Lemonick S (2019) Machine learning can have human bias. Chem Eng News 97(6). https://cen.acs.org/physical-chemistry/computational-chemistry/Machine-learning-human-bias/97/i36

61. Allen G, Chan T (2017) Artificial intelligence and national security. Harvard Belfer Center, p 31
62. Taddonio P (2019) How China's government is using AI on its Uighur Muslim population. PBS Frontline, Nov 21, 2019. https://www.pbs.org/wgbh/frontline/article/how-chinas-government-is-using-ai-on-its-uighur-muslim-population/
63. China's Digital Authoritarianism: Surveillance, Influence, and Political Control, U.S. House of Representatives, Permanent Select Committee on Intelligence, committee hearing, May 16, 2019. https://docs.house.gov/Committee/Calendar/ByEvent.aspx?EventID=109462; Morgus R, Sherman J (2018) Authoritarians are exporting surveillance tech, and with it their vision for the internet, Council on Foreign Relations, Dec 5, 2018. https://www.cfr.org/blog/authoritarians-are-exporting-surveillance-tech-and-it-their-vision-internet; Qiang X (2020) The Road to Digital Unfreedom: President Xi's Surveillance State. J Democracy 3(1):53–67; Alfred Ng, How China uses facial recognition to control human behavior, C/Net, Aug 11, 2020. https://www.cnet.com/news/in-china-facial-recognition-public-shaming-and-control-go-hand-in-hand/
64. Regions will recognize by sight: Moscow video surveillance system will be launched in ten more cities. Kommersant (Russia), Sept 25, 2020. https://www.kommersant.ru/doc/4503379
65. Russia to Install 'Orwell' Facial Recognition Tech in Every School—Vedomosti. The Moscow Times (Russia), June 16, 2020. https://www.themoscowtimes.com/2020/06/16/russia-to-install-orwell-facial-recognition-tech-in-every-school-vedomosti-a70585
66. Russia Expands Facial Recognition Despite Privacy Concerns (2020) Human Rights Watch, Oct 2, 2020. https://www.hrw.org/news/2020/10/02/russia-expands-facial-recognition-despite-privacy-concerns. Stolyarov G, Tétrault-Farber G (2021) "Face control": Russian police go digital against protesters," Reuters, Feb 22, 2021. https://www.reuters.com/article/us-russia-politics-navalny-tech/face-control-russian-police-go-digital-against-protesters-idUSKBN2AB1U2; "Moscow's facial recognition cameras are identifying Navalny supporters: activists," South China Morning Press (Hong Kong), Feb 4, 2021. https://www.scmp.com/news/world/russia-central-asia/article/3120588/moscows-facial-recognition-cameras-are-identifying
67. Feldstein S (2019) The global expansion of AI surveillance. Carnegie endowment for international peace paper, Sept 17, 2019
68. Via Twitter Alessandra Bocchi @alessabocchi

The Impacts of Proliferation and Autonomy of Small Unmanned Aircraft Systems on Security

Tejas G. Puranik

Abstract Unmanned Aircraft Systems (UAS) have become a regular part of military operations and civilian life since the early 2000s. The proliferation of drone technologies has led to reduced costs and increased accessibility for individuals, states, and non-state actors. While extensive research and commentary have been made on the impacts of high-end military drones, the literature is comparatively sparse on the impacts of small UAS. With the regulations for civilian drones set to be finalized shortly, the potential impacts of small UAS on safety, privacy, and security need to be understood to have the right regulatory framework in place. This chapter deals with estimating the projected impacts of small UAS proliferation and increased autonomy on security. A robust analysis is presented by evaluating the disruptive potential of national security in various scenarios by analyzing the current and future trends of drone technologies, regulations, threats, and other important variables. The framework provided lays the groundwork for further studies into the impact of small UAS on security and hopes to inform future usage, perception, and policy surrounding these systems.

1 Introduction

Since the early 2000s, there has been rapid development in the use of unmanned aircraft systems (UAS), more commonly known as 'drones.' Drones have become a regular part of military and civilian life. The successful military deployment of drones has increased awareness and created public demand to operate UAS for a variety of non-military applications. Over 90 countries and non-state actors operate drones today, including at least 30 operating or developing armed drones. The postwar historical trend in aviation has been that research in military systems and applications precedes its percolation into the commercial and civilian sectors. To some extent, however, drones are the exception. Other than strictly military technologies such as

---

T. G. Puranik (✉)
Georgia Institute of Technology, Atlanta, GA, USA
e-mail: tpuranik3@gatech.edu

© The Author(s), under exclusive license to Springer Nature Switzerland AG 2021
M. E. Kosal (ed.), *Proliferation of Weapons- and Dual-Use Technologies*,
Advanced Sciences and Technologies for Security Applications,
https://doi.org/10.1007/978-3-030-73655-2_4

stealth, developments in commercial drones are driving down the costs and barriers to entry, particularly in the small UAS categories. The idea that drones can replace crewed flight in situations that are dull, dirty, or dangerous for the human pilot has led to increased research into drones' usage for various purposes beyond military use. Therefore, drones could significantly impact civilian tasks such as transportation, communication, agriculture, disaster mitigation, law enforcement, media, environment preservation, etc. Drones have already made their presence felt in specific scenarios (such as surveillance and counter-terrorism), and as the costs of operation and barriers to entry reduce, they seem poised to tackle problems in a variety of new domains.

The United States Department of Defense (DOD) defines a drone as—*"A powered, aerial vehicle that does not carry a human operator, uses aerodynamic forces to provide vehicle lift, can fly itself (autonomously) or be remotely piloted, can be expendable or recoverable at the end of the flight, and can carry a lethal or nonlethal payload"* [1]. However, the idea that a UAS is "unmanned" is a misnomer because current generation UAS are still operated remotely by a human pilot. Therefore, the DOD further defines UAS as *"A system whose components include the necessary equipment, network, and personnel to control an unmanned aircraft."* While the definition is broadly applicable to a variety of systems, the DOD classifies UAS into five broad categories in increasing order of their payload capabilities, gross weight, and mission types (micro/mini tactical, small tactical, tactical, persistent, penetrating). Figure 1 shows a schematic of the overall spectrum of UAS currently in everyday use and the categories defined by the US DOD.

A similar classification of UAS has been by various other agencies within the military and civilian domain and academia. NASA atmospheric research provides a 3-category classification based on a combination of maximum weight and airspeed capability [2]. This classification groups categories 1 and 2 from the DOD categories into a single group and creates two more groups out of category 3, 4, and 5 from the DOD categories. Clarke, [3] an expert in the field, provides a more straightforward bipartite classification (large and small) based on weight, with the small category further divided into nano, micro, and mini. The Center for a New American Security (CNAS) provides an operator-oriented classification into four categories based on accessibility and technological sophistication required to operate. The eventual categories that arise are similar to those created based on weight [4]. On the civilian side, the Federal Aviation Administration (FAA) has also defined the small unmanned

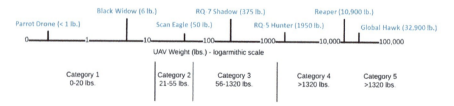

Fig. 1 Spectrum of UAS categories according to US DOD classification

aircraft systems for commercial and hobbyist use based on weight (category 1 & 2 of DOD classification). Thus, it is evident that while there is little consensus in the nomenclature of UAS classification, there is, in general, consistency in the eventual groupings that arise. Therefore, in this work, the categorization based on the DOD classification presented in Fig. 1 is followed.

At the large end of the spectrum, proliferation and increasing autonomy of category 4 and 5 UAS has already had profound impacts on the conduct of warfare and national strategy. For example, post 9–11, the US has conducted about 50 total counterterrorism strikes using armed drones from 2001 to 2008, which jumped up to about 450 from 2009 to 2014 [5]. Armed drones have been the subject of considerable research, scholarly work, and debate in recent years [6]. These studies include but are not limited to the technological capabilities, ethical and moral issues surrounding autonomous drones, regulatory issues, and proliferation. Many normative proposals have been made recommending everything from complete prohibition on one end to meaningful human control of autonomous drones at the other.

Meanwhile, at the low end of the UAS spectrum, small drones' capabilities have increased along with a simultaneous decrease in manufacturing costs [7]. Due to the proliferation of small drones, the increase in market-size has attracted further investment and caused a leap in the functionality-to-cost ratio. he so-called hobbyist drones available for purchase in either pre-assembled or customizable component form enable several capabilities that were formerly the monopoly of large states' military. Estimates from the FAA indicate that the total number of registered small UAS as of October 2017 was more than 900,000 [8]. This number is predicted to grow up to 4 million by the year 2020 according to agency forecasts [9]. Therefore, the proliferation of small UAS is an important contemporary issue that needs to be better understood. While many studies are available for large UAS, as they have been around for much longer, relatively few exist relating to small UAS proliferation. Much of the existing literature on drones has focused on challenges arising from the proliferation of high-end military-grade systems when, in reality, a far wider range of drones is already available to states, non-state actors, and individuals [10]. Therefore, this work aims to focus on the impact of small UAS proliferation. Henceforth small UAS will be used to refer to the categories of drones focused on in this work. These comprise category 1 and 2 from the DOD definitions, i.e., drones up to a weight of 55 lbs. with some flexibility on this threshold.

In addition to understanding the effects of drone proliferation, an important capability that is currently maturing is autonomous operations. The increased autonomy of lethal weapons-equipped drones has raised the alarm in parts of the security community [11]. Similarly, increased autonomous operations are being tested across the UAS spectrum, including small UAS operations. While autonomy can have different meanings in different contexts, in the UAS domain, it has a particular meaning. For current generation drones, a human operator is in constant oversight in almost all the levels of autonomous operations (hence the popular term Remotely Piloted Aircraft). The International Organization for Standardization defines robot autonomy as the ability to perform intended tasks based on current state and sensing, without human intervention [12]. The following discussion tries to identify how this technology is applied at different levels of sophistication in the military and civilian UAS landscape.

The military drone environment identifies four to five levels of autonomy. These are human-operated, human-delegated, human-supervised, mostly autonomous, and fully autonomous [3]. The amount of direct human control exercised becomes progressively lower as each level progresses. In the military context, one of the most debated aspects of autonomous UAS operations is the launch of an attack. This action is typically not delegated to the drone for any level other than the highest level of autonomy. However, because of the advanced sensors and technology available on large drones, most routine functions such as maintaining control, navigation, loitering, etc. can be carried out autonomously. On the other hand, for small drones, three broad levels of autonomy are identified [13]—*sensory-motor* autonomy (translate high-level human commands into actions like navigation, hold position, etc.), *reactive* autonomy (maintain current position or trajectory in the presence of external perturbations, take-off and land), and *cognitive* autonomy (perform simultaneous localization and mapping; resolve conflicting information, plan, etc.). A summary of the levels of autonomy for small UAS as provided by Floreano [13] is provided in Fig. 2.

In the military domain, classification of autonomy focuses more on the presence or absence of a human element as most of the sophisticated large drones already have plenty of autonomous operations capabilities. On the other hand, in small UAS operations, especially those that encompass operations in Fig. 1, the focus of automation is more on the functional capability of the drones. This is because these smaller systems do not yet have many of those capabilities (except for drones at the larger end of the small UAS spectrum). Therefore, while the classification is useful for initial analysis, this capabilities gap should be noted when extrapolating the analysis provided here or using a similar classification elsewhere. Of the three types of autonomy identified, sense-and-avoid capabilities or reactive autonomy are sought after as this has been identified as one of the important to full integration of small UAS in the airspace [14].

Levels of autonomy: requirements, availability, and readiness for market					
	Exteroceptive sensors	Computational Load	Supervision Required	Readiness Level	Validated on Drone Type
Sensory-motor autonomy	None or few	Little	Yes	Deployed	All types
Reactive autonomy	Few or sparse	Medium	Little	Partly deployed	Fixed Wing, rotorcraft, and flapping wing
Cognitive autonomy	Several and high density	High	None	Not yet deployed	Mostly rotorcraft

Fig. 2 Summary of levels of autonomy in small UAS recreated based on Floreano et al. [13]

2 Motivation

The proliferation of small UAS has raised several concerns within the security community. As this technology continues to become more accessible, improvised drones carrying explosives or chemical or biological agents will be increasingly within reach of virtually any state, non-state actor, or individual. The FAA has initially provided regulations (14 CFR Part 107) [15] for small UAS operations for vehicles under 55 lbs. While these regulations provide a starting point mandating visual line-of-sight operations of small UAS, a road map for the gradual integration into the national airspace system of civil unmanned drones that can fly beyond the operator's line of sight is expected by 2028 [16]. Some countries, including Australia, Canada, France, Switzerland, and the United Kingdom have national regulations that are already in place for small UAS operations in their airspace [17]. France allows beyond-line-of-sight operations on a case-by-case basis whereas Switzerland allows autonomous operations as long as the operator can regain control. The US's current regulations have introduced the first step towards integrating UAS in the national airspace, however, many hurdles remain. The volume of aircraft in the US airspace (which contains an order of magnitude more aircraft than any other nation) [18] adds complexity to the task of safely integrating UAS. Some of the other hurdles include the lack of standard command and control protocol, no dedicated secure frequency for UAS operations, and the inability to detect and avoid obstacles (including other aircraft or drones).

The civilian uses of drones are still only in their infancy, and therefore there are relatively few examples of harm caused by drones to date [19]. Nevertheless, numerous incidents have been recorded recently, which highlight the potential issues that might arise in the near term future due to the proliferation of small UAS. A few of these have been highlighted here from the military as well as civilian domain for the purpose of illustration.

On August 25, 2010, the US Navy lost control of a UAV and could only intervene after it had flown 37 km toward, and then over, Washington DC airspace [20]. During a UAS incident in July 2017, a drone was spotted near London's Gatwick airport's approach path and caused delays of up to three hours and increased disruption on all airports in the vicinity [21]. This type of incident could result in a particularly precarious situation that could be capitalized by non-state actors elevating a seemingly harmless incident to one that could potentially endanger hundreds of lives by creating dangerous conditions for civilian air traffic. In 2013 a security researcher modified a Parrot AR Drone 2 to automatically detect and disconnect another UAV from its ground station and then reconnect it to an alternative ground station [22]. Various authorities in the U.S., Germany, Spain, and Egypt have foiled at least six potential terrorist attacks with small drones since 2011 [23]. Of course, the well-known military incident that caused great concern was when an American RQ-170 Sentinel drone was captured by Iranian forces in 2011 and brought down by its cyber-warfare unit that commandeered the aircraft and safely landed it [24]. These are but a few examples on an expanding list of incidents and near-misses involving drones.

As with any new technology, adverse occurrences involving drones tend to be sensationalized, especially in the media. W While the number of reported incidents seems to be accurate, the potential impact of near misses tends to be exaggerated for small UAS generally. A robust understanding therefore needs to include a more realistic evaluation of possible impact.

At all levels of technological sophistication, small UAS are increasingly available to responsible and disruptive actors alike. Therefore, military agencies such as the Department of Defense as well as civilian agencies like Homeland Security, FAA, and NASA are interested in the implications of proliferation. The ability to influence the perceptions and responsible operation of UAS as well as develop deterrence strategies in the case of use by disruptive actors will be required to develop a robust national security strategy towards small UAS.

3 Security Puzzle and Research Questions

Whereas small UAS can be utilized by a number of industries as identified earlier, the typical functions carried out by these systems can generally be classified into various operations including but not limited to load delivery, surveillance, physical measurements, connectivity, or passenger transport. This list will change as new technologies like multi-modal drones and foldable drones which are in the basic research stage currently, likely become a reality in a few years. Unless properly used and regulated, drones can pose a risk to *security*, *safety*, and *privacy* in various ways. The vulnerabilities in these three domains and how they are related to each other is further examined here (Fig. 3).

3.1 Security: Use by Non-state Actors

Non-state actors such as insurgents, terrorists, and transnational criminal organizations can employ small UAS to undermine important infrastructure. Although small UAS currently do not have the payload capability or sensors to carry heavy lethal weapons, they can nevertheless be used lethally in a variety of ways by non-state

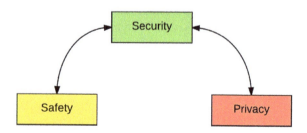

Fig. 3 Potential areas where small UAS operations can pose a risk

actors. The first is in terms of "bringing the detonator," in which the drone is used to target a site that already has a large concentration of explosive material such as aircraft and vehicles, fuel depots, chemical facilities, and ammunition dumps. At these sites, even a few ounces of explosives delivered precisely could initiate a much larger secondary explosion. The second way is to use explosively formed penetrators (EFPs), weighing as little as a few pounds to damage or destroy armored and protected targets [25]. UAS can also be used as cheap precision-guided weapons to disperse chemical or biological payloads in crowded locations such as football stadiums. Some small UAS, such as the Switchblade by AeroVironment, has been proposed to be deployed as expendable 'kamikaze' drones that attack an enemy target kinetically [26]. These systems blur the line between missiles and UAS. Finally, multiple drones operating in swarms can be used for any of the purposes outlined earlier to magnify the impact and improve the likelihood of successfully overwhelming defenses and striking a target [27]. Due to their size, construction material, and flight altitude, hobbyist drones are difficult to defend against if their presence in a particular area is unknown or unexpected.

3.2 Security: Cybersecurity

Communications between civilian UAS and their controllers are typically unencrypted and therefore susceptible to jamming, hacking, or spoofing attacks [28]. Researchers at the University of Texas demonstrated that a GPS spoofer could hijack a UAV by altering the UAV's perceived location [29]. Signals between drones and remote pilots or GPS satellites are subject to a considerable amount of interference—whether environmental, accidental and intentional. SkyJack, created by hacker Samy Kamkar, and is a software package meant to take control of drones using another drone [30]. Data security is also a challenge as a regulatory framework must be adapted for the protection of data collected by small UAS, a lot of which is in the form of videos and images. These concerns point to the need for autonomous vehicle systems to be developed to mitigate such dangers and be equipped with defensive measures such that they can respond automatically and dynamically to both accidental and deliberate defects and attacks.

3.3 Safety

One fundamental requirement for operation in the US National Airspace System (NAS) is to preserve the safety of the public and infrastructure. Two types of critical hazards can typically arise—ground impact and mid-air collision [31]. Ground impact of UAS as light as a few pounds can lead to fatal injuries [32] or cause lasting damage to public infrastructure. The reliability of the avionics technology onboard small UAS is nowhere near that of military-grade drones or large commercial aircraft.

Thus, they present many more failure modes and will need thorough testing and validation before being safe and seamless integration into the airspace. According to a study, small drones pose a more serious threat to large commercial airplanes than bird strikes [33]. Therefore, while midair collisions might only lead to the loss of the UAV for its operator, it can endanger hundreds of lives on-board commercial aircraft with which it might collide. Sense-and-avoid capabilities would need to increase considerably for this to be prevented. Clarke [34] has discussed possible means of minimizing the risk to safety through natural and regulatory barriers.

3.4 Privacy

Typical surveillance applications of drones include environmental monitoring, tracking of livestock and wildlife, measurement of meteorological phenomena, and observation of large-scale human constructions such as buildings, energy infrastructure sites, etc. Drones have been increasingly used by media for journalism [19] and by law-enforcement agencies and homeland security agencies for applications such as border protection [34]. This increasing use of drones has further eroded individual privacy which was already occurring with the proliferation of smartphones. UAS surveillance may target an area, or one or more objects, including people. Use of drones for surveillance can have many detrimental effects on the expectation of privacy derived from the Fourth Amendment of the US Constitution after Katz v. United States (1967) [35]. Further, negative impacts arise at the psychological level on individuals, at the social level on groups and societies, at the economic level on innovators, and at the political level on democracies [36].

Integrating public and civil UAS into the National Airspace System (NAS) by itself carries certain national security implications such as security vetting for certification and training of UAS-related personnel, addressing cyber and communications vulnerabilities, and maintaining/enhancing air defense and air domain awareness capabilities in an increasingly complex and crowded airspace. Due to their size and materials used, small UAS are typically invisible to the naked eye and radar, introducing risk of reduced quality data available to air traffic controllers. Even large drone operations' safety is nowhere near the same level as has been achieved, and is expected, with manned commercial aviation services [37].

The boundaries between safety, privacy, and security become fuzzy when UAS are used with nefarious intent. Non-state actors or states might use small UAS in ways that threaten the public's safety or privacy, creating a security issue. Therefore, it is necessary to tackle these issues as interconnected rather than separate and assess their combined impact in different scenarios. In some cases, existing security frameworks applied to manned aircraft may be applicable. Other security concerns may require development of new frameworks altogether. In the context of the larger problem of weapons technology proliferation, the security issues raised here connect with other topics of interest being pursued, including delivery mechanisms for chemical and biological weapons, civilian GPS vulnerabilities, and cybersecurity. The above considerations lead to several research questions that need to be addressed as small UAS proliferation grows. Some of the important ones tackled in this chapter are:

- How robust are upcoming technologies in the small UAS domain with respect to their projected impact in different scenarios?
- Which scenarios might need deterrence frameworks to be developed to contain threats emerging due to different reasons?
- What are the limitations of autonomy in the near and far term for small UAS?

4 Methodology

Prior authors have summarized the impact of current-generation drones in different contexts [3]. Fig. 4 provides a summary of their interpretations and shows that this impact is not symmetric. While the primary focus of their work was on large and military armed drones, this chapter aims to understand how this impact would change in terms of cutting-edge technologies applied to category 1 and 2 drones of less than 56 lbs.in these and other contexts. While prior authors' impact assessments seem accurate for armed drones, they do not address certain scenarios that are of interest in the scope of small UAS (notably dense urban environments). Additionally, it is noted that in previous studies, the impacts were examined via state-level analysis. However, for small UAS proliferation, this level of analysis is inadequate as use by non-state actors and individuals would not receive attention commensurate with their potential impact.

In such a problem it is difficult to develop a single theory that can successfully explain each category of drones with sufficient depth due to the diversity in industries, applications, and capabilities. Therefore, a *building-block* approach is applied for this task. In such a study, the focus is on categories within the overall spectrum with the

Overall Consequences of Current Generation Drone Proliferation	
Context	Consequences
Counterterrorism operations	High
Interstate war	Low
Crisis onset and deterrence	Moderate
Coercive diplomacy	Low
Domestic control and repression	High
Use by nonstate actors	Moderate

Fig. 4 Consequences of current-generation drones in different contexts (recreated based on Horowitz et al. [5])

intention of better explaining and predicting the impacts within those categories. Therefore, various scenarios of interest with respect to small UAS proliferation will be identified and evaluated.

To carry out a robust analysis of impact, not only are the technological capabilities important, but also the likelihood of specific strategic, operational, and tactical uses. Therefore, a study that evaluates current generation and future small UAS capabilities will involve speculative impacts based on reported literature and extrapolation of present generation capabilities. It is reasoned that the future assessment beyond 10 years is riddled with uncertainty not just from extrapolation but also from the increasingly rapid pace at which the technology is evolving. Therefore, the impact of current and next (2025 timeframe) generation small UAS and the near future (2030 timeframe) projection is evaluated separately in each scenario to account for decreasing accuracy over time. The following discussion outlines scenarios of interest and the dependent and independent variables considered for each.

4.1 Dependent Variables

Various scenarios of interest arise while studying small UAS proliferation which are not particularly applicable for the larger UAS categories and vice versa. Perhaps the most interesting scenario for small UAS is dense urban environments such as megacities where they can have a particularly large impact. On the other hand, due to the (currently) limited payload and range capabilities of small UAS, scenarios such as counterterrorism operations or high-intensity conflict in contested airspace might not be those where small UAS proliferation could have much impact. The list of scenarios explored here is presented below.

- Dense urban environments (megacities)
- National Airspace System (airports).

In each case, the dependent variable is assessed with qualitative rankings of low, medium, or high with respect to the disruptive impact on national security. The afore-mentioned spheres of influence—safety, security, and privacy—of small UAS proliferation provide the basis for assessing each scenario.

4.2 Independent Variables

The proliferation risk presented by small UAS can be measured in terms of various metrics and independent variables (IVs) grouped into different categories that could constitute a predictive model's components in future work. Each variable is assigned a qualitative estimation (low, medium, high) by reviewing existing literature related to that variable. The qualitative estimate is obtained based on reviews, reports, scholarly articles, and other literature in the public domain. The impact of this variable on each scenario in the present is then identified. For the prediction of future impact on the same variable-scenario combination, the variable trend is extrapolated. Thus, the study aims to map how a variable affects each scenario (low, medium, or high). The different categories of independent variables and their current or predicted levels are enumerated here based on review of relevant literature and synthesis of this information.

4.2.1 Capability–Low

The capability of current generation small UAS is estimated in terms of its payload, range, endurance, and speed in this context. The payload carrying capacity of small UAS ranges from a few lbs. to around 25 lbs. Most current small UAS are unable to carry a payload greater than their own weight at their normal endurance. The maximum range and endurance capabilities of small UAS considered here are of the order of a few miles and an hour or two respectively [5]. The maximum speeds attainable by small UAS are typically lower (up to 80–100 mph) than large UAS (greater than 230 mph) [38]. Low capability indicates that current small UAS are limited in terms of these metrics relative to large UAS. In the near future (2030 timeframe) these capabilities are expected to improve (to *medium*) due to the improvements in battery technology, light-weight materials, and other technologies [2].

4.2.2 Operability–Low

Operability is a specific capability of UAS that is separated into its own category because it can dramatically effect UAS robustness in a particular scenario. Specific components of operability considered here are harsh weather operation operations, congested airspace operations, and portability. Among current generation small UAS, harsh weather operation is poor because of the light weight and slower speeds. One of the most important obstacles identified for current generation small UAS is poor sense-and-avoid capabilities [39].

These are important to operate in congested airspace in conjunction with other aircraft, and obstacles. On the other hand, most small UAS are extremely portable due to small size, lightweight materials, and in some cases removable components such as propeller blades. However, the operability overall is still low. The lack of a dedicated frequency spectrum for small UAS operations is another major hindrance to operability. Due to all these reasons, this variable is currently estimated at low. In the future, the potential introduction of technologies like foldable drones [40] and multi-modal drones, [41] as well as improvements in sense-and-avoid capabilities, operability is expected to improve to *medium* level.

4.2.3 Autonomy–Low

The present levels of autonomy for small UAS, identified in the chart earlier by Floreano et al., are not as advanced as large UAS. While a lot of research is being conducted on increased autonomy, limitations of size and sensors currently place this variable at a low level for small UAS. There are plenty of improvements expected in autonomous operations, however in the 2030 timeframe autonomous operations in small UAS are still not expected to reach very high levels. Public perception also has some impact limiting advancement of autonomous operations. It is conjectured that advancement in small UAS autonomy will remain *low* in the 2030 timeframe.

4.2.4 Affordability–Medium

The average cost of a drone in the small UAS category has decreased over the past few years [42]. More drones are now available in the sub-1000 USD price range making them affordable to a wider group of customers. While affordability was a major barrier in large UAS category that precluded its proliferation, it has now been lowered with the emergence of so-called hobbyist drone market. Affordability will explicitly affect which actors gain access to UAS systems whether for good or nefarious purposes. Therefore, this variable is currently estimated at a medium level and the cost trend points to further decreases, which will change affordability to a *high* value in the future analysis.

4.2.5 Proliferation–Medium

Despite the low capability and operability of current small UAS, there has been a significant proliferation increase in this category in the past 15 years or so. Recent market analyses have shown an overall increase in small UAS sales and registered hobbyist and commercial users [43]. The FAA has predicted that by the end of the year 2020, the number of small UAS is expected to be close to 4 million, nearly four times the present numbers [44].

Similar reports from other agencies such as Gartner have predicted that the number of drones manufactured in 2017 was almost 39% higher than the previous year [8]. Because of all these reasons, this variable is currently at *medium* level and the trends point to the expectation to be *high* in the near future due to low costs and new potential applications are regularly surfacing.

4.2.6 Regulations–Low

Current civilian UAS regulations are still being finalized by the FAA and are expected to be in place by 2028 [45]. In the present US regulatory environment, small UAS are permitted in a very limited set of scenarios in non-crowded areas [16]. Other countries have laid down some form of regulations for integration of small UAS. Because of the volume and complexity of the US airspace, this is expected to be a big challenge and progress towards the integration has been slow to-date. Due to these reasons, this variable is currently at low and is expected to increase to *medium* in the near future (2030 timeframe).

4.2.7 Crossover Threat–Medium

This variable deals with the potential dual-use of civilian UAS. In the context of this chapter, dual use refers to "*technology that can be used for beneficial or malicious purposes depending on intent.*" There are various ways in which small UAS can be used that can threaten national security. In the history of modern warfare, there have been few purely commercial technologies that so readily lend themselves to immediate weaponization as the sUAS [15]. The threat lies not only in the technology itself, but also in the degree to which that technology is sufficiently capable and available to all potential nefarious actors. Some of these were highlighted earlier in the chapter. The overall crossover threat that can be posed using current and future small UAS is tied quite closely with the capability, operability, and autonomy variables. However, the crossover threat variable is meant to capture the dual-use nature of small UAS being repurposed for violence. Threat level is measured not just by the potential ways in which small UAS can be repurposed but also the frequency and capacity for disruption of such events. Most of the recently reported incidents relating to small UAS repurposed for violence involve improvised uses of commercial off-the-shelf (COTS) UAS [46]. These uses involve intrusive, sometimes undetectable, and potentially lethal applications of small UAS. For example, the Raytheon Pyros glide bomb weighs only 6 kg (13.2 lb), while Lockheed-Martin's Shadow Hawk weapon weighs only 5 kg (11 lb). In the hands of an innovative user, the DJI S1000 is a highly capable sUAS that can fly a 9.5 kg (20 lb) payload for 15 min. This capability can enable a lone-wolf actor to perform precise kinetic strikes against targets in protected areas for less than $5000 [47].

While the possibility of kamikaze drones, swarming capabilities, and chemical and biological weapons is perhaps further away, crossover threat is currently estimated at a *medium* value. The main reason for this being medium not high is that so far no major incidents have occurred involving use of small UAS for disruption or death of a large number of people. In the near future (2030 timeframe), however, when the potential avenues of nefarious use can increase, the crossover threat will grow to a *high* level due to the increasing number of small UAS in operation.

5 Analysis

Previous studies in sUAS have analyzed the vulnerability of critical infrastructure to the projected technology trends [48]. However, these studies have typically provided a tech-centric view of sUAS proliferation threat. The analyses focused on whether sUAS add new threats to the vulnerability picture through new attack vectors or amplify existing threats.

In this study, using the independent variables provided above, their impact on two key scenarios is analyzed. Figures 5 and 6 indicate these projected impacts on the scenarios of interest at present and in the near future (2030 timeframe). The overall observation is that each variable *generally* affects the scenario in accordance with its own level. The impact of each variable on each scenario is divided into two types—disruptive or deterrent impact. The impacts tend to become higher or remain the same in future context for both the scenarios due to changes in the independent variable.

There are some interesting implications in each analysis. Firstly, it is observed that current generation small UAS overall have a low impact on both the scenarios considered here. However, as observed from the figures, the independent variables do have an asymmetric impact on different scenarios. For example, capability and operability can have a more significant impact on the NAS scenario than dense urban environments. This is mainly because the characteristics of each scenario are different (such as the vulnerability to potential threats). Autonomy is an interesting variable in

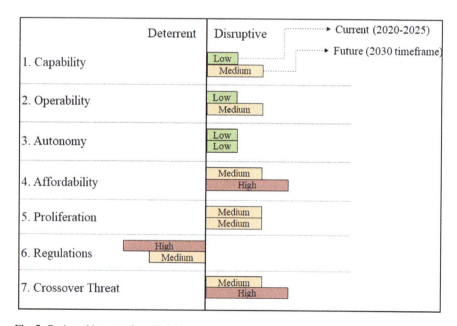

Fig. 5 Projected impact of small UAS on megacity scenario

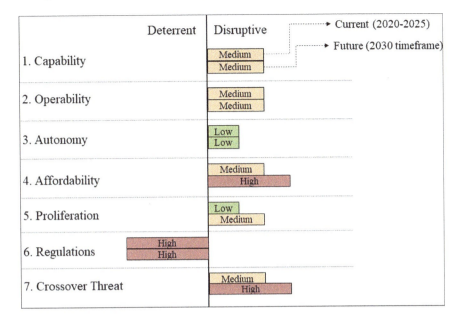

Fig. 6 Projected impact of small UAS on NAS—airports scenario

this framework and by the current and near future estimations is expected to remain low due to gaps in autonomous capabilities and public acceptability. Therefore, while it is expected to have a low impact in the current generation in both scenarios, it could assert more impact in the megacities scenario in the near future despite the capabilities remaining low. This is because, autonomous or semi-autonomous operations which are not completely at the level of safety and reliability required may, in congested areas lead to problems of safety and security.

Besides these tech-centric independent variables, other important variables that affect the disruptive impact are affordability and proliferation. Both variables have a medium to high impact because of the dramatic decrease in costs and increased accessibility to small UAS. Regulation is the only variable that has a high deterrent impact in both scenarios mainly because of the high number of restrictions currently placed on operations. It is expected to have a decreased deterrent impact in the future when more drone operations are allowed and the potential for using them for nefarious purposes increases. Upcoming regulations can be expected to allot specific frequency and spectrum for UAS operations as well as allow operations in such congested areas which could open the vulnerability of cyber-attacks on drones. These regulations, on the other hand, will continue to act as a significant deterrent in the NAS scenario as operations are already forbidden near airports and will continue to be so in updated regulations. Finally, the most important variable that has a large impact in both scenarios is the crossover threat. This is a measure of the dual-use nature of small UAS. Currently, most of the incidents/events being reported involve the improvised use of COTS drones for nefarious purposes. This crossover threat is

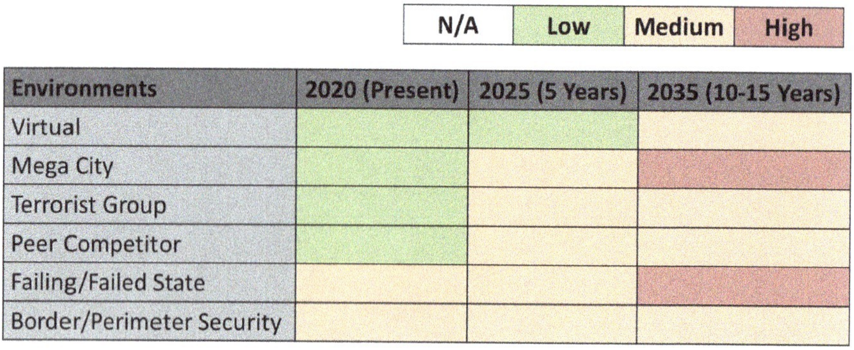

| | N/A | Low | Medium | High |

Environments	2020 (Present)	2025 (5 Years)	2035 (10-15 Years)
Virtual	Low	Low	Medium
Mega City	Low	Medium	High
Terrorist Group	Medium	Medium	Medium
Peer Competitor	Low	Medium	Medium
Failing/Failed State	Medium	Medium	High
Border/Perimeter Security	Medium	Medium	Medium

Fig. 7 Analytical chart showing impacts of small UAS in near and far term on various other scenarios

particularly disruptive even in the present-day scenario with restrictive regulations especially because small UAS are difficult to track in dense urban environments. Often, it is difficult to ascertain malicious intent, if any, of the drone user prior to an incident involving the drone happening. Due to all these reasons, crossover threat is deemed to be medium in the present and expected to climb to high values in the future for both scenarios.

In a similar manner, the framework presented here can be conceptually extended to other relevant scenarios that are not analyzed in detail in this chapter. Similar to the scenarios presented earlier, an analytical chart with the projected impact in different scenarios of interest from the national security perspective is created as shown in Fig. 7.

6 Swarms and Countermeasures

Apart from the independent variables explored earlier, another potentially disruptive technology that is currently upcoming is swarming. There are two main technologies upcoming in swarming literature—cooperative and coordinated swarming. If sUAS operate as a single body to perform a single function (cooperative swarming) [49] or if they can perform separate distinct tasks in coordination with each other (coordinated swarming). Coordinated swarming capability exists to some extent today but will need to be improved upon with the use of smart communication and information sharing between UAS. As defined by Scharre, "a swarm consists of disparate elements that coordinate and adapt their movements in order to give rise to an emergent, coherent whole" [50]. Based on current estimates, swarming capabilities and technology is currently at a nascent stage of research but progressing rapidly. Therefore, developments in this technology are a threat multiplier to each of the scenarios listed earlier.

The basic physical structure of the sUAS (including the use of advanced materials) hinders radar technologies, the primary component of the modern air defense. Additionally, concerning radar, sUAS are often indistinguishable from other airborne objects (specifically birds) [27]. Positive identification is a necessary component of engagement authority, especially when considering deployment of sUAS countermeasures on U.S. soil, including interdiction by law enforcement and the possibility of civilian casualties. Therefore, efficient countermeasures need to be devised that can be safely deployed at a low-cost. Currently, there do exist defense systems or countermeasures, both kinetic and non-kinetic in the nature of their deployment. However, most defense systems are—at least at this stage of development—restrictively expensive [46]. Countermeasures need to be effective as well as quick in response. To put this into perspective, a store-bought $1500 DJI Phantom 4, traveling at a max speed of 20 m/s (or ~45 mph) with an explosive payload equal to that of the weight of its camera (~0.75 lbs), will traverse one kilometer in just under 50 s (depending on weather conditions) to reach its target. Therefore, it is proposed that pro-active countermeasures need to be developed before the disruptive threat from small UAS leads to incidents that seriously harm national security.

7 Conclusions

UAS are an increasingly prominent feature of world politics as well as civilian life. At the same time, a thorough understanding of UAS (especially small UAS) in contemporary literature remains incomplete. Proliferation of small UAS is happening at a rapid pace as new potential applications are regularly surfacing. Preventing or inhibiting proliferation of low-cost drones is difficult, if not impossible, due to many active worldwide endeavors expanded their use in many different civil and military roles. For these reasons, it may be more useful to understand the intended applications as well as their potentially malicious uses to ensure development of appropriate policy, regulations, and countermeasures. This research presents an attempt to evaluate the impacts of small UAS proliferation and increasing autonomy on various scenarios. It is meant to help identification of threat areas and scenarios where regulation, policy, or counter-capabilities would need to be developed beyond those currently in existence. This work is not exhaustive since drone technology evolves rapidly but it is aimed at providing a framework for future analysis.

In the future, this chapter will hopefully contribute to a common analytical framework for studies on small UAS proliferation in other scenarios. The projected impact due to regulatory differences between different states in the near and far term can also be examined to provide a cross-cutting view of the problem. Reports have suggested that Europe, China, and Japan will press with small UAS development programs that compete with the US [46]. A decomposition of some of the independent variables (such as capability) might need to be done for other scenarios. However, care needs to be taken to not decompose the components too much as that would reduce the model's parsimony. UAS are a technology that is proliferating and taking proactive steps to ensure their safe and sustainable operations is important for ensuring national security.

References

1. US Department of Defense (2013) "Unmanned systems integrated roadmap FY 2013–2038." https://archive.defense.gov/pubs/DOD-USRM-2013.pdf
2. Fladeland M, Schoenung S, Lord M (2017) "Unmanned aircraft systems for atmospheric research". White paper, NCAR/EOL
3. Clarke R (2014) Understanding the drone epidemic. Comput Law Secur Rev 30(3):230–246
4. Sayler K (2015 A world of proliferated drones: a technology primer. Center for a new American security (CNAS)
5. Horowitz MC, Kreps SE, Fuhrmann M (2016) Separating fact from fiction in the debate over drone proliferation. Int Secur 41(2):7–42
6. Fuhrmann M, Michael CH (2017) "Droning on: explaining the proliferation of unmanned aerial vehicles." Int Organ 71(2):397–418. Horowitz MC, Sarah EK, Matthew F (2016) "Separating fact from fiction in the debate over drone proliferation." Int Secur 41(2):7–42. Canellas MC, Rachel AH (2015) "Toward meaningful human control of autonomous weapons systems through function allocation." In: Technology and society (ISTAS), 2015 IEEE international symposium on. IEEE, pp 1–7. Sharkey N (2011) "The automation and proliferation of military drones and the protection of civilians." Law, Innov Technol 3(2):229–240. Marchant GE., Braden A, Ronald CA, Edward TB, Jason B, Lyn MG, Orde K et al (2011) "International governance of autonomous military robots."
7. Vergouw B, Huub N, Geert B, Bart C (2016) "Drone technology: types, payloads, applications, frequency spectrum issues and future developments." In: The future of drone use. TMC Asser Press, The Hague, pp 21–45
8. Gettinger D, Michel AH (2017) "Drone registrations: a preliminary analysis." Fed Aviat Adm
9. Federal Aviation Administration (2016) "Aerospace forecast FY 2016–2036". https://www.faa.gov/data_research/aviation/aerospace_forecasts/media/FAA_Aerospace_Forecasts_FY_2016-2036.pdf
10. Sayler K (2015) A world of proliferated drones: a technology primer. Center for a new American security (CNAS)
11. Zenko M, Sarah EK (2014) Limiting armed drone proliferation. Council on Foreign Relations, New York
12. International Organization for Standardization (2012) "Robots and robotic devices —vocabulary ISO 8373:2012"
13. Floreano D, Wood RJ (2015) Science, technology and the future of small autonomous drones. Nature 521:460–466
14. Huerta M (2018) "Integration of civil unmanned aircraft systems (UAS) in the national airspace system (NAS) roadmap." Federal aviation administration. Retrieved 19 Apr 2013
15. Code of Federal Regulations, title 14, chapter I, subchapter F, part 107, https://www.ecfr.gov/cgi-bin/text-idx?SID=e331c2fe611df1717386d29eee38b000&mc=true&node=pt14.2.107&rgn=div5
16. US Department of Transportation (2013) "Integration of civil unmanned aircraft systems (UAS) in the national airspace system (NAS) roadmap" Government accountability office report on unmanned aerial systems. https://www.gao.gov/assets/680/671469.pdf
17. Finn RL, Wright D (2012) Unmanned aircraft systems: surveillance, ethics and privacy in civil applications. Comput Law Secur Rev 28(2):184–194
18. General Aviation Manufacturer's Association Database. https://gama.aero/wp-content/uploads/2016-GAMA-Databook_forWeb.pdf

19. Clarke R, Lyria BM (2014) The regulation of civilian drones' impacts on public safety. Comput Law Secur Rev 30(3):263–285
20. Elisabeth B (August 25, 2010) "Navy drone violated washington airspace". The New York times. https://www.nytimes.com/2010/08/26/us/26drone.html
21. "Drone 'put 130 lives at risk' after near-miss with plane approaching Gatwick", The telegraph, October 15, 2017. https://www.telegraph.co.uk/news/2017/10/15/drone-put-130-lives-risk-near-miss-plane-approaching-gatwick
22. Jonathan F (December 9, 2013) "Sky jack: the drone that hijacks other drones in mid-air". New atlas. https://www.gizmag.com/skyjack-hijacks-otherdrones/30055/
23. Nicas J (September 18, 2013) "Criminals, terrorists find uses for drones, raising concerns," The wall street journal. https://www.wsj.com/articles/criminals-terrorists-find-uses-for-drones-raising-concerns-1422494268. Gallagher S, "German chancellor's drone 'attack' shows the threat of weaponized UAVs," ArsTechnica.com. https://arstechnica.com/information-technology/2013/09/german-chancellors-drone-attack-shows-the-threat-of-weaponized-uavs/
24. "Obama says US has asked Iran to return drone aircraft" (December 13, 2011) CNN.com, https://edition.cnn.com/2011/12/12/world/meast/iran-us-drone/index.html
25. Hammes TX (2016) "The future of conflict." In: Hammes TX (ed) Charting a course. National Defence University Press
26. Hennigan WJ (2012) "Pentagon soon to deploy pint-sized but lethal switchblade drones." Los angeles times
27. Paul S (2014) The coming swarm: the cost-imposing value of mass, vol 2. Center for a New American Security, Washington, DC. https://s3.amazonaws.com/fles.cnas.org/documents/CNAS_CostImposingValueofMass_Scharre.pdf.pdf
28. Rivera E, Baykov R, Guofei Gu (2014) A study on unmanned vehicles and cyber security. Texas A&M University, USA
29. Shepard DP, Bhatti JA, Humphreys TE, Fansler AA (2012) Evaluation of smart grid and civilian UAV vulnerability to GPS spoofing attacks. Proc ION GNSS Meet 3:3591–3605
30. Jonathan F (December 9, 2013) "SkyJack: the drone that hijacks other drones in mid-air". New atlas. https://www.gizmag.com/skyjack-hijacks-otherdrones/30055/
31. Weibel RE, John Hansman R (2004) "Safety considerations for operation of different classes of UAVs in the NAS." In: AIAA 4th aviation technology, integration and operations forum, AIAA 3rd unmanned unlimited technical conference, workshop and exhibit
32. la Cour-Harbo A (2017) Mass threshold for 'harmless' drones. Int J Micro Air Veh 9(2):77–92
33. Smith WH, Freddie L Main III (2015) "The real consequences of flying toy drones in the national airspace system." Fort worth. Aero kinetics aviation, Texas https://www.eurocockpit.be/system/files/2017-05/Aerokinetics%20study%20on%20Toy%20drones%202015.pdf
34. Tremayne M, Clark A (2014) New perspectives from the sky: unmanned aerial vehicles and journalism. Digit Journalism 2(2):232–246
35. Haddal CC, Jeremiah G (2010) "Homeland security: unmanned aerial vehicles and border surveillance." Library of congress Washington Dc congressional research service
36. Katz v. United States
37. Clarke R (2014) The regulation of civilian drones' impacts on behavioral privacy. Comput Law Secur Rev 30(3):286–305
38. James Herrera G, Dechant JA, Green EK (October 2, 2017) "Technology trends in small unmanned aircraft systems (sUAS) and counter-UAS: a five-year outlook," Institute for defense analyses, IDA paper P-8823, November 2017. Vito Dronelli, "7 drones that can lift heavy weights [2017 edn],". dronesglobe.com. https://www.dronesglobe.com/guide/heavy-lift-drones/
39. James Herrera G, Dechant JA, Green EK (November 2017) "Technology trends in small unmanned aircraft systems (sUAS) and counter-UAS: a five-year outlook." Institute for defense analyses, IDA paper P-8823
40. Valavanis KP, Vachtsevanos GJ (2015) "Future of unmanned aviation." In: Handbook of unmanned aerial vehicles. Springer, Netherlands, pp 2993–3009

41. Floreano D, Stefano M, Jun S (2017) "Foldable drones: from biology to technology." In: SPIE smart structures and materials + nondestructive evaluation and health monitoring. International Society for Optics and Photonics, pp 1016203–1016203
42. Bachmann RJ, Boria FJ, Vaidyanathan R, Ifju PG, Quinn RD (2009) A biologically inspired micro-vehicle capable of aerial and terrestrial locomotion. Mech Mach Theory 44(3):513–526
43. Joseph F (2018) "How much do drones cost?". 3dinsider.com. Retrieved April 24. https://3dinsider.com/drone-cost/
44. Glaser (April 14, 2017) "DJI is running away with the drone market", recode.net. https://www.recode.net/2017/4/14/14690576/drone-market-share-growth-charts-dji-forecast
45. Gartner press release (Feb 9, 2017) "Gartner says almost 3 million personal and commercial drones will be shipped in 2017". https://www.gartner.com/newsroom/id/3602317
46. Anthony T, David T (April 1, 2017) "The rise of the commercial threat: countering the small unmanned aircraft system". Joint force quarterly 85. National Defense University Press
47. Tom O'connor "ISIS has no air force, but it has an army of drones that drop explosives." newsweek.com, Retrieved April 24, 2018. https://www.newsweek.com/isis-air-force-army-drones-drop-bombs-585331
48. Patterson DR (2017) Defeating the threat of small unmanned aerial systems. Air Space Power J 31(1):15–26
49. James Herrera G, Dechant JA, Green EK (Nov 2017) "Technology trends in small unmanned aircraft systems (sUAS) and counter-UAS: a five-year outlook." Institute for defense analyses, IDA paper P-8823
50. 1000 Drones perform spectacular formations in guangzhou," CRIENGLISH.com. Accessed April 21, 2018. https://english.cri.cn/12394/2017/02/13/2021s951725.htm

Development and Proliferation of Flexible and Wearable Electronics: Opportunities and Challenges for National Security

Federico Pulvirenti

Abstract The United States dominance in science and technology is under threat due to large foreign investment in the development of dual-use technologies with a primary civil-commercial use but which could be directly misapplied to pose a significant threat with broad potential consequences to national security. In the last two decades, rising powers like China have increased their spending in domestic research activities. In late 2017, China diverted millions of dollars to finance applied research at universities based in Australia, a traditionally strong U.S. ally in the South Pacific. Among the disruptive technologies the Chinese investment aims to develop, "flexible and wearable technologies" (FWEs) stand out given the limited U.S. efforts to dominate an industry where there is no clear leader. To invert the current trend, to control proliferation of FWEs, and to maintain the technological advantage the U.S. economy and the military enjoy, the prevailing scholarship suggests the creation of U.S. based consortia linking universities, companies, and the federal entities. However, the hypotheses that consortia are the ideal institutions to favor diffusion of FWEs technologies and primarily confine diffusion domestically rest on empirical arguments. Analysis of more than 9000 patent records shows consortia promote FWEs diffusion if the countries involved are strong innovators, but it is not possible to prove that FWEs will diffuse locally. The U.S. could adopt a second mover strategy and acquire intellectual property (IP) developed by consortia to establish leadership in FWEs. Last, there is need for more effective international agreements to regulate IP developed through consortia.

F. Pulvirenti (✉)
Georgia Institute of Technology, Atlanta, Georgia
e-mail: fpulvirenti@gatech.edu

1 Introduction

1.1 Cardwell's Law

Historically a nation's dominance in science and technology (S&T) is limited in time, and as one nation flagged, another one or another set of nations would take over the torch. Although the philosopher David Hume made similar remarks already in the eighteenth century, [1] this observation was renamed as Cardwell's law, after late British historian Donald Cardwell who in the early 1970s studied innovation levels across different nations over time [2]. In his 2016 analysis, political scientist Zak Taylor confirms once again the validity of Cardwell's law and attempts to study why certain countries are better at innovating then others [3].

First, Taylor shows that a country's innovation level is independent of population or economy size. Indeed, countries like Sweden and Switzerland are strong innovators but have relatively small populations and gross domestic products. There is also no correlation between military spending and capability and rates of innovation. To cite again Sweden and Switzerland, yet further extending our focus to Japan, Germany and Canada, none of these countries has substantially invested in military research after World War II (WWII). On the other hand, nations with large weapon productions, such as Italy and Russia, exhibit medium to low innovation rates.

Contrary to popular belief, being "first-movers" in S&T does not guarantee long-lasting advantages over competitors, even if maintaining labs and curating established research and development (R&D) programs cost less than building new ones from the ground up. A rampant example is Japan, a country with limited technical capabilities at the end of WWII that transformed itself into a high-tech giant in the 1970s, contributing to more than 70% of the world's semiconductor materials production by 1989 [4]. Another success story of a primarily agricultural country turned innovation leader is the U.S.

1.2 The U.S. S&T Dominance

During its first hundred years, the U.S. was a predominantly agricultural country with limited S&T ambitions. Science was regarded as a personal hobby more than a national priority or an opportunity to lead the world to the forefront of innovation [3]. However, during the second industrial revolution this young country shifted gears, excelling in mining, transportation, and chemical production. American research institutions delivered high quality graduates and inventions. But WWII and the Cold War offered the U.S. a chance for world domination in S&T [3]. In part driven by the Nazi persecutions in Europe against minority groups and in particular against the Jews, top scientists like Albert Einstein and Enrico Fermi moved to American universities, enabling ground-breaking discoveries. Research by economist Petra Moser shows how U.S. patents increased by 31% in fields common among Jewish scientists. Moreover, these highly skilled immigrants attracted new researchers who then trained other aspiring scientists and engineers, propagating for decades the influence of this exodus on the American innovation landscape [5].

The external threat posed by a fascist invasion first and by a Soviet one later, pushed R&D efforts to unprecedented heights. New industries saw the light and the U.S. became a global leader in weapons development, telecommunications, computing, biotechnology, etc. Figure 1 shows the number of Nobel Prize winners for the United States and for the United Kingdom in scientific disciplines as of 2017.

Not only is the U.S. the country with most winners in physics, chemistry, and physiology or medicine, but it also significant outperforming the runner up country, the United Kingdom. Although the quality of U.S. innovation is high, it is worthwhile noting that Nobel Prizes are awarded for past discoveries and the data in Fig. 1 may not capture the current S&T environment. Indeed, as the possibility of a nuclear conflict with the Soviet Union became unlikely, American stance in R&D started to totter. After a booster at the dawn of the twenty-first century due the growth in usage and adaptation of the Internet by enterprises and consumers, [7, 8] the U.S. S&T competitiveness deteriorated further urging Congress to commission reports in 2005 and 2010 to assess the nation S&T outlook [9].

The reports found that most of the patents developed in the U.S. are currently licensed to foreign firms, and fewer American students opt for scientific or technical graduate degrees. These findings are correlated to reduced resource allocation to train the next generation of STEM (Science, Technology, Engineering and Math) professionals, a weaker US dollar, high public debt, and an internationally relocated manufacturing sector [10]. Concurrently, rising powers like China have stepped up their efforts to become the next S&T superpower, as per Cardwell's law [11, 12].

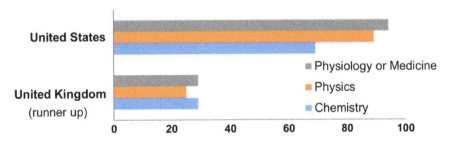

Fig. 1 Number of Nobel Prize winners in physiology or medicine, physics and chemistry per country. The two countries with most Nobel laureates are considered. Adapted from The Telegraph [6]

1.3 China as the Next S&T Superpower?

China has enjoyed over the last five decades conspicuous foreign investments (on the order of billions of USD) by high-tech firms with the purpose of producing goods at lower prices. This has resulted in a shift of the manufacturing base from the U.S. and Europe to China, and even double-digit economic growth, in terms of gross domestic product (GDP). Since the early 2000s Chinese spending in R&D has increased significantly and is now comparable to R&D spending of the European Union [13].

China is taking a clear stance in S&T; as of 2017 it publishes more scientific papers than any other country, if we exclude the U.S., specifically in the field of computer science and engineering. This increase in publication output is correlated to a strong commitment to graduate education in S&T. Chinese institutions have awarded more Ph.D. degrees in the natural sciences and engineering than any other country [13].

However, the quality of a technical education at an undergraduate level in China may not be as high as that received in the most developed E.U. countries and in the U.S. [14] Researchers at Stanford University found that Chinese primary and secondary schools produce students with some of the strongest critical thinking skills in the world. Nevertheless, the study reveals that Chinese students enrolled in computer science and engineering programs at eleven mainland universities, lose their advantage in critical thinking in college [15]. This outcome may be associated with three factors: poor emphasis on engaging teaching at the college level, a lack of motivation among students post-matriculation, and the slowing economy [14]. Students report that the energetic and demanding teaching they are accustomed to in primary and secondary schools disappears when they reach college. Chinese universities tend to reward professors for their research achievements not for their teaching abilities. Moreover, after years of preparation preparing for the "gaokao," the national exam that determines admission to Chinese universities, students are not as pressured to study when they reach college for two reasons. While almost all students graduate within four years, one-fifth of university graduates remains unemployed post-graduation and many accept low-paying jobs due to a slowing economy [14].

In an attempt to possibly make up for the skills they failed to acquire in college, top Chinese students tend to apply to U.S. universities, benefit from U.S.-based resources to realize their full scientific potential, and return to the homeland [13]. In the short-term, this flow of scientists benefits the U.S., whose dominant position in science is based on its openness to the best talents of all nationalities, who contribute to U.S. science, technology and economic success. However, it still needs to be determined how such leak of skilled Chinese personnel moving back to China will affect American competitiveness in the long-term future, as China becomes more and more self-sufficient [13]. Some have argued that while China's S&T capabilities are increasing, it remains a minor player relative to other strong innovators [16].

Chinese patents have grown in number, but the quality of Chinese innovation has grown less rapidly, especially on a per capita basis. Most of the Chinese patent filings have been for utility models and industrial designs, which are obtained faster and need to meet lower standards than patents for new products or processes. In addition, the citations-weighted data on STEM publications position Chinese science in the same league as Thailand's. Nevertheless, the data that Taylor reports are limited to publications released up to 2011 [16]. The scientific landscape is evolving fast and soon China could claim a seat among the most innovative countries. While the U.S. domestic debate has shifted from STEM promotion under the Obama presidency to attempts to increase taxation for graduate students under President Trump's mandate, China successfully tested the world's first quantum satellite communication [17, 18].

Building on CRISPR gene-editing, China announced seven human trials to treat cancer and other ailments in 2017 [19]. Remarkably, CRISPR is a technique developed in the U.S. in 2012, but the first-in-U.S. trials were only performed in 2019 and 2020 by the University of Pennsylvania Health System [20, 21].

1.4 Dual-Use Technologies of Concern

Quantum satellite communication and CRISPR gene editing are examples of dual-use technologies that have a primary civil-commercial use but could be directly misapplied to pose a significant threat with broad potential consequences to public health and safety, the environment, or national security [22]. These emerging technologies are often so sophisticated that the scientists who develop them cannot predict how their intellectual property will be used. To further complicate the issue at a policy level, a high level of specialization is required to understand the impact of such research, and the complexity of controlling rapidly evolving technologies. The U.S. Department of Commerce has listed the dual-use technologies it controls on the Commerce Control List [23].

1.5 Non-State Actors

Non-state actors are non-sovereign entities that exercise significant economic, political, or social power and influence at a national, and in some cases international, level [24]. The definition of non-state actors cannot be unequivocal and universal [25]. Some definitions include trade unions, community organizations, religious institutions, ethnic groupings, terrorist groups, and universities in addition to the players outlined above. In the context of this chapter, non-state actors indicate universities, private companies and consortia.

1.6 The Keys of Innovation

In "The Politics of Innovation," Taylor identifies three keys to defy Cardwell's law: the presence of strong domestic institutions, comprehensive policies, and external threats. Some literature [26] commends to strengthen institutions and policies in order to promote innovation, and while institutions and policies are necessary pillars, they are not enough to lead to high rates of innovation. He argues that competition causes innovation, and countries innovate the most when they are competing with one another on the international scene, as they are driven by a "creative insecurity." If external threats are absent, domestic efforts tend to be directed to ideological battles and political debates over distribution of resources [27].

This chapter will mostly focus on diffusion of dual-use technology, as defined by the NIH, [22] in an attempt to understand how to better design policy that protects partnerships between non-state actors and foreign governments, and how to possibly spark creative insecurity in the U.S. and its allies.

2 Relevance and Importance

2.1 The Torch Program

China is posing itself as the next S&T superpower and it is trying to bridge the technological gap with other countries by developing cutting-edge technologies through the Torch program. Established in 1988, the Torch program is an innovation partnership between Chinese companies and Chinese universities. Modeled after Western consortia, the program has been largely financed by the Chinese government to form high-tech start-ups, which now accounts for 11% of the country's GDP and for 50% of China's R&D spending [28]. Steve Blank, an adjunct professor in management science and engineering at Stanford University, claims the Chinese government has run the program in a unique way, almost like if Torch was a start-up itself. To paraphrase Blank, by iterating and pivoting as it learned and discovered, Torch completely disconnected itself from the central government bureaucracy, and was able to thrive in China's ever-changing economy [29]. There are now more than thirty Torch program software parks. The program can be dissected in four components: innovation clusters, technology business incubators, seed funding and venture guiding fund. The idea is to be able to promote innovation by geographically concentrating explicit and tacit knowledge, as well as copious resources, and assisting scientists and engineers in the development of their ideas from the inception to the marketplace. Incubators provide start-ups with free rent, office space, and open access to intellectual property developed at domestic universities. Companies of the caliber of Lenovo, Huawei, and Suntech Power were originally start-ups developed within the Torch program incubators [28].

In 2017, the Torch program started to collaborate with the University of New South Wales (UNSW), [28] a public university in a country that is a strong U.S. ally in the South Pacific, an area where China has poorly-hidden military aspirations [30].

2.2 From S&T to Politics—China's Thirst for Power

China has reclaimed more than 2900 acres of land since December 2013, more than any other country claiming sovereignty over nearby natural islands, namely the Paracel and Spratly Island chains [31]. China's maritime dispute can be traced back to the Sino-Japanese War of 1894. According to experts at the Council on Foreign Relations, encouraged by a rise in military capabilities and a strong economy, China is building artificial islands to increase its potential power projection in the region of thriving trade. Given the high commercial traffic in the area, miscalculations by sea captains could trigger a military conflict and a crisis management system is essential [30]. Therefore, if the U.S. wants to retain its "soft power" in the Asia–Pacific region, it is important to retain strong ties with allies such as Japan and Australia.

The creation of the Torch precinct in Australia raises several concerns from a security and economic standpoint. Although none of the technologies that will be developed can be openly used for military applications, there is a possibility that some of the discoveries and inventions could give China a military advantage in the Asia–Pacific over the U.S. and its allies.

2.3 The U.S. Military

While China is developing cutting-edge technologies, and is eager to expand its area of influence, what is the U.S. doing to maintain its technological superiority? The U.S. military is increasingly reliant on technologies developed for markets largely independent of the DoD influence [32]. Given today's relatively free flow of capital, information, and skilled personnel, the world has evolved to the point that it is impossible for the U.S to sustain the qualitative military-technology superiority it enjoyed during the Cold War. The rapid migration of the technological state-of-the-art to the civilian marketplace requires the DoD to rethink its relationship with industry or risk closing the gap or falling behind adversaries better prepared to accommodate the new military-technology landscape. Only by intentionally synchronizing the prerogatives of the civilian and military technology markets can the U.S. ensure preferential access to the most advanced products and capabilities to support the nation's defense objectives [33]. But to create an effective and long-lasting collaboration with industry, the DoD needs to establish conditions of mutual benefit for the military and the private sector.

On the other hand, the DoD needs to phase down some of the older technology it currently owns. Instead of focusing on innovative ways of discarding or substitute technology, the DoD sought incremental upgrades in technology it already possessed [34]. Nevertheless, advances in materials science and nanotechnology threaten to produce radical change in the conduct of warfare in the near future. Coincidentally, one of the world centers of excellence in materials research is UNSW [35].

2.4 Flexible and Wearable Electronics

Among the technologies of interest to the Torch division at UNSW, flexible and wearable electronics (FWEs) stand out [36]. This field of technology is disruptive for two main reasons. First, flexible and wearable electronics enable new product designs with a wide range of applications from healthcare and consumer goods, to power generation from renewable sources and national security [37]. Second, flexible hybrid-organic electronics can be manufactured using simple and scalable processes that rely on printing and lithography at a reduced cost compared to rigid silicon-based devices [38]. The portable, lightweight, low-power and potentially low-cost nature of FWEs makes this type of technology suitable for implementation in humanitarian aid efforts in areas that affected by conflict or natural disasters. On the other hand, military operations can also benefit from the use of foldable devices [39]. For example, supply lines during conflicts tend to be vulnerable to attacks from adversaries. Flexible devices could allow combat units that may become isolated to be able to have sources of power to recharge electronics, stay connected with support units, and potentially treat soldiers in need of medical help.

Europe, North America, and East Asia are the three zones in which major efforts are under way to develop flexible and wearable electronic products. Although countries located in each zone enjoy significant competitive strengths, no region has established a clear leadership in the industry [37]. In recent years, China has made significant efforts to acquire intellectual property from European, American, and Australian non-state actors (e.g., private companies and universities) by giving in return access to its market [12]. Proliferation of dual use technologies, like flexible and wearable electronics, could potentially jeopardize America's future economy dynamism and the technological superiority the U.S. military enjoys [28]. Within the technological context of flexible electronics, the goal of this chapter is three-fold:

(1) Evaluating the sufficiency of international agreements to control detrimental effects of cross-border collaborations among non-state actors (universities and private companies), and between these non-state actors and foreign governments;
(2) Understanding how to effectively control appropriation and proliferation among rising powers of ground-breaking technology;
(3) Assessing how to adapt the U.S. Department of Defense (DoD) to benefit for example, from self-powered smart garments that could regulate body temperature or charge electronic devices.

2.5 Intellectual Property Regulations

After WWII an agency within the United Nations, known as the World Intellectual Property Organization (WIPO), became responsible for regulating and enforcing intellectual property rights (IPRs). WIPO was established in 1967, but it was not until the 1980s that the U.S. Congress made IPRs a priority within U.S. foreign policy [40]. In 1988 the Office of the U.S. Trade Representative started to identify countries with effective IPRs regulations and to compile findings in an annual "Special 301 Report." [41] In 1995 the first successful and enforceable IPRs law in the international arena, the so-called Trade-Related aspects of Intellectual Property Rights (TRIPS), became effective.

In China, copyright protection is regulated by the 1990 "Copyright Law of the People's Republic of China," last amended in 2010 [42]. Patents and utility models and industrial designs are covered by the "Patent Law of the People's Republic of China," first adopted in 1984 and last amended in 2008. Interestingly, according to the "China Patent Law" patent rights will not be granted for scientific discoveries, for methods for the diagnosis or treatment of diseases, and for substances obtained by means of nuclear transformation [42].

The scarce level of intellectual property protection in China and yet the large number of collaborations between this rising power and the rest of the world is alarming, specifically when the world S&T dominance is at stake. Guidelines or code of conducts for intercontinental R&D collaborations, as provided by the European Union to universities and public research organizations in its member states, are just not enough to counter unwanted technology proliferation [43]. In a time when non-state actors become more independent from governments, there is a clear need to involve innovation centers such as universities, companies, etc., and foreign governments in international agreements to prevent the proliferation of dual-use technologies.

3 Method

Since American firms need to give the Chinese rights to their intellectual property in order to have access to desirable Asian market, scholars propose the creation of consortia for FWEs development [38, 39]. Based on success stories of consortia like Sematech, which galvanized resurgence of U.S. leadership in the semiconductor industry in the 1990s, [44] the hypothesis advanced in the literature is that consortia will bring together small and medium-sized enterprises (SMEs), government funding and procurement, and skilled personnel [38, 39, 44]. Consortia are thought to bring advantages in fields where technological and commercial risks are substantial and where no single company, no matter how large and well endowed, can command the resources and full range of technologies needed to successfully commercialize new ones of general-purpose. As Vernon Ruttan claims, no single firm will have sufficient incentive to make large investments necessary to develop the next general-purpose technology [45]. However, general-purpose technologies will have by definition large effects on subsequent innovation and the diffusion of these technologies, and their underlying knowledge, will be high [46]. Hence, it is possible to advance the following hypothesis:

H1   Consortia will generate general-purpose technologies that are likely to diffuse more than technologies developed by companies or universities.

Moreover, scholars claim that consortia will promote local manufacturing and technology development by enabling local companies to have priority access to the IP generated within the consortia, as observed in the case of the Flexible Display Center at the Industrial Technology Research Institute of Taiwan. Thus, it is possible to advance a second hypothesis:

H2   Technologies developed by consortia will preferentially diffuse domestically, rather than internationally.

If H2 holds true, the results of the present project would be in agreement with the literature. Since qualitative SWOT (Strength, Weaknesses, Opportunities, Threats) analysis was previously used to support the argument that consortia will preferentially foster technological diffusion locally rather than internationally, [39] there is room to quantitatively support or confute this argument for the first time.

3.1 *Identification of Variables and Data Collection*

To quantify diffusion of military technology, Jon Schmid [47] uses forward citations of patents and patents developed by the top fifty military technology-patenting organization. Military technology is classified under the Derwent classification code W07 [48]. Flexible and wearable electronics are a general-purpose technology, data collection was focused on patents with specific Derwent classification codes, taking into account the possible applications of FWEs:

(1)   A82: Coatings
(2)   A85: Electrical applications of polymers
(3)   A89: Optical equipment
(4)   A96: Plastics for medical applications
(5)   F08: Flexible sheet materials
(6)   G05: Printing processes
(7)   L03: Electro-chemical features of semiconductors
(8)   M13: Coating material with metals
(9)   P54: Shaping metal
(10) P55: General soldering
(11) P81: General optics
(12) P85: General cryptography

(13) Q34: Packaging elements
(14) Q71: Lightning
(15) Q78: Heat exchange
(16) S01: Electrical instruments
(17) S02: Engineering instrumentation
(18) S06: Electrophotography
(19) T01: Electronic data processors
(20) T02: Hybrid simulators
(21) T03: Data recording
(22) T04: Magnetic, optical and smart cards
(23) T06: Process and machine control
(24) V04: Printed circuits and connectors
(25) V06: Small electric machines and their controllers
(26) V07: Light control
(27) U11 - U14: Discrete devices and processes (LEDs, solar cells, thermo-electrics)
(28) U21: Electronic switching circuits
(29) U22: Frequency conversion
(30) W01: Secret data communication
(31) W03: Remote control
(32) W04: Video recording systems
(33) W06: Air control systems, radar
(34) W07: Electrical military equipment and weapons
(35) X15: Solar energy
(36) X16: Electrochemical storage
(37) X22: Automotive electrics, lightning and instrumentation
(38) X26: Portable lightning devices.

To test H1, the number of patents and patent citations (dependent variables) were measured as a function of university, company, and consortium. The country of origin of the institutions is a control. By sampling the number of patents and patent citations for non-state actors in four developed countries, the U.S., Germany, Australia, and China; we should be able to observe that non-state actors in countries that are strong innovators (the U.S., Germany, and China) will receive a higher total number of foreign citations compared to non-state actors in countries that are mid-level innovators (Australia). Note that including China as a strong innovator goes against Taylor's classification of the country's innovation capabilities. However, recent achievements by the Chinese lead to belief that the Asian country is actually realizing its innovation potential. Data collection will bring further insight on whether China should or should not be classified as a strong innovator. The decision to include Germany and Australia in the study, next to the U.S. (world S&T leader) and China (rising power), stems from the fact that Germany is a stable U.S. ally, and Australia is a U.S. ally that China wants to highly influence, given the recent Torch partnership and Chinese Communist Party interferences in Australian politics [49]. The author has identified the following consortia of interest per country so far:

(1) United States: Flexible Electronics and Display Center at Arizona State University,
(2) Germany: So-Light,
(3) China: Nano and Advanced Materials Institute Limited (NAMI),
(4) Australia: Victorian Organic Solar Cell Consortium.

It is too early to include the Torch precinct at UNSW in the data collection, given its recent formation and the time it takes for patents to be granted.

To provide a clear quantification of the level of innovation associated with the formation of a given consortium, the number of patents and patent citations pre- and post-consortium formation were measured only for companies and universities that are taking part to the same public–private partnership.

To validate H2, the number of domestic and international licensees (dependent variables) could be measured as a function of consortium (independent variable).

4 Analysis

4.1 The American Consortium—Flexible Electronics and Display Center

The Flexible Electronics and Display Center (FEDC) at Arizona State University was launched in 2004 as a $43.7 million, five-year cooperative agreement between the Army Research Laboratory (ARL) and Arizona State University. The agreement was then renewed in 2009 for an addition $50 million over an extra five-year period [50]. The FEDC website shows that up until 2016 the research partnership continued, and after that it is unclear if the public–private partnership is still currently active [51]. FEDC has attracted more than thirty industrial partners and research institutions, and FEDC reached important technological achievements, such as the production of a flexible e-paper prototype in 2008 [52] and of the world's largest flexible organic light-emitting diode in 2012 [53]. Since some of these major partners of FEDC were simultaneously active in other consortia (e.g., Boeing is part of the Network Centric Operations Industry Consortium (NCOIC) since 2004), [54] comparing number of patents and patent citations among universities, companies, and the consortium would lead to a spurious correlation.

The assignee of the patents associated with the FEDC consortium is the Arizona Board of Regents, a body corporate of the State of Arizona, acting for and on behalf of Arizona State University. By analyzing the number of patents and patent citations assigned to the Arizona Board of Regents from 1974, the year Xerox produced the first e-paper display, until right before the creation of the Flexible Electronics and Display Center, it is possible to see that the FEDC consortium has triggered significant innovation in the FWEs field. Both the number of patents and patent citations associated with the selected Derwent classification codes reported above,

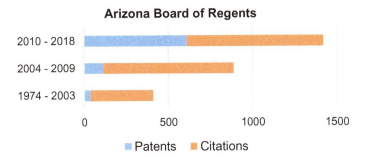

Fig. 2 Number of patents and patent citations granted before (1974–2003) the creation of FEDC, during the first five-year funding cycle of FEDC (2004–2009), and over its last cycle (2010–2018). Data collected through the Web of Science database by selecting specific Derwent classification codes associated with flexible and wearable electronics

increase sharply after the creation of the consortium. The absolute value of the number of patent citations (371 for patents released between 1974 and 2003; 772 for patents released between 2004 and 2009; 809 for patents release between 2010 and 2018) show how FEDC has been a strong innovator during both of its two five-year funding cycles. Note that the second funding cycle went from 2010 until 2018, hence beyond the five years mentioned in the initial press release of 2004, [50] for two reasons. First, there is evidence of FEDC-related research activity on a flexible x-ray detector in 2016; [55] and second, it is reasonable to assume that any patents assigned with the Arizona Board of Regents filed in 2016 would probably be granted within eighteen months or longer, [56] justifying the second funding cycle to end in 2018. Since the number of patents granted to the Arizona Board of Regents between 2010 and 2018 are more than five times higher than the number of patents granted between 2004 and 2009, it is likely that the number of forward citations for patents filed in FEDC's second funding cycle will further increase.

4.2 The Chinese Consortium—Nano and Advanced Materials Institute Limited

How does the Flexible Electronics and Display Center compare to a consortium based in China? Unlike the U.S., until 2014 China lacked most of the equipment and materials infrastructure to support manufacture of flexible displays, as well as a mature science research base. However, in contrast to the U.S. and the European Union, where no major manufacturer of flexible displays has emerged, China is experiencing an investment rush by companies seeking to enter the production of active-matrix organic light-emitting diodes (AMOLED) displays [57]. China's market demand and the government willingness to finance large-scale investment in production capacity, has played a major role in the creation of a consortium, made up by the Printed Electronics Fund Ltd. and the Chiangzhou Industrial Institute of Printed Electronics [58]. To the best of the author's ability, it is not possible to retrieve any patent associated with such consortium using databases such us Web of Science and Google Patents, as of April 2018 (Fig. 3).

Nevertheless, it is possible to collect patents associated with the Nano and Advanced Materials Institute Limited (NAMI), an R&D center created by the government of Hong Kong in 2006 to bridge the gap between scientific research and application [59]. The Hong Kong University of Science and Technology, one of the top thirty universities in the world, [60] owns NAMI. The latter collaborates with a large number of Chinese companies (e.g., KaShui, Joneson Environmental Technologies Ltd, Hip Hing, etc.) and won nine gold medals at the 45th International Exhibition of Inventions of Geneva in 2017, [61] which is considered to be the world's most important event dedicated to inventions [62]. However, the number of patents (39) and citations (158) that NAMI's patents received since its inception are particularly small if compared to those received by the Flexible Electronics and Display Center. On the other side, after the creation of NAMI in 2006 the Hong Kong University of Science and Technology (HKUST) has produced more patents related to flexible and wearable electronics, and these patents have received more forward citations than those patents granted between the foundation of the university (1991) and 2005.

Hence, Fig. 3 may capture the essence of Chinese paradox. Public–private partnership trigger innovation, but in China these partnerships tend to be more public-public [63]. Moreover, the large number of forward citations (1251) HKUST received between 2006 and 2018 justifies placing China in the strong innovator category, as far as flexible and wearable electronics are concerned.

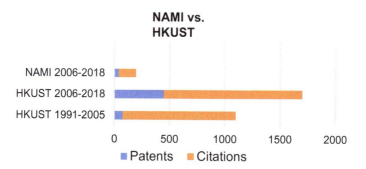

Fig. 3 Number of patents and patent citations granted to NAMI and the Hong Kong University of Science and Technology before (1991–2005) and after (2006–2018) the creation of NAMI. Data collected through the Web of Science database for HKUST and the Google Patents database for NAMI, by selecting specific Derwent classification codes associated with flexible and wearable electronics

4.3 The German Consortium—So-Light

Eight companies, two universities, and one public research institutions from Germany launched the public–private partnership So-Light in 2009 [64]. The German Ministry of Education and Research (BMBF) provided the consortium with €14.7 million to address the complete value chain of organic light-emitting diodes (OLEDs), from materials research and production to OLED-lightning applications [65]. The eight companies were Novaled, Sensient, Aixtron, Ledon OLED Lighting, Fresnel Optics, Hella, Siteco, and BMG MIS. The academic partners were the University of Muenster and the University of Padeborn/L-Lab, and last, the Fraunhofer Center for Organics, Materials and Electronic Devices Dresden (COMEDD). Fraunhofer is Europe's largest application-oriented research organization, focusing on health, security, communication, energy, and the environment [66]. The outcomes of the consortium exceeded expectations, and Novaled later decided to launch products based on the prototypes developed throughout the collaboration [65]. Novaled was purchased by Samsung for $347 million in 2013 [67] (Fig. 4).

Patent analysis focused on the period the consortium was active (2009–2014), and the five years immediately before its creation (2003–2008). Expanding the time range from 2009–2014 to 2009–2018 does not fundamentally change the outcome of the analysis, as Fig. 5 shows. The number of patents and patent citations associated with Germany institutions and commercial enterprises represents more than 75% of the total amount of patents (9090) and patent citations (31,198) analyzed in this study, confirming that Germany is a strong innovator in the field of flexible and wearable electronics. Both the number of patents and patent citations increase post-consortium creation only for the University of Muenster (World Rank: 356) [68] and the University of Padeborn (World Rank: 806) [69]. While the number of patents increases post-2009 for both companies and the Fraunhofer research institute, the number of patents citations does not. This trend in patent citations may reflect the presence of

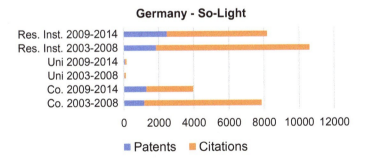

Fig. 4 Number of patents and patent citations granted to the companies, universities and the research institution (Fraunhofer COMEDD) associated with So-Light before (2003–2008) and after (2009–2014) the formation of the consortium. Data collected through the Web of Science database, by selecting specific Derwent classification codes associated with FWEs

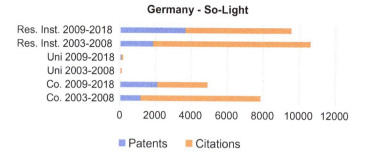

Fig. 5 Number of patents and patent citations granted to the companies, universities and the research institution (Fraunhofer COMEDD) associated with So-Light before (2003–2008) and after (2009–2014) the formation of the consortium. Data collected through the Web of Science database, by selecting specific Derwent classification codes associated with FWEs

a larger competition from other countries in the field of flexible and wearable electronics (FWEs), [39] while the influence of the 2008 financial crisis is excluded given that Germany weathered the crisis well [70]. Even if the number of citations does not increase for companies and the Fraunhofer institute post-consortium creation, the number of citations post-2009 for companies (2665) and research institutions (5713) combined represent more than 27% of the total number of citations of this study's dataset. Innovation in FWEs may slow down post-2009 in Germany, but it stays strong.

4.4 The Australian Consortium—Victorian Organic Solar Cell Consortium

Smaller than the So-Light consortium in Germany, the Victorian Organic Solar Cell Consortium is a public–private partnership between one research institution, CSIRO; two universities, Monash University (World Rank: 55) [71] and the University of Melbourne (World Rank: 41) [72]; and four companies, BlueScope Steel, Innovia Films, Innovia Security, and Robert Bosch South East Asia [73]. CSIRO stands for the Commonwealth Scientific and Industrial Research Organization, which is an independent agency of the Australian Federal Government that manages scientific research in Australia. The first project associated with the consortium can be traced back to 2011 [74]. Hence, the analysis of patents was focused on capturing roughly the same number of years before (2003–2010) and after (2011–2018) the creation of the consortium. Figure 6 illustrates how the number of patents granted to the four companies and two universities increases after the creation of the Victorian Organic Solar Cell Consortium (VOSCC), while it remains constant for CSIRO. None of the institutions experienced an increase in patent citations post-2011. It is possible that the limited participation of companies (half the number of the companies that

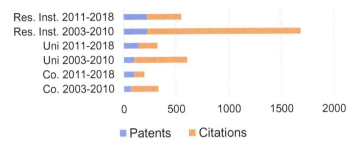

Fig. 6 Number of patents and patent citations granted to the companies, universities and the research institution (CSIRO) associated with the Victorian Organic Solar Cell Consortium before (2003–2010) and after (2011–2018) the formation of the consortium. Data collected through the Web of Science database, by selecting specific Derwent classification codes associated with FWEs

took part in So-Light) to the VOSCC and that their poor innovation capabilities play a role in the proliferation of technology. Indeed, the number of patents and patent citations of the VOSCC companies before 2011 are respectively 6% and 4% the So-Light companies equivalent, showing how little innovative the companies were. Therefore, classifying Australia as middle-level innovator is in agreement with prior work [75].

Analysis of FWEs-related patents and patents citations shows that H1 holds true only if the countries where consortia are formed are strong-level innovators, since major industry players can be involved in the public–private partnership.

4.5 Validating H2: Technologies Developed by Consortia Will Preferentially Diffuse Domestically

A very small number of patent licenses are recorded in the U.S. Patent and Trademark Office's Assignment database, which is a public record of patent ownership rights [76]. Since there is no legal requirement to record licenses, most of them are not. However, "confirmatory licenses" tend to be recorded in databases like the USPTO's Assignment or others, because such licenses are given to the U.S. government in exchange for public funding [77]. Given the reservations companies have to disclose the details of the technologies used in their products, it is possible to track patent licensing only through press releases, databases that determine royalty rates, and litigation settlement documents. For example, each of the German companies Novaled, Osram's LEDVANCE, and BMG MIS took part at a given time to a consortium [64, 78]. The German enterprises all developed innovative technologies through public–private partnerships, but the companies' IP were later acquired by Samsung, [67] MLS, [79] and Luminator Technology Group, [80] respectively. Thanks to press releases, it is possible to track the diffusion of relevant FWEs technology developed by a consortium internationally, rather than domestically. However, different conclusions may be drawn for other FWEs patents.

Few patent reform bills have included provisions seeking to require increased transparency around patent ownership [81, 82]. At the time of writing, there is no means to track the diffusion of each patent developed through public–private partnerships. Hence, H2 cannot be validated.

4.6 FWEs: Threats and Benefits to the U.S. DoD

Based on what has been discussed so far, there is no clear leader in the field of flexible and wearable electronics. China, a peer competitor of the U.S., is currently ramping up its efforts to establish its hegemony in the industry. Given the rapid technological development of FWEs and China's military aspirations, the threat to the U.S. is currently medium and will increase in the next 5–10 years. Terrorist groups also pose a threat to the U.S. national security.

Although the threat is low now, terrorist groups are expected to gain access to FWEs as their commercial application spreads worldwide in the medium-long term [83]. Armed groups could disrupt political order in failing states, similarly to what ISIS did in Syria and Iraq. As summary of the threat assessment is shown in Fig. 7.

Nonetheless, FWEs could provide the U.S. with a strategic advantage. FWEs are an example of a major technology trend called the Internet of Things (IoT), which aims at connecting different types of devices and networks together to increase data sharing [84]. As the aerospace and defense industry adopt more FWEs, more data will be stored, sent, and retrieved from them. Ongoing R&D work centers on securing the networks and data information. However, once it is understood how to properly secure certain type information, and once weak spots in network security are identified, it

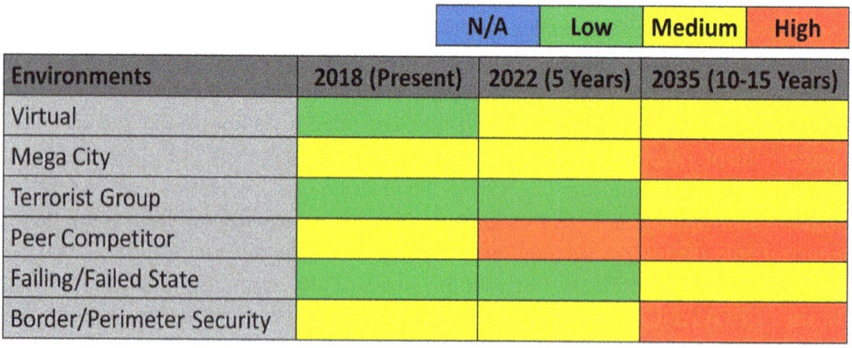

	N/A	Low	Medium	High
Environments	**2018 (Present)**	**2022 (5 Years)**	**2035 (10-15 Years)**	
Virtual	Low	Medium	Medium	
Mega City	Medium	Medium	High	
Terrorist Group	Low	Low	Medium	
Peer Competitor	Medium	High	High	
Failing/Failed State	Low	Medium	Medium	
Border/Perimeter Security	Medium	Medium	High	

Fig. 7 Threat assessment of the destructive impact/threat of flexible and wearable electronics in different environments over time

could be possible to use this knowledge to launch cyber-attacks or influence election outcomes abroad.

Last, FWEs delivers tactical advantages that are relevant in megacities and along borders. Flexible and wearable electronics increase connectivity among soldiers while decreasing armed personnel reliance on the supply lines [37]. These attributes can help sustain longer operations and increase operations effectiveness. Major technology manufacturing and development efforts are underway, although implementation in the defense industry has been there for a decade.

5 Conclusions

The absence of efficient international regulations controlling research partnerships between non-state actors and foreign governments or enterprises is evidenced in the literature. Particularly alarming it is the scarce protection of intellectual property in China, where scientific discoveries do not enjoy patent protection. To define efficient tools to control diffusion of dual-use technologies, it is necessary to study diffusion of general-purpose technologies, and specifically the diffusion of flexible and wearable electronics (FWEs). The U.S. has not established a clear leadership in the FWEs industry, and given the large range of applications of FWEs, the U.S. risks to erode the technological advantage of its military. The prevailing literature claims that formation of consortia will favor the development and the local diffusion of general-purpose technologies, as opposed to university and company-based R&D efforts. While the present literature supports this claim by means of qualitative analysis, the author suggests using patent citations. The latter is an established quantitative tool to study diffusion of military technologies. Creating consortia increases the number of patents granted in four different countries, with varying levels of innovation capability. Creating consortia leads to different outcomes in terms of number of forward citations, depending on the country considered. If a consortium is created in a country that is a strong innovator (i.e., the U.S., China, and Germany), university patents related to flexible and wearable electronics will receive more forward citations. The same argument may not necessarily be true for companies involved in the same consortium as universities; these companies will maintain excellent innovation capabilities. If a consortium is created in a country that is a mid-level innovator (i.e., Australia), innovation capabilities are likely to remain limited. This outcome could change whether key industry partners are attracted to the public–private partnership.

Beyond tracking patent citations, it is important to understand who the licensees of these patents are. At the time of writing, there is no means to track the diffusion of each patent developed through consortia. However, the U.S. could adopt a second-mover strategy and license patents develop through consortia in other countries, as several civilian companies have done in the past. In conclusion, FWEs constitute both a threat and an opportunity for the DoD, given the applications of these devices to increase connectivity among soldiers and among devices, to decrease reliance on supply lines, and to potentially breach into information systems. It is important to keep in mind that the key for innovation is not just in the institutions or diplomatic tools (treaties), but it is also in creative insecurity. Policymakers and military leaders need to shift the conversation back to S&T and invest in understanding our peer competitors in depth.

6 Next Steps

Model refinement and expansion of data collection are necessary. Large patent datasets and reports associated with FWEs are available for pay [85]. Since consortia in the field of FWEs have only been established within the last ten-fifteen years, it may be still premature to use forward citations as a tool to assess proliferation of FWEs. Other possible dependent variables that could be used are spending in basic education, country perception of national security situation, intellectual property regime relative to universities and companies.

7 Novelty

This chapter represents the first attempt to validate whether technologies developed by consortia will tend to diffuse more than technologies developed by universities and companies alone. Diffusion of intellectual property generated by consortia, research institutions and companies was studied by measuring the number of patent citations relevant to FWEs. Moreover, this work highlighted that it is currently not possible to claim local proliferation of IP developed by consortia based on patent data. The results of this work inform policy makers on the lack of regulations on scientific discovery in China, the advantages of creating consortia, and the potential threats and benefits of FWEs. Future work could also inform companies whether relocating their manufacturing base from China back to their homeland, is a strategic move. Relocation of manufacturing may prevent proliferation of sensitive IPs, while an international agreement is not in place.

References

1. Hume D (1742) On the rise and progress of the arts and sciences. In: Essays, moral and political, vol. 1, Part 1, Essay 14
2. Cardwell DSL (1972) Turning points in western technology: a study of technology, science, and history. Science History Publications, New York
3. Taylor MZ (2016) Chapter 1—The puzzle of cardwell's law. In: The politics of innovation: why some countries are better than others at science and technology. Oxford University Press, pp 10–32
4. Kodama F (1991) Analyzing Japanese high technologies. Printer Publishers, London

5. Moser P, Voena A, Waldinger F (2013) German-Jewish emigres and U.S. invention. SSRN, 1–59, https://doi.org/10.2139/ssrn.1910247
6. Kirk A. (2015) Nobel prize winners: which country has the most nobel laureates"? The telegraph. https://www.telegraph.co.uk/news/worldnews/northamerica/usa/11926364/Nobel-Prize-winners-Which-country-has-the-most-Nobel-laureates.html
7. Reich RB (2010) Aftershock: the next economy and America's future. Alfred A. Knopf, New York
8. Atkinson RD, Ezell SJ (2012) Innovation economics: The race for global advantage. Yale University Press, New Haven, CT
9. National Research Council (2005) Rising above the gathering storm: energizing and employing america for a brighter economic future. National Academies Press, Washington, DC
10. National Research Council (2010) Rising above the gathering storm, revisited: rapidly approaching category 5. National Academies Press, Washington, DC
11. National Research Council (2012) Improving measures of science, technology, and innovation. National Academies Press, Washington, DC
12. Kliman D, Krejsa H (2017) Is China leaping past Us"? Politico. https://www.politico.com/agenda/story/2017/09/11/china-leaping-past-us-000509
13. Veugelers R (2017) China is the world's new science and technology powerhouse. Brink. https://www.brinknews.com/the-challenge-of-chinas-rise-as-a-science-and-technology-powerhouse/
14. Hernández JC (2016) Study finds Chinese students excel in critical thinking. Until College. The New York Times. https://www.nytimes.com/2016/07/31/world/asia/china-college-education-quality.html
15. Yi H, Li G, Li L, Loyalka P, Zhang L, Xu J, Kardanova E, Shi H, Chu J (2017) Assessing the quality of upper-secondary vocational education and training: evidence from China. Comp Educ Rev. https://doi.org/10.1086/696920
16. Taylor MZ (2016) Chapter 3—Cardwell's law in action. In: The politics of innovation: why some countries are better than others at science and technology. Oxford University Press, pp 66–70
17. Aron J (2016) China launches world's first quantum communications satellite. New Scientist. https://www.newscientist.com/article/2101071-china-launches-worlds-first-quantum-communications-satellite/
18. Popkin G (2017) China's quantum satellite achieves 'Spooky action' at record distance." Science. https://www.sciencemag.org/news/2017/06/china-s-quantum-satellite-achieves-spooky-action-record-distance
19. Rana P (2017) China pushes ahead with human gene-editing trials. Wall Street J. https://www.wsj.com/articles/china-pushes-ahead-with-human-gene-trials-1493380057
20. Galeon D (2018) The first American CRISPR trial in humans will target cancer. Futurism. https://futurism.com/first-american-human-crispr-trial-target-cancer/
21. Stadtmauer E (2020) CRISPR-engineered T cells in patients with refractory cancer. Science 367:6481. https://doi.org/10.1126/science.aba7365
22. National Institutes of Health (2020) Office of science policy. Dual use research of concern. Accessed in December 2020. https://osp.od.nih.gov/biotechnology/dual-use-research-of-concern/
23. Bureau of Industry and Security (2018) U.S. Department of commerce. Commerce control list (CCL). Accessed in April 2018. https://www.bis.doc.gov/index.php/regulations/commerce-control-list-ccl
24. National Intelligence Council (2007) Nonstate actors: impact on international relations and implications for the United States. https://www.dni.gov/files/documents/nonstate_actors_2007.pdf
25. European Commission (2020) The definition of non-state actors (NSAs). Accessed in December 2020. https://webgate.ec.europa.eu/fpfis/mwikis/aidco/index.php?title=Special:Pdfprint&page=9EDF:_Types_of_non_state_actors
26. Acemoglu D, Robinson JA (2012) Why nations fail: the origins of power, prosperity and poverty. Crown Publishers, New York

27. Taylor MZ (2016) Chapter 1—The puzzle of Cardwell's law." In: The politics of innovation: why some countries are better than others at science and technology. Oxford University Press, pp 20–22
28. Furze A, Lim L (2017) 'Faustian bargain': defence fears over Australian university's $100m China partnership. The Guardian. https://www.theguardian.com/australia-news/2017/sep/19/faustian-bargain-defence-fears-over-australian-universitys-100m-china-partnership
29. Blank S (2013) China's torch program: the glow that can light the world. https://steveblank.com/2013/04/11/chinas-torch-program-the-glow-that-can-light-the-world-part-2-of-5/
30. Dingli S, Economy E, Haass R, Kurlantzick J, Smith SA, Tay S (2017) China's maritime disputes. Council on Foreign Relations. https://www.cfr.org/interactives/chinas-maritime-disputes?cid=otr-marketing_use-china_sea_InfoGuide#!/chinas-maritime-disputes?cid=otr-marketing_use-china_sea_InfoGuide
31. Department of Defense (2015) Asia-Pacific maritime security strategy. https://www.defense.gov/Portals/1/Documents/pubs/NDAA%20A-P_Maritime_SecuritY_Strategy-08142015-1300-FINALFORMAT.PDF
32. U.S. Senate Permanent Subcommittee on Investigations (2014) Defense acquisition reform: where do we go from here? Staff Report. https://www.gpo.gov/fdsys/pkg/CPRT-113SPRT90719/pdf/CPRT-113SPRT90719.pdf
33. Harrison AJ (2016) DOD 2.0: high tech is eating the pentagon.In: Proceedings Magazine of the U.S. Naval Institute 1, 42/2/1356. https://www.usni.org/magazines/proceedings/2016-02/dod-20-high-tech-eating-pentagon
34. Blanken L, Lepore J, Rodriguez S (2018) America's military is choking on old technology. Foreign Policy. https://foreignpolicy.com/2018/01/29/americas-military-is-choking-on-old-technology/
35. Top Universities QS Global Rankings (2020) Accessed in December 2020. https://www.topuniversities.com/universities/university-new-south-wales-unsw-sydney#sub
36. Torch University of New South Wales (2020) UNSW research capabilities: next generation materials and technologies. Accessed in Dec 2020. https://www.torch.unsw.edu.au/unsw-research-capabilities/next-generation-materials-and-technologies
37. Kettunen J, Kaisto I, van den Kieboom E, Rikkola R, Korhonen R (2011) Promoting entrepreneurship in organic and large area electronics in Europe. Valtion Teknillinen Tutkimuskeskus (VTT). https://www.vtt.fi/inf/pdf/tiedotteet/2011/T2579.pdf
38. Dodabalapur A, Arias AC, Frisbie DC, Gamota D, Marks TJ, Wood C (2010) European research and development on hybrid flexible electronics. WTEC Panel Report, v, xv.
39. National Research Council (2014) The flexible electronics opportunity. The National Academies Press, Washington, DC. https://doi.org/10.17226/18812
40. Sloan SS, Alper J (2014) Institute of medicine; national academy of engineering; national academy of sciences; national research council (U.S.); planning committee for the work-shop on culture matters: an approach to international research agreements; policy and global affairs and government-university-industry research roundtable. 2014. In: Chapter 6: intellectual property. culture matters: international research collaboration in a changing world : summary of a workshop, National Academies Press, pp 33–39
41. Office of the United States Trade Representative (2017) Special 301 report. https://ustr.gov/sites/default/files/301/2017%20Special%20301%20Report%20FINAL.PDF
42. World Intellectual Property Organization (2014) Outline of the legal and regulatory framework for intellectual property in the people's Republic of China (PRC). Accessed in April 2018. https://www.wipo.int/wipolex/en/outline/cn.html
43. Knowledge Transfer Working Group of the European Research Area Committee (2012) European research area guidelines on intellectual property (IP) management in collaboration agreements between European and Non-European Partners. https://ec.europa.eu/research/innovation-union/pdf/international_cooperation_guidelines_erac_kt_group.pdf
44. Grindley P, Mowery DC, Silverman B (1994) SEMATECH and collaborative research: lessons in the design of high-technology consortia. J Policy Anal Manage. https://doi.org/10.2307/3325495

45. Ruttan VW (2006) Is war necessary for economic growth? Oxford University Press, Oxford
46. Ruttan VW (2006) Is war necessary for economic growth? Historically Speaking 7:17–19
47. Schmid J (2017) The diffusion of military technology. Defence Peace Econ. https://doi.org/10.1080/10242694.2017.1292203
48. Derwent Innovations Index (2017) Clarivate Analytics, 2017. https://images.webofknowledge.com/images/help/DII/hp_database.html
49. Garnaut J (2018) How China interferes in Australia. Foreign affairs. https://www.foreignaffairs.com/articles/china/2018-03-09/how-china-interferes-australia
50. Derra S (2004) ASU, army open new flexible display center. Arizona State University. https://www.asu.edu/feature/includes/spring05/readmore/flexdisplay.html
51. Flexible Electronics and Display Center (2020) Arizona state university. Accessed in Dec 2020. https://flexdisplay.asu.edu/publications
52. Murph D (2008) HP and ASU demo bendable, unbreakable electronic displays. Engadget. https://www.engadget.com/2008/12/08/hp-and-asu-demo-bendable-unbreakable-electronic-displays/
53. Flexible Display Center at Arizona State University. The flexible display center produces largest flexible Color OLED display manufactured with mixed oxide thin film transistors. Market Wired. https://www.marketwired.com/press-release/flexible-display-center-produces-largest-flexible-color-oled-display-manufactured-with-1662878.htm
54. Esposito R (2004) One for all, all for one. Boeing is part of key network-centric group. Boeing Frontiers Online. https://www.boeing.com/news/frontiers/archive/2004/november/i_ids6.html
55. Nicodemo A (2016) Researchers building durable X-ray detector with broad health-care implications. Arizona State University. https://asunow.asu.edu/20160815-solutions-flexible-future-todays-technologies-asu
56. Eric W (2012) How long does it take to get a patent? Erickson Law Group, PC. Accessed in April 2018. https://www.ericksonlawgroup.com/law/patents/patentfaq/how-long-does-it-take-to-get-a-patent/
57. National Research Council (2014) Chapter 6—East Asia. In: The flexible electronics opportunity, The National Academies Press, Washington, DC, pp 182–200. https://doi.org/10.17226/18812
58. Institute of Printed Electronic Industry (2017) Accessed in April 2018. https://en.czipei.com/news_detail/newsId=434.html
59. Nano and Advanced Materials Institute Ltd (2020) Accessed in Dec 2020. https://www.nami.org.hk/en/nami/introduction.html
60. Top Universities QS Global Rankings. Accessed in December 2020. https://www.topuniversities.com/universities/hong-kong-university-science-technology
61. Nano and Advanced Materials Institute Ltd. (2017). Geneva award booklet. file:///C:/Users/Utente-PC/Downloads/2017_Geneva_Award_Booklet.pdf
62. International Exhibition of Inventions of Geneva. (2018) Palexpo. Accessed in Dec 2020. https://www.palexpo.ch/en/agenda/international-exhibition-inventions-geneva
63. Bloomberg News (2017) In China public-private partnerships are really public-public. https://www.bloomberg.com/news/articles/2017-02-27/in-china-public-private-partnerships-are-really-public-public
64. LEDs Magazine (2009) So-light project brings together Germany's OLED Community. https://www.ledsmagazine.com/articles/2009/12/so-light-project-brings-together-germany-s-oled-community.html
65. LEDinside (2014) German OLED project so-light successfully concludes. https://www.ledinside.com/news/2014/1/german_oled_project_so_light_successfully_concludes
66. Fraunhofer (2020) Accessed in Dec 2020. https://www.fraunhofer.de/en/about-fraunhofer/profile-structure.html
67. Whitney L (2013) Samsung to buy OLED maker novaled for $347 Million. ClNet. https://www.cnet.com/news/samsung-to-buy-oled-maker-novaled-for-347-million/
68. Top Universities Global Rankings (2020) Accessed in Dec 2020. https://www.topuniversities.com/universities/westfalische-wilhelms-universitat-munster

69. Ranking Web of Universities—Germany (2020) Accessed in Dec 2020. https://www.webometrics.info/en/Europe/Germany%20
70. Palmer R (2016) Is the global economic crisis about to hit Germany? The Trumpet. https://www.thetrumpet.com/14235-is-the-global-economic-crisis-about-to-hit-germany
71. Top Universities Global Rankings (2020) Accessed in Dec 2020. https://www.topuniversities.com/universities/monash-university
72. Top Universities Global Rankings (2020) Accessed in Dec 2020. https://www.topuniversities.com/universities/university-melbourne
73. CSIRO (2020) Printable solar cells for lightweight energy. Accessed in Dec 2020. https://www.csiro.au/en/Research/MF/Areas/Innovation/Flex-Electronics/Printed-Solar-Cells
74. Jones D (2014) Printing solar cells—A manufacturing proposition for Australia. Australian government—Australian renewable energy agency (ARENA). https://arena.gov.au/assets/2014/11/Printing-solar-cells-public-dissemination-report.pdf
75. Taylor MZ (2016) Chapter 8—Creative insecurity-olson's nemesis. In: The politics of innovation: why some countries are better than others at science and technology. Oxford University Press, pp 238–267
76. Patent Assignment Search (2020) U.S. Patent and Trademark Office. Accessed in December 2020. https://assignment.uspto.gov/patent/index.html#/patent/search
77. iEdison.gov (2016) Provide a confirmatory license that gives the government certain rights to invention in iEdison. Accessed in Dec 2020. https://era.nih.gov/iedison/provide_license.htm
78. LEDs Magazine (2010) TOPAS 2012 consortium targets innovative OLED lighting. Accessed in Dec 2020. https://www.ledsmagazine.com/articles/2010/01/topas-2012-consortium-targets-innovative-oled-lighting.html
79. LEDinside (2016) Chinese consortium including MLS acquires Osram's LEDVANCE business for EUR 400M. Accessed in Dec 2020. https://www.ledinside.com/news/2016/7/mls_acquires_osrams_ledvance_business_for_eur_400m
80. Cision PR Newswire (2015) Luminator technology group acquires BMG MIS. Accessed in Dec 2020. https://www.prnewswire.com/news-releases/luminator-technology-group-acquires-bmg-mis-300162008.html
81. S. 1720—113th Congress (2013–2014) Patent Transparency and Improvements Act of 2013. Accessed in Dec 2020. https://www.congress.gov/bill/113th-congress/senate-bill/1720
82. American Intellectual Property Law Association (2013–2014) Patent litigation legislation in the 113th congress. https://www.aipla.org/advocacy/congress/113C/Pages/patentlitigation.aspx
83. Alexander D (2015) Pentagon teams up with Apple, Boeing to develop wearable tech. Reuters. https://www.reuters.com/article/usa-defense-tech/pentagon-teams-up-with-apple-boeing-to-develop-wearable-tech-idUSL1N11302F20150828?rpc=401
84. Howard C (2015) Widespread use of wearable technology. Mil Aerosp Electron. https://www.militaryaerospace.com/articles/print/volume-26/issue-9/technology-focus/widespread-use-of-wearable-technology.html
85. Cintelliq (2018) Organic and printed electronics. A ten year review of the patent landscape: 2008–2017. Accessed in Apr 2018. https://www.cintelliq.com/research/report/organic-printed-electronics/

Assessment of Potential Security Threats from Advances in Neurotechnology

Sathya Balachander

Abstract Neurotechnology has experienced rapid growth and progress, and this could be attributed to the advances in the fundamental understanding of human brain activity, coupled with access to high technology. Additionally, it is a "dual use" technology as it has immense medical applications that could benefit the public and could also pose significant threat to the public safety and health. As the nature how wars are being fought change, neurotechnology can be used in military and counterintelligence applications, thus benefiting both the civilian and the military realm. Using three emerging neurotechnologies as case studies, this chapter addresses the potential medical and military applications of these technologies, while speculating on potential misuses. The possibility of exploiting neurotechnology by various actors for nefarious purposes is analyzed, along with hypothesizing the current, near, and far future use of neurotechnology in different environments.

1 Introduction

Neuroscience refers to a range of disciplines that pursue research on the nervous system, the brain, and the underlying biochemistry of cognition to better understand the behavior, disease, development, and the process of reasoning, perception, and awareness. Extensive work to uncover the brain's function and the structure dates back decades. In the 1960s, the term 'neuroscience' was introduced by scholar Francis Otto Schmitt. Combining fields like biology, chemistry, psychology with developments in imaging, research to better understand the functioning of normal and abnormal brains grew. Neuroscience encompasses different areas from molecular neuroscience to computational biophysics to experimental psychology.

The origins of neuroscience research date back to the nineteen century. In 1815, Jean Pierre Flourens and his team developed an experimental method to study motor function, sensibility, and behavior by performing localized lesions on living animals (pigeons and rabbits) [1]. These experiments helped identify the function of the brain.

S. Balachander (✉)
UAB, Birmingham, USA

© The Author(s), under exclusive license to Springer Nature Switzerland AG 2021
M. E. Kosal (ed.), *Proliferation of Weapons- and Dual-Use Technologies*,
Advanced Sciences and Technologies for Security Applications,
https://doi.org/10.1007/978-3-030-73655-2_6

The continuing interest and understanding of neurons became increasingly accurate during the twentieth century. In 1952, Alon Lloyd Hodgkin and Andrew Huxley presented their model, Hodgkin-Huxley model, to describe how nerve cells function. They used squid giant axons to demonstrate how action potential, mechanism through with cells communicate, are initiated and propagated [2].

The scientific study of the nervous system, including the brain, increased significantly, especially due to the advances in other fields such as molecular biology, psychology, physiology, anatomy, developmental biology, mathematical modeling and computational technology, and the pairing of neuroscience and technology have paved way to neurotechnology. In this chapter, neurotechnology is used in the context of applying the knowledge of neuroscience to fundamentally influence/alter/impair the brain by using technological advancements. This includes technologies that are designed to improve and repair the nervous system and the brain, and ones that allow researchers and clinicians to visualize the brain. The advent of brain imaging started the first of many developments in neurotechnology [3]. The depth and knowledge in the basic and applied sciences have increased to a level that now neurotechnology is used in many areas, from controlling depression to improving stroke victim's motor coordination [4].

2 Neurotechnology

2.1 Interest in Advancing Neurotechnology

Investments in research and development in neuroscience and technology are substantial. In 2013, President Obama announced a BRAIN Initiative (Brain Research through Advancing Innovative Neurotechnologies), and $200 million a year was appropriated for brain related research and development by Congress. The underlying idea driving the BRAIN Initiative is to create significant developments in the field of neuroscience analogous to what the Human Genome Project was to genetics. The BRAIN Initiative included impressive goals to integrate principles of theory, modeling, statistics, and computation with basic neuroscience to produce sophisticated systems [5].

As of 2019, National Institutes of Health funding levels have increased to more than $424 million and have been awarded to over 180 new BRAIN Initiative awards [6]. This upward trend is expected to continue in the following years and will increase to $500 million per year for FY21-25 [7]. Since the launch of this program more than a billion dollars has been funded towards research and advancements in this area.

Research as part of the BRAIN Initiative is being funded and executed throughout the federal government, by either intramural or extramural projects. DARPA (Defense Advanced Research Projects Agency) is involved directly with the BRAIN initiative and has allocated $95 million to support various projects. For example, DARPA has teams working in advanced projects such as Neural Engineering Systems Design

(NESD), with the goal of producing advanced neural devices with improved fidelity, resolution, and precision sensory interface [8]. The National Science Foundation (NSF) has budgeted $72 million to support the BRAIN Initiative and other related projects [9, 10]. One such example is the Brain-Inspired Concepts and Designs which covers an umbrella of different projects that aims to developing novel conceptual paradigms and innovative technologies [11].

Another federal agency, the Intelligence Advanced Research Projects Activity (IARPA) is working on testing and validating non-invasive neural interventions to improve human performance in information-rich environments [12]. They have invested in projects that reverse-engineer algorithms of the brain to motivate and better perform complex information processing tasks. To speed up the process of commercializing it, the Food and Drug Administration (FDA) is working on streamlining the 'regulatory framework to improve the efficiency, consistency and predictability' of all such technologies that would be used in clinical studies [13]. Success coming from any of these research organizations will likely provide medical benefits to patients, civilian and military personnel.

2.2 Dual Use Nature of Neurotechnology

The National Institutes of Health (NIH) define dual use research as "research areas, that based on current understanding, can reasonably be anticipated to provide knowledge, information, products, or technologies that could be directly misapplied to pose a significant threat to public health and safety" [14]. In the context of neurotechnology, dual use would include technologies that are used for beneficial purposes but could be misused for nefarious purposes. Neurotechnologies are often "dual use" in nature, having both medical/scientific applications and use in military/counterintelligence application. Some of the case studies highlighted in this chapter will demonstrate how such technologies might be misused. It is important, that the potential for the latter be assessed in order to make decisions affecting future research, development, deployment, and policy at the domestic and international level.

For the sake of being consistent, for this chapter, the dual nature of neurotechnology will be classified in two categories—(a) technologies that provide beneficial medical applications and (b) neurotechnology applications that could be used for hostile reasons. Although there are many subcategories that can be categorized under neurotechnology, emphasis of this chapter will be on Brain-Machine Interface (BMI) or Brain-Computer Interface (BCI), as our lives are increasingly getting integrated with machines in more and more ways than it has ever been possible. Hence, this chapter will attempt to explore some of the ways in which neurotechnology could be misused.

2.3 Neurotechnology and Security

The military dominance of the U.S. and the changing character of warfare, often facilitated by advances in science and technology, has fostered an environment where wars or conflicts fought by non-traditional means are more prevalent [15]. In 2014, the United States National Academies published a study titled "Emerging and Readily Available Technologies and National Security," which lists new technologies that are readily accessible to the military and increasingly available globally [16]. Notable among those technologies are prosthetics with enhanced capabilities and stimulating drugs to enhance cognitive performance. More recently, the National Defense Strategy pointed out that new commercially made technology will be game changers in reshaping the character of war [17]. These advancements would be used to boost national security and change the landscape of military weapons.

Certain aspects of neuroscience and neurotechnology have been applied in the military. Significant research has been carried out on areas of cognitive performance. They range from controlling factors that affect sleep and stress to augmented reality that can be used for nutrition and training [18, 19]. These applications have been used for lie-detection, and are currently used for training and rehabilitation by using augmented reality [20]. Neurotechnology is also assisting the military in medical applications [21, 22]. For example, transcranial direct current stimulation (tDCS) which was originally developed to treat psychiatric conditions, have been shown to improve the ways in which Air Force members process information while multi-tasking. In this study, just by increasing brain stimulation for longer than 30 s, the participants demonstrated a significant improvement in information processing and displayed enhanced multitasking performance [23]. These routes might perhaps be implemented to stimulate the brain function.

Due to advances in technology, such as computers and miniaturization of electronic devices, there are numerous benefits that the army can exploit in the future from neurotechnological applications. An example of that would be the use of helmet mounted-electroencephalogram (EEG) device to monitor the brain activity and to augment a human's ability to detect a potential threat anywhere in the wide field of view when seen through a binocular. The objective of this program, Cognitive Technology Threat Warning System (CTTWS), is to identify potential features of interest using the brain signal, and then warn the soldier to direct their attention to the potential threat [24]. This threat detection system incorporates cognitive visual processing algorithms that identify potential targets and cue images for the user using a 120-megapixel, 120-degree field view electro-optical video camera. Tests demonstrated a greater than 90% success in target recognition rate [25].

Advances in neuroscience and neurotechnology may improve the capability of military personnel to meet the challenges of the modern battlefield. Presence of medical supplements, non-invasive modifications of brain effectiveness for training and sleeplessness, and neuropharmaceuticals have been used. An example of this, would be in the area of pain management. By inducing Transcutaneous Electrical

Nerve Stimulation (TENS) directly on the inflicted area, it activates opioid and serotonin, which helps in relieving pain. This technology is available in a wearable form to relieve chronic pain to treat wound pain [26, 27]. Use of prosthetics would be another example. DARPA's Revolutionizing Prosthetics have created a fully functional upper limb that responds to neural control. Surviving military service members with severe battlefield injuries can utilize prosthetics to regain limb functions [28].

For non-medical applications, brain-machine interface, is used to augment normal performance by using an external device linked to nervous system. EEG-based BCIs are being used as wearable accessories for gaming and entertainment activities. For example, companies Emotiv and Neurosky offer a wireless headset for daily use, that can be connected to smart phone or personal computers [29]. These can be used in gaming or for entertainment purposes as they could potentially eliminate the need for external keyboards or mouse [30, 31].

There is also the new strategy, The Third Offset [32]. The goal of the Third Offset was to "identify and invest in innovative ways to sustain and advance America's military dominance for the twenty-first century" [33]. The 2018 National Defense Strategy highlighted the importance of The Third Offset Strategy by noting that the U.S. national security will likely be "affected by rapid technological advancements and the changing character of war. New technologies include advance computing, "big data" analytics, artificial intelligence, autonomy, robotics, directed energy, hypersonics, and biotechnology-the very technologies that ensure we will be able to fight and win the wars of the future." [34] The combination of these technologies constitute neurotechnology and they could contribute to increasing the military advantage. The following sections specifically highlight three emerging neurotechnologies and their potential applications.

2.3.1 High-Definition Artificial Retina

DARPA's program Neural Engineering System Design (NESD) aims to develop high-resolution neurotechnology that can mitigate the effects of injury or disease [35]. An innovative project that falls under this program is the High-Definition Artificial Retina (HDAR) which is developed by the research team at Fondation Voir et Entendre (The Seeing and Hearing Foundation) in Paris, France. The team is working on translating techniques from optogenetics (use of light to control living cells) to enable communication between visual cortex and a camera based HDAR that can be worn over the eyes, like sunglasses [36]. They are building a model where information would be transmitted from a camera to an external device worn on the head, which is responsible for transforming the images into simulation patterns which can then be wirelessly be communicated to a high-density micro-LED array for the visual cortex. This would require overcoming challenges of processing vast amount of data collected by the retina. The team plans on developing a neuromorphic event-based camera system to capture only relevant content from dynamic scenes, scenes that change substantially from frame to frame. Scientifically, this research will help in mapping out how the eye and brain work together to process vision. Although, it has yet to be seen if a product could be generated from this project as it is difficult to translate this research but not impossible.

Assuming HDAR project come to fruition, HDAR might be employed to assist in intelligence gathering in a stealthy manner, as heavy camera equipment becomes dispensable. There has been significant progress made in this field of retinal implants and artificial vision [37]. HDAR technology could become valuable in places that have high security as artificial retina will not trigger security alert. Additionally, these lenses can transmit information wirelessly allowing for recording real time events. Another application of HDAR might be for surveillance. In a military context, it could aid surveillance and other efforts. Concurrently, one can imagine the use of HDAR by law enforcement, criminals, stalkers, or others to use such technology for surveillance of civilians. Domestic surveillance is a long-contested issue, and HDAR with other technologies will make them complicated. In the future, merging HDAR with artificial intelligence (AI) system could create a powerful system. For example, within eight months of developing an AI-augmented algorithm, intelligence analysts were utilizing it to identify objects from any video feed coming from small drones [38]. This is a stepping stone for bigger and successful future projects of human–machine interface. This AI enabled program called as Project Maven is assisting U.S. Special Operations Command intelligence analysts identify objects in video from small scale drones. Before this program came to fruition, the intelligence team had to use algorithms and spend thousands of hours analyzing video captured by drones. By integrating AI, the need for manual intelligence analysis is drastically reduced, and this may allow significantly increased speeds of detection and targeting a threat.

2.3.2 Neuroprosthetics

A prosthesis is used to reestablish wholeness to the body when it is missing a part like a limb or an eye. The need for prosthetic is neatly captured in 'The J.E. Hanger Story'. J.E. Hanger was the first amputee of the Civil War. Amputation was performed to save his life. On returning home, he constructed the 'Hanger Limb,' which he used until his death and was commissioned to develop prosthetic limbs for veteran soldiers from 1861 till his death. The company he established is now a $1 billion entity that serves veterans and civilians alike [39]. Artificial limbs were mass produced during World War I due to the enormous number of causalities.

Emerging prosthetics function as brain-machine interface to restore function to patients with extreme paralysis, enabling return to performance of daily life activities. High-density electrocorticography (ECoG) arrays are placed in the brain to increase intracortical microstimulation of the somatosensory cortex which could help gain sensation and control the prosthetic fingers in the arms [40, 41]. This is significant, as it helps the user to control finger movements of a robotic arm individually in real-time with enhanced sensitivity. Another emerging field in this avenue is Modular Prosthetic Limb (MPL), which is a cutting-edge technology innovation using mechanical, electrical, and biological sciences [42]. MPL is capable of functioning like a human arm and hand and is the world's most sophisticated upper-extremity prosthesis. It is an efficient program to help the clinicians provide any part required by the patients. MPL will function very similar to a human arm, and this technology significantly improves the quality of life for civilians and aids in robotic arm for military personnel.

More advanced research has been possible on the prostheses themselves by exploiting benefits of compact sensor, actuator, and energy-storage technologies. Example of an advanced type of this prosthetic is "Luke Arm." Luke arm uses microprocessors that are small, and can provide sufficient power to control the electronics, batteries, motors and wiring. Additionally, it weighs only 3.6 kg. Clinical trials began in 2008, and within five years it received FDA approval. Currently it is commercially available, although at a steep price of $100,000 from Mobius Bionics [43]. This could be used for ex-service members of the military to regain their sense of movement using a prosthetic arm.

Most of these prosthetic and robotic arms require a remote access capability to control. Having this remote access capability creates security issues as they may be susceptible to hacking. In 2012 it was shown that Medtronic insulin pumps, widely used by diabetic patients, could be disrupted by instructing the pump to alter the insulin dosage [44]. Implantable cardiac defibrillators or pacemakers are vulnerable to manipulation by delivering shocks that could lead to heart shocks [45]. This vulnerability was fictionalized in the second season of the series, *Homeland,* in which the character of the US Vice President was assassinated by such a tactic [46].

2.3.3 fMRI/EEG

Neural implant recordings are currently being done through direct electrical measurements of neurons through either an external device or by implanting an electrode array in the brain. All the technologies have trade-off characteristics such as size, number of implanted electrode arrays, durability, portability, and invasiveness. Brain imaging tools such as positron emission tomography (PET) and functional magnetic resonance imaging (fMRI), when used in combination with electroencephalograms (EEGs) provide spatial and temporal information on brain function. Using non-invasive methods, these technologies can be used to study the brain functioning. Limitations of non-invasive methods in EEG result in less efficient or degraded signal. By using electrocorticographic electrodes, which are placed directly on the surface of the brain, enhanced signal strength and specificity can be obtained.

In order to solve the issue of durability, size and low power, a research team has recently explored the possibility of using thousands of 10–100 μm scales, free-floating, independent sensor nodes that they call neural dust that can detect and report the local electrophysiological data [47]. They also have utilized a subcranial interrogator that establishes power and communication links with thousands of free-floating, independent sensor nodes, which they call 'neural dust'. Unlike other systems that rely on electromagnetic waves, neural dusts rely on ultrasound as it provides more power and enables efficient transfer of energy. The underlying concept is to implant these neural dusts anywhere in the body and have a path over the implanted site send ultrasonic waves to send and receive information from the dusts for a desired application [48]. Scientifically, the use of neural dust is conceivable, but it involves an invasive process of surgically planting thousands of neural dusts in the different parts of the body. It is hard to imagine the absence of side-effects when using this technique. A potential misuse of this technology could be remote guidance or control of these neural dust. Research has been done in remote controlling of animals that could be used for search and rescue operations during natural disaster recovery [49, 50]. By applying external stimuli or by manipulating the signals could trigger a response that would prove catastrophic for people with these neural dusts.

EEG is a classic example of how neurotechnology is beneficial in the medical field [51]. EEG is a monitoring method to record the electrical activity of the brain. This can be invasive, by placing patching electrodes on the scalp, or it can be noninvasive, such as by placing electrodes externally on the scalp. A team at Imperial College London has devised an earbud-like EEG device that is affordable and comfortable [14]. This ear-EEG uses a noise-blocking earplug made of memory foam that conforms to the shape of a user's ears, thereby enabling excellent contact with the skin inside of the ear canal [52]. The sides of ear plugs are attached to two soft silver-coated electrode which transmit high-quality EEG signals. This would help in monitoring the brain signals in real-time and could assist in indicating any deviation from normal patterns of brain activity. Although the military could use this to track the sleep patterns, mental state and fitness for duty, currently the technology is not sophisticated enough to have a small device that is capable of functioning as that of a high-end EEG. As all technologies are increasingly becoming wireless, the signals that the electrodes help in emitting and the software component that communicates with the EEG could be disrupted or hacked and disrupt the communication between the electrodes and the software [53].

Research developments in areas of computation, neuroscience, and neurotechnology have driven the growth of the brain-machine interface (BMI) market, which is predicted to have a $1.46 billion market by 2020 [54]. The BMI field started about 40 years ago. A pivotal BMI experiment was performed by researchers at the University of Washington, Seattle, in which electrodes were implanted in the brains of rhesus macaque monkeys to monitor the activity of their neurons [55]. When a neuron fired at a specific rate, the electrical signal was detected by an electrode, which caused an audible chirping noise. When this happened, the monkey received a treat. Within a few trials, the test monkeys learned to intentionally fire more neurons to receive more treats. This study proved that neuronal activity can be conditioned and that this principle could be applied for other activities. Ever since there has been a lot of interest in research as well as in producing technology that uses BMI-like mechanism to create medical products that can significantly enhance an affected individual's life [56]. A typical BMI has three components: a biophysical interface, a signal decoder, and the device that uses the signal. A neural interface is a biocompatible sensor that can detect the signal of a firing neuron in the brain. The sensor is wireless and durable so that it can be placed in the brain and left for an appreciable time in a typical configuration. The second component is an external decoder that converts the neuronal activity into output signals. It typically takes the form of a computer program or algorithm. The third component is the "machine," such as a prosthetic limb, monitoring device, or a smart phone, that uses the signals from the decoder to control the machine [57]. In an ideal application, an apparatus could be controlled by just thinking about it.

3 Analysis of Risks from Using Neurotechnology for Nefarious Purposes

The U.S and the world face internal and external threats that may come in different form or fashion. The number of conflicts in the world has been sharply increasing since 2010, while still much lower than previous decades. The conflicts increasingly are affecting civilian population [15, 58]. Advanced neurotechnologies offer a smarter way of analyzing threats and combating them. Some of the factors that should be considered for the use of neuotechnological applications for nefarious purposes have unique challenges. As an emerging field, a critical challenge on the experimental research side is the credibility of results. For example, two independent research teams that utilized the same technique (direct electrical stimulation) came to different conclusions. One study shows the electrical stimulation improves memory, [59] and another one asserted that it impairs memory [60]. Despite the lack of clear evidence, companies have started to produce wearable accessories to treat chronic pain [31]. Thus, there is a large amount of uncertainty in assessing the use of neurotechnology in the future. Keeping that in mind, the possibility of employing advanced neurotechnologies for nefarious purposes in different environments (virtual, mega city, border/perimeter security) and by different actors (terrorist groups, peer competitors, failing/failed state) against different time periods (current, five years and 10–15 years from now) will be discussed (Table 1).

Table 1 Analysis of risks from using neurotechnology for nefarious purposes in different environments

Criteria	Present	5 Years	10-15 Years
Virtual	Medium	Medium	High
Mega City	Low	Medium	High
Terrorist Group	N/A	Low	Medium
Peer Competitor	High	High	Medium
Failing/Failed State	Low	Medium	Medium
Border/Perimeter Security	N/A	N/A	N/A

3.1 Assessing Use of Neurotechnology in Different Environments

Augmentation of neurotechnologies to improve physical and cognitive condition in humans have consistently been improved. Sight, one of the five senses, can be restored and extended to see beyond the range of visible light into non-visible radiation [61]. In the virtual environment, there is a likelihood that the technology could be used for hostile purposes, as shown in Table 1. While they have been no reports of patients being harmed this way, it is still a possibility and the risk of patient harm could be significant. FDA has issued warnings to patients, medical device companies and hospitals that "cybersecurity vulnerabilities may allow a remote/virtual user to take control of a medical device and change its function, cause denial of service, or cause information leaks or logical flaws, which may prevent a device from functioning properly or at all" [62, 63] and have the potential to create chaos. It has been shown that pacemakers and implantable cardiac defibrillators are vulnerable to radio attacks, potentially leaving them powerless [64]. For example, in 2007 doctors disabled the wireless option to former Vice President Dick Cheney's pacemaker fearing a terrorist could assassinate the him by sending a signal to the device [65]. Although there were no direct or indirect threats, it was a precautionary step taken to avoid potential attack. Additionally, there are several devices that are vulnerable to disruptions, and it has been shown that a remote user can shut off or alter the settings of an implanted device, such as insulin pump without the user's knowledge [66].

A lot of a nation's population is densely populated in mega cities. Attacking mega cities can cause a domino effect that spread throughout the region and has the potential to cripple the country. Currently, there are twenty four mega cities and by 2025 at least twenty seven cities will be classified as mega cities [67]. In the United States, there are 57.23 million people residing in rural areas compared to about 272.91 million people living in urban areas [68]. To ensure maximum damage, it is conceivable that mega cities and urban areas could be targeted. Increase in neurotechnological applications will result in increase in the number of people using them for medical purpose and for general convenience as well. For example, a Swedish and an American company are offering free chip implants for their employees [69, 70]. The implanted chips help employees to enter the office building, to buy food, and sign into their computers. This is a rising trend and as more people get implanted, the easier it might be to hack the radio frequency and cause damage [71]. It is possible to imagine a scenario of mass hacking these chips, which could result in physical harm.

3.2 Assessing Use of Neurotechnology by Different Actors

Not all countries have the capability to develop or implement neurotechnology. Countries that can invest and commit to the development of these technologies can gain a lot. Some of the factors that could be the drivers for neurotechnology would be the capital available for research and development, availability of materials, presence of skilled personnel, and laws/policies enabling such progress in neurotechnology [72]. Alternative ways for a state to acquire access to advanced neurotechnnology, either for research purposes or for implementing them, will be through technology transfer, international collaboration or even through direct purchase. Additionally, technology has evolved due to the free-flow of capital, knowledge, and talent working on high-tech marketplace, which means that there are realistic chances of out-inventing the competition. A significant second-mover advantage exists in technology competition [73]. Former President and CEO of the 3 M company, L.D. DeSimone has asserted, "Not so very long ago, a technological breakthrough could generate margins of leadership that would last for years. Today, the grace period of market dominance for new products and technologies is short-and getting shorter" [74]. This is applicable for neurotechnology as well. In the medical sector, competitors like China and India will emerge. For example, China has about 230 million people with cardiovascular disease, and India is soon becoming the diabetes and cardiovascular disease capital of the world [75]. This highlights the demand for new neurotechnology applications and this could lead to inventing smarter and efficient devices for medical intervention. Hence, it is highly likely that there would be competition between peer countries to outpace one another. This would lead to the probability of utilizing neurotechnology as one of the modes of conflict.

While being a dual use technology, ethical factors must be considered for the use of neurotechnology. An entire field, "neuroethics," has evolved that focuses on ethical issues that emerge from understanding and used of neuroscience and technology [76]. Taking brain-machine interface as an example, there are strict laws and regulations limiting human experimentation in the U.S., but in other countries this might not be the case. For example, China has relaxed policies. China has edited genes of human embryos [77]. Hence, it is possible that research or technology being developed in the U.S. but be utilized by other countries against the U.S. due to the relaxed laws and regulations in that country. In failed or failing states, it is conceivable that neurotechnology could be used in similar cases. For terrorist groups, as indicated in Table 1, it would be difficult to get access to high-end neurotechnological tools. Neurotechnology devices are expensive, and hence may not be the primary method used by terrorist groups to carry out an attack. Although, when and if in possession of those devices, they may be used for hostile reasons. Unlike physical attack, rise in neurotechnology devices could certainly lead to cyberattack and attack through electromagnetic interference [78].

4 Conclusions

Intersection of multiple branches of science have helped create a better understanding of the functioning of brain and thus making significant progress in neuroscience and technology. Brain to brain communication, once thought as science fiction, have become a reality. A recent study has demonstrated the first multi-person non-invasive direct brain to brain interface for collaborative problem solving [79]. As seen in this chapter, neurotechnology have high potential to be used for good and for bad reasons. It provides clinical benefits, for civilian and military personnel, while also having the potential to be misused for hostile reasons. Additionally, it can be used in combination with other emerging technologies like the artificial intelligence and that could have exponential applications, for better or for worse. It is certainly difficult to map the future growth of neuroscience and neurotechnology. It is also going to be a challenge to proactively bset laws for monitoring and enforcing measures regarding the use of neurotechnology, especially in avenues such as brain to brain interface. In terms of future work, analyzing the current guidelines for regulation of emerging technologies like neurotechnology could be helpful. Having an index of the current neurotechnology devices and updating that regularly, while simultaneously speculating on the possible applications, both positive and negative, could help in identifying potential risks.

References

1. Pearce JMS (2009) Marie-Jean-Pierre Flourens (1794–1867) and cortical localization. Eur Neurol 61(5):311–314
2. Schwiening CJ (2012) A brief historical perspective: Hodkin and Huxley. The Journal of Physiology 590(11):2571–2575
3. Filler AG (1961) The history, development, and impact of computed imaging in neurological diagnosis and neurosurgery: CT, MRI, DTI. Nat Precedings
4. Lazarou I, Nikolopoulos S, Petrantonakis PC, Kompatsiaris I, Tsolaki M (2018) EEG-based brain-computer interfaces for communication and rehabilitation for people with motor impariment: a novel approach of the 21st century. Front Hum Neurosci 12–14
5. The Brain Research through Advancing Innovative Neurotechnologies (BRAIN) (2013) National Institutes of Health. https://acd.od.nih.gov/documents/reports/BRAIN-Interim-Report.pdf
6. New BRAIN Initiative Awards Accelerate Neuroscience Discoveries, Press Release by the National Institute of Mental Health (2019) https://www.nimh.nih.gov/news/science-news/2019/new-brain-initiative-awards-accelerate-neuroscience-discoveries.shtml
7. The BRAIN Initiative, BRAIN 2025: A Scientific Vision (2014) https://braininitiative.nih.gov/sites/default/files/pdfs/brain2025_508c.pdf
8. "Towards a High-Resolution, Implantable Neural Interface," Defense Advanced Research Projects Agency (2017) https://www.darpa.mil/news-events/2017-07-10
9. National Science Board (2014) Science and Engineering Indicators. National Institutes of Health, https://www.nsf.gov/statistics/seind14/content/etc/nsb1401.pdf
10. The BRAIN Initiative, https://braininitiative.nih.gov/ and https://obamawhitehouse.archives.gov/the-press-office/2013/04/02/fact-sheet-brain-initiative
11. National Science Foundation, "BRAIN: Brain Research through Advancing Innovative Neurotechnologies. https://www.nsf.gov/news/special_reports/brain/initiative/
12. Research Programs at IARPA. https://www.iarpa.gov/index.php/research-programs
13. Food and Drug Administration Strategic Priorities 2014–2018, Sept 2014. https://www.fdanews.com/ext/resources/files/07/07-14-14-priorities.pdf
14. Dual Use Research of Concern: Recent Policy Development, National Institutes of Health (2012). https://acd.od.nih.gov/documents/06142012_DualUseResearchofConcern.pdf

15. Sharpening the American Military's Competitive Edge, National Defense Strategy of the United States of America (2018). https://www.defense.gov/Portals/1/Documents/pubs/2018-National-Defense-Strategy-Summary.pdf
16. Emerging and Readily Available Technologies and National Security (2014) National Academies Press, pp 65–78
17. National Defense Strategy of the United States of America (2018). https://www.defense.gov/Portals/1/Documents/pubs/2018-National-Defense-Strategy-Summary.pdf
18. Committee on Opportunities in Neuroscience for Future Army Applications, National Research Council (2008).
19. Monitoring Metabolic Status (2004) Predicting decrements in physiological and cognitive performance, committee on metabolic monitoring for military field applications. Institute of Medicine, NAS 2004
20. Carmigniani J, Furht B, Anisetti M, Ceravolo P, Damiani E, Ivkovic A (2010) Augmented reality technologies, systems and applications. Multimedia Tools Appl 51(1):341–377
21. Matthews PM, Honey GD, Bullmore ET (2006) Applications of fMRI in translational and clinical practice. Nat Rev 7(732)
22. Munakata Y, Casey BJ, Diamond A (2004) Developmental cognitive neuroscience: progress and potential. Trends Cogn Sci 8(122)
23. Nelson J, McKinley RA, Phillips C, McIntire L, Goodyear C, Kreiner A, Monforton L (2016) The effects of transcranial direct current stimulation (tDCS) on multitasking throughput capacity. Front Hum Neurosci 10(589)
24. DARPA's Cognitive Technology Threat Warning Systems (2009) Archived https://web.archive.org/web/20080204203721/ https://www.darpa.mil/baa/BAA07-25.html
25. Dr. Doug Kirkpatrick (2007) Cognitive technology threat warning system (CT2WS). https://www.wired.com/images_blogs/dangerroom/files/doug_kirkpatrick_ct2ws_31307.pdf
26. DeSantana JM, Walsh DM, Vance C, Rakel BA, Sluka KA (2008) Effectiveness of transcutaneous electrical nerve stimulation for treatment of hyperalgesia and pain. Curr Rheumatol Rep 10(6):492–499
27. Getting the Most out of Your Quell (2015) Quell, NeuroMetrix
28. Dr. Al Elmondi, "Revolutionizing prosthetics," Defense Advanced Research Projects Agency. https://www.darpa.mil/program/revolutionizing-prosthetics
29. Ienca M, Haselager P (2016) Hacking the brain:brain-computer interfacing technology and the ethics of neurosecurity. Ethics Inf Technol 18(2):117–29
30. Yuan BJ, Hsieh CH, Chang CC (2010) National technology foresight research: a literature review from 1984 to 2005. Int J Foresight Innov Policy 6(1):5–35
31. Powell C, Munetomo M, Schlueter M, Mizukoshi M (2013) Towards thought control of next-generation wearable computing. Int Conf Brain Health Inform
32. Wong YH (2016) Approaching future offsets. RAND
33. Pellerin C (2016) DoD strategic capabilities office is near-term part of third offset. Defense Media Activity
34. Department of Defense (2018) Summary of the 2018 national defense strategy of The United states of America, p 3. at https://dod.defense.gov/Portals/1/Documents/pubs/2018-National-Defense-Strategy-Summary.pdf
35. Towards a High-Resolution, Implantable Neural Interface (2017) Defense advanced research projects agency. https://www.darpa.mil/news-events/2017-07-10
36. Neural Engineering System Design (NESD) (2017) Defense advanced research projects agency (DARPA). https://www.darpa.mil/program/neural-engineering-system-design
37. Mills JO, Jalil A, Stanga PE (2017) Electronic retinal implants and artificial vision: journey and present. Nat Rev 31:1383–1398
38. Weisgerber M (2017) Pentagon's new algorithmic warfare cell gets its first mission: Hunt IIS. Defense One
39. Hanger Clinic. https://www.hanger.com/doing/Pages/default.aspx
40. Hotson G, McMullen DP, Fifer MS, Johannes MS, Katyal KD, Para MP, Armiger R, Anderson R, Thakor NV, Wester BA (2016) Individual finger control of a modular prosthetic limb using high-density electrocorticography in a human subject. J Neural Eng 13(2)

41. Flesher SN, Collinger JL, Foldes ST, Weiss JM, Downey JE, Tyler-Kabara EC, Bensmaia SJ, Schwartz AB, Boninger ML, Gaunt RA (2016) Intracortical microstimulation of human somatosensory cortex. Sci Translationary Med (2016)
42. Burck JM, Bigelow JD, Harshbarger SD (2011) Revolutionizing prosthetics: systems engineering challenges and opportunities. John Hopkins APL Tech Dig 30(3)
43. Mobius Bionics. https://www.mobiusbionics.com/luke-arm/
44. Barnaby J (2011) McAfee, Research presented at "Hacker Halted" conference. https://www.theregister.co.uk/2011/10/27/fatal_insulin_pump_attack/
45. Halperin D, Heydt-Benjamin TS, Ransford B, Clark SS, Defend B, Morgan W, Fu K, Kohno T, Maisel WH (2008) Pacemakers and implantable cardiac defibrillators: software radio attacks and zaero-power defenses. IEEE Symp Secur Priv
46. Homeland TV show, Showtime (2012). https://vimeo.com/63176830
47. Seo D, Carmena JM, Rabaey JM, Alon E, Maharbiz M (2013) Neural dust: an ultrasonic, low power solution for chronic brain-machine interfaces. Neurons Cognition, arXiv 2013
48. Seo D, Neely RM, Shen K, Singhal U, Alon E, Rabaey JM, Carmena JM, Maharbiz M (2016) Wireless recording in the peripheral nervous system with ultrasonic neural dust. Neuron 91(3):529–539
49. Li Y, Panwar SS, Mao S (2006) A wireless biosensor network using autonomously controlled animals. IEEE Net
50. Song W, Yuan K, Han T, Chai J (2006) Remote controlled biostimulator and animal behavior analysis system. In: Proceding of the SPIE 6031 60310W
51. Kranczioch C, Zich C, Schierholz I, Sterr A (2014) Mobile EEG and its potential to promote the theory and application of imagery-based motor rehabilitation. Int J Psychophysiol 91(1):10–15
52. Goverdovsky V, Looney D, Kidmose P, Mandic DP (2015) In-ear EEG from viscoelastic generic earpieces: robust and unobstrusive 24/7 monitoring. IEEE 16(1):271–277
53. Simms AP (2014) Reading and wirelessly sending EEG signals using arduinos and XBee radios to control a robot. Electrical Engineering Thesis at the University of Arkansas at Fayetteville
54. Vishwa G (2016) Brain computer interface market economy, Global opportunity analysis and industry forecast- 2013–2020. https://www.alliedmarketresearch.com/brain-computer-interfaces-market
55. Fetz EE (1969) Operant conditioning of cortical unit activity. Science 163(3870):955–958
56. Rosenfeld JV, Wong YT (2017) Neurobionics and the brain-computer interface: current applications and future horizons. Med J Aust 206(8):363–368
57. Carmena J (2017) Dust in the machine, California Magazine. https://alumni.berkeley.edu/california-magazine/fall-2017-bugged/dust-machine
58. Alexandre M (2015) Conflict and violence in the 21st Century. World Bank Group
59. Suthana N, Haneef Z, Stern J, Mukamel R (2012) Memory enhancement and deep-brain stimulation of the entorhinal area. N Engl J Med 366:502–510
60. Jacobs J, Miller J, Lee SA, Coffer T, Watrous AJ, Sperling MR, Sharan A, Worrell G, Berry B, Lega, Jobst BC, Davis K, Gross RE, Sheth SA, Ezzyat Y, Das SR, Stein J, Gorniak R, Kahana MJ, Rizzuto DS, Direct electrical stimulation of the human entorhinal region and hippocampus impairs memory. Neuron 92(5):983–990
61. Planker D, Restoration of sight to the blind: optoelectronic retinal prosthesis. https://www.stanfordedu/~palanker/lab/retinalpros.html
62. Cybersecurity vulnerabilities in a widely-used third-party software component may introduce risks during use of certain medical devices: FDA safety communication. U.S. Food & Drug Administration (2019). https://www.fda.gov/medical-devices/safety-communications/urgent11-cybersecurity-vulnerabilities-widely-used-third-party-software-component-may-introduce
63. FDA informs patients, providers and manufacturers about potential cybersecurity vulnerabilities for connected medical devices and health care networks that use certain communication software. U.S. Food & Drug Administration (2019) https://www.fda.gov/news-events/press-announcements/fda-informs-patients-providers-and-manufacturers-about-potential-cybersecurity-vulnerabilities

64. Pacemakers and Implantable Cardiac Defibrillators: Software Radio Attacks and Zero-Power Defenses (2008) IEEE symposium on security and privacy
65. Yes, terrorists could have hacked Dick Cheney's heart (2013) Washington Post. https://www.washingtonpost.com/news/the-switch/wp/2013/10/21/yes-terrorists-could-have-hacked-dick-cheneys-heart/
66. Attack Surface: Healthcare and Public Health Sector (2012) National cybersecurity and communications integration center. https://info.publicintelligence.net/NCCIC-MedicalDevices.pdf
67. Liotta PH, Miskel JF (2012) The real population bomb: Megacities, global security and the map of the future. Dulles, Potomac Books.
68. Erin D, Size of urban and rural population of the United States from 1960 to 2020. Statista. https://www.statista.com/statistics/985183/size-urban-rural-population-us
69. Carolyn M (2017) US company is putting microchips in its employees. VOA Learning English. https://learningenglish.voanews.com/a/microchip-employees-us-company/3967947.html
70. James B (2017) Cyborgs at work: employees getting implanted with microchips. Associated Press. https://apnews.com/article/4fdcd5970f4f4871961b69eeff5a6585
71. Sarah G (2020) Microchipping employees: a rising trend in the future of work? Learn Technol. https://trainingindustry.com/articles/learning-technologies/microchipping-employees-a-rising-trend-in-the-future-of-work/
72. The Global Technology Revolution 2020 (2006) In-depth analyses, national security research division, RAND
73. Carpenter G, Shanker V (2013) The Second-mover advantage. KellogInsight. https://insight.kellogg.northwestern.edu/article/the_second_mover_advantage
74. Spreng B (2002) How much R&D is not available? https://apps.americanbar.org/contract/federal/randcomm/0402pres/spreng.pdf
75. World Health Organization. https://www.wpro.who.int/china/mediacentre/factsheets/cvd/en/
76. Stanford Encyclopedia of Philosophy. https://plato.stanford.edu/entries/neuroethics/
77. Liang P, Xu Y, Zhang X, Ding C, Huang R, Zhang Z, Lv J, Xie X, Chen Y, Li, Sun Y, Bai Y, Songyang Z, Ma W, Zhou C, Huang J (2015) CRISPR/Cas9-mediated gene editing in human tripronuclear zygotes. Protein Cell 6(5):353–372
78. Report of the Commission to Assess the Threat to the United States from Electromagnetic Pulse (EMP) Attack, Critical National Infrastructures (2008). https://www.empcommission.org/docs/A2473-EMP_Commission-7MB.pdf
79. Jiang L, Stocco A, Losey DM, Abernethy JA, Prat CS, Rao RPN (2019) BrainNet: a multi-person brain-to-brain interface for direct collaboration between brains. Sci Rep. 16, 9(1):6115

The Future of Chemical Warfare: How Urbanization and Proliferation of Delivery Mechanisms Create the Need for In-Situ Defense

Colton M. Moran

Abstract A future increase in chemical warfare is a likely possibility due to advancements in delivery mechanisms, new urban battle fronts, and population growth. Chemical warfare agents have the potential to be more lethal and effective than they have throughout history. It is suggested that two well established technologies, adsorbents and non-woven fibers should be further investigated to create an affordable and scalable protective wear that can be easily deployed in the field for rapid protection.

1 Introduction

In a world of evolving technologies, demographics, countries, and ideologies, conflict has and will occur. A consistent response throughout history to conflict is the evolution of weapons to gain a distinct advantage over one's opponent. In today's age, the most notorious of weapons a state or non-state actor could wield is a nuclear device. Though these weapons possess destructive capabilities, they bear a strong deterrent due to the extreme consequences that follow their employment. The barrier to entry for nuclear weapons due to developing enrichment technologies and long-range capabilities is also quite high. These factors are why only two nuclear devices have been used in war and haven't been deployed during conflict since 1945. Though not on the same scale in absolute destructive capabilities in a single strike as nuclear weapons, chemical weapons provide a much lower barrier to entry, significant lethality, and have observed repeated uses over the past 100 years. Chemical weapons provide a relatively easy synthesizable agent with immense power to cause damage, both physically and psychologically. Such weapons have been poorly used, in respect to optimization, throughout history and to this day receive less notoriety than other weapons of mass destruction (WMD). Unlike other WMD, chemical weapons have been consistently used in some fashion during conflict and are still being employed

---

C. M. Moran (✉)
Georgia Institute of Technology, Atlanta, GA, US
e-mail: cmoran@exponent.com

© The Author(s), under exclusive license to Springer Nature Switzerland AG 2021
M. E. Kosal (ed.), *Proliferation of Weapons- and Dual-Use Technologies*,
Advanced Sciences and Technologies for Security Applications,
https://doi.org/10.1007/978-3-030-73655-2_7

today. Their repeated application has caused more collective deaths than nuclear devices throughout history, with little progress in optimization for their deployment. Though CWA are primed for proliferation in the coming years, the White House is proposing cuts to chemical and biological programs in the Department of Defense FY 2021 budget [1]. These cuts are proposed during a pandemic that has repeatedly shown how vulnerable the United States and the world is to weapons that possess analogous characteristics and mechanisms. Such budget cuts in at a time where fundamental strides need to be made towards mitigation measures against the looming threat of CWA proliferation are at the very least characterized as unwise. Current restrictions to chemical and biological defense programs can have a cascading effect in the future where the risk of exposure to CWA is a likely outcome.

This chapter highlights the history of chemical weapons, current international policies and an argument that projects a future increase in their application. Future use of CW will be analyzed through correlations with population growth and how those trends may influence conflict and urbanization, as well as proliferation of delivery technologies creating more effective use of chemical warfare agents. As a result of a plausible increases in chemical warfare, a defensive mechanism that can be deployed in-situ based on combining existing technology is reviewed.

2 Overview of Chemical Weapons

2.1 Historical Employment of Chemical Weapons

Throughout history, chemical weapons (CW) have been used during conflicts, ranging from poison on projectiles to the release of deadly nerve agents among unsuspecting crowds. Along with their use, comes fear from the groups being targeted, power to those who use them, and condemnation from many actors around the world who observe it. This trend can be observed throughout history when chemical weapons are involved, and it reached a critical point in the first world war. Chemical weapons saw their peak use in World War I (WWI), which was a pivotal point in history effecting the perception of chemical warfare agents (CWA) and future policies on them [2]. Though the four year war features the highest concentration of casualties related to chemical weapons at a staggering 1.3 million, their lethality and deployment mechanisms were rudimentary at best [3]. The main chemicals used during this time frame where sulfur mustard ($ClCH_2CH_2)_2S$, phosgene ($COCl_2$) and chlorine (Cl_2). Sulfur mustard, which involves a relatively simple synthesis utilizing two common reagents, sulfur dichloride and ethylene, can lead to cellular toxicity manifesting itself in a variety of physiological effects [4]. Phosgene also involves a simple synthesis using two common reagents, carbon monoxide and chlorine, in a catalytic bed filled with activated carbon as the catalyst [5]. Phosgene represented the deadliest of chemical weapons in WWI with the capacity to kill at concentrations of 5 part per million (ppm) and was responsible for nearly 85% of the deaths involving chemical warfare agents [6]. Chlorine was the most heavily used agent in the war even though it was severely limited due to its lethal dose, visible indicators of its presence, and a density greater than that of air. The lethal dose of chlorine is 1000 ppm, which made it extremely difficult to obtain high enough concentrations in the open battlefield to cause fatalities [7]. The yellow-green appearance of the gas made it easily visible for soldiers being exposed so they could run or deploy defensive tactics. The density of the gas propels it to sink, allowing an individual standing up to avoid the worst of exposures, though the same density mismatch had a strategic advantage in removing individuals in trenches to expose them to enemy fire as well.

The deployment of chemical agents during WWI was also handicapped due to ignorance of the agent's physical properties and under-developed technologies surrounding safe handling of the material and effective disbursement. Many attempts to use CWA were unsuccessful due to the miscalculation of factors involved. In one such instance German troops were deploying dianisidine chlorosulfate on British forces with artillery shells, which inadvertently incinerated the irritant leaving the British forces unaware that they were being attack with chemical weapons [8]. Another failed delivery involved xylyl bromide in Russia, where Germans fired off 18,000 shells filled with the CWA. After the CWA was released it was rendered useless by the frigid atmosphere keeping the agent from vaporizing to the gas phase, which is the desired state for exposure. Incidents such as these handicapped the effectiveness of chemical weapons throughout the war. One of the most notorious and "successful" attacks occurred on April 22nd 1915 in Ypres, Belgium. Fritz Haper, the individual charged with kick-starting German chemical warfare, went to the front lines of the battlefield with 5730 chlorine cylinders, nearly 170 metric tons, and waited two weeks for the wind to shift in his favor [9]. The cylinders were opened by hand allowing chlorine to be released in the air in the form of a deadly toxic cloud, killing thousands on both sides. Though this attack was deadly, the casualties caused were severely hindered due to the uncontrollable dispersal behavior of wind, immense dilution of the gas in open atmosphere, and a relatively small population density of people present at the interface of exposure.

With all these factors in play; primitive CWA, failed attacks due to ignorance of CWA properties, poorly optimized "successful" attacks as a result of battlefield conditions, and poor delivery mechanisms, WWI still remains the deadliest use of chemical weapons to date. The most effective attribute of CWA during WWI was the psychological effects they had on both soldiers and citizens back home. Instilling fear in soldiers with subsequent confusion during attacks which could manifest itself as a sociogenic illness and a terror mentality in civilian populations via media outlets sensationalizing CWA attacks [10]. Both the physical and psychological factors played an important role during the four year war.

Due to causalities and psychological consequences of chemical weapons during WWI a major step was taken to ban their use in 1925 during the Geneva Protocol. It was an important step towards curtailing CWA use, but it still lacked enforcement, non-proliferation content and strong commitment by participating countries with an important but limited ban on the use of chemical weapons in war. Even with this protocol in place CWA were still utilized by members of the agreement 65 years later, setting an unnerving precedent for international treaties [11].

The Iran-Iraq War from September 1980 to August 1988, also known as the Persian Gulf War, was the second major milestone for the utilization of CWA, representing the first major war with the extensive use of nerve agents against military and civilian populations. Saddam Hussein, Iraqi's president, utilized sulfur mustard and nerve agents against poorly trained Iranian forces causing nearly 100,000 fatalities including those who died immediately and those who died from long term complications. This CIA based estimate does not including civilian populations contaminated in nearby towns, decedents of those directly affected, or survivors with severe mental or physical impairments which could severely inflate the casualty estimate [4, 11]. An example of how devastating Iraq's use of chemical weapons were can be highlighted in the town of Halabja. Iraqi warplanes dropped nerve agents and sulfur mustard to the extent of approximately 5000 causalities, which were mostly civilian, displaying a frightening disregard for human life and efficiency of CWA [11]. Throughout the majority of the war, major powers took little to no initiative in addressing or stopping Iraq's flagrant use of CWA. The first six U.N. Security Council resolutions addressing the conflict did not mention chemical weapons. Not until February 24, 1986 did the world truly begin to acknowledge the Geneva Protocol violations with resolution 582 noting "…the use of chemical weapons contrary to obligations." indicating the Geneva Protocol and both countries respective membership [12]. The lack of response and enforcement of the one key requirement in the Geneva Protocol, not using CWA in war, predicts favorable outcomes for a country who deploys such agents in the future if history truly does repeat itself.

2.2 Current International Policy Overview on Chemical Weapons

Due to causalities and psychological consequences of chemical weapons during WWI and further expedited due to the Iran-Iraq war, the international community put into motion the creation of a comprehensive convention involving chemical weapons. In 1980 the Conference of Disarmament began the writing of a convention that displayed significant rules and regulations on all aspects of chemical warfare. After overcoming a surfeit of obstacles the Chemical Weapons Convention (CWC) was signed on the 13th of January, 1993 in Paris by 130 countries and entered into force on April 29th, 1997 creating the Organization for the Prohibition of Chemical Weapons (OPCW) [2]. In the first 10 years of its existence the CWC accrued 182 member states and oversaw the destruction of over 25,000 metric tons of CWA. The OPCW itself has been viewed as a successful entity with recognition worldwide for its efforts in eliminating CW including a Nobel Peace Prize in 2013. Currently there are 192 members of the CWC with Egypt, North Korea, South Sudan and Palestine being the major entities yet to sign or accede to the CWC.

The mission of the OPCW is a simple concept, to prevent chemistry from ever again being used for warfare. The achievement of such a goal is much more complex, in which they have four key aims which are addressed in the Articles of the CWC. The first of which is destroying existing chemical weapons in a responsible manner. Articles IV and V directly address the obligation each participating state has in destroying their respective CWs and CW facilities. Destruction technologies have been developed for CWs involving both high temperature technologies such as incineration and "low"-temperature technologies used to convert CW to benign materials. Facilities must instantly be shut down and destroyed or converted to an alternative production plant, in both cases inspections will take place. Article V also entails detailed timeframes for destruction/conversion from plans to fulfillment of agreements which ranges from an arbitrary, as soon as possible, to a max of ten years after the enforcement of the CWC. In order to stop future production, the OPCW also prohibits future construction of a plant that has the capacity to produce CWs.

The second goal is to monitor chemical industries to prevent new weapons from re-emerging. Article VI specifically goes over the rights of states to develop and use toxic chemicals and their precursors but requires monitoring, verification, and if listed in Schedule 1 of the Annex on Chemicals, an inspection. This is an important improvement on any previous agreement because it directly addresses a systematic way to prevent future stockpiling of weapons and due to its language, if a state if found in violation, the OPCW has the ability to enforce sanctions such as those discussed in article XII. Article VII also helps push states towards full commitment to destroying and monitoring CW and precursors by stating each state party shall adopt measures, within its constitution, to fulfill CWC requirements. It also places liability on states for entities in their respective territories, again adding liability for states to monitor non-state actors.

Providing assistance and protection to States Parties against chemical threats is the third objective of the OPCW. This objective was extremely important to gain almost unanimous co-operation of states with respect to the CWC. Heavily emphasized in Article X are the rights for states to research and develop methods of protection against chemical agents as well the right of each state to request aid or protection against the use or threat of CW. What this effectively did was provide positive security guarantees to all those involved in the CWC, which is a strong counter argument for states with reservations about giving up their CWs in case they found themselves under an attack involving chemical agents. This is especially attractive for smaller states that now have great powers involved in their protection. It is worth noting that since the CWC entered into force, chemical attacks have occurred during civil strife in Syria (not a state party to the CWC at the time) and there has not been a major world conflict where mass deployment of CWs could feasibly occur between states participating in the CWC, therefor gauging the impact of this organization/convention is difficult. As previously mentioned though, one metric it has excelled at is facilitating the destruction of mass amounts of CW and routinely inspecting facilities pertaining to dangerous agents to prevent development or stockpiling. The United States and Russia alone have verified destruction of over 70,000 metric tons to-date [13].

The final aim of the OPCW is to promote international cooperation to strengthen implementation of the CWC and therefore promote the peaceful use of chemistry internationally. This goal is subtle yet important for international safety and future advancements in fields derived from chemistry. Though it is not explicitly addressed in the Articles of the CWC, many sections of the previous three aims cover how international cooperation is essential and mandated in order to create harmony for the future of chemistry. The deliberately tedious crafting of the CWC with its in-depth articles, timelines, regulations and cooperation along with its enforcement set a strong deterrent for future use of chemical weapons and peaceful yet monitored use of chemistry. This convention would suggest a strong case for a stop to the future use of chemical weapons since its 1997 enforcement, though this is not the case.

2.3 Conflicts Involving Chemical Weapons Since the CWCs Entry into Force

Syria's civil war, originating in 2011, has entailed a plethora of verified chemical attacks from both sides of the conflict starting on October 17, 2012 in Homs with the deployment of Agent 15 [14]. The largest reported attack in recent years was the Ghouta Chemical Attack on August 12, 2013 where the nerve agent sarin was released. The attack saw more than 3600 injuries, 355 of whom reportedly died within hours, with reports from different nations citing final causalities ranging from 350 to 1500 people, making it the most lethal chemical weapons attack since the Iran-Iraq war [14]. The use of chemical weapons in the Syrian civil war invites another dangerous precedent for future inter-state conflicts involving the effectiveness of CWAs, international response to their use, and in some cases the ease in which the materials are synthesized or acquired.

A new realm of chemical weapons utility has also been realized starting in August 2015 via chemical terrorism. August 2015 was the first confirmed chemical attack by the Islamic State of Iraq and Syria (ISIS). It was confirmed that Kurdish forces had been hit with sulfur mustard wounding 35 soldiers [15]. Following these attacks were incidents involving chlorine with February 2016 seeing two attacks totaling 285 injuries. More recent verified CW attacks since this article was written included an attack on April 4th 2017 in the town of Khan Sheikhoun centralized to a rebel held Idlib province. The attack killed at least 70 people and injured over 200, all of whom displayed signs of suffocation, convulsions, and foaming from the mouth which are direct indicators of a nerve agent [15]. Another The attack on April 7th 2018, occurred in Douman, a district in eastern Ghouta in Damascus, Syrian Arab Republic. The attack claimed dozens of lives and an OPCW fact finding mission confirmed the use of chlorine during the attack [15]. More recent attacks included a chlorine attack on May 19th, 2019 in the Latakia province, Syria. The attack was carried out by the Assad regime and marks the continued use of CWAs in modern times [16].

A wide view of the magnitude and volume of chemical attacks still occurring today by non-state actors, which are by definition not members of the CWC, can be seen when one observes the history of chemical attacks over the last decade in the middle east. To-date over 54 chemical attacks have been attributed to ISIS, with up to 71 allegations, creating a dangerous precedent for the future use of CWA [17]. These types of attacks, alongside the history of attacks during the Syrian civil war, which is a state actor, are direct evidence that chemical warfare is not a thing of the past and are a very real and present threat during conflicts. Also of note is the disagreement among world powers in regards to authorizing sanctions against those using chemical weapons, with a veto seen on Feb 28th 2017 from Russia and China on implementing sanctions [18]. The current reality where chemical weapons are used in war with political strife among external nations impeding action toward perpetrators, paints a dark reality for chemical warfare and the role such weapons may play in the future.

3 Contributing Factors to CWA Proliferation

3.1 Population Growth and Its Impact on War

In the arena of chemical warfare, four distinct types of conflict have been discussed in this chapter. The largest being the hegemonic war (WWI) displaying the first widespread use of chemical weapons. This type of war is not considered in the analysis of future conflict involving CWA due the large number of variables involved. Three conflict types will be examined and how they correspond to increase in the world's population. The first of which is designated as a small power vs small power conflict represented by the Iran-Iraq War which entailed the frequent use of blister and nerve agents. The second conflict is civil war with regards to Syria, and the last type of conflict covered is terrorism. Though terrorist actions are not considered formally war, their employment of chemical weapons is considered within this chapter's analysis.

Studies have shown these types of conflicts can be directly correlated with changes in population. This discussion of population is not stating population growth causes these conflicts but rather that certain types of population growth are well associated with political and economic strife [19]. These correlations with population for all conflicts covered are to be realized through generations of change, shaping areas by altering variables such as demographics and gender ratios. Examining terrorism, it is important cite that terrorist organizations have seen somewhat of an evolution with Islamic fundamentalist meaning historical trends are not adequate by themselves to predict how CWs can be employed by terrorist organizations. This change can be attributed to youth bulges, a high proportion of the adult population aged 15–24, in many Islamic states [20, 21]. Males in particular, as part of these youth bulges, are joining jihadist movements creating a large influx of recruits that have the potential to

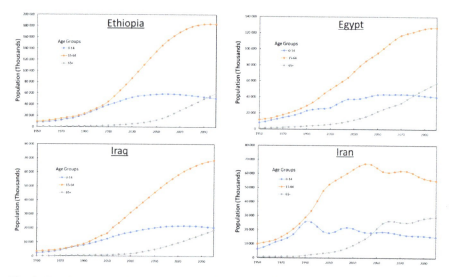

Fig. 1 Broad range population projections adapted from UN world population prospects 2019. Dates range from 1950 to 2100

add funds, knowledge, and manpower behind the movement [22, 23]. Fig. 1 shows future trends of youth bulges for developing countries and forecasts this type of phenomena is not an isolated occurrence. A notable accelerated parallel to this change would be refugee migration, due to war or other natural causes, which can realize an influx of individuals into areas displaying sharp differences in the demographic composition. These changes in population can ultimately affect the balance of the population and therefor the balance of power in a given region. When power is shifting conflict can readily follow and chemical weapons are a strong source of power for a small force trying to establish itself.

3.2 Conflict Types

Small power conflicts have been associated with increased populations citing a few variables that lead to increased tensions. With limited resources, an increase in populations can fuel conflict between states due to a perceived unbalanced use of non-renewable sources such as water or farmland between regions [24]. A growing population will also lead to an influx of labor into the economy. If the economy is not robust that gives a surplus of educated youths in an urbanizing environment. This urbanization can lead to a shift in power among major demographics which appear to increase the risk of conflict [24].

In respect to civil war, rapid changes in ethnic groups are the main variable of concern that can be directly tied into growth rate of populations and youth budges. This rate is intrinsically tied to the fertility rate of different ethnic and religious groups which will likely be unbalanced giving one group a surplus [23]. This surplus leans towards the minority demographic feeling threatened which can cause turmoil amongst individuals in the state and fuel civil unrest. A few outcomes of youth bulges correlate with civil unrest and ultimately conflict. Rapid urbanization can create an employment deficit pushing youth towards gangs, heterodox ideologies, and religions, while unrealistic expectations of life derived from a media's enhanced portrayal can lead to discontent and a push for change or revolution [23]. Such revolutions or movements are well associated with increases in young populations such as the English Revolution, the French Revolution, Student Movement in China, and the American's Civil Rights Movement and others in the twentieth century [24]. With some of these heading towards violence and others reform. A study in 2009 by Bradley Thayer reported 88 countries experiencing youth bulges with 60 of those respective countries displaying significant social tensions [23]. As Thayer mentions, this observation does not mean social unrest will lead to civil war, but it can be used as a strong indicator of such an event.

With the knowledge of how increased population is correlated with terrorism, small power conflict, and civil war; it is important to observe the trend of population growth in the next 80 years, spanning multiple generations. The current population of the world is ~7.7 billion people and estimated to increase to over 11.2 billion by 2100 [25]. A large portion of this projected growth is in undeveloped regions were economies may not be resilient enough to withstand the growth that can lead to conflict. These historical trends correlating conflict with increasing populations paired with a large projected growth in the next 80 years provides a realistic future were small power conflict, civil war, and terrorism could see an increase in frequency. Based on chemical weapons use since the CWC was entered into force, these types of conflicts can be correlated with the employment of chemical agents during a struggle for power. Therefore, it is reasonable to say a likely increase in the use of chemical weapons over the next 80 years is a plausible outcome.

3.3 Dense Urban Terrain and Chemical Warfare

Parallel to the growth of the world's population is the increase in number of people living in urbanized areas. In 1900 only 15% of the world's population resided in cities, which has grown to over 50% today [26]. This change in residency has led to the creation of megacities throughout the world; megacities are urban environments that contain more than 10 million residents, which include 30–47 cities as of late 2017 depending on the criteria used to classify the city [27]. It has been well documented that the new frontier for the modern soldier will be dense urban environments which provide an entirely new class of obstacles [27]. These types of cities are estimated to increase along with their respective population densities, adding new targets and areas that are more and more susceptible towards deadly chemical attacks.

An important example of how dense urban environments can provide huge tactical advantages to small groups is Mosul, Syria. Mosul was seized by ISIS in June 2014, accompanied by two separate failed attempts to retake the city by Peshmerga forces in 2015 and 2016 [28]. Though Mosul is not a megacity, it begins to display how the change in urban warfare can favor smaller forces. A few thousand ISIS fighters were able to withstand 100,000 US backed troops for nearly 9 months using guerilla-style warfare involving drones, mortars, unsophisticated homemade explosives, and the cover of the city itself. Though the city was eventually recaptured, the operation sustained heavy causalities with an estimated 7000 fatalities and 22,000 individuals wounded [28]. The capturing of Mosul by ISIS and the strong resistance put forth towards forces fighting to liberate the city illustrates how non-state actors can claim power and assert authority by exploiting urbanization.

One caveat to using chemical weapons is their residence time after employment. A deterrent to their use would be the contamination of the building/area they were used in. If the CWA was left with no consideration to neutralization or decontamination it could make reclamation or occupation of the area difficult. For common CWA, simple removal processes can be implemented when an area with a known containment needs to be repopulated. Depending on the agent, the process will typically include time for diffusion, steam, water, alkaline solution, or adsorbents [7]. The process of cleaning up an area after exposure to chemical weapons is significantly simpler than defending against them during armed combat.

During the battle for Mosul, chemical weapons were sparingly used by ISIS, but other technologies such as drones were heavily relied upon. As previously mentioned, chemical weapons that have been deployed throughout history have seen limited optimization in their delivery. During war significant inefficiencies were seen such as reliance on wind for dispersal, failed deployment of the agents for various reasons, and vast dilution in open atmosphere when the chemical was successfully released, which severely hinder the lethality of the weapon. Proliferation of technologies such as drones and the onset of megacities with dense populations provide an entirely new view on how lethal chemical weapons can be in warfare.

Drones provide a relatively cheap and well established aerial delivery mechanism that can carry anywhere from 5 to 40 lb payloads, all the way up to a possible 1764 lb with enhanced payload drones from emerging technologies [29]. These drones that can be equipped with cameras to create a delivery mechanism that will allow accurate release of CWA, subsequently increasing the concentration of the agent via targeted exposure and increasing the overall lethality/effectiveness of the weapon. The same argument can be made for the triggered release of toxins utilizing remote technologies. A crude video set-up with a remote opening mechanism and a fan could create problematic booby traps for any counter insurgency operation moving through urban terrain. It is also worth noting that CWA, unlike traditional explosives, have the capacity to keep the surrounding infrastructure intact, which does not degrade the cover insurgents are utilizing and represents an added benefit if a group is able to take control of an intact city compared to a city reduced to rubble by kinetic means. The proliferation of technologies around the optimized delivery of chemical weapons integrated with high density populations in urban environments provides a new and deadly arena for the resurrection of chemical weapons.

4 Future Defense Mechanisms for Chemical Weapons

4.1 Current State of Technology

There currently are well developed protective measures to chemical weapons involving catalytic conversion of nerve agents, adsorptive technologies for air filtration and integrated chemical resistance in combat gear [30, 31]. Though these technologies have matured they still remain costly to produce and must be preemptively integrated into military equipment to provide chemical protection and resistance. In a future where chemical weapons may play an increased role as discussed in the previous sections, it would be a costly endeavor to retrofit all current military equipment to enable chemical resistance. Therefore, it is proposed that a combination of current technologies into a sprayable protective cloth or layer is highly desirable.

There are three main areas of research that are well establish that can be extrapolated from to create such a sprayable protective apparatus. The first entails porous matrices with high surfaces areas such as metal organic frameworks (MOFs), zeolites, and carbon materials. These adsorbents have the well-established capacity to selectively trap or break down toxic chemicals as they pass through, allowing for protection and filtration during a chemical attack [32, 33]. Visualized in Fig. 2 is a cartoon of a typical process a MOF would go through to adsorb a toxic chemical. This process utilizes the high surface area of the framework to provide an ample amount of adsorptive surface and catalytic sites for the respective containment and conversion of CWA providing a protective layer of material between the hazardous environment during exposure and the individual. There is an inherent drawback when it comes to utilizing these types of adsorptive materials due to their typical powered form. These types of powders are difficult to handle, can create pressure drop due to packing density in airways, and are not optimized to be quickly utilized in their parent form for protective purposes. They typically need to be integrated, post-synthetically, into materials to create chemically resistant apparel or cartridges for personal protective gear aka "gas" masks.

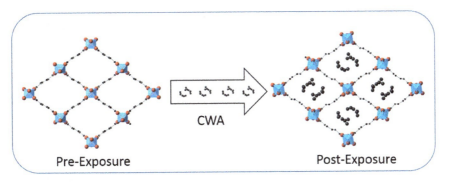

Fig. 2 Representation of a MOF (MIL-53(Al)) adsorbing CWA

4.2 New Mitigation Technologies

To overcome the drawback of the powdered form of adsorptive materials support structures have been examined. In order to meet the needs of a protective sprayable material that can be applied in-situ many of these supports are not suitable. Of the potential supports, non-woven fabrics that can be created via synthetic organic polymers offer the most feasible support matrix for a quickly deployable adsorptive agent. It has been demonstrated that non-woven fabrics can utilize monomeric species in a polar solution in tandem with a spray gun or a general propulsion mechanism to create tightly woven fabric material with enough durability that they can be worn after being directly sprayed on [34, 35].

This type of technology utilizing volatile solvents and aerosol technology provides the possibility for a support matrix to be applied in-situ during a chemical attack. An important issue with utilizing solvents revolves around the solvent's capability with biological material. A solvent such as chloroform is unusable due to its toxicity. This parameter narrows down potential candidates and polymers that are currently established but can be overcome. The use of acetone and ethyl acetate has shown to be both bio-compatible and efficient solvents for fiber formation. Both adsorptive materials and non-woven fabrics continue to be studied independently of one another but combining the two technologies can create an entirely new defense mechanism in the world of chemical warfare. Such a combination creates a powerful potential solution to chemical attacks, but it will entail ample research to optimize the integration of the porous material into the support.

Questions analogous to how the adsorptive particles change the properties of the applied non-woven fabric will need to be addressed. Research on how MOFs can be incorporated into a polymer or a fabric matrix have been well documented in literature, which provides insight into techniques to produce well dispersed particles throughout the support material with a variety of adsorbents and hosts [36, 37]. Therefore, combining these two technologies to create a sprayable protective cloth that can be used on any current equipment, bare skin, or directly as a mask for air filtration is an achievable prospective solution. Such a material would be self-contained in a can and would be easily transportable, applicable, and adaptable to a variety of situations in which an individual could be exposed to a chemical agent.

Though it is not the focus of this article, a detection matrix, analogous to the adsorptive spray matrix would be of great benefit for some chemical agents that are difficult to detect via an individual's senses alone. These two defense mechanisms would provide a scalable level of protection for both military and civilian populations. Current personal protection equipment is effective, typically involving activated carbon as a filtering cartridge or woven into military gear during production to add chemical resistance. Though effective, the current industry standard for adding chemical resistance is an expensive process and is not economically efficient for scale-up. Due to the current production method of PPE, the state of chemically resistive gear is not conducive to a market that involves civilian use. Therefore, a disruptive technology such as the one proposed would be beneficial in reducing the cost of chemically resistant gear while allowing for scalability.

5 Threat Assessment of CWA up to the Year 2035

As previously mentioned, many factors point towards the plausible increase in CWA employment due to forecasts of future conflicts. A large factor that has not been discussed, is the role of political stability of a state. Political stability can be defined as "the health of authority, resilience, legitimacy, and replacement in a political object" [38]. Throughout the historical use of CWA, the states that have employed significant use of CWA display signs of low political stability, as previously defined. This can be used as an indicator moving forward to suggest what regions or state actors may be susceptible to becoming involved in the employment of chemical agents. Figure 3 displays data from the World Bank on the political stability and violence in different regions around the world. Regions marked in red are located in the lower 90th percentile for political stability and absence of violence/terrorism. Notably, the majority of recent CWA incidents previously discussed are from countries currently marked in the bottom percentiles. This data suggests many regions/states display low political stability, indicating a multitude of geographic locations that have the potential for future conflicts. This factor of political stability, precedents set by Syria,

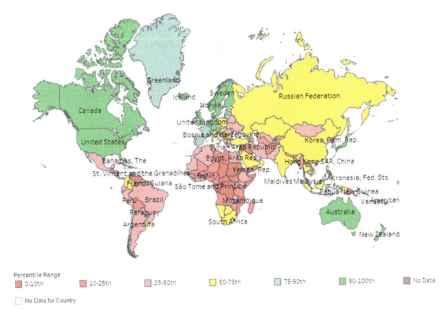

Fig. 3 International map of political stability and absence of violence generated from data collected by the World Bank

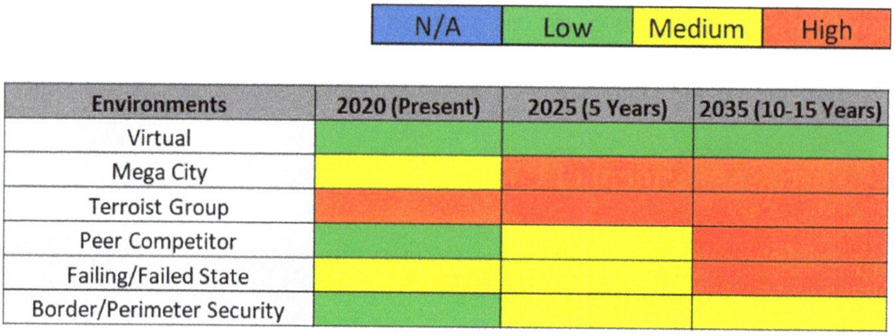

| | N/A | Low | Medium | High |

Environments	2020 (Present)	2025 (5 Years)	2035 (10-15 Years)
Virtual	Low	Low	Low
Mega City	Medium	High	High
Terroist Group	High	High	High
Peer Competitor	Low	Medium	High
Failing/Failed State	Medium	Medium	High
Border/Perimeter Security	Low	Medium	Medium

Fig. 4 Threat assessment for six different environments forecasted out to 2035

Iran, and Iraq for CWA use, along with the proliferation of technologies surrounding the deployment of CWA points towards the conclusion that the United States military and countless civilians may be in combat areas where chemical weapons are relevant and deadlier than ever.

Having covered the general forecast of chemical weapons in the future, the next logical question is which frontier will chemical agents present themselves as a threat. Figure 4 is an assessment of six separate environments where CWA may play a role in the future. It should be noted that green means lower probability but not absent, while red means CWA have a high potential to be employed in this environment and/or have increased utility as well as lethality in such an environment.

The three environments that present the highest threat are mega cities, perimeter security and terrorist groups. Mega cities and terrorist groups were highlighted previously in the text, while perimeter security can be viewed as a niche environment that can be applied to any physical conflict. CWA provide a deadly deterrent with a high cost of entry when used as a weapons buffer that can slow down the largest of forces. This gives a distinct advantage to smaller groups looking to control the flow of adversaries into combat regions. Failing or failed states is difficult to classify because it depends on the state in question, and the likelihood its constituents or entities operating inside of the state would resort to CWA employment. This creates a somewhat grey area; however, all cases present at least a moderate threat simply due to instability in the region. Peer competitors and virtual environments areas of concern but in the near future their risk is not the largest threat. Peer competitors such as China and Russia have always been within the magnitude of capabilities of the US for chemical weapons so the question revolves less around the proliferation of technology and stability of the region and more so with the economic and political relationship each state shares with the United States, which is not investigated in this research. It should be noted that Russia has reportedly used Novichok (nerve agent) multiple times in recent years for targeted assassinations, therefore CWA are still relevant for peer competitors, but currently not on the scale this chapter is addressing. Virtual environments do not provide immediate threats to health but can be used as a platform to promote fear and panic via graphic imaging and descriptive articles of the damage CWA have. This can induce panic in regions where the threat of their employment is real, creating potential chaos. As previously mentioned, one of the most damaging aspects of CWA is the physiological aspect they bring to war.

6 Conclusions

The deadly memory of chemical weapons employed throughout history has created multiple international treaties condemning their use, while their full potential has not nearly been reached due to poor dispersion and delivery. This means without direct development of CWA their threat and lethality can be increased through proliferation of separate technologies. With the Chemical Weapons Convention in force there are still CWA being created and used on both military and civilian targets as of 2019, mostly in regions relating to Syria or Iraq. The flagrant use of these agents and insignificant or absent consequences to the perpetrator are setting deadly precedents for those looking to employ chemical warfare agents in the future. As highlighted at the beginning of the chapter, the proposed cuts to chemical and biological programs in the Department of Defense FY 2021 budget is an ill-advised move when considering the topics outlined in this chapter regarding the increasing probability of CWA use and increased lethality in newly immerging environments.

By examining the correlation of small power conflicts, civil war, and terrorism with population growth, it can be asserted that in the next 80 years the world may see more of these types of conflicts in correlation with youth bulges of certain demographics. Observing the type of conflicts that have involved chemical weapons in the past 40 years, which are the small power conflict of Iran-Iraq, civil war in Syria, and terrorism, it is reasonable to assert that an increase in such conflicts could likely results in an increase in the utilization of chemical weapons.

Outside of observing historical trends and how they may correlate with future disputes, population growth in tandem with urbanization has also created a new battlefield for more optimal use of chemical warfare agents. The rapid growth of megacities provides a unique advantage to small forces trying to display power. The well-developed urban landscape, high densities of civilians and constricted air space provide a significantly more optimized environment for the release of chemical weapons than seen throughout history. The capture of Mosul opens a new chapter in how a city can be used as an effective terrain for insurgents all while displaying to the world that a city can still be captured, which sets another unfavourable precedent for future state and non-state actors. While chemical weapons did not play a large role in Mosul, proliferation of technologies around their dispersion, provide an attractive and possibly more effective alternative to traditional weapons in the urban environment.

Living in a current reality where the use of chemical weapons is evident and a future where their use and lethality can see an increase, advances in defensive measures should be pursued. Current technology involving chemical protection is well developed but can be expensive and a large portion of the equipment is pre-engineered for chemical resistance. To retrofit all personnel's belongings that could see future chemical agents with current technology would require a substantial investment, leaving some current equipment obsolete for use in dense urban environments where attacks may occur. Therefore, the investment into the combination of two developed technologies, adsorptive materials and sprayable non-woven fabrics would be advantageous. Such a material would provide protection that can be deployed in the field on current equipment, used directly as a mask, or applied to any situation where a protective layer is necessary. This spray would circumnavigate the need to manufacture new equipment allowing for large scale production that could be used for both military and civilian populations. By creating such a defense mechanism, the attractive features of chemical weapons would begin to be negated by both reducing their effectiveness and the fear caused by their utility with protection that is readily available.

References

1. Donnelly JM Amid pandemic, Pentagon would cut 'chem-bio' protections. https://www.rollcall.com/2020/07/13/defense-department-spending-chemical-biological-programs-russia-china/. Accessed 15 Nov 2020
2. Perry Robinson J (1998) The negotiations on the chemical weapons convention: a historical overview
3. Schneider BR (1999) Future war and counterproliferation: US military responses to NBC proliferation threats. Greenwood publishing group
4. Nokhodian Z, ZareFarashbandi F, Shoaei P (2015) Mustard gas exposure in Iran-Iraq war—a scientometric study. J Educ Health Promot 4:56
5. Schneider W, Diller W (2000) Phosgene. In: Ullmann's encyclopedia of industrial chemistry. Wiley-VCH GmbH & Co. KGaA
6. Heller C (1984) Leavenworth papers no. 10, chemical warfare in world war I: the American experience, 1917–1918. Fort leavenworth, Ka. ns., combat studies institute. pp 7–9
7. Fitzgerald GJ (2008) Chemical warfare and medical response during world war I. Am J Public Health 98(4):611–625
8. Mauroni AJ (2007) Chemical and biological warfare: a reference handbook. ABC-CLIO
9. Croddy E (2002) Chemical and biological warfare: a comprehensive survey for the concerned citizen. Springer Science & Business Media
10. Wessely S, Hyams KC, Bartholomew R (2001) Psychological implications of chemical and biological weapons: long term social and psychological effects may be worse than acute ones. BMJ: Brit Med J 323(7318):878
11. Karsh E (2002) The Iran-Iraq war, 1980–1988. Osprey publishing, vol 20
12. Ali J (2001) Chemical weapons and the Iran-Iraq war: a case study in noncompliance. Nonproliferation Rev 8(1):43–58
13. Chadwick A, Lee PA (2018) Chemical weapons elimination. environmental health in the 21st century: from air pollution to zoonotic diseases, vol 2. p 90
14. Pita R, Domingo J (2014) The use of chemical weapons in the syrian conflict. Toxics 2(3):391
15. Chemical-Weapons attack in syria was largest such event since (2013) Disarmament affairs chief tells security council, meetings coverage and press releases. https://www.un.org/press/en/2017/sc12777.doc.htm. Accessed 11 Dec
16. Kimball D Timeline of syrian chemical weapons activity, 2012–2020. https://www.armscontrol.org/factsheets/Timeline-of-Syrian-Chemical-Weapons-Activity. Accessed 15 Nov 20
17. ISIS used chemical weapons '52 times'. https://www.straitstimes.com/world/middle-east/isis-used-chemical-weapons-52-times. Accessed 12 Nov 2017

18. Sengupta S Russia and U.S. clash over syria in security council vote. https://www.nytimes.com/2017/02/28/world/middleeast/united-nations-security-council-syria-sanctions-russia-trump.html. Accessed 4 Feb 2018
19. de Sherbinin A (1995) World population growth and US national security. In Each Issue 24
20. Lam D (2007) The demography and economics of the world's "youth bulge." World Bank Dev Outreach 9(2):6–8
21. Arif G, Chaudhry N (2008) Demographic transition and youth employment in Pakistan. Pak Dev Rev 27–70
22. Gunaratna R (2002) Inside Al Qaeda: global network of terror. Columbia University Press
23. Thayer BA (2009) Considering population and war: a critical and neglected aspect of conflict studies. Philosophical transactions of the royal society of London. Ser B, Biol Sci 364(1532):3081
24. Goldstone JA (2002) Population and security: how demographic change can lead to violent conflict. J Int Aff 3–21
25. Roser M "Future population growth". https://ourworldindata.org/future-population-growth#citation
26. Glaeser EL (2017) 1 urban transformations and the future of cities. In: The post-urban world: emergent transformation of cities and regions in the innovative global economy. p 15
27. Khalili L (2017) Pacifying urban insurrections
28. Smith B, Brook-Holland L, Page R (2014) Islamic state of Iraq and the levant (ISIS) and the takeover of Mosul. SNIA 6915:4
29. Fly with a legend. GRIFF aviation. https://griffaviation.com/. Accessed 4 Feb 2018
30. Smith BM (2008) Catalytic methods for the destruction of chemical warfare agents under ambient conditions. Chem Soc Rev 37(3):470–478
31. Lodewyckx P (2006) Adsorption of chemical warfare agents. Interface Sci Technol 7:475–528
32. Mondal SS, Holdt HJ (2016) Breaking down chemical weapons by metal-organic frameworks. Angew Chem Int Ed 55(1):42–44
33. Mondloch JE, Katz MJ, Isley WC III, Ghosh P, Liao P, Bury W, Wagner GW, Hall MG, DeCoste JB, Peterson GW (2015) Destruction of chemical warfare agents using metal–organic frameworks. Nat Mater 14(5):512–516
34. Torres M, Luckham P (2012) Non-woven fabric. Google patents
35. Torres M, Luckham P (2003) Non-woven fabric. Google patents
36. Zhao J, Gong B, Nunn WT, Lemaire PC, Stevens EC, Sidi FI, Williams PS, Oldham CJ, Walls HJ, Shepherd SD, Browe MA, Peterson GW, Losego MD, Parsons GN (2015) Conformal and highly adsorptive metal-organic framework thin films via layer-by-layer growth on ALD-coated fiber mats. J Mater Chem A 3(4):1458–1464
37. Rocío-Bautista P, Pacheco-Fernández I, Pasán J, Pino V (2016) Are metal-organic frameworks able to provide a new generation of solid-phase microextraction coatings?—a review. Analytica Chimica Acta 939(Supplement C):26–41
38. Margolis JE (2010) Understanding political stability and instability. Civil Wars 12(3):326–345

Dragonflies in the African Bush: Security Ramifications of Low-Cost Light Attack/Air Reconnaissance Aircraft Proliferation and the Chinese Aviation Industry

Christopher Long

Abstract The adaptation of civilian agricultural aircraft into a military attack and reconnaissance role represents a potential proliferation risk to US interests in areas of low-intensity conflict, particularly if the Chinese aviation industry builds on initial investments made by Chinese state-owned enterprises. Judging the likelihood of this shift, however, remains difficult. While not a high-tech threat, this type of aircraft has the potential to disrupt US diplomatic and military operations, as well as economic interests, in areas where advanced air-defense systems are not present, exploiting a narrow capabilities gap between these and man-portable countermeasures. The rapid advances Chinese firms have made in the international military UAV market and recent domestic reforms poise them uniquely to capitalize on the market for this type of aircraft, particularly in the African theater, and the issue begs closer attention from US military and intelligence institutions.

1 Introduction

The notion of the humble turboprop agricultural aircraft—the crop-duster or "air tractor"—pressed into military service by strapping missiles and guns to its wings may seem an odd duck when discussing the disruptive potential of technology proliferation. Existing examples of such planes are neither high-tech nor cutting-edge. They are largely ad-hoc adaptations of civilian technology and some off-the-shelf commodity hardware that was new technology perhaps twenty years ago, repackaged and marketed with a low price point as the decisive factor. The United States Air Force (USAF) won't fly many of them due to the lack of expected safety features such as ejection seats that have become *de rigueur* throughout its fixed-wing attack aircraft fleet, and their crippling vulnerability to any capable modern air defense system (ADS).

C. Long (✉)
Georgia Institute of Technology, Atlanta, GA, USA
e-mail: calong@gatech.edu

This chapter aims to demonstrate that the "armed crop-duster" concept presents a significant potential proliferation risk to US interests in regions of low-intensity conflict, where the lack of modern air defenses allow these aircraft to exploit the gap between the limitations of small arms and man-portable air defense systems (MANPADS) and the capabilities of more advanced countermeasures. The aircraft present a military option that has advantages versus the use of armed UAVs, carving out a narrow but exploitable niche in which to flourish. Further, low-cost attack aircraft represent an export opportunity that China's military aviation industry stands ready to capitalize on, as they have successfully with their development of military drones such as the Wing Loong I and II. As the Chinese aviation export industry has demonstrated, it is in a good position to exploit features in the geopolitical landscape that may inhibit or delay sales from market leaders US and Russia, making it difficult for either nation or the international community to limit proliferation of these types of aircraft. Recent, large Chinese aerospace sales to Saudi Arabia, the UAE, Nigeria, and other nations in the regions where US forces are increasingly being called on to operate will mean that the US military will be in close contact with these types of aircraft, whether fielded by allied, neutral or adversary forces.

2 Theory and Background

Innovation isn't something that always occurs at the leading edge of technology, nor does it always bring new capabilities to the field so much as consolidate existing ones in an economical package to make them ubiquitous. The AK-47 counts its enormous impact on the world not because it was the first or best performing in its class, but because it was durable, cheap and increasingly easy to manufacture. More than seventy years on, it remains a worldwide potent threat despite its age, accounting for perhaps one-fifth of all small arms worldwide only a decade ago [1].

Histories of transformative technologies often focus on the innovation, research, and design story of a technology's emergence but neglect the subsequent evolutionary changes arising from simple everyday use and adaptation to new purposes, both of which serve to make discoveries widespread and accessible. Similarly, US offset strategies have guided American defense research to continuously exploit the nascent phase of emerging technologies, but this focus may minimize the fact that many adversaries—particularly those without the capital to invest in R&D on the same scale—concentrate the bulk of their efforts on making tried and true technology cheaper and easier to maintain, precisely because a follow-on strategy profits them the most. The period of maximum impact for any particular technology corresponds not to its inception but its period of peak usage—"typically decades away from invention, or indeed innovation" [2]. For example, most Americans tend to view the automobile as the key civilian transportation technology innovation of the twentieth century, but for much of the rest of the world it has been the humble bicycle, which dwarfs the worldwide production of automobiles: 100 million annually versus 40 million cars is a recent statistic. Near the end of the twentieth century, between China,

Taiwan and India as many bicycles were built annually as had been worldwide in total from 1900 to 1950 [3].

As technology is diffused through the world it re-contextualizes itself to the problems and perceptions of each new audience; while a prop-driven attack aircraft may appear to American eyes an artifact of the Vietnam conflict, in less-developed nations it remains a potent means of exercising power at a distance. Technologies considered well behind the innovation curve by the developed world often lead organically to local, hybridized innovations such as the ubiquitous 'technical' armed pickup truck of Africa and the Middle East that continue to transform their environment. The work of Thomas Hughes, Trevor Pinch, Wiebe Bijker, and collaborators on the social construction of technology provides a solid grounding to observe and assess this changeable nature of tech as it moves through the world—often it is not the intrinsic properties of a technology but the outlines of the problem it's brought to bear on for each new set of users that holds more importance in assessing impact [4].

There has long been a tight interlinkage between developments in civilian technology and the changing face of warfare—the First World War would not have been the catastrophe of human cost it was without the parallel developments of machinists and chemists in private industry before and during the conflict, and the outcome of WWII cannot be understood without considering physicists' efforts that forever altered the international calculus of force. More than one scholar has echoed the compelling argument that "the key themes [of twentieth century military history] are the industrialization and civilianization of war since the late nineteenth century," [5] with mass production, "total war" mobilization, and rapid adaptation of civilian technologies to wartime needs proving the decisive factor in victory or defeat during the World Wars—from Liberty ships to mass communication.

Renewed peacetime attention given to dual-use technologies—those designed with both a peaceful civilian and military or defense-oriented use in mind—to attract innovation and reduce R&D outlays has served the West well in recent years. Again, however, it remains vital to carry this perspective beyond the clean rooms and drawing boards of US research institutions and consider instances where civilian and military technology might be joined and adapted to new purposes in the real world. In this hybrid environment, where tried and true civilian technology made cheap and accessible by continual refinement and economies of scale meets established, still-deadly military tech, the inexpensive fixed-wing attack and reconnaissance aircraft finds its niche.

3 Historical Precedents

Militarizing civilian crop-dusters to serve as reconnaissance or ground attack aircraft is by no means a novel concept. The key appeal of this approach has always been it's low-cost, an aim achieved by modifying civilian airframes, usually agricultural turboprop aircraft, to carry weapons, armor, and sensors. The United States has long been involved in efforts in this arena for purposes of counter-drug or counter-insurgency (COIN) operations, dating back at least into the 1980s and the Department of State's Narcotics Eradication Delivery System (NEDS) aircraft program, which armored Ayres Thrush crop-dusters to counter narcotics cultivation in Latin America and Southeast Asia [6]. Over time this merger of agricultural aviation (ag-av) and military aviation technology has grown around the COIN mission, leading to a number of US-sponsored foreign aid programs to provide similar aircraft to allies, as well as commercial development for the military export market by firms such as Brazil's Embraer with its well-regarded Super Tucano[7]. The USAF recently ran its Light Attack/Armed Reconnaissance (LAAR) and Light Attack Experiment (OA-X) programs to evaluate these types of aircraft for allied use in theaters of war where advanced air defenses are not typically present [8].

Notably, however, the low-cost element here is relative—USAF requirements for pressurized cockpits, ejection seats, and other features commonplace in military aviation have all but excluded adapted agricultural aviation aircraft from final selection in favour of purpose-built aircraft on the model of the Super Tucano. These specifications mandate a purchase and operational price-point well below American aircraft operating in similar roles, such as the Rockwell B1-B Lancer bomber and Fairchild Republic A-10 Thunderbolt II attack aircraft (themselves both built in the 1970s), but one that is nearly double that of adapted ag-av aircraft being marketed for export elsewhere [9]. This cost disparity may limit the potential appeal for any USAF-endorsed LAAR platform to allies seeking a cheaper or more readily available (from a bureaucratic regulatory perspective) solution, as China has demonstrated with its ability to woo potential MQ-9 Reaper drone customers to its own Wing Loong aircraft [10]. Michael Horowitz's adoption-capacity theory of military power holds that cost, not capability, is more often key when it comes to predicting proliferation—even an inferior product can achieve widespread military adoption if it is available at a far cheaper price [11].

4 China's Export Military Aviation Industry

Regional antagonism between China and its Asian neighbors over the South China Sea and other border disputes, coupled with its bloated and sluggish state-run military aviation industry, had previously been predicted to stymie Chinese efforts to expand its military aviation export industry at the expense of its main competitor in that sector, Russia [12]. Recent international fallout for China's foreign relations related to the COVID-19 pandemic has not brightened these prospects. Nonetheless, China has historically taken steps to reform and streamline its chief aviation firms under its state-owned Aviation Industry Corporation (AVIC), seeking to exploit opportunities underserved by Russian and US exports. It has tightened ties between AVIC and Poly Group Corporation, a large Chinese state-owned enterprise (SOE) conglomerate that controls, among many other subsidiaries, Poly Technologies—the largest arms exporter in China [13]. This followed earlier reforms that consolidated the separate

AVIC I and AVIC II SOEs that had been operating in parallel from 1998 to 2008, in an effort to reduce redundancy and increase AVIC's overall capacity for innovation among new lines of research [14].

The looming presence of massive, established SOEs such as AVIC in the Chinese defense sector has been regarded by analysts as a limiting factor in Chinese innovation in defense R&D—with little competitive pressure from private firms, the environment was thought to be less fertile ground for new development than that of its Western counterparts. Here, too, reforms have sought to make room for small private enterprises in the military R&D dynamic: in 2016, Chinese military procurement contracts opened to private firms for the first time, encouraging competitive bidding with the traditional SOEs on thousands of R&D contracts [15]. Particular attention has been given to encouraging development within the aviation sector, evidenced by a 2011 five-year plan citing reform in the Chinese aviation industry as a priority target, which resulted in the relaxation of rules that had inhibited private/general aviation ventures within the country [16]. Whether this trend will continue is presently an open question—as the Chinese economy has struggled to respond to the effects of the recent pandemic, President Xi Jingping has signaled an intent to bring Chinese private industry under tighter control by the communist regime [17]. How this directive will be implemented and its effects on arms and aviation exports remains to be seen.

Much of this emphasis on expanding the role of the private sector in technology development revolves around a question that has gripped the Chinese domestic political mindset: (in their words) why has there been no Chinese Steve Jobs? China's steadily expanding espionage operations have been extremely successful in extracting foreign R&D and funneling it into Chinese defense SOEs. Indeed, in diplomatic negotiations with the US, the Chinese seem to see no distinction between industrial espionage to the benefit of private firms, as Americans view the term, and state espionage generally, so tightly intertwined are Chinese intelligence operations and the SOEs/private entities in their defense industry. However, Western analysts as well as the Chinese themselves have noted that despite a steady influx of 'acquired' R&D, Chinese firms have had relatively little success in spurring follow-on development of the foreign technologies they've attained from these sources, often only realizing the next generation of a technology when Chinese intelligence returns to pilfer it once more. With growing international attention on Chinese espionage operations and technology theft by nations such as Canada, the United States, Australia and several European Union member states, the regular inflow of foreign-developed technologies may become more inhibited in the future [18].

In this light, the question of the "Chinese Steve Jobs" is one that the regime has addressed by expanding the opportunities for private firms in defense R&D and increasing competition with the traditionally dominant SOEs [19]. While competition on capital-heavy programs such as the Chinese fifth-generation fighter program may prove unfeasible for small private firms, emerging sectors of the military aviation export economy such as unmanned aerial vehicles (UAVs) and light attack/aerial reconnaissance (LAAR) aircraft present opportunities within the reach of smaller firms, particularly those with direct funding or finance assistance from the Chinese state. One such firm is Frontier Services Group, which received significant investment from the state-owned China International Trust Investment Corporation (CITIC) Group, the largest Chinese commercial/industrial conglomerate, umbrella organization of smaller SOEs such as Poly Group, and a key financial partner on large AVIC ventures such as the Jian-10 fighter aircraft [20].

5 Background: Frontier Services Group

Frontier Services Group (FSG) is a company with an interesting history—created in Hong Kong in 2014 under the chairmanship of Erik Prince, former head of private military contractor (PMC) Blackwater, with an injection of money from CITIC as its second largest shareholder (purportedly 20% of the company) and a significant element of its board and upper management, which includes several top CITIC executives and former Chinese Ministry of Public Security officials [21]. Prince, a former US Navy SEAL, made a reputation for himself while offering paramilitary training facilities, PMC services, and logistical support for US forces engaged in the war on terrorism until incidents involving Blackwater employees under criminal indictment for their actions in Iraq prompted his departure from the company in 2009 [22]. After the US State Department cooled on the widespread use of PMCs, he reoriented himself towards providing many of the same services to Chinese SOE-associated infrastructure projects and firms via FSG [23]. Prince's initial focus for FSG was Africa, a region where China has recently made significant strides in both commerce and power projection, including its recent opening of a People's Liberation Army (PLA) Navy base in Djibouti, its first overseas military outpost. The PLAN Djibouti base has been linked both to China's "One Belt and One Road" (OBOR) or "Belt and Road Initiative" (BRI, the official translated acronym) to expand its regional trade network and the "string of pearls" effort to secure Chinese sea trade and naval strength in the Indian Ocean [24]. Not coincidentally, the "string of pearls" ports and BRI projects are areas where FSG has secured numerous contracts in recent years.

Though Prince claims that FSG is involved only in logistics, infrastructure construction, and transportation and that he is no longer in the business of military training or security services, there is ample evidence that FSG is engaged in the same sorts of activities in which Blackwater specialized [19]. Prince refers to his new partnership with CITIC as representative of China's "appetite to take frontier risk, that expeditionary risk of going to those less-certain, less-normal markets" [22]. "Less-normal" in this context may be reasonably construed as a euphemistic allusion to China's pursuit of business partnerships with regimes where questionable human rights records have made military export contracts with US firms politically difficult or unlawful to execute. What is clear is that FSG and Chinese overseas interests have been tightly intertwined since its outset, and that the firm has adeptly pursued opportunities in line with the Chinese government's overarching plans in the African and South/Southwestern Asian theaters. This is in accord with a March 2016 FSG board meeting confrontation between disputing corporate elements led by a retired

US Navy Admiral on one side and by Prince and CITIC's representatives on the other, where dissenting board members were allegedly told outright that FSG "had been created to support China's global economic plan" [25].

One of FSG's first pursuits was what Prince envisioned as a private military air force employing low-cost LAAR aircraft of its own creation, in conjunction with an Austrian firm that provided technical implementation services. His intention was to create an extremely low-cost platform derived from the COIN aircraft designs previously pursued by US projects such as NEDS, adding commodity parts to provide advanced intelligence, surveillance, and reconnaissance (ISR) and weapons-carrying capabilities. His plan was to market the mercenary air fleet as a service with FSG-employed pilots at the controls. His first attempt to secure a contract with South Sudan to provide security for its mining operations fizzled when international arms control and journalistic attentions fell on the project and complicated delivery, but not before two proof-of-concept prototypes were developed and a spinoff firm, Light Armed Surveillance Aircraft (LASA) Engineering of Bulgaria, was created to produce and market the planes themselves. Tellingly, Prince's former firm Blackwater had been fined by the US in 2006 for doing business with then-separatist, now-leader of an independent South Sudan Salva Kiir, the same man with whom FSG had been attempting to broker a contract [26].

6 The Low-Cost Light Attack/Armed Reconnaissance Aircraft Concept

The internal FSG presentation on its LAAR aircraft cites three key priorities: that it be highly rugged and require little infrastructure to function, that it be cheap above all else, and that it skirt the fringes of export constraints such as the US International Traffic in Arms Regulations (ITAR) [27] that had limited or slowed the adoption of similar products by potential clients such as UAE. To fulfill these goals, FSG based its new project around an American Thrush 510 aircraft, designed for crop-dusting and distantly related, via several corporate closures and consolidations, to the Ayres Thrush aircraft that the US State Department had used for its NEDS program in the 1980s [28]. With its low cost, extended loiter time, and a design built for short, unimproved rural runways, the Thrush provided a solid foundation for the new mission FSG hoped to adapt it to. Roughly, the base Thrush aircraft had only half the performance capabilities of an Embraer Super Tucano—half fuel endurance, half engine horsepower, half cruise speed—though it came at a fraction of the price, as little as six-figures versus several million USD. FSG arranged to have two of the aircraft modified in Austria to add armor to the engine and cockpit, protect its fuel tanks from explosions and fires, install an off-the-shelf ISR "pod" that also had a target designator for laser-guided munitions, and supply custom wing-mounted hardpoints (locations for attaching armaments or accessories to the aircraft) that could carry a range of NATO or Warsaw Pact munitions [29].

The aircraft was a feat of jury-rigged engineering improvisation—according to internal design documents, a special provision for attacks executed during daylight was necessary when the pilot, expected to typically operate in darkness wearing night-vision goggles/NVGs, wouldn't be able to see the targeting laser from the aircraft. To compensate, a cheap EOTech rifle sight was bolted to the nose of the aircraft to indicate point of aim [30]. Night operation and altitude were the planned defense against MANPADS and small arms fire. In the dark, the ISR's camera system doubled as a target finder if the pilot couldn't make it out via his NVGs. A simple lever-actuated mount swung the ISR pod below the radius of the propeller during flight so its target laser wouldn't be interrupted by the prop blades. The data link to the ISR system was designed to work over generic Wi-Fi or 3G/4G cellular networks, accessible via a planned iPad app that clients would be able to link up to in real-time, wireless service permitting. These relatively crude examples of inventiveness on FSG's part underscored the recurring theme of its core concept presentation—it was not building a plane to fight a modern war but one to fight in a Vietnam-era threat environment and do so as cheaply as possible [31].

The choice of a crop-duster held other advantages in chasing a low bottom line. The demands of agricultural application aviation (crop dusting) groomed a certain sort of pilot for the job—those skilled in dangerous low-altitude flying, the precision dropping of pesticides and other agricultural chemicals (often via GPS guidance) on small fields, and flying in unfavorable weather conditions due to the tight schedule imposed by crop spoilage, etc. The role of a crop-dusting pilot was a more dangerous profession than most in civilian aviation—an NTSB report notes that from 2001 to 2010, agricultural flight operations ranked sixth or seventh in hours flown among US general aviation but third in total number of accidents despite consistently high levels of experience in terms of flight hours logged by agricultural pilots [32]. If ever there were a civilian pilot job tailored to prepare for a transition into flying military attack aircraft, crop-dusting would be it—providing FSG an inherent head start in pilot training and recruitment. With commercial UAV use in the agricultural sector experiencing brisk year over year growth and steady development of new, more capable drones, there is likely to be a growing pool of ag-av pilots looking for new work, as well.

While FSG's plans for a private air force seem to have been scuttled after the spotlight fell on their operation and US regulators began questioning their activities in light of a lack of relevant export licenses, the planes themselves survived. They were transferred to the new LASA Engineering spinoff in Bulgaria, where Prince had allegedly planned to procure and install armaments from the local arsenal firms. According to leaked emails between Erik Prince and the CFO of the Austrian firm that had begun building the armed Thrush prototypes, LASA was explicitly designed as a front company set up to conduct business on FSG's and the affiliated Austrian firm's behalf [25]. In the end, US and EU arms control regulations as well as the beleaguered legacy of mercenary outfits Blackwater and Executive Outcomes [33] contributed to derailing Prince's plans for a private mercenary air force. While he has since unsuccessfully floated the concept to the Afghani government, via a company set up under FSG's former director of operations and aviation, [34] international appetite for this type of PMC air service has diminished considerably since the heyday of Blackwater. Meanwhile, however, LASA has continued marketing the weaponized Thrush, now known as the LASA T-Bird [35]. Given FSG's funding and stated commitment to acting in support of the Chinese global economic plan, it is likely that development of the low-cost LAAR platform is endorsed by elements of the CITIC Group. While China is a signatory of both the 1989 UN Mercenaries Convention and the 2008 Montreux Document that would theoretically preclude support for a private military air force of the sort Prince proposed, this certainly would not prevent Chinese firms from developing and selling a product like the T-Bird.

Recent sanctions instituted by the United States that bar the transfer of technology with possible military applications to Chinese firms may attenuate China's designs on plunging into high-tech aviation development and make a more low-cost, low-technology product like LAAR aircraft more attractive. Much of China's aviation industry at the high end relies on foreign imports, whether it's Russian engines for its new J-20 fighter or American electronics for the Comac C919 passenger jet it had hoped would allow it to compete with Boeing and Airbus in the transportation sector. Development of the C919 seems to have ground to an abrupt halt as Comac is no longer able to acquire American engines and electronics necessary for its production [36].

7 Analysis: Disruptive Potential of Low-Cost LAAR Aircraft

In weighing the hypothetical impact of a cheaply weaponized crop-duster style of LAAR aircraft, parallel consideration of a similar sector in which Chinese military aviation firms have been successful is fruitful. The first important attribute to judge impact is cost—given China's ability to deliver products such as their Wing Loong drone at costs significantly undercutting (by 50%) their Western equivalents, it seems likely that an effort by AVIC, a subsidiary, or even a private Chinese defense R&D firm to enter the LAAR aircraft market could further drive down prices. This could be accomplished by swapping the Thrush airframe for a lower cost domestic Chinese ag-av airframe such as the analogous Hongdu N-5, which in its Canadian license-built variant already beats the Thrush turboprop's North American price by nearly 25%, and it can be built for even less in China [37]. According to the central tenet of adoption-capacity theory, low cost will be key to rapid proliferation.

Seeking a historical parallel to gauge China's capacity to enter and exploit the market for LAAR aircraft, the example of military UAVs springs readily to mind. While the two products might seem to be in direct competition—indeed, crop-dusting aircraft and commercial UAVs contest each other quite vigorously in ag-av—LAAR aircraft and armed UAVs readily coexist despite their common traits because they lie in different zones on a spectrum of tradeoffs within military aviation as a whole. A traditional jet-powered fighter-bomber, such as the Xian JH-7, has a relatively expensive development cycle, high capabilities in speed and armament compared to a LAAR craft or UAV, a very high operational cost (thousands of dollars per flight hour) and training requirements, and low unrefueled endurance relative to the other two options. A UAV, on the other hand, has very low operational costs (though considerable setup/infrastructure costs) and high endurance, allowing some models to loiter in an area for 36 hours or more [38]. The low-cost LAAR option falls somewhere in the middle of these two options—slightly more expensive to operate than the UAV but significantly less than a traditional military aircraft, with loiter times of up to 12 hours [39]. The LAAR aircraft's ability to function in rugged, undeveloped environments and the flexibility of having a human pilot in the cockpit, [40] though not one so expensive to train as the traditional military option, carves out a unique niche for the airplane relative to UAVs or larger, more sophisticated craft. In fact, one of China's larger clients for the Wing Loong drone, the UAE, has been operating its drones in the Libyan and Yemeni conflicts alongside a (more expensive) LAAR plane based on a different model of Thrush, called the Iomax Archangel, and an older ag-av adapted LAAR airframe built by Air Tractor [41].

Given that Chinese drones are already being used alongside these LAAR aircraft, domestic development of such an airframe might present an attractive opportunity for AVIC or another Chinese firm to diversify and expand sales to established clients. Through the financial support CITIC has provided to the low-cost LAAR concept through FSG, the groundwork may already be laid for such a shift. Chinese firms such as Shaanxi BaoHe Defense Technology, which supplies military exports to nations as varied as Bolivia and Tajikistan, already produce relatively simple, inexpensive military aircraft such as the Lieying gyrocopter for the PLA [42]. In their pursuit of UAV contracts, China's various military aviation export firms have consistently taken advantage of US or Russian reluctance to provide military exports to certain clients (based on overriding political or economic concerns) as an opportunity to substitute their own products for sale. Thus, it seems equally feasible that a Chinese-built LAAR aircraft might show up in the hands of a nominal US ally as it might one of its adversaries—wherever there is a profit to be made. Used by allied states in the COIN role originally envisioned for the LAAR concept, this may be a boon for US interests—one the State Department has attempted to foster in several nations by encouraging allies such as the Afghani Air Force to purchase similar aircraft. FSG originally framed their Thrush as a product "that can break the paradigm of attrition warfare in low intensity conflict," [43] however, this can break both ways. In an area without allied ADS, aircraft designed for COIN operations can readily be turned to insurgency or other purposes.

8 The Political Dimension

A recent period of dynamic change in Chinese international diplomacy and trade practices makes judging their likelihood of proliferating a technology such as cheap LAAR aircraft a complex assessment. Chinese SOEs have been historically aggressive in marketing arms and war materiel to African and Middle Eastern clients: sales of arms from China to African nations tripled during the 1990s and continue to rise. Though the Congressional Research Service reported China was the #6 supplier of arms worldwide through 2001, 83% of its sales went to the developing world demonstrating a strong bias towards sales to states and actors without advanced domestic R&D capabilities [44]. China's increasingly assertive posture along its land and maritime borders has purportedly constrained its ability to market arms to many of its regional neighbors, further narrowing the scope of its sales outreach to African and Middle Eastern nations where it can compete with Russian arms on cost [45].

China has been witnessed selling arms to both sides of African conflicts on at least two occasions—the Ethiopia-Eritrea War in 1998–2000 and the intermittent Sudanese civil war of the 2010s [46]. Expanded military sales have in some instances been pursued with the backing of Chinese state leadership. President Xi has expressed a desire to modernize production and build sales outreach for AVIC and other defense SOEs to compete with US-based industry leaders Boeing and Lockheed-Martin [47]. Occasionally, arms-industry SOEs seem to have acted on their own initiative and against the prevailing ambitions of the Chinese government. There was a politically embarrassing episode where South African port facilities rejected a shipment of arms from Poly Group meant for Zimbabwe's Mugabe regime, a transfer that apparently occurred without the prior knowledge of Chinese state leadership. On at least two occasions during the South Sudanese civil war, while the Chinese diplomatic corps was shepherding disarmament and ceasefire agreements through the UN Security Council, UN arms control officials reported that Chinese SOEs such as Norinco were selling arms to the breakaway South Sudan republic [48]. These trends suggest a nation that is not always in absolute control or full awareness of its arms export industry, despite recent attempts at reform [49].

China's strategies in the developing world have evolved rapidly with the transitions from presidents Jiang to Hu to Xi. Both Hu and Xi cultivated increasing economic and political influence within the African continent and among Latin American states, proving increasingly willing to stray from the traditional Chinese foreign diplomatic principle of non-interference when Chinese economic interests took precedence [50]. This trend of economic concerns coming to the fore has been referred to as the corporatization of Chinese foreign policy—where SOEs have been driving Chinese foreign engagement by entering into risky business ventures overseas and then obligating their government to act on their behalf through public and political pressure [51]. The need for steady and secure international trade is particularly pressing due to China's dependence on foreign energy: Africa has supplied up to 33% of China's oil imports [52]. Other drivers include a hunger for natural resources to supply China's still-growing manufacturing base and markets to sell its products. Between 2001 and

2007 China experienced almost seven-fold growth in international commerce with both Africa and Latin America [53]. Chinese trade with African states has grown enormously since 2000 and it is now the largest single-state trade partner with the African continent [54]. It has further evidenced willingness to deprioritize rhetorical goals when they've gotten in the way of commerce, apparently with the expectation that increased economic ties will bring partners more firmly into its orbit, as in the case of Senegal. China circumvented its ban on doing business with national governments holding diplomatic ties to Taiwan by contracting directly with Senegalese provincial governments, and several economically fruitful years later it was able to persuade Senegal to formally break ties with Taipei [55]. Perhaps the most profound evidence of its growing willingness to eschew non-interference is the establishment of its first overseas military base in Djibouti, where PLA Navy forces have been stationed to provide regional security for the nearby shipping lanes and, by extension, Chinese economic interests in Africa [56].

This first shift towards having an overseas military presence was striking for several reasons, even in light of the increased risk profile of its SOEs' overseas ventures. Under President Xi's unfolding BRI initiative, China has increasingly invested heavily in overseas development from Africa to its own western frontier. At the same time, the Chinese state has shown a marked preference towards keeping PLA activities separate from the economic activity of Chinese firms whenever possible. Though both Xi and the Chinese Ministry of Foreign Affairs have acknowledged security threats to Chinese enterprises and nationals supporting BRI abroad, this has not translated to ongoing, proactive support from the Chinese military, outside reactions to acute emergency [57]. Instead, Beijing has pursued security guarantees from host nations where Chinese-financed development is taking place, such as the 15,000 strong Pakistani Army force protecting Chinese contractors in the Pakistani tribal areas [58]. Where weak states are unable to provide such guarantees, private-sector security arrangements between SOEs and a variety of contractors are typically substituted instead [59].

9 China's Private Security Market

Overall, the domestic private security contractor (PSC) market in China is not as highly developed as that of Western PSCs and private military contractors (PMCs), and this presents something of a conundrum for Chinese firms. While Chinese security firms are highly preferred by SOEs with the view that they will maintain the secrecy of Chinese proprietary business data. Chinese law imposes criminal liability, up to and including life imprisonment, for Chinese nationals disclosing SOE information to foreigners, [60] so this is a pressing concern. However, domestic private security capability is not yet equal to the needs of BRI projects abroad. Chinese law absolutely prohibits the arming of non-PLA nationals, [61] even overseas, leading Chinese PSCs to seek out foreign employees, whether from Western PSCs/PMCs or locally-recruited forces such as African militants, or to partner with established

Western firms [62]. This hybrid Chinese-Western PSC environment has led to the creation of Chinese-chartered firms such as Erik Prince's FSG, who himself was one of a very few foreign guests and a widely lauded attendee at the 2016 Chinese PSC Association annual meeting [63]. Firms that employ a mix of Western and Chinese personnel often seek to transfer Western skills to Chinese PSCs. This can be seen in another area where FSG has been actively engaged, administering training camps for security contractors in Xinjiang and other restive Chinese border provinces.

The growing demand for security for BRI projects has catalyzed a rapid series of changes in the Chinese PSC market and regulatory environment. The Ministry of Foreign Affairs has increasingly tightened control over these Chinese PSCs to ensure that they retain a principally domestic character—PSCs with armed personnel (again, anyone carrying a weapon for Chinese firms must be foreign-born employees) must be either entirely state-owned or have at least 51% capital investment from a Chinese SOE to incorporate [64]. Ex-PLA or ex-PAP (Chinese Armed Police) personnel dominate the management hierarchy of domestic PSCs, closely tying them to the Chinese military and state security apparatus [65]. Though the growing China PSC industry remains, today, largely focused on an internal market, particularly in its restive Muslim provinces such as Xinjiang, BRI has begun to change the dynamic and foster growth among a small subset of Chinese security firms with international ambitions. Of over five thousand registered Chinese PSCs existing in 2017, less than a dozen are judged by the industry as capable of mounting operations overseas, [66] but Africa has become increasingly seen as the testing ground for Chinese PSC firms looking to internationalize [67]. Though not yet able to compete with Russian or Western PSCs/PMCs in many areas, Chinese firms operating in an intensively competitive environment have begun to separate low-cost, low-skill firms from more specialized PSCs marketing capabilities including drones, satellite and aerial reconnaissance data gathering, and intelligence analysis, allowing for higher-paying overseas security contracts [68]. In this niche, the notion of PSCs operating Chinese-built LAAR in the manner Erik Prince envisioned for FSG may find ready footing (at least in a reconnaissance role).

10 Futures in Risk Mitigation

Whether China expands PLA involvement in providing overseas BRI security, as it did at Djibouti, or its regulatory environment continues to evolve to make room for Chinese security outfits to operate in the more kinetic fashion of Russian or Western PSCs is an unknown. Both approaches have their advantages for China—direct state control over the PLA on one hand, and a layer of semi-plausible deniability through PSCs on the other that might shelter China from a degree of political fallout in a crisis or misstep. Whatever the approach, it is clear the Chinese will continue to have to mitigate their risks in overseas ventures. The nation currently has active investments or contracts of more than US$1b in 12 of the top 20 failed/failing states of the world,

[69] and in Africa, in particular, political backlash from their partnerships has put Chinese SOEs and nationals under scrutiny and subjected them to recurring violence.

Close engagement with African elites has aroused the ire of separatist, rebel, and terrorist movements throughout the continent, [70] and China's tech- and skills-transfer of media-monitoring and suppression methods to repressive African regimes such as Zimbabwe has provoked angry local responses [71]. Chinese leadership has shown no qualms about supporting potentially repressive regimes (by Western standards) that are able to ensure local and regional stability, despite the painful lesson of Libya. Chinese firms there held over US$20b in contracts with the Gaddafi regime, of which only US$2-3 m were recovered in insurance payouts after his ouster and death [72]. In the aftermath of Gadhafi's ouster, Chinese business connections to the former regime have made it difficult for China to establish cordial relations with the present Libyan government [49]. Additionally, China has been accused of attempting to offload low-skill, high-pollution industries to Africa and Southeast Asia due to rising labor costs and environmental consciousness at home, hardening overseas labor relations and inspiring several incidents of violence [73]. Lastly, increasing displays of wealth and prosperity abroad has resulted in the targeting of Chinese employees overseas by the piracy and kidnap & ransom (one of the fastest growing criminal ventures at present) "industries," [74] exacerbated by a widely observed Chinese SOE tendency to fulfill high ransom demands quickly to avoid protracted negotiations, which has only made Chinese nationals a more lucrative and attractive target to kidnappers [75]. It is unlikely that international fallout relating to China's role in the Covid-19 pandemic will do much improve to these security challenges abroad. With these trends unfolding, it seems inevitable that China will have to pursue more complex and widespread security arrangements to support BRI's continued development.

It is in this context that a Chinese SOE or small, privately-owned defense firm pursuing LAAR development might feasibly depress the cost-floor of this platform simply by taking an interest. Without knowing the internal deliberations of CITIC, it is impossible to say whether the leadership there has any sustained interest in furthering support of FSG's aircraft development, but domestic experts within the Chinese PSC community and academic observers both believe that the economic links between PSCs and military-oriented SOEs such as Poly Group and Norinco are likely to increase if limitations on arming Chinese PSC employees overseas are modified or lifted [76]. Whether this never occurs in favour of increasing PLA engagement with BRI security, occurs years down the road, or is an imminent undertaking can only be known presently to those in the Chinese Communist Party leadership.

There has been much speculation over the potential of military drones to increase the lethality of warfare by lowering the risk and political cost of executing an attack from the air. This disconnect between aggression and a consequence in friendly lives lost has certainly opened up a range of new options for actors who recently acquired armed drone fleets, such as Iran. Iranian drones were shot down twice by American aircraft over the summer of 2017 after approaching or dropping bombs near a US overseas training outpost [77]. This debate is less relevant when trying to draw a parallel to low-cost LAAR aircraft because they are designed to be manned.

As an economic cost vs. capacity question, however, there may be common note that carries through—Iran has aimed to threaten superior US naval forces in the Strait of Hormuz via swarm tactics designed to overwhelm via "large numbers of relatively unsophisticated systems on land, at sea and in the air" [78]. Certainly cheap LAAR aircraft could figure prominently in planning for this kind of mass asymmetric warfare.

The largest threat represented by widely proliferated LAAR aircraft, however, is not in areas where the US military presence is strong but where it is weak. Without the high infrastructure costs associated with medium to large drones (control facilities, improved runways, satellite bandwidth), the cheap LAAR concept provides a subset of the capabilities of drones or more advanced manned aircraft at a fraction of the cost. This immediately makes for an attractive option for regimes of limited means or insurgencies and other non-state actors with little money to spend. While no match for US airpower or air defense assets, inexpensive LAAR aircraft could certainly menace US military training or advising operations, special forces operations without an accompanying ADS umbrella, or US commercial and industrial interests overseas. The low cost of entry puts it within reach of a host of potential hostile entities that otherwise would not possess any air combat capabilities whatsoever. While there may be one or two well-supported terrorist organizations—Hezbollah, for example—capable of fielding advanced armed drones (though several have utilized small commercial drones for aerial reconnaissance or IED-delivery purposes), there are potentially many more that could afford to fly a weaponized crop-duster from a primitive dirt airstrip to great effect.

If we consider these risk and emerging threat environments, then, it is in the terrorist and failed or failing state scenarios where LAAR represents the greatest risk. From an economic and political standpoint, the threat to US interests from China as a peer competitor must also be appreciated. The range of development environments among the emerging megacities of the mid-twenty-first century means some will be better prepared (with ADS, for example) to fend off a LAAR or drone threat than others. At the borders of nation-states, LAAR are already extensively used by UAE and others for border security—or border penetration, such as when Columbian aircraft attacked a FARC camp inside Ecuador and triggered a South American arms race in 2008 [79]. Within the cyber or virtual environment, obviously, aircraft such as these have little impact other than potentially serving as a vehicle for cyber intrusion of infrastructure via onboard electronics—but this is a corner case. This threat assessment is summarized in Fig. 1.

11 Conclusions

The prospect of low-cost, widely proliferated LAAR aircraft both broadens and diversifies the range and source of risk facing US interests, and developments in this area should be monitored closely. Particularly, the potential for China to make a strong move into this market represents an area of concern. The Chinese military

Environments	2018 (Present)	2022 (5 Years)	2035 (10-15 Years)
		N/A Low Medium High	
Virtual	N/A	N/A	N/A
Mega City	Low	High	High
Terrorist Group	Low	Medium	Medium
Peer Competitor	Medium	High	High
Failing/Failed State	Medium	Medium	Medium
Border/Perimeter Security	Low	Medium	High

Fig. 1 Summary of the threat from proliferation of LAAR in different environments and by different adversary types

export aviation industry is far from a monolithic entity, even in the heyday of its largest SOEs, and its increasing diversity and volatility increases the potential for Chinese firms to break out into new market segments such as LAAR aircraft. To the extent possible, it would befit US intelligence to keep a closer ear on Chinese developments in the area of military UAVs and LAAR aircraft, even if only through open-source intelligence channels. China is rapidly solidifying its role as one of the largest investors in drone R&D as well as a major player in military aviation export and seems steadily on track to take more market share away from Russian interests as they progress. Their weapons will only become more prevalent globally in the coming years.

As demonstrated by FSG, there are some grey areas between the US ITAR and the multilateral Missile Technology Control Regime (MTCR, which covers drones as well) that LAAR exports could potentially slip through. China is itself not a signatory of MTCR, though it has pledged to support the original 1987 accord. As recently as 2004, it applied to become a member of MTCR only to be rejected due to concerns over its military export policies [80]. There may remain opportunities at the US State Department or other agencies to diplomatically shore up some of the gaps by which civilian, commercial aircraft being converted to military use might skirt international arms regulations, as well as to revisit the MTCR issue with China, incorporating dialog on drones and LAAR aircraft on the international export market. That LAAR aircraft and drones are being currently deployed operationally alongside one another in the Middle East and North Africa begs open discussion that addresses both concerns.

The US is once more faced with an innovation that, like military UAVs, it initially developed only to see it adopted by a rival and potentially widely produced and proliferated. Many criticisms have been levelled at the Bush and Obama administrations during the early years of drone warfare in the war on terrorism for not moving quickly to encourage international agreements and domestic export standards that might limit the global spread of armed drones. Today, military UAVs are in active development and production by Iran, Turkey, China, India, Pakistan, Israel, numerous EU states and other nations that present pressing security concerns for American political and military leaders. While cheap LAAR aircraft do not represent as comprehensive a threat as armed drones, the US is currently in a "strike while the iron is hot" moment with regard to their development, with an opportunity to take decisive action before broad proliferation puts the issue beyond our ability to influence.

References

1. Killicoat P (2007) Weaponomics: the global market for assault rifles. World Bank policy research working paper no. 4202. p 3
2. Edgerton D (2006) The shock of the old—technology and global history since 1900. Profile Books, London, p 4
3. Edgerton D (2006) The shock of the old—technology and global history since 1900. Profile Books, London, p 45
4. MacKenzie D (1987) Missile accuracy: a case study in the social processes of technological change. In: Bijker WE, Hughes TP, Pinch T (eds) The social construction of technological systems. MIT Press, Cambridge MA, pp 195–222
5. Edgerton D (2006) The shock of the old—technology and global history since 1900. Profile Books, London, p 138
6. Trevithick J (2014) The U.S. state department has its own air force. And it's surprisingly big. The Week. https://theweek.com/articles/445676/state-department-air-force-surprisingly-big. Accessed 1 Oct 2020
7. FitzGerald T, Long G, Ogier T et al (2010) Building up military muscle. Latin Trade 18(6), p 27; Keltz MA (2014) Getting our partners airborne—training air advisors and their impact in-theater. Air Space Power J 28(3):5–6
8. Mizokami K (2017) One of these planes will be the air force's new light attack aircraft. Popular Mechanics. https://www.popularmechanics.com/military/aviation/news/a27751/oa-x-light-aircraft/. Accessed 1 May 2018
9. Hasick J (2008) Arms and innovation: entrepreneurship and alliances in the twenty-first century defense industry. University of Chicago Press, Chicago, p 41; Mizokami K (2017) One of these planes will be the air force's new light attack aircraft. Popular Mechanics. https://www.popularmechanics.com/military/aviation/news/a27751/oa-x-light-aircraft/. Accessed 1 May 2018
10. Brimelow B (2017) Chinese drones could swarm the market and that could be bad for the US. Business insider. https://www.businessinsider.com/chinese-drones-swarm-market-2017-11. Accessed 22 April 2018
11. Horowitz MC (2010) The diffusion of military power—causes and consequences for international politics. Princeton University Press, Princeton, p 16
12. Mehta A (2015) For military aviation, China not yet rising. DefenseNews. https://www.defensenews.com/digital-show-dailies/paris-air-show/2015/06/14/for-military-aviation-china-not-yet-rising/. Accessed 23 April 2018
13. Nunns C (2013) China's poly group: the most important company you've never heard of. Public radio international. https://www.pri.org/stories/2013-02-25/chinas-poly-group-most-important-company-youve-never-heard. Accessed 15 April 2018; Cendrowski S (2016) China reshuffles 8 state-owned giants in race against rising debt. Fortune September 2016. p 2
14. Krolikowski A, Raska M (2013) China's military aviation industry: in search of innovation. In: SITC research briefs. https://escholarship.org/uc/item/8t12095f. Accessed 20 April 2018
15. Grevatt J (2016) China opens military R&D to the private sector. Jane's Defence Ind 33(9):2–3
16. Sarsfield K (2013) China relaxes restrictions for private flight operators. Flight International December 2013, p 22
17. He L (2020) Xi Jinping wants China's private companies to fight alongside the communist party. CNN. https://www.cnn.com/2020/09/22/business/china-private-sector-intl-hnk/index.html. Accessed 29 Sep 2020

18. Gates M (2020) An unfair advantage: confronting organized intellectual property theft. ASIS International. https://www.asisonline.org/security-management-magazine/articles/2020/07/an-unfair-advantage-confronting-organized-intellectual-property-theft/. Accessed 28 Sep 2020
19. Mulvenon J (4 Dec, 2017) Myths and realities of Chinese espionage. Paper presented at School of History & Sociology speaker series, Georgia Institute of Technology
20. Nunns C (2013) China's poly group: the most important company you've never heard of. Public Radio International. https://www.pri.org/stories/2013-02-25/chinas-poly-group-most-important-company-youve-never-heard. Accessed 15 April 2018; Xinhua News (2007) China AVIC I sets up finance unit. In: China Daily. https://www.chinadaily.com.cn/china/2007-04/08/content_845707.htm. Accessed 24 April 2018
21. Parello-Plesner J, Duchatel M (2015) China's strong arm—protecting citizens and assets abroad. Routledge, London, p 54
22. Feith D (25 Jan, 2014) The weekend interview with Erik Prince: out of Blackwater and into China. Wall Street J
23. Arduino A (2018) China's private army: protecting the new silk road. Palgrave Macmillan, Singapore, p 157. https://doi.org/10.1007/978-981-10-7215-4
24. Calamur K (July, 2017) China's first overseas military base. The Atlantic. p 2
25. Scahill J, Cole M (2016) Echo papa exposed—inside Erik prince's treacherous drive to build a private air force. The Intercept, 11 April 2016. https://theintercept.com/2016/04/11/blackwater-founder-erik-prince-drive-to-build-private-air-force/. Accessed 12 April 2018
26. Scahill J, Cole M (2016) Echo papa exposed—inside Erik prince's treacherous drive to build a private air force. The Intercept, 11 April 2016. https://theintercept.com/2016/04/11/blackwater-founder-erik-prince-drive-to-build-private-air-force/. Accessed 12 April 2018; Arduino A (2018) China's private army: protecting the new silk road. Palgrave Macmillan, Singapore, p 154. https://doi.org/10.1007/978-981-10-7215-4
27. DiMascio J, Osborne T (2017) The new crop of low-cost ISR or attack aircraft. Aviation Week and Space Technology, 12 July 2017. https://aviationweek.com/defense/new-crop-low-cost-isr-or-attack-aircraft. Accessed 2 April 2018
28. Federal Aviation Administration (2014) Type certificate data sheet No. A3SW, Revision 19. Department of Transportation, Washington DC
29. Scahill J, Cole M (2016) Echo papa exposed—inside Erik prince's treacherous drive to build a private air force. The Intercept, 11 April 2016. https://theintercept.com/2016/04/11/blackwater-founder-erik-prince-drive-to-build-private-air-force/. Accessed 12 April 2018; DiMascio J, Osborne T (2017) The new crop of low-cost ISR or attack aircraft. Aviation Week & Space Technology, 12 July 2017. https://aviationweek.com/defense/new-crop-low-cost-isr-or-attack-aircraft. Accessed 2 April 2018
30. Frontier Services Group (2016) Thrush weaponization blueprint. In: Scahill J, Cole M Echo papa exposed—inside Erik Prince's treacherous drive to build a private air force. The Intercept, 11 April 2016. https://theintercept.com/2016/04/11/blackwater-founder-erik-prince-drive-to-build-private-air-force/. Accessed 12 April 2018, p 15
31. Frontier Services Group (2016) Thrush weaponization blueprint. In: Scahill J, Cole M (eds) Echo papa exposed—inside Erik prince's treacherous drive to build a private air force. The Intercept, 11 April 2016. https://theintercept.com/2016/04/11/blackwater-founder-erik-prince-drive-to-build-private-air-force/. Accessed 12 April 2018, p 7
32. National Transportation Safety Board (2014) Special investigation report on the safety of agricultural aircraft operations. NTSB, Washington DC, pp 1–2
33. Executive Outcomes was a South African PMC that flew its own private air force in Africa during the 1990s
34. Snow S, Wolf M (2017) Blackwater founder wants to boost the Afghan air war with his private air force. Military Times, 2 August 2017, p 2
35. de Cherisey E (2017) Paris air show 2017: LASA engineering unveils its T-Bird armed surveillance aircraft. Jane's 360, 23 June 2017, p 1

36. Zhou C (2019) US trade war could impact China's ability to manufacture rival to Airbus, Boeing, designer says. South China Morning Post, 22 October 2019. https://www.scmp.com/economy/china-economy/article/3034028/us-trade-war-could-impact-chinas-ability-manufacture-rival. Accessed 1 Oct 2020
37. Lewis P (1998) China signs for Canadian N-5 production. FlightGlobal, 22 April 1998. https://www.flightglobal.com/news/articles/china-signs-for-canadian-n-5-production-35718/. Accessed 15 April 2018
38. Hasick J (2008) Arms and innovation: entrepreneurship and alliances in the twenty-first century defense industry. University of Chicago Press, Chicago, p 41
39. Lavender B (2017) How much does it cost?. In: Ag2AirUpdate. https://www.agairupdate.com/how-much-does-it-cost/. Accessed 18 April 2018; Frontier Services Group (2016) Thrush weaponization blueprint. In: Scahill J, Cole M (eds) Echo papa exposed—inside Erik prince's treacherous drive to build a private air force. The Intercept, 11 April 2016. https://theintercept.com/2016/04/11/blackwater-founder-erik-prince-drive-to-build-private-air-force/. Accessed 12 April 2018, p 3
40. N.b.: Apparent Chinese enthusiasm for incorporating artificial intelligence (AI) into tactical decision-making by autonomous drones themselves may diverge sharply from their potential clients. This schism may represent another potential reason to prefer the manned LAARP concept over some of the more advanced Chinese drones being developed
41. IHS Jane's (2015) Yemeni pilots carry out airstrikes with AT-802 turboprops. Jane's 360, 28 October 2015, p 1; Pickering M (2017) UAE Thrush T-660 'Archangel' crashes off Yemeni coast. Military Aviation Review, 11 Sep 2017, p 1
42. Global Times (2019) Gyroplane can send stealth missions: report. Global Times, 8 October 2019. https://www.globaltimes.cn/content/1166283.shtml. Accessed 1 Oct 2020
43. Frontier Services Group (2016) Thrush weaponization blueprint. In: Scahill J, Cole M (eds) Echo papa exposed—inside Erik prince's treacherous drive to build a private air force. The Intercept, 11 April 2016. https://theintercept.com/2016/04/11/blackwater-founder-erik-prince-drive-to-build-private-air-force/. Accessed 12 April 2018, p 1
44. Shinn DH (2009) Military and security relations: China, Africa, and the rest of the world. In: Rotberg RI (ed) China into Africa: trade, aid, and influence. Brookings Institution Press, Washington DC, pp 160, 162. https://doi.org/10.1017/S0022278X11000395
45. Metha A (2015) For military aviation, China not yet rising. DefenseNews. https://www.defensenews.com/digital-show-dailies/paris-air-show/2015/06/14/for-military-aviation-china-not-yet-rising/. Accessed 23 April 2018.
46. Eisenman J, Kurlantzick J (2006) China's Africa strategy. Current Hist 105(691):222; Large D (2016) China and South Sudan's civil war, 2013–2105. Afr Stud Q 16(3–4):40–41
47. Arduino A (2018) China's private army: protecting the new silk road. Palgrave Macmillan, Singapore, pp 119–120. https://doi.org/10.1007/978-981-10-7215-4
48. Alden C, Hughes CR (2009) Harmony and discord in China's Africa strategy: some implications for foreign policy. China Q 199:563–584. https://doi.org/10.1017/S0305741009990105; Large D (2016) China and South Sudan's civil war, 2013–2105. Afr Stud Q 16(3–4):40–41
49. Parello-Plesner J, Duchatel M (2015) China's strong arm—protecting citizens and assets abroad. Routledge, London, p 53
50. Forsythe M, Sanderson H (2013) China's superbank: debt, oil, and influence—how China development bank is rewriting the rules of finance. Wiley-Bloomberg Press, Singapore, p 117; Alden C, Hughes CR (2009) Harmony and discord in China's Africa strategy: some implications for foreign policy. China Q 199:568. https://doi.org/10.1017/S0305741009990105; Thrall L (2015) China's expanding African relations—implications for U.S. national security. RAND, Santa Monica, pp 71–72. https://doi.org/10.7249/RR905
51. Parello-Plesner J, Duchatel M (2015) China's strong arm—protecting citizens and assets abroad. Routledge, London, p 51
52. Shinn DH (2009) Military and security relations: China, Africa, and the rest of the world. In: Rotberg RI (ed) China into Africa: trade, aid, and influence. Brookings Institution Press, Washington DC, p 182. https://doi.org/10.1017/S0022278X11000395

53. Jiang W (2009) China's emerging strategic partnerships in Africa. In: Rotberg RI (ed) China into Africa: trade, aid, and influence. Brookings Institution Press, Washington DC, pp 50–64, 53. https://doi.org/10.1017/S0022278X11000395
54. Thrall L (2015) China's expanding African relations—implications for U.S. national security. RAND, Santa Monica, pp 24–25. https://doi.org/10.7249/RR905
55. Alden C, Hughes CR (2009) Harmony and discord in China's Africa strategy: some implications for foreign policy. China Q 199:566. https://doi.org/10.1017/S0305741009990105; Eisenman J, Kurlantzick J (2006) China's Africa strategy. Current Hist 105(691):220
56. Arduino A (2018) China's private army: protecting the new silk road. Palgrave Macmillan, Singapore, pp 75, 79. https://doi.org/10.1007/978-981-10-7215-4
57. Arduino A (2017) China's belt and road initiative security needs—the evolution of Chinese private security companies. In: RSIS working paper series, Rajaratnam School of International Studies, Singapore, p 37
58. Arduino A (2017) China's belt and road initiative security needs—the evolution of Chinese private security companies. In: RSIS working paper series, Rajaratnam School of International Studies, Singapore, pp 5–6
59. Thrall L (2015) China's expanding African relations—implications for U.S. national security. RAND, Santa Monica, pp 52, 60. https://doi.org/10.7249/RR905
60. Arduino A (2018) China's private army: protecting the new silk road. Palgrave Macmillan, Singapore, p 36. https://doi.org/10.1007/978-981-10-7215-4
61. Wuthnow J (2006) Securing China's belt and road initiative: dimensions and implications. US-China Economic and Security Review Commission, Washington DC, p 6; Arduino A (2015) Security privatization with Chinese characteristics—the role of Chinese private security corporations in protecting Chinese outbound investments and citizens. In: RSIS policy reports, Rajaratnam School of International Studies, Singapore, p 11
62. Arduino A (2018) China's private army: protecting the new silk road. Palgrave Macmillan, Singapore, pp 36, 125, 165. https://doi.org/10.1007/978-981-10-7215-4
63. Arduino A (2017) China's belt and road initiative security needs—the evolution of Chinese private security companies. In: RSIS working paper series, Rajaratnam School of International Studies, Singapore, p 16
64. Arduino A (2018) China's private army: protecting the new silk road. Palgrave Macmillan, Singapore, p 35. https://doi.org/10.1007/978-981-10-7215-4
65. Arduino A (2017) China's belt and road initiative security needs—the evolution of Chinese private security companies. In: RSIS working paper series, Rajaratnam School of International Studies, Singapore, p 13
66. Arduino A (2017) China's belt and road initiative security needs—the evolution of Chinese private security companies. In: RSIS working paper series, Rajaratnam School of International Studies, Singapore, pp 7, 12
67. Arduino A (2018) China's private army: protecting the new silk road. Palgrave Macmillan, Singapore, p 103. https://doi.org/10.1007/978-981-10-7215-4
68. Arduino A (2017) China's belt and road initiative security needs—the evolution of Chinese private security companies. In: RSIS working paper series, Rajaratnam School of International Studies, Singapore, p 9; Arduino A (2018) China's private army: protecting the new silk road. Palgrave Macmillan, Singapore, p 165. https://doi.org/10.1007/978-981-10-7215-4
69. Thrall L (2015) China's expanding African relations—implications for U.S. national security. RAND, Santa Monica, pp xiv-xv. https://doi.org/10.7249/RR905
70. Alden C, Hughes CR (2009) Harmony and discord in China's Africa strategy: some implications for foreign policy. China Q 199:570–571. https://doi.org/10.1017/S0305741009990105
71. Eisenman J, Kurlantzick J (2006) China's Africa strategy. Curr Hist 105(691):223
72. Arduino A (2018) China's private army: protecting the new silk road. Palgrave Macmillan, Singapore, pp 72–73. https://doi.org/10.1007/978-981-10-7215-4
73. Alden C, Hughes CR (2009) Harmony and discord in China's Africa strategy: some implications for foreign policy. China Q 199:567–568. https://doi.org/10.1017/S0305741009990105

74. Wuthnow J (2006) Securing China's belt and road initiative: dimensions and implications. US-China Economic and Security Review Commission, Washington DC, p 5; Shinn DH (2009) Military and security relations: China, Africa, and the rest of the world. In: Rotberg RI (ed) China into Africa: trade, aid, and influence. Brookings Institution Press, Washington DC, p 178. https://doi.org/10.1017/S0022278X11000395
75. Arduino A (2018) China's private army: protecting the new silk road. Palgrave Macmillan, Singapore, p 136. https://doi.org/10.1007/978-981-10-7215-4
76. Arduino A (2018) China's private army: protecting the new silk road. Palgrave Macmillan, Singapore, p 120. https://doi.org/10.1007/978-981-10-7215-4
77. Borger J (20 June 2017) US shoots down second Iran-made armed drone over Syria in 12 days. The Guardian
78. Axe D (2016) Commentary: here's how the US Navy will defeat Iran's speedboats. Reuters, 30 August 2016. p 2
79. FitzGerald T, Long G, Ogier T et al (2010) Building up military muscle. Latin Trade 18(6):25
80. Boese W (2004) Missile regime puts off China. Arms Control Association. https://www.armscontrol.org/act/2004_11/MTCR. Accessed 12 April 2018

Exploring the Spread of Offensive Cyber Operations Campaigns

Holly M. Dragoo

Abstract What constitutes an act of war has evolved throughout time but is largely agreed upon by most actors either by treatise or various global norms. Established rules of engagement apply to naval, ground, air, and even aerospace battle domains. International consensus on the rules doesn't apply to cyber warfare, however, making for a murky international climate rife with tension, ambiguity, and plausible deniability. For this paper, data on national cyber programs for all UN-recognized 195 countries was coded looking for identifiable trends or interesting observations. Over 80 countries have some form of military-driven offensive cyber program. Intuitive associations that countries with a high percentage of internet users and high GDP per capita were not indicative of whether or not a country had an active offensive cyber operations campaign; nor was military size or the presence of a criminal code for cybercrimes. There was a loose association of national cybersecurity strategy and offensive cyber operations (OCO) programs, but of course it is one-directional: it's not guaranteed that countries with a national cyber strategy have OCO programs. Other observations include: states share threat intelligence regionally more than they do internationally, and sharing agreements generally mirror political security alliances. With the rapid spread and lack of determining factors, we can confirm the choice to pursue OCO is a political one.

1 Background

What constitutes an act of war has evolved throughout time but is largely agreed upon by most actors either by treatise or various global norms. Established rules of engagement apply to naval, ground, air, and even aerospace battle domains. International consensus on the rules doesn't apply to cyber warfare, however, making for a murky international climate rife with tension, ambiguity, and plausible deniability [1].

H. M. Dragoo (✉)
Georgia Institute of Technology, Atlanta, Georgia

© The Author(s), under exclusive license to Springer Nature Switzerland AG 2021
M. E. Kosal (ed.), *Proliferation of Weapons- and Dual-Use Technologies*,
Advanced Sciences and Technologies for Security Applications,
https://doi.org/10.1007/978-3-030-73655-2_9

What constitutes an act of war in cyberspace and how to respond proportionately is a comparatively newer and ongoing debate. Assuming a threshold can be agreed upon, responses necessitate accurate attribution and a calculation of a proportionate counteraction, which is an approximation at best when there is no loss of life. Complicating the issue, the Law of Armed Conflict (LOAC) allows for responses to cyberattacks be physical in nature, which in so doing escalates conflict rapidly [2]. This is a major issue for both political and military leaders, as nations struggle to determine what those thresholds are in defense strategies and doctrine [3].

Part of the complexity about offensive cyber operations (OCO) is attributable to how easily they can be confused with cybercriminal activity or intelligence gathering operations. Often, only the end result is the distinguishing factor that classifies intent behind an event. According to Chris Inglis, from his essay *Illuminating the New Domain: The Role and Nature of Intelligence, Surveillance and Reconnaissance (ISR) in Cyberspace*: "… the first 90 percent of cyber reconnaissance (i.e. ISR), cyber defense and cyberattack consisted of the common work of finding and fixing a target of interest in cyberspace. The remaining 10 percent of a given cyber action was deemed to be all that separated the three possible outcomes of reconnaissance, defense, and attack." [4].

Fundamentally, to exploit a network for overt military, covert intelligence, extortionist, or profiteering motives requires the same expertise in malware, network technology, and incremental degrees of target knowledge. Arguably this is not the case with kinetic acts of war, or terrorism. Responding to a cyberattack under this construct places perilous importance on accurate information and individual leaders' aptitude for understanding technical details. Without that understanding or situational awareness, decision-making suffers—oftentimes by uncertainty in the political realm, but always in timeliness. Not only does this have troubling ramifications in international humanitarian law (a term used interchangeably with the LOAC), but ambiguity seeds confusion and greatly slows the decision-making process [5].

Thousands of cyberattacks happen daily, everywhere. No sector is immune, from healthcare, financial services, critical infrastructure, and retail, to government networks worldwide. Ransomware attacks against enterprises are on the rise with increasingly high demands and more frequently, retaliatory information disclosures when organizations refuse to pay. Losses reportedly total in the billions of dollars and incalculable intellectual property theft and risk to municipal and national security [6]. This high-stakes climate has prompted governments to revise cyber defense postures and seek collaborative opportunities beyond their own borders to address the common threats. One such call for international norms in cyberspace is the Budapest Convention on Cybercrime—which has 65 ratified members and counting as of this writing [7]. Even the North Atlantic Treaty Organization (NATO) has officially declared that its famous Article 5 collective defense clause can be used in the event of a cyberattack on one of the 30 member nations [8]. This is likely an attempt to deter would be attackers in the same manner that the original NATO kinetic strike back security pact did. Building norms and institutions in this space is beneficial, but it takes time and consensus to achieve—neither of which is prominent in cybersecurity.

As this dynamic policy space has evolved, so too has deterrence theory. The popular trend to analogize cyber warfare to nuclear warfare simply crumbles on inspection [9]. What was once a space clearly dominated by a nuclear club of few members (those with the scientific knowledge and vast resources to develop and maintain a nuclear stockpile), has now morphed into a free-for-all market of easily attainable, affordable cyber weapons. With barriers to entry into the cyber realm quite low, state-run offensive cyber programs have proliferated in recent years, making for a strategic dilemma that is almost the inverse of the cold war-era nuclear club. Allyship is a strong force that can be used to mitigate shared threats on the battlefield, as countless nuclear security pacts have demonstrated, but in cyber warfare, linked states tend to expand the list of vulnerabilities and attack surfaces between partners, not necessarily build up stockpiles in a collective arsenal.

For deterrence and coercion to work, a nation must be able to clearly communicate a credible, verifiable threat to an adversary. In the nuclear world, this was easy—a public show or test of a bomb. When an adversary is shown what consequences await a given set of actions, options narrow, and a path forward can be chosen (or not as it may be). In cyberspace, the very act of disclosing what capacity a nation has for dispensing credible threats requires a level of specificity that is precisely what enables the adversary to shore up their defenses. In many cases the only real vulnerability isn't the specific technological threat posed by the aggressor, but rather the oppressive scale of how challenging it is for networks of any size to standardize endpoint security and synchronize configuration updates/settings management. This idiosyncrasy nullifies deterrence tactics, leaving us with a growing number of states seeking to arm themselves with cheap technologies that can have potentially devastating effects, and few exemplary forms of regulation or governance.

So why do states pursue OCO at all? Max Smeets suggests in his writing "The Strategic Promise of Offensive Cyber Operations" that the decision for states to pursue OCO capacity may in fact be unrelated to deterrence, but it may simply be to increase a state's menu of options for achieving specific policy goals. "They can serve as a force multiplier as well as an independent strategic asset" [10]. A good example of this is in the 2020 dispute between Egypt and Ethiopia over the Grand Dam project. Construction of the dam on the Nile river in Ethiopia will bring significant economic benefits and power to the resource-starved country, but the Nile is the sole source of water to agrarian Egypt and it's 100 million residents. Ethiopia has claimed to be victim of a campaign of cyber harassment, defacements on official dam-related websites and an unsuccessful cyberattack attempted by the Cyber_Horus Group, affiliated with Egyption nationals, but not confirmed to be linked to the government [11]. Full attribution to the threat actors is immaterial here as the ambiguity works to Egypts advantage, keeps conflict to a minimum, provides plausible deniability, and yet likely achieves some policy goals of the government, to delay or degrade progress on the dam. It's unlikely other types of strategic assets available to official decision-makers could have achieved the same effects; let alone with minimal casualties and/or escalation.

Broadly, publications on cybersecurity tend to fall in one of a few categories: how to defend networks; current threat/law/breach trends; aggregate statistics on cyberattacks and intellectual property theft; or vulnerabilities in consumer goods and emerging technologies. To a lesser extent, there are pieces on policies affecting privacy issues or product standards, but there isn't much literature on how governments are incorporating cybersecurity strategies into domestic or foreign policy, or military doctrine [12]. In part this is because books (in particular) about anything cyber-related are quickly outdated and partly because legal frameworks, legislative bodies, and politicians don't adapt as quickly as technology evolves. Other factors, such as security classification—research and development work, and network defense tactics—often reside behind the wall of official secrecy. The purpose in looking at this topic is to characterize what types of states pursue offensive cyber operations (OCO) (is there a type?), expand the dialogue on the proliferation of OCO, and aggregate disparate data outside classified channels. Hopefully the compilation of data points and accompanying analysis can confirm theories and be used as a resource for other proliferation or cybersecurity researchers.

2 Motivation

Fear-mongering about the potential for countries to levy war in novel ways has gone unchecked, often by people citing a few genuinely scary events as having the potential to become the new normal in a 'wild west' cyber dystopia. The 2015 Russian cyberattacks on the Ukrainian power grid or the 2016 hack on a still-undisclosed water treatment facility (that was likely ineffective criminals at work but could also easily be a test run for state OCO) are frequently referenced as examples of how easy it would be for an attacker, even acting as a lone wolf, to affect large swaths of a civilian population with malicious intent [13]. Conventional wisdom suggests terrifying, valid scenarios abound, but there's really only a handful of countries with the credible capacity to threaten such an attack, let alone levy one. Or are there? More and more we are seeing countries advertise investment in OCO capabilities; even traditionally benign or pacifist nations are coming forward with voluntary disclosures of military elements prepared to pursue adversaries in cyberspace [14]. Why is this? It is possibly a shift towards an attempt at deterrence in cyberspace. Deterrence and uniform messaging of consequences to potential attackers is important to a strong cyber defense.

Having a declared deterrence policy does not (and will never) prevent cyberattacks from happening, and it commits nations to certain costs to maintain credibility (or risk being perceived as weak). However, apart from criminal code penalties and hardening networks—that can be ineffective with foreign or state-sponsored aggressors—the sheer volume of attacks and impunity with which attackers operate suggest there are no real costs that will deter potential attackers [15]. Yet countries still pursue OCO investment; the deterrence value is either perceived, or prestige-driven. The absence of specific criteria for determining what an act of war vis-à-vis an 'act of aggression' looks like in cyberspace only exacerbates this problem. No action, or a delayed action in response to a cyber event (or even a kinetic event) can reveal a disjointed defense posture or give the impression attacks will be tolerated. Psychological value aside, governments simply can't afford to continue bypassing political response to cyber events given the likelihood of their occurrence and increasing severity of political impact.

At this time, there is no *known, publicly available* [16] example of a political response plan designed to handle fallout from a large-scale cyber breach on a military or government network (or critical infrastructure) in the United States. Presumably one would not be too different from a natural disaster or other battle damage recovery plan, but it would be nice to confirm this. Even without a plan, time sensitivity to the original aggression is key; a retaliatory cyberattack loses relevance if the strike is delivered 6 months ex post facto. In the wake of such an attack, many states would be reluctant to engage in a (proportionate) cyber-focused counterattack due to lack of resources, mobilization capacity, and control over escalation. Chief among these factors is controlling escalation. What happens if a big, well-equipped Nation A attacks comparatively smaller, ill-equipped Nation B in cyberspace? If Nation B retaliates, it will likely only do so in ways to avoid escalation it can't afford, even if the calculus includes a physical response. That is, if it takes any action at all. Additionally, to retaliate in kind requires an in-depth understanding of adversarial network topology, its vulnerabilities, and a certainty that the target in question is in fact the entity that attacked, not a (witting or not) proxy for a different actor. Often the process of attribution alone can stymie reaction times.

Attacks that required the type of calculus described above can be seen in these examples: the 2019 hack on the Chilean company Redbanc (which manages the entire national ATM infrastructure) by the DPRK-sponsored Lazarus Group; the 2015 French TV5Monde hack by Russia masquerading as an Islamic group called the Cyber Caliphate; and most poignantly the 2007 multi-sector Russian cyber assault on Estonian government, financial, and media networks. In the DPRK/Chile case, it's not known what retaliatory actions were taken, if any. The current capacity of the Chilean government to conduct OCO is unknown, but they are a member of the Organization of American States (OAS), which has active cyber defense and threat intelligence sharing institutions in place. France and Estonia are both NATO members, and could have filed for an Article Five defense petition from the collective, but they did not - even when attribution was as clear and quick. In all three cases, public 'outing' of the aggressors was the only real recourse available to the victims in the given time constraints.

Since near real-time counterstrikes in cyberspace are impracticable, conflicts often get disclosed to the press in an attempt to publicly shame the attacker, or they go unanswered. Humiliation is a powerful and centuries-old tactic, though, one that may actually be a cause to use OCO, not just an effect of it, as Max Smeets points out [10]. However, collective action, or the threat thereof, appears to be gaining traction as an alternative. In 2018, NATO established a Cyber Operations Center for member states to coordinate and execute operations [17]. These groups appear to help de-escalate tensions and assist in capacity building by increasing readiness with a proactive defense posture.

Stakeholders in these scenarios range from critical infrastructure providers to law enforcement agencies to Ministries of Foreign Affairs, but this research primarily focuses on Ministry of Defense perceptions and motivations. Most cyberattacks focus on the victims and coordinated mitigation response as that is, according to the National Institute of Standards and Technology (NIST) Guide for Cyber Event Recovery, the first order of business should an attack happen [18]. After quarantining the site of the attack, the next most important step is determining attribution. Attribution is difficult, but key to enabling official responses in all scenarios. Why did the attack occur? If criminal activity can be ruled out, adversarial militaries (often inextricably linked to intelligence services) are assuredly the aggressors. Identifying why increasing numbers of militaries are choosing to openly adopt overt OCO programs may shed some light on why some attacks happen and how to be proactive in defending against them.

3 Methodology

Questions driving this research include the following: What types of states pursue OCO? Are there any statistical profile data about countries or regions that can be shown to be driving the rapid spread of declared OCO programs? What can we learn from the collective countries who have declared campaigns? Are there predictive indicators for whether a country will pursue OCO in military doctrine? Lastly, do regional cybersecurity groups impact the proliferation of military OCO?

Quantitative research for this project begins with a survey of four primary independent variables: state capacity for offensive cyber military or intelligence collection campaigns; how many may have attempted to develop national cybersecurity strategy documents; national-level computer emergency response teams/computer security incident response teams (CERT/CSIRTs); and legal frameworks that address crime in cyberspace. These particular factors demonstrate a nation's commitment to addressing the complexities of economic, military, and legal aspects of cyberspace, and therefore can be seen as potential precursors but not necessarily prerequisites or causative drivers of OCO programs. Put another way, not all nations have cybersecurity strategies and conduct OCO; but almost all nations that conduct OCO have some minimal form of an overarching cyber strategy (though there are exceptions). To contextualize these variables, basic economic data such as GDP per capita, percentage of Internet users, and size of the national military have been included. Looking at these primary factors as independent variables along with the contextual data will help to gauge a country's likelihood to pursue OCO campaigns or collaborate in international organizations focused on cybersecurity concerns (the dependent variables).

For consistency, this research focuses on the military aspects of cyber warfare, a type of technology and personnel skill set that can be used for both civilian and military purposes; commonly referred to as "dual-use" technology. As such, in evaluating source material it becomes keenly important to distinguish who is conducting the cyber activities. Whenever sources suggested said activities were being conducted by national police or gendarmerie, those data points were disregarded. While there might be privacy or authoritarian concerns in these countries, it was more frequently the case that they did not have a military and would be therefore unlikely to prosecute international attacks. Conversely, anytime a record indicated the military was conducting cyber surveillance on its own population, this activity was counted as having OCO capabilities, since the effort to convert these technical tools and staff to battle-ready forces would likely be minimal.

By highlighting the similarities and differences among regional groups, this research attempts to ascertain if there are trends or irregularities that warrant explanation or further research. Data presented here has been manually coded for 193 countries drawing from a litany of publicly available sources but relying heavily on press releases from ministries of defense and the like wherever possible. Questioning the veracity of the claims made by any official mouthpiece is valid, but for these purposes is irrelevant; again, the *threat of attack is just as useful as the capacity to attack*.

For this research, a lot of useful statistics came from the International Telecommunications Union (ITU) Cyber Wellness Profiles such as the listing of national strategy documents, percentage of Internet users, and CERTs registered by state [19]. While the ITU data required some verification for changes over time, it largely overlapped with several independent articles and other data sources like the CIA World Factbook and the UN Institute for Disarmament Research (UNIDIR) [20, 21]. Population and GDP per capita figures came from the UN Department of Economic and Social Affairs [20]; and the military strength numbers came from *The Military Balance 2019* by the International Institute for Strategic Studies (IISS). The UN Conference on Trade and Development (UNCTAD) has wonderfully current and comprehensive data on cybersecurity legislation by country that was also instructive [22].

4 Data and Analysis

Initial reflections from the data on the four primary variables show that out of 193 total countries, there are 96 with declared OCO (50%), 138 (72%) have national cybersecurity strategies in some form, 126 (65%) have national-level CERTs, and 169 (88%) have laws that cover cyberspace intrusions [23].

From the outset, we can see that percentage of the population with access to the Internet is not a factor in determining if a country will pursue OCO. India only has 20% of its population connected, Pakistan 17%, and Zimbabwe has 27%, and all three have declared offensive cyber capabilities. Egypt (57%), Honduras (32%), and Algeria (49%) add evidence to this assertion and suggest it is not specific to one region. Thus, while the expectation is to see well-connected, tech-savvy countries to be the primary actors in the OCO arena, a statistically significant group—almost a quarter (23%)—of all OCO countries have less than half the population with access to the Internet, preventing any gross generalizations about access to technology/infrastructure, wealth, or other resource allocations.

GDP per capita and total population, on their own, are obviously not indicators that a country might have OCO: 64% of all countries claiming to have OCO have a population of more than 10 million, and 43% have a GDP of more than $20,000 per capita. From this, it can be derived that small countries are just as likely to be interested in investing in OCO as large countries—and interestingly, that low income doesn't seem to be an obstacle for those with a desire to pursue OCO [24]. Correlation is certainly not causation, but one could theorize based on this data that the lower income countries that are investing resources in OCO programs are doing so as an affordable military deterrent than costly research like advanced weapon systems or nuclear programs. When factoring in the bonus of societal impact from upgraded telecommunications infrastructure and a highly-trained cybersecurity workforce, the incentives to invest in OCO are clear for both civil and military reasons [25].

A note about the military variable: for purposes of this research, I chose to classify countries with less than 10,000 soldiers (total ready reserve plus active duty) as having "no" military. Doing so helps refine the data pool, since I have defined OCO as military in nature, then by extension these countries do not have OCO. Most countries have armed forces of some kind, even if it is functioning more like a national police force, but militaries of this size often don't have the capacity to fund or prioritize an OCO program, let alone hire qualified staff for standard network defense. Keeping this in mind, of the 193 countries surveyed, 56 have no military at all (or a force of less than 10,000) [26]. Unsurprisingly, these are nations high in poverty rates and relatively unplugged with 83% of them having a GDP of less than $20,000 per capita, and 57% have less than 50% of the population with Internet access.

While the data doesn't say much independently, looking at data by regionally-focused treaty groups (in no particular order), reveals a few trends.

NATO, for example, has 30 members, 90% of which have declared OCO programs or capabilities. A comprehensive approach to cybersecurity is commonly held, and in 2016 the organization itself embraced cyberspace as a valid attack vector in which to invoke the famous defense pact clause, Article 5, of the Treaty [27]. All of the NATO members have laws that cover cybercrime, national cybersecurity strategies, CERTs, and public-private partnerships established. The focus of these programs is international and security-minded, not surveillance-based. With membership primarily including six of the wealthiest economies and best-funded militaries, these numbers are unsurprising [28] (Fig. 1).

The Arab League is a regional group and voting block focused on policies and economic integration of Arabic-speaking nations. It has 21 members, 17 (81%) of which have declared OCO capacity. Of the four countries who do not, Kuwait and Djibouti enjoy substantial security cooperation agreements with the US (also China in the case of Djibouti), including substantial provisions for cybersecurity. Just over half (12 members) have chosen to dedicate their programs to domestic surveillance activities, which is unsurprising as 8 are run as dictatorships or monarchical societies, and most do not have any form of cyber defense public-private partnership (PPP). As for criminal legislation, 100% of the Arab League nations have enacted laws that cover cybercrime, which is an increase of over 30% in just two years, which

Exploring the Spread of Offensive Cyber Operations Campaigns

Flag	Country	Population	Internet Users (%pop)	GDP per capita	Active Duty + Reserve	Military (Y/N)	OCO (Y/N)	CIRT (Y/N)	Nat'l Strategy	Criminal Law (Y/N)	NATO
	Albania	2,877,797	70%	$5,353	8,500	Y	Y	Y	Y	Y	Y
	Belgium	11,607,826	90%	$46,117	31,650	Y	Y	Y	Y	Y	Y
	Bulgaria	6,929,706	68%	$9,738	34,300	Y	N	Y	Y	Y	Y
	Canada	37,864,223	93%	$46,195	109,273	Y	Y	Y	Y	Y	Y
	Croatia	4,096,433	79%	$14,853	36,550	Y	Y	Y	Y	Y	Y
	Czech Republic	10,715,004	81%	$23,102	23,200	Y	Y	Y	Y	Y	Y
	Denmark	5,799,967	98%	$59,822	60,200	Y	Y	Y	Y	Y	Y
	Estonia	1,326,401	90%	$23,660	34,400	Y	Y	Y	Y	Y	Y
	France	65,332,284	83%	$40,494	383,600	Y	Y	Y	Y	Y	Y
	Germany	83,863,869	88%	$46,259	207,650	Y	Y	Y	Y	Y	Y
	Greece	10,404,846	76%	$19,583	366,850	Y	Y	Y	Y	Y	Y
	Hungary	9,650,845	80%	$16,476	59,800	Y	Y	Y	Y	Y	Y
	Iceland	342,046	99%	$66,945	250	N	N	Y	Y	Y	Y
	Italy	60,439,467	74%	$33,190	365,100	Y	Y	Y	Y	Y	Y
	Latvia	1,878,700	86%	$17,836	22,110	Y	Y	Y	Y	Y	Y
	Lithuania	2,709,301	82%	$19,456	40,950	Y	Y	Y	Y	Y	Y
	Luxembourg	629,593	97%	$114,705	1,500	N	N	Y	Y	Y	Y
	Montenegro	628,200	73%	$8,832	12,050	Y	Y	Y	Y	Y	Y
	Netherlands	17,148,932	93%	$52,448	45,800	Y	Y	Y	Y	Y	Y
	Norway	5,437,711	98%	$75,420	63,250	Y	Y	Y	Y	Y	Y
	Poland	37,828,668	85%	$15,595	191,200	Y	Y	Y	Y	Y	Y
	Portugal	10,185,058	75%	$23,145	263,850	Y	Y	Y	Y	Y	Y
	Romania	19,193,766	74%	$12,920	176,300	Y	Y	Y	Y	Y	Y
	Slovakia	5,460,446	83%	$19,329	15,850	Y	Y	Y	Y	Y	Y
	Slovenia	2,078,938	83%	$25,739	14,700	Y	Y	Y	Y	Y	Y
	Spain	46,753,305	91%	$29,614	211,300	Y	Y	Y	Y	Y	Y
	Turkey	84,664,105	74%	$9,043	890,700	Y	Y	Y	Y	Y	Y
	United Kingdom	68,016,054	93%	$42,300	228,350	Y	Y	Y	Y	Y	Y
	United States	331,723,851	88%	$65,118	2,205,050	Y	Y	Y	Y	Y	Y

Fig. 1 Data on NATO countries

demonstrates intent and suggests substantial investment is forthcoming. However, just 48% have established national-level CERTs, likely due to the large role cooperative defense agreements such as the Arab Convention (aka The Arab Convention on Combating Information Technology Offenses), the Organization of The Islamic Cooperation-Computer Emergency Response Team (OIC-CERT), among others, that make resource pooling possible among members (Fig. 2).

The *African Union (AU)* is a continental union of all 55 African states dedicated to the collective defense, socio-economic prosperity, and political alignment of its members. Only one fifth of the 55 members have declared OCO programs, and one state's status is difficult to determine from publicly available sources. On the other

Flag	Country	Population	Internet Users (%pop)	GDP per capita	Active Duty + Reserve	Military (Y/N)	OCO (Y/N)	CIRT (Y/N)	Nat'l Strategy	Criminal Law (Y/N)	AL
	Egypt	103,045,021	57%	$3,020	1,314,500	Y	Y	N	Y	Y	Y
	Iraq	40,572,741	75%	$5,955	338,000	Y	Y	N	Y	Y	Y
	Jordan	10,248,255	67%	$4,330	180,500	Y	Y	N	Y	Y	Y
	Kuwait	4,296,814	100%	$32,032	48,300	Y	N	N	Y	Y	Y
	Lebanon	6,825,847	78%	$7,784	80,000	Y	Y	N	Y	Y	Y
	Libya	6,902,891	22%	$7,684	57,000	Y	Y	Y	Y	Y	Y
	Mauritania	4,695,049	21%	$1,678	20,850	Y	Y	N	Y	Y	Y
	Morocco	37,071,105	74%	$3,204	395,800	Y	Y	Y	Y	Y	Y
	Oman	5,157,241	92%	$15,474	47,000	Y	Y	Y	Y	Y	Y
	Qatar	2,901,944	100%	$64,782	21,500	Y	Y	Y	Y	Y	Y
	Saudi Arabia	35,021,580	96%	$23,140	251,500	Y	Y	Y	Y	Y	Y
	Somalia	16,058,347	2%	$127	19,800	Y	N	N	N	N	Y
	Sudan	44,228,395	31%	$442	209,300	Y	Y	Y	Y	Y	Y
	Syrian Arab Republic	17,642,082	34%	$2,033	239,000	Y	Y	Y	Y	Y	Y
	Tunisia	11,862,145	67%	$3,318	47,800	Y	Y	Y	Y	Y	Y
	United Arab Emirates	9,930,714	99%	$43,103	63,000	Y	Y	Y	Y	Y	Y
	Yemen	30,069,715	27%	$968	40,000	Y	Y	N	N	Y	Y

Fig. 2 Data on the Arab League countries

end of the spectrum, another fifth do not even have cyber criminal legislation on the books. This low number is likely explained by the lack of digital infrastructure, with 24 countries showing less than 20% of the population with reliable access to the Internet, and 17 countries with GDP per capita figures under $1,000. Food security, clean water, and public health concerns are recurrent issues in the region that rightfully get prioritized above cyber defense needs. When capacity building groups do get to prioritize cybersecurity, they focus on national strategic policies, legal and telecommunications infrastructure; not so much on enforcement mechanisms or even domestic surveillance. The situation is changing, however, as 22 AU states also have established domestic CERTs. All of these CERTs partner with the top-level domain registrant AFRINIC, and umbrella organization AfricaCERT. These groups have increased collaboration and network defense substantially among AU members, by establishing communication channels in government and telecommunications industry partners, and investment in education and workforce training [29].

Ironically, in 2014, the AU drafted a cybersecurity strategy for the collective, covering basic principles for personal data protection and electronic commercial transactions [30]. Only 8 states have ratified the convention though, out of 14 signatories, each with no discernable cyber commitments such as cyber strategies, laws, or CERTs. This discrepancy suggests there may be less obvious barriers to engaging in cyberspace cooperation that happen to coincide with significant developmental challenges (Fig. 3).

The *Shanghai Cooperation Organization (SCO)* is an intergovernmental alliance comprised of 12 Eurasian state members and observers [31], also cooperating on political, economic and security issues. This group, and a partner group of militaries called the Cooperative Security Treaty Organization (CSTO) [32] have recently formally agreed to start sharing cyber threat intelligence, tools, etc. and initiate a Cyber Shield program [33]. It remains to be seen what this Cyber Shield will look like beyond "active defense," but all SCO members already have declared OCO programs, focused on both international activities and domestic network traffic— with the exception of Afghanistan, which is receiving substantive cyber support from NATO's International Security Assistance Force (ISAF). Additionally, all SCO states have laws that cover cybercrime, and 63% of SCO countries have a national cybersecurity strategy. Kyrgyzstan is the only state that does not have a national CERT (Fig. 4).

The *Association of SE Asian Nations (ASEAN)* has started a Cyber Capacity Programme, designed to help its 10 members (and 2 observer nations) generate model legislation, strategy, and improve cyber incident response. Member state delegations and their CERTs participate in workshops at working and leadership levels annually. The Programme has been quite successful in improving the numbers: all 10 members have cybercrime laws in force, CERTs stood up, and 7 have national strategies drafted with public-private-partnerships in place. This is a dramatic change in two years when less than half did. Trying to derive meaning from this small sampling of data points is challenging as the basic profile data for this group runs the gamut from the extremely small kingdom of Brunei (less than 1 million population) to over 110 m people in the Philippines; from 11% of the populace wired for the Internet in Papua New Guinea

Flag	Country	Population	Internet Users (%pop)	GDP per capita	Active Duty + Reserve	Military (Y/N)	OCO (Y/N)	CIRT (Y/N)	Nat'l Strategy	Criminal Law (Y/N)	AU
	Algeria	44,136,123	49%	$3,948	467,200	Y	Y	Y	N	Y	Y
	Angola	33,249,993	14%	$2,974	117,000	Y	N	N	N	Y	Y
	Benin	12,241,117	12%	$1,219	12,050	N	N	Y	Y	Y	Y
	Botswana	2,368,090	41%	$7,961	9,000	N	N	Y	Y	Y	Y
	Burkina Faso	21,116,759	16%	$775	11,450	Y	N	Y	Y	Y	Y
	Burundi	12,021,687	3%	$261	51,050	Y	N	N	N	Y	Y
	Cameroon	26,790,804	23%	$1,498	24,400	Y	N	Y	N	Y	Y
	Cape Verde	558,129	57%	$3,604	1,200	N	N	N	N	Y	Y
	Central African Republi	4,859,481	4%	$468	8,150	N	N	N	N	N	Y
	Chad	16,602,009	6%	$710	34,850	Y	N	N	N	N	Y
	Comoros	876,427	8%	$1,394	500	N	N	N	N	Y	Y
	Côte d'Ivoire	26,619,876	36%	$2,286	27,400	Y	N	Y	N	Y	Y
	Democratic Republic of	90,574,419	9%	$545	134,250	Y	N	N	N	N	Y
	Djibouti	993,221	56%	$3,409	13,100	Y	N	N	N	Y	Y
	Egypt	103,045,021	57%	$3,020	1,314,500	Y	Y	Y	Y	Y	Y
	Equatorial Guinea	1,420,121	26%	$8,132	1,450	N	N	N	N	N	Y
	Eritrea	3,564,762	1%	$643	321,750	Y	N	N	N	N	Y
	Eswatini (Fmr. Swazilan	1,164,450	29%	$3,911	0	N	N	N	N	Y	Y
	Ethiopia	116,018,817	19%	$858	138,000	Y	N	Y	N	Y	Y
	Gabon	2,245,682	50%	$7,667	6,700	N	N	N	N	N	Y
	Gambia	2,441,971	20%	$751	800	N	N	N	Y	Y	Y
	Ghana	31,312,587	38%	$2,202	15,500	Y	N	Y	Y	Y	Y
	Guinea	13,262,394	22%	$1,064	12,300	Y	N	N	N	Y	Y
	Guinea-Bissau	1,985,272	4%	$698	4,450	N	N	N	N	N	Y
	Kenya	54,212,731	23%	$1,817	29,100	Y	Y	Y	Y	Y	Y
	Lesotho	2,148,408	30%	$1,158	2,000	N	N	N	N	Y	Y
	Liberia	5,101,999	8%	$622	2,010	N	N	N	N	N	Y
	Libya	6,902,891	22%	$7,684	57,000	Y	Y	Y	Y	Y	Y
	Madagascar	27,955,192	5%	$522	21,600	Y	N	N	N	Y	Y
	Malawi	19,314,994	14%	$412	14,900	N	N	N	Y	Y	Y
	Mali	20,467,343	13%	$891	17,800	Y	N	N	N	Y	Y
	Mauritania	4,695,049	21%	$1,678	20,850	Y	Y	N	Y	Y	Y
	Mauritius	1,272,437	64%	$11,204	2,550	N	N	Y	Y	Y	Y
	Morocco	37,071,105	74%	$3,204	395,800	Y	Y	Y	Y	Y	Y
	Mozambique	31,579,471	21%	$492	11,200	Y	N	Y	N	Y	Y
	Namibia	2,557,776	37%	$4,958	15,900	Y	N	N	N	N	Y
	Niger	24,536,043	5%	$555	10,700	Y	N	N	N	Y	Y
	Nigeria	208,037,661	7%	$2,230	215,000	Y	N	Y	Y	Y	Y
	Rwanda	13,069,530	22%	$802	35,000	Y	Y	Y	Y	Y	Y
	Sao Tome and Principe	220,766	30%	$1,995	300	N	N	N	N	Y	Y
	Senegal	16,907,175	30%	$1,447	18,600	Y	N	N	Y	Y	Y
	Seychelles	98,481	59%	$17,402	420	N	N	N	N	Y	Y
	Sierra Leone	8,036,711	13%	$505	8,500	N	N	N	Y	Y	Y
	Somalia	16,058,347	2%	$127	19,800	Y	N	N	N	N	Y
	South Africa	59,583,765	56%	$6,001	80,400	Y	Y	Y	Y	Y	Y
	South Sudan	11,251,847	8%	$1,120	185,000	Y	N	N	N	Y	Y
	Sudan	44,228,395	31%	$442	209,300	Y	Y	Y	Y	Y	Y
	Tanzania	60,367,278	16%	$1,122	108,400	Y	N	Y	Y	Y	Y
	Togo	8,351,044	12%	$676	9,300	N	N	N	N	Y	Y
	Tunisia	11,862,145	67%	$3,318	47,800	Y	Y	Y	Y	Y	Y
	Uganda	46,263,990	22%	$777	56,400	Y	Unk	Y	Y	Y	Y
	Zambia	18,576,679	14%	$1,291	19,500	Y	N	Y	Y	Y	Y
	Zimbabwe	14,945,692	27%	$1,464	50,800	Y	Y	N	Y	Y	Y

Fig. 3 Data on African Union countries

to 95% in Brunei; and GDP per capita figures ranging from $1,300 in Timor Leste to $65,000 in Singapore.

The remarkable fact is that 80% do have OCO capabilities now, with Laos and Brunei as the holdouts plus both observer states, none of which have militaries save Laos. Interestingly, this figure actually remains the same even when looking at the broader ASEAN Regional Forum (ARF), with almost triple the participants (26 diplomatic partners plus the EU). Japan has a substantial presence in the ARF on cyber issues, reflected in the bi-lateral cybersecurity agreements with five core ASEAN states. ASEAN is the only regional group with such an influential, singular partner in the bilateral space (Figs. 5 and 6).

One of the most comprehensive regional cybersecurity sharing programs is the *Organization of American States (OAS)*, the world's oldest regional political forum,

Fig. 4 Shanghai Cooperation Organization country data

Flag	Country	Population	Internet Users (%pop)	GDP per capita	Active Duty + Reserve	Military (Y/N)	OCO (Y/N)	CIRT (Y/N)	Nat'l Strategy	Criminal Law (Y/N)	SCO
	Afghanistan	38,928,346	11%	$502	323,000	Y	N	Y	Y	Y	O
	Armenia	2,965,384	68%	$4,623	259,100	Y	Y	Y	Y	Y	DP
	Azerbaijan	10,172,370	80%	$4,794	381,950	Y	Unk	Y	Y	Y	DP
	Belarus	9,447,985	83%	$6,663	444,850	Y	Y	Y	Y	Y	O
	Cambodia	16,803,557	41%	$1,643	191,300	Y	Y	Y	N	Y	DP
	China	1,441,296,983	54%	$10,262	3,205,000	Y	Y	Y	Y	Y	Y
	India	1,384,984,120	20%	$2,104	5,126,450	Y	Y	Y	Y	Y	Y
	Iran	84,375,195	70%	$5,520	2,010,000	Y	Y	Y	Y	Y	O
	Kazakhstan	18,859,317	82%	$9,731	70,500	Y	Y	Y	Y	Y	Y
	Kyrgyzstan	6,563,291	38%	$1,309	20,400	Y	Y	N	N	Y	Y
	Mongolia	3,297,437	51%	$4,295	154,200	Y	Y	Y	N	Y	O
	Nepal	29,306,995	21%	$1,071	111,600	Y	N	Y	Y	Y	DP
	Pakistan	222,462,762	17%	$1,285	935,800	Y	Y	Y	N	Y	Y
	Russian Federation	145,952,809	83%	$11,585	3,454,000	Y	Y	Y	Y	Y	Y
	Sri Lanka	21,446,328	34%	$3,853	353,100	Y	Y	Y	Y	Y	DP
	Tajikistan	9,615,321	22%	$871	16,300	Y	N	N	N	Y	Y
	Turkey	84,664,105	74%	$9,043	890,700	Y	Y	Y	Y	Y	DP
	Uzbekistan	33,643,979	55%	$1,725	68,000	Y	Y	Y	Y	Y	Y

Fig. 4 Shanghai Cooperation Organization country data

Flag	Country	Population	Internet Users (%pop)	GDP per capita	Active Duty + Reserve	Military (Y/N)	OCO (Y/N)	CIRT (Y/N)	Nat'l Strategy	Criminal Law (Y/N)	ASEAN
	Brunei Darussalam	438,951	95%	$31,087	8,400	N	N	Y	Y	Y	Y
	Cambodia	16,803,557	41%	$1,643	191,300	Y	Y	Y	N	Y	Y
	Indonesia	274,587,605	48%	$4,136	1,075,500	Y	Y	Y	Y	Y	Y
	Laos	7,313,719	26%	$2,535	129,100	Y	N	Y	N	Y	Y
	Malaysia	32,516,363	84%	$11,415	431,800	Y	Y	Y	Y	Y	Y
	Myanmar	54,548,118	24%	$1,408	513,000	Y	Y	Y	N	Y	Y
	Papua New Guinea	9,009,423	11%	$2,845	3,600	N	N	Y	N	N	O
	Philippines	110,122,324	43%	$3,485	334,450	Y	Y	Y	Y	Y	Y
	Singapore	5,868,421	89%	$65,233	1,468,091	Y	Y	Y	Y	Y	Y
	Thailand	69,863,324	67%	$7,808	699,550	Y	Y	Y	Y	Y	Y
	Timor-Leste	1,327,686	27%	$1,294	2,280	N	N	N	N	N	O
	Vietnam	97,654,249	69%	$2,715	5,522,000	Y	Y	Y	Y	Y	Y

Fig. 5 ASEAN country data

Flag	Country	Population	Internet Users (%pop)	GDP per capita	Active Duty + Reserve	Military (Y/N)	OCO (Y/N)	CIRT (Y/N)	Nat'l Strategy	Criminal Law (Y/N)	ASEAN
	Australia	25,609,233	87%	$54,907	78,100	Y	Y	Y	Y	Y	DP
	Bangladesh	165,286,322	13%	$1,856	220,950	Y	Y	Y	Y	Y	DP
	Brunei Darussalam	438,951	95%	$31,087	8,400	N	N	Y	Y	Y	Y
	Cambodia	16,803,557	41%	$1,643	191,300	Y	Y	Y	N	Y	Y
	Canada	37,864,223	93%	$46,195	109,273	Y	Y	Y	Y	Y	DP
	China	1,441,296,983	54%	$10,262	3,205,000	Y	Y	Y	Y	Y	DP
	Democratic People's Republic of Ko	25,819,508		$583	7,769,000	Y	Y	N	N	Y	DP
	India	1,384,984,120	20%	$2,104	5,126,450	Y	Y	Y	Y	Y	DP
	Indonesia	274,587,605	48%	$4,136	1,075,500	Y	Y	Y	Y	Y	Y
	Japan	126,336,681	91%	$40,247	317,150	Y	Y	Y	Y	Y	DP
	Laos	7,313,719	26%	$2,535	129,100	Y	N	Y	N	Y	Y
	Malaysia	32,516,363	84%	$11,415	431,800	Y	Y	Y	Y	Y	Y
	Mongolia	3,297,437	51%	$4,295	154,200	Y	Y	Y	N	Y	DP
	Myanmar	54,548,118	24%	$1,408	513,000	Y	Y	Y	N	Y	Y
	New Zealand	4,836,828	91%	$42,084	11,300	Y	Y	Y	Y	Y	DP
	Pakistan	222,462,762	17%	$1,285	935,800	Y	Y	Y	N	Y	DP
	Papua New Guinea	9,009,423	11%	$2,845	3,600	N	N	Y	N	N	O
	Philippines	110,122,324	43%	$3,485	334,450	Y	Y	Y	Y	Y	Y
	Republic of Korea	51,290,879	96%	$31,762	6,708,000	Y	Y	Y	Y	Y	DP
	Russian Federation	145,952,809	83%	$11,585	3,454,000	Y	Y	Y	Y	Y	DP
	Singapore	5,868,421	89%	$65,233	1,468,091	Y	Y	Y	Y	Y	Y
	Sri Lanka	21,446,328	34%	$3,853	353,100	Y	Y	Y	Y	Y	DP
	Thailand	69,863,324	67%	$7,808	699,550	Y	Y	Y	Y	Y	Y
	Timor-Leste	1,327,686	27%	$1,294	2,280	N	N	N	N	N	O
	United States	331,723,851	88%	$65,118	2,205,050	Y	Y	Y	Y	Y	DP
	Vietnam	97,654,249	69%	$2,715	5,522,000	Y	Y	Y	Y	Y	Y

Fig. 6 ASEAN Regional Forum country data

comprising 35 member states in North, Central and South America. In 2004, the OAS General Assembly set lofty goals to establish CERT organizations in every member state for a "hemispheric watch and warning network," cultivate the development of national cybersecurity strategies, and facilitate law enforcement collaboration on cybercrime [34]. The endeavor appears successful as only 38% are without a CERT, and only 4 countries remain without cybercrime legal statutes. OAS is the only group studied with a web portal set up as a resource for practicing network defenders with links to practical tools and current points of contact for inter-governmental outreach [35].

Almost half of the OAS states (15) do not meet the threshold in this research for having a standing military, reducing the pool of potential candidates for having OCO to 20. Of these 20, 11 have declared OCO investments; this is only 32% of the total OAS complement. Similar to ASEAN, OAS members have some of the highest GDP per capita nations, largest militaries, populations, and some of the smallest. Of the variables included in this research, no obvious trends or correlations were observed (Fig. 7).

In April of 2018, as a part of its national cybersecurity strategy, the Australian Cyber Security Center founded the *Pacific Cyber Security Operational Network (PaCSON)*, one of the first regional international organizations focused exclusively on cybersecurity. Member composition consists of 12 Pacific Island states, none of which have militaries, save for Australia and New Zealand, which happen to both have declared OCO programs. While publicly available data is sparse since the organization's founding, it appears civil in structure, with intent to share

Flag	Country	Population	Internet Users (%pop)	GDP per capita	Active Duty + Reserve	Military (Y/N)	OCO (Y/N)	CIRT (Y/N)	Nat'l Strategy	Criminal Law (Y/N)	OAS
	Antigua and Barbuda	98,197	73%	$17,790	260	N	N	Y	Y	Y	Y
	Argentina	45,347,550	74%	$10,006	105,450	Y	Y	Y	Y	Y	Y
	Bahamas	394,716	85%	$32,923	1,300	N	N	Y	Y	Y	Y
	Barbados	287,509	82%	$18,148	1,040	N	N	Y	Y	Y	Y
	Belize	400,305	47%	$4,815	2,350	N	N	N	Y	Y	Y
	Bolivia	11,731,645	44%	$3,552	71,200	Y	N	N	N	N	Y
	Brazil	213,104,572	70%	$8,717	2,069,500	Y	Y	Y	Y	Y	Y
	Canada	37,864,223	93%	$46,195	109,273	Y	Y	Y	Y	Y	Y
	Chile	19,170,410	82%	$14,897	161,900	Y	Y	Y	Y	Y	Y
	Colombia	51,063,722	65%	$6,432	516,050	Y	Y	Y	Y	Y	Y
	Costa Rica	5,111,117	81%	$12,238	9,800	N	N	Y	Y	Y	Y
	Cuba	11,324,608	62%	$8,822	1,234,500	Y	Y	N	Y	Y	Y
	Dominica	71,986	70%	$8,300	0	N	N	Y	N	Y	Y
	Dominican Republic	10,887,403	75%	$8,282	71,050	Y	N	N	Y	Y	Y
	Ecuador	17,738,106	54%	$6,184	158,750	Y	Y	Y	N	Y	Y
	El Salvador	6,497,852	34%	$4,187	51,400	Y	N	Y	N	Y	Y
	Grenada	112,657	59%	$10,966	0	N	N	N	Y	Y	Y
	Guatemala	18,037,535	41%	$4,620	106,900	Y	N	Y	Y	Y	Y
	Haiti	11,453,672	32%	$755	200	N	N	N	N	N	Y
	Honduras	9,962,579	32%	$2,575	82,950	Y	Y	N	N	Y	Y
	Jamaica	2,965,719	55%	$5,582	4,930	N	N	Y	Y	Y	Y
	Mexico	129,430,315	70%	$9,863	417,550	Y	Y	Y	Y	Y	Y
	Nicaragua	6,653,343	28%	$1,913	12,000	Y	N	N	Y	Y	Y
	Panama	4,339,405	64%	$15,731	26,000	N	N	Y	Y	Y	Y
	Paraguay	7,164,541	69%	$5,415	191,200	Y	N	Y	Y	Y	Y
	Peru	33,127,184	60%	$6,978	346,000	Y	N	Y	Y	Y	Y
	Saint Kitts and Nevis	53,199	81%	$19,897	450	N	N	N	N	Y	Y
	Saint Lucia	183,895	51%	$11,611	0	N	N	N	N	Y	Y
	Saint Vincent and the Grenadines	110,940	21%	$7,464	0	N	N	N	N	Y	Y
	Suriname	588,507	49%	$6,855	1,840	N	N	Y	N	Y	Y
	Trinidad and Tobago	1,401,095	77%	$17,277	4,050	N	N	Y	Y	Y	Y
	United States	331,723,851	88%	$65,118	2,205,050	Y	Y	Y	Y	Y	Y
	Uruguay	3,478,016	77%	$16,190	22,400	Y	N	Y	Y	Y	Y
	Venezuela	28,452,815	64%	$16,055	351,000	Y	Y	Y	Y	Y	Y

Fig. 7 OAS country data

working-level threat indicators of compromise (IoCs) among national CERTs, and collectively respond to regional incidents.

It may be futile to speculate about the future of such a group, but it's not hard to imagine collective cyber defense arrangements evolving from such a treaty. Hypothetically speaking, the computing power, network architecture or asset positioning of the small states could provide force multiplying aspects to the two countries with militarized OCO capacity; and conversely, Australia and New Zealand could furnish strike back capabilities for vulnerable states with little capacity to respond to cyber events. From a strategic view, this type of arrangement could be a very effective way to balance power dynamics in cyberspace with little additional investment beyond the current paperwork in place (Fig. 8).

The Caribbean Community, formalized into the economic and political group known as *CARICOM*, has no military among any of its 10 member states. Apart from workforce training and cybersecurity initiatives, there is no militarized OCO investment, as to be expected. Judging by the press reviewed in this research, this is most likely due to a lack of infrastructure and the prioritization of other basic needs. The data is included here for continuity and transparency (Fig. 9).

Flag	Country	Population	Internet Users (%pop)	GDP per capita	Active Duty + Reserve	Military (Y/N)	OCO (Y/N)	CIRT (Y/N)	Nat'l Strategy	Criminal Law (Y/N)	PaCSON
	Australia	25,609,233	87%	$54,907	78,100	Y	Y	Y	Y	Y	Y
	Fiji	898,721	50%	$6,220	9,500	N	N	Y	Y	Y	Y
	Kiribati	120,118	15%	$1,655	0	N	N	N	Y	Y	Y
	Marshall Islands	59,190	39%	$3,788	0	N	N	N	Y	N	Y
	New Zealand	4,836,828	91%	$42,084	11,300	Y	Y	Y	Y	Y	Y
	Palau	18,094	27%	$15,859	0	N	N	N	N	N	Y
	Papua New Guinea	9,009,423	11%	$2,845	3,600	N	N	Y	N	N	Y
	Samoa	55,191	34%	$4,316	0	N	N	N	Y	Y	Y
	Solomon Islands	693,178	12%	$2,128	0	N	N	N	Y	Y	Y
	Tonga	106,097	41%	$4,364	500	N	N	Y	Y	Y	Y
	Tuvalu	11,792	49%	$4,059	0	N	N	N	Y	Y	Y
	Vanuatu	309,824	26%	$3,058	0	N	N	Y	Y	N	Y

Fig. 8 PaCSON country data

Flag	Country	Population	Internet Users (%pop)	GDP per capita	Active Duty + Reserve	Military (Y/N)	OCO (Y/N)	CIRT (Y/N)	Nat'l Strategy	Criminal Law (Y/N)	CARICOM
	Antigua and Barbuda	98,197	73%	$17,790	260	N	N	Y	Y	Y	Y
	Bahamas	394,716	85%	$32,923	1,300	N	N	Y	Y	Y	Y
	Barbados	287,509	82%	$18,148	1,040	N	N	Y	Y	Y	Y
	Belize	400,305	47%	$4,815	2,350	N	N	N	Y	Y	Y
	Dominica	71,986	70%	$8,300	0	N	N	N	Y	N	Y
	Grenada	112,657	59%	$10,966	0	N	N	N	Y	Y	Y
	Guyana	788,025	37%	$5,468	4,070	N	N	Y	N	N	Y
	Haiti	11,453,672	32%	$755	200	N	N	N	N	N	Y
	Jamaica	2,965,719	55%	$5,582	4,930	N	N	Y	Y	Y	Y
	Saint Kitts and Nevis	53,199	81%	$19,897	450	N	N	N	N	Y	Y
	Saint Lucia	183,895	51%	$11,611	0	N	N	N	N	Y	Y
	Saint Vincent and the G	110,940	21%	$7,464	0	N	N	N	N	Y	Y
	Suriname	588,507	49%	$6,855	1,840	N	N	Y	Y	N	Y
	Trinidad and Tobago	1,401,095	77%	$17,277	4,050	N	N	Y	Y	Y	Y

Fig. 9 CARICOM country data

5 Challenges

Several challenges presented themselves in coding the data for this project. Chief among them was determining whether operational focus of a military unit was domestic surveillance, intelligence collection or cyber warfare. A state declaring they had a "cyber training exercise" could mean any number of things from law enforcement detecting hacking methods to totalitarian information control over a social network, or it could be monitoring international network traffic. Intent behind the technology used by the state helped determine what their offensive cyber force looked like and corresponding development level [36]. Generally speaking, all variants of surveillance are included—be it domestically or internationally focused—because the equipment and expertise needed is roughly the same.

Furthermore, it was also hard to distinguish between intelligence collection activity and warfare preparatory work that facilitates battlespace situational awareness (aka "battlespace prep"). Dr. Herb Lin, Senior Research Scholar on cyber issues at the Hoover Institution, sums it up well: "Access paths to the target for a given cyber weapon must be established in advance, and such access paths must be maintained and concealed until the weapon is used. If it is not concealed, the adversary may well eliminate that path and thus negate the weapon's effectiveness against the target until another access path is found." [37]. Of course, there are no publicly available accounts discussing intelligence operations details, but the ambiguity further complicates the task of classifying an organization as pure military, civilian intelligence, law enforcement, or a staff support agency that happens to perform those functions in advance.

Since this chapter is focused on OCO as an orchestrated effort embraced by military doctrine, national police forces that have the capacity to conduct cyber operations should not be counted as states with OCO capabilities. The key here is *who* is conducting the activity. The ambiguity between intelligence, surveillance, and OCO was counted in all regards if it was conducted by armed forces. If it was by national police, however, it was not counted. Omitting these activities typically only affected nations with small populations and military forces numbering less than 10,000 people. Fiji was one such state, and several sources characterized their national capabilities as "offensive"—but they did not have a military, so international cyberattack readiness of any kind was unlikely; a few sources also reported Fiji as having no cyber capacity whatsoever.

In many cases, sources implied cybersecurity strategies were only "offensive" or "defensive" in nature but no evidence existed to corroborate the polarity or even confirm operations of any kind (foreign or domestic) were happening. In fact, the Japanese constitution prohibits the development of offensive forces of any kind, and espouses a legal system that views all cyberattacks as cybercrime, not armed attacks [38]. Hence the Japanese Defense Force's (JDF) Cyber Defense Unit (CDU) stood up in 2014 with the mandate to stick to defensive posturing. Yet, because the programs are managed by armed forces, and Prime Minister Shinzo Abe himself declared that the famous Article 9 of Japan's pacifist constitution does not apply to cyber forces, it can be perceived to be an offensive capability [39]. This also happened often with small states like Mauritania, whose military also functions as law enforcement and/or critical infrastructure management [40]. Ultimately, however, the dual-use nature of this technology nullifies the distinction, since the equipment and expertise serves at the pleasure of the governing leaders. It would not take long to repurpose a strictly defensive cyber campaign to include offensive capabilities or a full campaign, making for a low latency factor.

Inconsistent data from sources was a rampant problem—even correcting for the date of issue. For example, the ITU would claim that Uzbekistan had no CERT, but then CERT.org would list UZ-CERT as an active member team participant, within the same year. In some cases, it was simply a product of the rapidly changing cyberspace environment over the last 5 years as states continue to evolve and upgrade their infrastructures. Other times, though, it was a maddening circle of doubt that required more sources to confirm or disprove data points.

6 Conclusions

Trying to characterize the nature of what types of states develop OCO or determine what key traits they may share is not simple. Intuitively, states with OCO "should be" better able to defend against and prosecute attacks; by extension, having this military tool might exacerbate or simply be a reflection of the gap between the rich and poor countries [41]. Instead, the data presented here indicates that wealth and technical infrastructure are not predictors of whether a society invests in OCO, surprisingly. The only thing they can correlate to is if a society *does not* have OCO (or a military, et al.). However, the fact that almost half of all nations claim to have even a minimal level of investment suggests that perhaps it's precisely the affordability and/or dual-use nature of OCO that make it an attractive option to include in a defense strategy. OCO is inherently versatile—it can be used as a perceived deterrent, political tool, or as a means of building prestige/regime legitimacy and it draws from technical expertise and equipment that doubles for standard network defense or intelligence operations. As far as resourcing goes, countries need only be concerned that they have qualified staff to maintain program viability. For many, that alone is hard, but that is another feature of an OCO campaign—it does not have to be a big program to have measured effect.

Even reviewing 'regime type' as a variable provided no substantive insights into whether or not states pursued OCO. Of the 4 communist states, Laos was not pursuing OCO (or at least publicly disclosing it). Out of the 10 constitutional and absolute monarchies, 5 had declared OCO capacity. When adding parliamentary constitutional monarchies to the list, the figure jumps from 50% to 64%. Interestingly, when accounting for only those monarchies with a standing military, 100% of them have capacity to execute OCO campaigns. When looking at variations of democratic societies from federal republics to presidential republics and parliamentary democracies, 100% of 85 nations have militaries, and of those, 64% have OCO capabilities.

While it doesn't indicate participation levels, having an OCO campaign does not seem to hinder state collaboration in cybersecurity. In fact, states with some of the largest, most aggressive campaigns are some of the most involved in collective sharing agreements (e.g., Russia, UK, US). This could be out of a perceived need to balance cyber capabilities (power) against a shared foe, such as stated in the 2020 agreement for shared research and development in cyber defense between Estonia and the US [42], or out of collaborative pursuit of innovating cyber technologies, such as the case with the Indo-French Bi-lateral Cyber Dialogue [43]. Another observation is that nations that do not have OCO programs often partner with states who do, frequently for law enforcement purposes like in the REMJA [44] Working Group on Cyber Crime under the Organization of American States (OAS) umbrella. This is mostly for the benefit of shared expertise or other incentives and is not an example of a defense commitment. Another good example of this is the Israeli agreement to exchange cyber threat information and training (along with an increase in trade) with 7 states in Sub-Saharan Africa [45]. Details about these arrangements or how effective they have been are hard to find publicly, but the number of them will likely expand in the near term.

International cooperation is limited in its capacity to equip states for thwarting attacks and hardening networks, but it is still important. Policy and legal groups are just not ready to replicate in vast numbers; ambiguities are too great, consensus is elusive, and norms and trust have not reached critical mass yet. That said, numerous high-profile attacks and data exposures in the private sector have demonstrated the value of sharing threat intelligence, new technologies and analytic techniques, and training staff; which in itself is establishing a set of expectations and norms [46]. Data presented in this research shows immense participation in collaborative international groups, but the locus tends towards regional interests, and are mostly at the working/technical level, not in strategic policy or legal arenas. Regions often have comparable economies of scale and face similar threats, so it makes sense that should extend to cyberspace, especially as malicious network traffic knows no sovereign borders and might utilize infrastructure from a neighbor to conduct an attack on a state's assets. CERTs are particularly well suited for this type of collaboration, and some states such as Kuwait are forgoing having a national CERT altogether in favor of the inter-state one.

> Right now, no comprehensive international treaty exists to regulate cyberattacks. Consequently, states must practice law by analogy: either equating cyberattacks to traditional armed attacks and responding to them under the law of war or equating them to criminal activity and dealing with them under domestic criminal laws. [47]

Simply having a penal code in place does not stop criminal activity. So too, it is with declaring an offensive cyber capability—it will not be enough to deter all attacks from happening, but it may weed out opportunists or those with inferior capabilities. Nations that have suffered massive fallout from state-sponsored cyberattacks understand that passive defenses, even with hardened, high-end infrastructures, are not enough to stop a motivated or advanced persistent threat (APT) actor. There is no higher authority or international order to appeal to for recompense in the event of a devastating attack. Hence, states are compensating with declaratory postures or military doctrinal revisions and investing in OCO programs. Doing so establishes clear boundaries and consequences. While there is no such thing as 100% security, OCO programs offer a credible threat of an active response to an attack, which is a more effective deterrent than prosecution and potential extradition (or not, in many cases). Since they are cheaper and faster to grow than other advanced weapons systems, states of all income and technology levels are hastening the widespread proliferation of OCO as the trendy deterrent: a weapon of mass disruption.

7 Future Work

A lot can be done in this research space down the road. Inconsistencies in source material can be attributed to a number of factors, but it would be beneficial to try to conduct the same research in native languages where this was most challenging. The data may not actually be available publicly, but it's worth confirming this.

Further quantitative analysis might yield interesting results if the likelihood of a state having OCO could be divined in a probabilistic manner from its other attributes. For instance, does having a national cybersecurity strategy and cybercriminal laws have any value in predicting the odds of a state having an OCO program based on population size, military size, or other factors. This would be different from the research presented in this chapter in that the calculations would be based on statistical models rather than presented as tabular relational data.

Additionally, it would be beneficial to investigate what state partnerships exist that are sharing cybersecurity tools, IoCs, and expertise to see if any patterns or anomalies appear. It may be predictable to expect results to be grouped by region or historical alliances, but some surprising affiliations may emerge. By extension, a more in-depth study of international public-private partnerships and threat intelligence sharing agreements could be fruitful. Finding out how many groups are operationally-focused such as CERT/CSIRT forums versus policy coordination groups like OSCE there are, and what precisely is being shared would help gauge what (if any) power dynamics affect state collaboration or security priorities.

References

1. National Research Council (2009) Technology, policy, law, and ethics regarding US acquisition and use of cyberattack capabilities. National Academies Press
2. Int'l and Operational Law Dept., US Army Judge Advocate General's Legal Center and School (2015) Law of armed conflict deskbook, 5th edn. US GPO, Charlottesville, VA
3. Levi M (2017) The worldwide struggle to claim cyber sovereignty, 26 Sept 2017. The Cipher Brief. Accessed 21 Nov 2017. https://www.thecipherbrief.com/worldwide-struggle-claim-cyber-sovereignty

4. Lin H, Zegart A (2018) Bytes, bombs, and spies. The Brookings Institution, Washington, DC, p 41
5. Schmitt MN (Ed) Tallinn manual 2.0 on the international law applicable to cyber operations. Cambridge University Press
6. Symantec Corporation (2018). Internet security threat report 2018. [online] Symantec Corp., Mountain View, CA. Available at: http://resource.symantec.com/LP=5538?cid=70138000000rm1eAAA. Accessed 2 Apr 2018
7. Council of Europe (2001) Convention on cybercrime. Treaty Office. ETS #185. Accessed 20 Oct 2020. https://www.coe.int/en/web/conventions/full-list/-/conventions/treaty/185/signatures?p_auth=Q4qZFBiR
8. Stoltenburg J (2019) NATO will defend itself. Prospect. Accessed 20 Oct 2020. https://www.prospectmagazine.co.uk/content/uploads/2019/08/Cyber_Resilience_October2019.pdf
9. The Flawed Analogy Between Nuclear And Cyber Deterrence—Bulletin Of The Atomic Scientists (2016) Bulletin of the atomic scientists. Accessed 30 Nov 2020. https://thebulletin.org/2016/02/the-flawed-analogy-between-nuclear-and-cyber-deterrence/
10. Smeets M (2018) The strategic promise of offensive cyber operations. Strat Stud Q 12(3):90–113. Accessed 6 Nov 2020. https://www.jstor.org/stable/26481911
11. Zelalem Z (2020) An Egyptian cyber attack on Ethiopia by hackers is the latest strike over the grand dam. Quartz Africa. Accessed 15 Nov 2020. https://qz.com/africa/1874343/egypt-cyber-attack-on-ethiopia-is-strike-over-the-grand-dam/
12. This is changing, though, with white papers on deterrence in the cyber world, and political analysis of Russian hacking elections, among similar topics
13. Russon M-A (2016) Hackers Hijacking water treatment plant controls shows how easily civilians could be poisoned. International Business Times UK. Accessed 2 Apr 2018. https://www.ibtimes.co.uk/hackers-hijacked-chemical-controls-water-treatment-plant-utility-company-was-using-1988-server-1551266
14. Valentino-DeVries J, Lam TV, Danny Y (2017) Interactive graphics, WSJ.com. 2017. Cataloging the world's cyber forces. The Wall Street J. Accessed 21 Nov 2017. http://graphics.wsj.com/world-catalogue-cyberwar-tools/
15. Carr J (2012) Inside cyber warfare. O'Reilly, Beijing
16. It is possible there is some manner of response plan that exists in classified arenas, but it is likely to be agency-specific, and not comprehensive or agency-integrated
17. Pomerleau M, Here are the problems offensive cyber poses for NATO. FifthDomain.com. Fifth Domain. Accessed 8 Nov 2020. https://www.fifthdomain.com/international/2019/11/20/here-are-the-problems-offensive-cyber-poses-for-nato/
18. National Institute of Standards and Technology (NIST) (2016) Guide for cyber event recovery. US Dept. of Commerce, Gaithersburg, MD
19. International Telecommunication Union (2020) Cyberwellness profiles. ITU.int. Accessed 29 Nov 2020. https://www.itu.int/en/ITU-D/Cybersecurity/Pages/Country_Profiles.aspx
20. United Nations Institute for Disarmament Research (UNIDIR) (2013) The cyber index: international security trends and realities. UN, Geneva
21. Central Intelligence Agency (2020) The CIA world factbook. Cia.Gov. Accessed 20 Nov 2020. https://www.cia.gov/library/publications/the-world-factbook/geos/sm.html
22. UNCTAD (2020) Cybercrime legislation worldwide. Unctad.Org. Accessed 17 Nov 2020. https://unctad.org/page/cybercrime-legislation-worldwide
23. This ranges from regular penal code that extends to cyberspace, to telecommunications laws covering digital crimes, to laws specifically covering cybercriminal activity
24. Marczak B, Alexander G, McKune S, Scott-Railton J, Deibert R (2017) Champing at the cyberbit: ethiopian dissidents targeted with new commercial spyware. 6 December 2017. *The Citizen Lab*. Accessed 15 Oct 2020. https://citizenlab.ca/2017/12/champing-cyberbit-ethiopian-dissidents-targeted-commercial-spyware/
25. Libicki MC (2009) Cyberdeterrence and cyberwar. Rand Corporation, p 34
26. This does not include national police or domestic surveillance operations

27. NATO Cyber Defence (2018) North Atlantic treaty organization. https://www.nato.int/cps/en/natohq/topics_78170.htm
28. NATO Cooperative Cyber Defence Centre of Excellence (CCD COE) (2020) Cyber security strategy documents (listed by country. *CCDCOE*. Accessed 29 NOv 2020. https://ccdcoe.org/cyber-security-strategy-documents.html
29. Countries—AfricaCERT (2020) AfricaCERT. https://www.africacert.org/home/countries/
30. Convention on Cyber Security and Personal Data Protection, African Union, 27 June 2014
31. Mostly former Soviet states, Russia, India, and China
32. Very similar membership profile to the SCO
33. Orazgaliyeva M (2017) CSTO foreign ministers adopt measures to curb IT crime during minsk meeting. 18 July 2017. The Astana Times. Accessed 15 Dec 2017. https://astanatimes.com/2017/07/csto-foreign-ministers-adopt-measures-to-curb-it-crime-during-minsk-meeting/
34. Directorio Certs Inicio (2020) Sites.Oas.Org. Accessed 29 Nov 2020. https://www.sites.oas.org/cyber/en/pages/default.aspx
35. Bienvenido Al Departamento De Cooperacion Jurídica (2020) Oas.Org. Accessed 29 Nov 2020. http://www.oas.org/juridico/english/cyber_lin
36. Gandhi R, Sharma A, Mahoney W, Sousan W, Zhu Q, Laplante P (2011) Dimensions of cyber-attacks: cultural, social, economic, and political. IEEE Technol Soc Mag 30(1):28–38
37. Lin H (2017) A continuing need for stealth with loud cyber weapons. 18 July 2017. Lawfare. Accessed 3 Oct 2020. https://www.lawfareblog.com/continuing-need-stealth-loud-cyber-weapons
38. Gady F-S (2017) Japan's defense ministry plans to boost number of cyber warriors. The diplomat. Accessed 3 Nov 2020. https://thediplomat.com/2017/07/japans-defense-ministry-plans-to-boost-number-of-cyber-warriors/
39. Rueda M (2015) Ecuador escalates cyber war by deploying army of twitter trolls. 30 January 2015. Splinternews.Com. Accessed 12 Nov 2020. https://splinternews.com/ecuador-escalates-cyber-war-by-deploying-army-of-twitte-1793844931
40. Robertson M, Riley M (2017) The post-snowden cyber arms hustle. Bloomberg.Com. Accessed 3 Oct 2020. https://www.bloomberg.com/news/features/2017-01-18/the-post-snowden-cyber-arms-hustle
41. Gartzke E (2014) making sense of cyberwar. Belfer Center for Science and International Affairs, Harvard Kennedy School, January, Policy Brief, pp 41–73
42. Thompson E (2020) US Army, Estonia sign historic agreement for collaborative research in cyber defense. Army.mil. Accessed 3 Nov 2020. https://www.army.mil/article/239023/us_army_estonia_sign_historic_agreement_for_collaborative_research_in_cyber_defense
43. Government of France (2019) Indo-French bilateral cyber dialogue (Paris, 20 June 2019). France Diplomacy. France Ministry of Foreign Affairs. Accessed 1 Nov 2020. https://www.diplomatie.gouv.fr/en/french-foreign-policy/security-disarmament-and-non-proliferation/fight-against-organized-criminality/cyber-security/article/indo-french-bilateral-cyber-dialogue-20-06-19
44. Meetings of Ministers of Justice or Other Ministers or Attorneys General of the Americas (REMJA)
45. Lusaka Times Staff (2016) Zambia: Israel and 7 African Countries agree to collaborate on security and economic matters. Lusakatimes.Com. Accessed 29 Nov 2020. https://www.lusakatimes.com/2016/07/05/israel-and-7-african-countries-agree-to-collaborate-on-security-and-economic-matters/
46. Sofaer A, Clark D, Diffie W (2009) Cyber security and international agreements. In: National research council, proceedings of a workshop on deterring cyberattacks
47. Carr J (2012) Inside cyber warfare. OReilly, Beijing

The Interplay Between Frugal Science and Chemical and Biological Weapons: Investigating the Proliferation Risks of Technology Intended for Humanitarian, Disaster Response, and International Development Efforts

Michael Tennenbaum and Margaret E. Kosal

Abstract The attempt to create cheap, easy-to-use scientific equipment made for anyone, anywhere has made significant progress in the last decade in what innovators call frugal science. The emerging technology developed by frugal science to increase access to the experimental practice of the physical sciences through low cost and low electricity equipment and to lower the cost of medical devices so as to expand their application to impoverished areas is a subject of concern along with most other emerging technologies. While designed to help both kids generally and scientists in impoverished areas reach parity with their experimentalist counterparts in the developed world, the question remains: Will terrorists exploit such technology to develop chemical or biological weapons (CBW)? In order to address this question, we develop an analytical framework that assesses the overall threat of CBW terrorism. Through evaluation of terrorist motivations, capabilities, and other influencing factors, this framework analyses how emerging technologies, such as frugal science, affect motivated terrorist organizations in their pursuit of CBW. We use as a case study al-Qaeda's CBW programs in the 1990s and early 2000s to demonstrate the small effect frugal science would have on the significant sociotechnical barriers faced by terrorist organizations. Results not only inform intelligence practitioners, law enforcement, and policy makers about the dual-use implications of emerging technologies, but also indicate the utility of this framework in future analyses and studies.

The authors thank Haston Gerencir for his invaluable research and writing assistance.

M. Tennenbaum · M. E. Kosal (✉)
Georgia Institute of Technology, Atlanta, Georgia
e-mail: margaret.kosal@inta.gatech.edu

1 Introduction

As the relatively new field of frugal science expands, its role in national security needs to be addressed. Recent developments into more open humanitarian aid technology could change how chemical and biological weapons proliferate. Some of the technologies available for implementation in humanitarian aid programs can be used beyond their intended purpose and the potential for alternative use is larger for more fundamental technologies. Though frugal innovations have the potential to be misused, the risk is low. Frugal laboratory equipment has low throughput and it would be difficult to use to create biological or chemical weapons at an effective scale. There are also industrial chemicals that are used as a part of humanitarian aid efforts that can be misused but restricting their use causes more harm than it prevents. Both types of aid technologies have the potential to be abused but limiting either could weaken national security by decreasing stability.

Foreign aid is an integral component of the United States' foreign policy. It helps maintain influence and promote stability both of which strengthen national security [1]. Aid comes in many forms from military to financial to material and from many sources from the state to the individual level. It arises as long-term infrastructure building and as short-term relief efforts. In promoting stability, aid that affects medical and civil infrastructure is of prime importance as these have large impacts of people's lives. Humanitarian aid is particularly focused on affecting the people's lives and wellbeing. The Organisation for Economic Co-operation and Development (OECD) describes humanitarian aid as action that "saves lives, alleviates suffering and maintains human dignity following conflict, shocks and natural disasters[,]" [2] and The World Health Organization echoes this sentiment as well, "Humanitarian Assistance: Aid that seeks, to save lives and alleviate suffering of a crisis-affected population [3]."

Unfortunately, we do not live in a post scarcity world, and so cost of foreign aid tempers what type and how much aid can be sent. As a result of this, there is a drive to create less expensive versions of aid technologies particularly when dealing with medical systems. There have been several approaches to decreasing the cost of aid technology mainly focusing on medical diagnostic technology, sanitation, and food [4–7]. For example, there has been significant research recently into developing cheaper alternatives to current medical diagnosis technology [8]. This work has tried to incorporate cell phones instead of large computers to make it more mobile [9] and has also tackled the problem of portability and cost of the equipment used in diagnosis.

In trying to make less expensive medical diagnostic devices there are two main approaches- make small inexpensive single use devices that can be manufactured at scale, or design laboratory equipment that is inexpensive [10–12]. The first leads to lab-on-a-chip (LOC) style devices and the second to low cost laboratory equipment, both of which are a part of frugal science. LOCs can be glass, plastic, or paper; single use or reusable; and single purpose or multipurpose. At the moment, most are single purpose glass based single use devices, but there is much ongoing work pushing the limit of what can be done. Work is being done on flexible sensor patches to replace current expensive monitoring devices [13]. There are also people working on printing single use diagnostic medical devices on paper [8]. This brings down the cost of production by allowing for roll-to-roll processing production of devices.

These new avenues of research fall within the relatively recent field of frugal science. That is science "designed to generate knowledge (and technology based on that knowledge) with cost as an integral part of the subject [5]." This cost focus can take the form of cost per single use device but it can also mean designing low-cost versions of general laboratory equipment, a microscope for example [6]. This low-cost laboratory equipment goes beyond single purpose and provide a general way of building and maintaining a diagnostic medical lab inexpensively. So far, there have been multiple low-cost microscopes [14, 15] and low-cost centrifuges [12, 16] produced with more equipment possible in the future [17]. These low-cost technologies are already being developed for use as part of humanitarian aid efforts [8, 11, 13, 18].

Technologies put in place as part of humanitarian aid efforts have great potential to improve stability in other countries [19, 20]. As the technologies put in place become cheaper and more advanced/generalized the potential for dual use increases. Distribution of more open technologies lays the groundwork for the potential proliferation of chemical and biological weapons. This proliferation could cause instability negating the intended effect of the aid program.

2 The Idea of Frugality

Frugal science is an area within the scientific domain designed to generate knowledge—and technology based on that knowledge—with cost as an integral part of the subject, while ultimately designing scientific instruments that are affordable to people in "resource-poor regions [21, 22]." Although frugal technology is a niche industry, the innovations stemming from frugal inspirations has led to the development of a wide array of products. For example, frugal science has influenced the microfluidic technology. In short, microfluidics is the science and technology of systems that process or manipulate small amounts of fluids, using channels with dimensions of tens to hundreds of micrometers [23]. After the initiation of microfluidics in the 1980s, and later in the 1990s for biodefense research [24], microfluidics began taking a more frugal approach in 2007 as George Whitesides, an innovator of microfluidics, invented patterned paper as a platform for inexpensive, low-volume, portable bioassays [25]. This creation has since influenced research, as well as actual products, on microfluidic designs based on frugal innovation technology.

Other frugal chemical and biological innovations include simpler technologies such as the Foldscope and Paperfuge. Created in 2014 by frugal science innovator, Manu Prakash, the Foldscope harnesses the magnitude of a desktop microscope, but is made out of paper and materials costing only ninety-seven cents [22]. Similar in concept, Dr. Prakash also created a hand-powered device, called a Paperfuge because of the prototype's paper disc, with the capabilities of doing a thousand-dollar commercial centrifuge's job for just twenty cents [22]. Yet, one of the most identifiable developments stemming from this concept, other than the frugal products themselves, is the rapid advancement of frugal science through the years.

2.1 Trends in Frugal Science

After looking closely at frugal science over the last ten to fifteen years, there are five identifiable trends. First, since Whitesides' initial development of microfluidic devices based on patterned paper in 2007, frugal science in the areas of chemistry and biology has catapulted to the top in terms of research, design, and popularity. Although microfluidic devices were created in the 1970s, extensive research, design, methodologies, and fabrication methods have only quickly grown in the last two decades [26]. In fact, in 2009, MIT named Whitesides' research product as one of the top ten breakthrough technologies of the year [27]. Since the breakthrough in microfluidics- commonly referred to as using lab-on-a-chip (LOC) because recent developments enable the small fluids and reactions to occur on small lab chips-researchers have developed various applications for microfluidic LOC technology pertaining to frugal science. For example, only a year after Whitesides' creation, Manu Prakash was able to create his own LOC technology with the main driver being frugality. In his research study he indicates that, "rather than focusing and relying on large, bulky, and expensive systems to operate the process, microfluidics develops automated liquid handling in integrated micro-chips; brings the capability within reach to experimentalists and biologists" [28]. Ultimately, his discoveries can reduce the size, cost, and complexity of microfluidic platforms [28].

Frugal technology's growth is not limited to just research either. The development of microfluidics has increased in scope and applicability outside of the laboratory. For example, the breakthroughs in frugal technology have incentivized developments in areas such as glucose detection [29], the detection of chemicals in explosive devices [30], and chemical and biological analysis through point-of-care diagnostics [31]. Thus, the initial research that served as the foundation for chemical and biological frugal technology in 2007 has turned into a substantial field with multiple developments and applications in a matter of years.

The second trend deals with simpler, less-complex frugal tools that have been created so that they can be used by anyone, anywhere. As was mentioned above, Manu Prakash developed laboratory equipment such as the Foldscope and Paperfuge using frugal innovation. Prakash, along with several of his colleagues at Stanford, are also working on creating inexpensive chemistry kits used not only for humanitarian efforts to test water and snake bites, but also kits for kids to play with and create their own experiments [32]. His creativity has inspired others to develop similar products intended to reach impoverished communities around the world. For example, MIT's Little Devices Group [33] and the University of California's Tekla Labs create, develop, and ship cheap lab equipment to hospitals in the developing world [34].

There are even international contests, such as those sponsored by the European Commission, to create frugal science tools that can be used in any environment [35].

Third, a growing trend in frugal innovation is the development of such cheap technologies on a mass scale. In the MIT top ten breakthrough technology report, when commenting on Whitesides' microfluidic technology, MIT indicated that the researchers "hope the advanced version of the test can eventually be mass produced using the same printing technology that churns out newspapers". Whitesides and his colleagues were not far off in their aspirations. Since 2009, researchers have been developing methods that could allow the microfluidic designs to be mass produced, even on an industrial level. For example, researchers have analyzed methods to fabricate and create microfluidic assays on a mass scale [36–38]. Methods such as ink-jet printing have demonstrated significant potential to commercially produce microfluidic paper-based assays. Just recently, a research team validated a first-of-its-kind portable diagnostic technology at a refugee camp in northwestern Kenya using ink-jet and 3D printing [39]. This demonstrates that Whitesides' desire to mass produce frugal science only a decade ago is coming to light. Furthermore, frugal science chemistry kits and Foldscopes have been donated by the thousands as Prakash's team has contributed 60,000 products to over 135 countries [40]. In essence, the path is being paved for the commercialization and mass scale production of frugal science technology.

Fourth, over the past several years, the explicit and tacit knowledge required for frugal technologies has spread across international boundaries. One notable example is the development of the LOC technology to detect aviation bird flu. In 2007, two institutes in Singapore successfully developed and deployed LOC technology that can detect the avian flu in a fraction of the time for a fraction of the cost compared to other methods [41]. Since then, several universities and companies across the world have developed their own chips or have further advanced the research. Using the same type of platform established in Singapore in 2007, two laboratories have since launched a similar style microfluidic chip that can detect up to nine avian flu viruses simultaneously [42].

Furthermore, other cases exemplify that those acquiring the products are more capable of using and understanding frugal technology as well. A major part of Tekla Labs' mission is to grow a worldwide community of likeminded researchers, educators, and students. The group is able to do so by creating and disseminating do-it-yourself (DIY) documents and instructions on the technology they provide in order to educate and inform users on how to construct and operate the equipment [43]. Additionally, as thousands of frugal science kits and tools have been used by people in the developing world, the simplicity of the technology is making it easy for anyone to assemble and repair on their own [44]. One example is the creation of the Foldscope. Since the creation of the Foldscope, clinics in Tanzania and Ghana have used the tool in diagnostics, while thousands of children across the globe have made their own Foldscopes to learn science [45]. These cases demonstrate that the inspiration to create frugal science has transpired into the increase in substantive research, knowledge, and know-how of using the equipment.

The final trend, which is one that is likely to emerge, is the use and accessibility of frugal science for humanitarian aid. Without proper understanding of U.S. aid distribution, some might conclude that money goes directly to the governments of the recipient countries [46]. However, only 4% of all funds in FY2014 went directly to the governments of recipient countries. In fact, most development and humanitarian assistance activities are not directly implemented by U.S. government personnel but through grants and loans to private sector entities such as individual personal service contractors, consulting firms, nonprofit nongovernment organizations, universities, or charitable private voluntary organizations (PVOs) [47]. It is these same types of implementors that predominantly research, develop, and disseminate frugal science products across the world.

While there are various forms of U.S. aid- military, political and strategic, non-military and security-assistance serving development and humanitarian purposes constituted 56% of the entire U.S. aid budget in FY2016 [48]. The specific programs within development and humanitarian purposes consist of: education, global health programs, emergencies resulting from natural disasters, problems resulting from conflicts associated with failed or failing states, HIV/AID crises, and sustainable food and water programs. These programs run parallel with several of the purposes and applications of frugal science: educating youth in impoverished countries, diagnosing diseases, and testing local drinking water. As these humanitarian and development issues continue to receive a majority of U.S. attention in terms of assistance, the development and incorporation of frugal science in these programs is even more likely. For example, health funding has increased 807% from FY2001 to FY2016 [49]. Education programs received $95 million in FY1997. This number rose to $1.2 billion in FY2016. Just as frugal science has grown in development, applicability, and popularity, so too has its potential for use through development and humanitarian assistance.

2.2 How Frugal Science Can Be Used to Create CBW

The applicability of frugal science spans across numerous domains: humanitarian aid, chemical and biological analysis, point-of-contact care, among many other helpful mechanisms. However, one area that has not been discussed is how frugal science could lead to a terrorists' chemical or biological weapons program. The rapid advancement in research, technological breakthroughs, know-how, and access to frugal science necessitates a better understanding as to how such progression could lead to exploitation. The aim of this section is not to indicate that frugal sciences are taking a turn for the worst, or that society will utilize the technology in detrimental ways. Rather, the focus of the section is to provide an awareness of the vulnerabilities of frugal science, especially as there are numerous unknown factors and paths that the advancement of frugal science might take. The following concerns are of speculation and possibilities that current technologies could have on terrorist CBW programs, as well as how recent trends in frugal science demonstrate the potential for devastating manifestations.

As previously stated, microfluidics is the science and technology of systems that process and manipulate fluids [23]. The advancement of LOC technology has allowed for this manipulation to occur on tiny microchips half the size of a postage stamp, with tiny channels used to guide the fluids [50]. When talking about microfluidic applications in 2006, George Whitesides demonstrated its current uses and capabilities, including: studying and understanding fast organic reactions, growing and observing cells in microbiology, and even testing and researching chemical synthesis and reactions [23]. The concern here is that terrorists could potentially use these microfluidic LOC technologies to develop their own chemical or biological laboratories. Terrorist organizations could test, synthesize, research, and even develop chemical or biological agents using this technology. When analyzed in the context of developments, trends, and frugality, the reality of a terrorist creating a CBW from frugal science is not far-fetched. For example, microfluidic chips have advanced to a level that allows a single chip to perform thousands of reactions in parallel in a matter of minutes [26]. This can allow a person or group of scientists, or terrorists, to conduct thousands of tests and reactions on a single chip in a timely manner. Furthermore, scientists such as Manu Prakash are working on microfluidic-based computers that can control millions of droplets simultaneously [50]. Prakash noted that, "the most immediate application might involve turning the computer into a high-throughput chemistry and biology laboratory" [50]. This invention would ultimately eliminate large laboratories with bulky test tubes needed to conduct chemical research, as each droplet on the chip could carry its own chemical reaction, becoming its own test tube. Thus, groups attempting to exploit such technology could potentially better understand and create their own CBW laboratory using frugal science.

Since each reaction and reagent of chemical and biological samples are in the micrometers [31], the scalability of microfluidics poses a problem for a CBW program. This issue can be solved with large-scale production and commercialization capabilities. Originally, several of the microchip prototypes were made of glass, silicon, or plastic [26, 51]. With recent advancements in LOC technologies, researchers have been able to create microfluidic chips that have the potential for more reactions, better efficiency, and mass production, primarily using paper-based chips [25, 26, 52]. When using paper as the main material for the chips, there are several methods to mass produce the LOC technology on a commercial scale [36–38]. This capability could allow terrorist organizations to obtain hundreds of microfluidic LOC devices, ultimately accumulating enough chemical or biological agents to amass a significant weapon. Additionally, another concern is with DIY chemistry kits and frugal technologies that have been donated to hundreds of countries across the world. While the kits are now only rudimentary in their development, it is worrisome to think about the potential advancement, properties, and capabilities of future chemistry sets. If the frugal science tools continue to progress through research and applicability, which trends indicate they will, then terrorist organizations could get their hands on even more advanced kits that were intended for the developing world.

While the inherent characteristics and applicability of frugal science could be used to create CBW, the accessibility and dissemination of the technology through humanitarian aid also poses significant security risks. When analyzing risks among charitable organizations, the U.S. Treasury Department stated that U.S.-based charities operating abroad, particularly in high-risk areas where terrorist groups are most active, the risks can be significant [53]. While protecting charities from terrorist abuse is a critical component of the global fight against terrorism, it is a difficult task because charities: often focus their relief efforts on areas of conflict where humanitarian need is urgently needed, but where terrorist groups may control territory or be particularly active; may have access to considerable sources of funds, including from donors who wish to support a charitable cause but are often unaware of or unlikely to question potential links to terrorism; enjoy the public trust and are often subject to minimal or modest government supervision, resulting in less oversight and transparency than in more-regulated sectors [54]. As a result, charities are targeted, exploited, and taken advantage of to support terrorist fundraising, logistical support, operations, recruitment, and weapons purchases.

The fear is that frugal science technology used to address these global challenges will be exploited by terrorist organizations as they have done to charities in the past. For example, World Vision, an international NGO that receives millions of dollars from over 100 countries, including the United States, was found diverting funds for humanitarian purposes to the terrorist arm of Hamas [55]. El-Halabi, the individual dispatched by Hamas to exploit the organization, established and promoted humanitarian projects and fictitious agricultural associations that acted as a cover for the transfer of money used to finance the terrorist organization and purchase weapons [55]. Terrorists could access frugal technology through charitable organizations in several ways. They could pose as legitimate recipients of aid as El-Halabi did, asking for and receiving frugal equipment to reconstruct the education system or help farmers in war-torn countries. Or, the frugal science tools that are handed out to legitimate local populations could be diverted to terrorist organizations. A recent and similar situation occurred with charities attempting to relieve people in ISIS held territory in Tikrit. An aid worker was attempting to help Iraq's suffering people by providing food. Yet, when asked if he considered if ISIS fighters had diverted aid meant for civilians, he confided that he did not actually know where the aid ended up [56]. Thus, terrorists could either pose as legitimate recipients of frugal science or take advantage of the lack of monitoring and security measures to divert frugal science tools intended for local populations.

3 Chemical and Biological Terrorism: Analytical Framework

The equation used in this study is Threat = Motivation * Capability. It is common to assess the risks of terrorist attacks using the Department of Homeland Security (DHS) risk assessment equation of Risk = Threat * Vulnerability * Consequence [57]. However, this study does not intend to analyze what happens after an attack, or in other words, the consequences of an attack by an adversary, which is defined as the effect of an event, incident, or occurrence [58]. Rather, this paper aims to understand the actual threat of an attack before it occurs, which can be conceptualized as Threat = Motivation * Vulnerability * Capability. Before moving forward, two clarifications need to be addressed. First, the analysis of vulnerability is beyond the scope of this paper. Vulnerability is the measure of the safeguards in place to prevent something from occurring and/or for protection, the ability to respond during an event, and the ability mitigate the effects after. Since the scope of vulnerability is broad and includes factors proceeding an actual attack, i.e. mitigations and responses to an attack, this particular analysis does not include the function of vulnerability. Second, this paper's threat equation is similar to that of how the DHS conceptualizes their threat assessment which is a combination of attackers' intent and capability [59]. Since their definition of intent is, "a state of mind or desire to achieve an objective [60]," this study broadens the spectrum of intention into motivation, both strategic and tactical. Therefore, the definitive equation for the paper is Threat = Motivation * Capability.

3.1 Motivation

The first variable that plays a major role within the threat of chemical and biological terrorism is motivation. The U.S. Department of Defense's definition of terrorism as of 2016 is, "The unlawful use of violence or threat of violence, often motivated by religious, political, or other ideological beliefs, to instill fear and coerce governments or societies in pursuit of goals that are usually political [61]." Experts of chemical and biological terrorism similarly define terrorism as, "the instrumental use or threatened use of violence by an organization or individual against innocent civilian targets in furtherance of a political, religious, or ideological objective [62]." In a brief comparison of both definitions, terrorism involves the use or threat of violence by an organization or people motivated by various beliefs or goals. While these definitions note political, ideological, and religious beliefs, further analysis is needed to fully understand the motivations of various types of terrorist organizations.

The motivations of terrorist organizations are complex and, in a way, tiered. The same motivation behind a group's desired end goals may or may not be the same motivation influencing their decision to carry out a particular tactic. Therefore, it is necessary to understand the various motivations of terrorist organizations in order to realistically consider the threat of a group using CBW. Military strategists and academics often use the concepts of ends, ways, and means. In fact, the frequently adopted definition of strategy is, "the process of achieving objectives (ends) through the purposeful application (ways) of available resources (means) while accounting for risk [63]." When thinking of the inspirations behind a group's long-term objectives, or ends, it is important to first look at terrorist's strategic motivations. Strategic motivation can be defined as a group's typology or ideology motivating them to strive for particular goals and ends. Thus, the first priority of understanding terrorist motivations is taking a closer look at overarching strategic motivations and typologies.

The typology of the group is the type of belief system, background, and ideology maintained by the organization [64]. As Rapoport and other scholars have indicated, different waves of terrorism have introduced groups with various ideologies and goals [65–67]. Terrorism in the late 1800s was marked by anarchist terrorists, who were then proceeded by anticolonial groups in the 1920s, new-left terrorist organizations in the 1960s, and then a religious wave of terrorists in 1979. Each of these types, or categories, of terrorists have their own goals, or ultimate long-term desires, whether they be regime change, territorial change, policy change, social control, and status quo maintenance [68]. However, the drive to achieve these goals lies in the group's typology, which can further be broken down as political, separatist, religious, and single-issue, retaliatory groups.

When discussing politically motivated terrorist groups, right-wing and left-wing political organizations immediately come to mind. Right-wing groups attempt to achieve one of several right-wing agendas: restore national greatness as radical nationalists, suppress particular social groups as nativists, expel or subordinate troublesome ethnic or cultural minorities as racists, or overthrow an existing system to establish a new order as neo-fascists [69]. On the other hand, there are left-wing groups. The left-wing terrorist wave began in the 1960s when terrorist groups began opposing American intervention in Vietnam [70]. These terrorists are motivated in uprooting what they claim are irredeemable social and economic inequities of the modern capitalist liberal-democratic state [71].

Outside of right and left-wing political groups, however, are separatist groups seeking to establish their own state or national community. Separatist groups can be further divided into anti-colonialists and irredentists. The anti-colonialist wave of terrorism began after WWI, when organizations wanted their own nationalist liberation movement and agenda instead of the all-encompassing empires or resulting political mandates [72]. This wave of terrorism has inspired groups such as Hamas and other irredentist groups who desire to (re)appropriate land from another state based on ethnic or historical claims [73]. Although they have small differences, both anti-colonialists and irredentists maintain some form of a separatist agenda.

Another major ideological factor of a group is religion. Religious motivation can come in two forms, political and apocalyptic. The former category, also known as religious fundamentalists, is motivated to forcibly insert religion into the political sphere and create their own state, and at times principles by which the New World will be established [74]. Whether the group intends to kill or subjugate non-believers, impose religious laws on society, or create a type of religious state, the overall goal is to incorporate religion into politics or vice versa. The latter of religious groups, apocalyptic terrorist organizations, seek to bring about Armageddon or the end of the world. The intent for these particular groups is to cleanse the world of the evil within it and please the higher deity in which they are based upon [75]. A common link between the two types of religious organizations is how religion itself is often used as a justifying mechanism for carrying out violent acts. One of the most well-known examples is Osama bin Laden's fatwas validating attacks against Americans.

Stating in a 1998 interview, bin Laden declared, "Acquiring weapons for the defense of Muslims is a religious duty [76]." Even unclassified CIA analyses on al-Qaeda strategy indicate, "Terrorism is a key component of al-Qa'ida's strategy and bin Laden cites Koranic references in an effort to justify it [77]." It is evident, then, that religious terrorism can be either political, apocalyptic, or even used to justify particular actions and goals.

Continually, terrorist groups might be motivated to use CBW in a retaliatory effect. Although more specific or reactionary, retaliatory groups' strategic intent often reflect terrorists' overarching motive and ideology [78]. Single issue groups are committed to acting as catalysts to change a policy or behavior, whether they are ecological groups, anti-abortion groups, animal rights activists, or other single-issue organizations [79–81]. In other words, their strategic intent is to react or respond to an event or policy in order to disrupt the government or bring attention to a matter hoping to incite change. Other strategic intents focus on protesting and responding to U.S. foreign policy or military operations. Take the bombing of a research facility belonging to Union Carbine in 1984, for example. The United Freedom Front, a group that protested U.S. involvement in South Africa and Central America, claimed responsibility for the attack that caused over $500,000 in damage [82]. Reports indicated that the group was motivated by "perceived injustice of imperialism around the world and specifically Union Carbide for business dealings in South Africa [83]." Whether the groups are responding to an event, protesting U.S. foreign policy, or are reacting to a single-issue related to the organization's ideology, the terrorists overall intent and motivation is retaliation.

The various typologies and strategic motivations behind terrorist organizations are found in Table 1. The number beside each typology is not a nominal value but a numeric assignment that is used within the analytical framework.

Now that the strategic motivations behind terrorists' end goals have been unveiled, the next step is to determine the motivations behind the purposeful application (ways) of available resources (means). Simply put, what motivates terrorist organizations to carry out particular actions or strategies over others when attempting to achieve their long-term objectives? In order to prevent a confusion of terms, this study uses operational motivation as the terminology to describe the motivation behind a particular strategy or plan of action.

Differentiating between operational and tactical motivation is important because CBW could be used as a tactic but could have implications on the overall strategy. Therefore, when analyzing the motivations for a plan of action, there needs to be a distinction between operational and tactical motivation. Operational and tactical motivations have been analyzed in literature, albeit separately or only assessing singular issues. On a theoretical level, for example, researchers have dissected various strategies of terrorists, from sabotaging the peace [86] to costly signaling [87, 88] to name but a few. Others explicitly examine specific goals of terrorist organizations or the tactics used to attain them. Studies such as Robert Pape's Dying to Win: The Strategic Logic of Suicide Terrorism [89], for example, brings attention to the motivations of groups using suicide terrorism as a tactic, as well as a means to a larger strategy. Edward Price's "The Strategy and Tactics of Revolutionary Terrorism" [90]

Table 1 Strategic motivations

Typology	Motivation/Aim
0-Right-wing	Political groups wishing to restore national greatness as radical nationalists, suppress particular social groups as nativists, expel or subordinate troublesome ethnic or cultural minorities as racists, or overthrow an existing system to establish a new order as neo-fascists [84]
1-Left-wing	Political groups wanting to uproot what they claim are irredeemable social and economic inequities of the modern capitalist liberal-democratic state [71]
2-Anti-colonial	Separatist organizations wanting their own nationalist liberation movement and agenda instead of the all-encompassing empires or resulting political mandates [72]
3-Irredentist	Separatist groups who desire to (re)appropriate land from another state based on ethnic or historical claims [73]
4-Religious	Organizations motivated to forcibly insert religion into the political sphere and create their own state [74]. Whether the group intends to kill or subjugate non-believers, impose religious laws on society, or create a type of religious state, the overall goal is to incorporate religion into politics or vice versa
5-Apocalyptic	Groups seeking to bring about Armageddon or the end of the world with the intent to cleanse the world of the evil within it and please the higher deity in which they are based upon [75]
6-Retaliatory	Single-issue groups committed to acting as catalysts to change a policy or behavior, whether they are ecological groups, anti-abortion groups, animal rights activists, or other single-issue organizations that protest and respond to U.S. foreign or military policy [79, 80, 85]

carefully investigates both operational and tactical motivation, but only through the lens of one long-term objective, revolution. While these examples contribute to a better understanding of motivations for terrorist strategies and tactics, it is difficult to find research that analyzes the two in a larger, encompassing framework.

Regarding CBW terrorism, scholars have circulated exhaustive research examining the motivations for pursuing or using such weapons. While the research creates a strengthened understanding of CBW terrorism and the overall threat, these studies typically focus on a single terrorist organization, event, or ideological group, making it difficult to extrapolate overarching motivations. Other work on CBW terrorism has indeed taken an all-inclusive approach to CBW terrorism, attempting to determine the true threat, motivations, and limitations of groups across the board [91–93]. Jonathan Tucker's Toxic Terror: Assessing Terrorist Use of Chemical and Biological Weapons systematically looks at historical cases of CBW terrorism and the reasons behind a group's decision to use such weapons. However, his work does not fully bring together a framework for understanding motivations for tactics and strategies and how CBW would be able to contribute to either, calling for further research to identify motivations associated with CB terrorism [94].

Other works, such as Ackerman, et al.'s Anatomizing Chemical and Biological Non-State Adversaries Identifying the Adversary, Final Report [92] or Nadine Gurr and Benjamin Cole's The New Face of Terrorism: Threats from Weapons of Mass

Destruction [93] provide promising foundations that carefully assess how CBW could be used in both tactics and operations of terrorist organizations, going so far to identify the groups most likely to use them. This paper incorporates their findings, along with previous influential literature on terrorist strategies and tactics, to create an all-encompassing framework that assesses the motivations behind terrorist operations and tactics.

Before incorporating CBW into either, however, it is important to clearly distinguish the differences between strategies and tactics and the motivations behind them. The goals of terrorist organizations are the ultimate desires of the group, which range from regime change, territorial change, policy change, social control, and status quo maintenance. The strategy is the plan of action, or purposeful application of its means, used to attain the goals [68]. Although trends in terrorist activity and organizations have oscillated through the years, there have been seven main terrorist operational objectives used to achieve their long-term desires: attrition, intimidation, provocation, deterrence, spoiling, outbidding, and total destruction [95–97].

The operational motivation for each particular plan of action, or strategy, is listed in Table 2. As was with typology, the number beside each operational motivation is used not as a nominal value but a numeric assignment.

Just as strategy is the plan to attain long-term desires, tactics are the actions taken within a strategy to help achieve the long-term goals, and more importantly, short term or proximate objectives [106]. The motivations behind tactics are diverse, depending on the strategy and goals the group wishes to achieve. For example, the

Table 2 Operational motivations

Strategy: operational	Motivation/Aim
0-Attrition	Wants to persuade the enemy that the group is strong and resolute enough to inflict serious costs, so that the enemy yields to the terrorists' demands [88, 98, 99]
1-Intimidation	Try and convince the population that the terrorists are strong enough to punish disobedience and that the government is too weak to stop them, so that people behave as the terrorists wish [100, 101]
2-Provocation	Aim to persuade the domestic audience that the target of attacks is evil and untrustworthy and must be vigorously resisted; to goad the target government into a military response that harms civilians within the terrorist organization's home territory [102]
3-Deterrence	Acts or threats of violence to deter the state or target audience from carrying out particular actions or policies [99]
4-Spoiling	To ensure that peace overtures between moderates on the terrorists' side and the target government do not succeed; to threaten or ruin peace agreements [103]
5-Outbidding	Use violence to convince the public that the terrorists have greater resolve to fight the enemy than rival groups, and therefore are worthy of support [100]
6-Total destruction	Seek high number of casualties; preserve the 'saved' and destroy the 'damned' [104, 105]

violent tactics of a revolutionary terrorist movement include armed robbery to gain supplies of weapons and money; military operations, or rather operations against the military, such as sniping, planting mines etc., to raise the costs of repression; and several others such as kidnapping, assassination, and indiscriminate attacks [107]. On the other hand, when using suicide terrorism as a tactic, the proximate goal and objective is to gain control of territory while the overarching strategy is attrition, a means to compel governments to change policy [108].

Although the repertoire of actions available to terrorists is extensive, groups are usually motivated by a select number of factors leading them to a particular tactic. Terrorist organizations are either motivated to: inflict severe damage (casualties or economic); gain recognition or attention (advertisement); disrupt or discredit the processes of government; affect public attitudes through sympathy or intimidation (psychological impact); provoke some sort of counter reaction from the target; and to gain popular support and dominate a popular movement [93, 109]. These tactical motivations are listed in Table 3.

Therefore, when understanding the reasons behind terrorists' use of a particular tactic, one can look at the tactical motivations of the group and speculate that the organization believed the means or method chosen was the best way to accomplish their proximate objective. In terms of analyzing CBW terrorism, there are various tactics that can be used to achieve proximate objectives, including: to inflict mass casualties, creating a psychological impact, assassination, propaganda, incapacitation, or contamination and area denial.

The relationships among tactics, operations, strategies, and motivations are illustrated in Fig. 1. Each of the terrorists' strategic motivations can be used in this model, which is demonstrated in an example in Fig. 2. In Fig. 2, the group maintains the overarching goal of overthrowing or uprooting the current government. Their typology, left-wing terrorist organization, is the strategic motivation behind their ultimate goal or end. The group then pursues a strategy that could likely bring about their ultimate desire. Thus, in order to uproot the government in power, the group hopes to convince the population of the terrorists' strength and government's weakness,

Table 3 Tactical motivations

Proximate objective	Motivation
0-Damage	Inflict severe damage (casualties and economic)
1-Advertisement	Gain recognition or attention
2-Disruption	Disrupt/discredit the process of government
3-Psychological impact	Affect public attitudes through sympathy, fear, or intimidation
4-Provocation	Provoke some sort of counter reaction from the target
5-Gain support	Gain support and dominate a popular movement

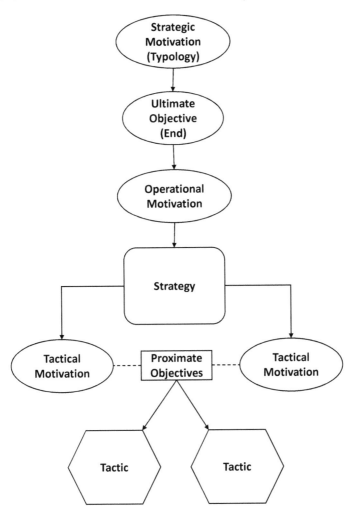

Fig. 1 Framework depicting relationships among different factors that affect terrorist decision-making

driving the organization to pursue a strategy of intimidation. Next, the terrorists must try and think of what action(s) could be taken to contribute to this strategy. In order to intimidate, the group insists on reaching more proximate objectives, inflicting severe damage or affecting public attitudes. These proximate objectives are then obtained through two potential tactics, mass casualty attacks or assassinations. Take assassinations for example. By assassinating leaders, police, or other governmental personnel and representatives, the public perception may be that the government is too weak to protect itself from terrorist organizations. On the other hand, a mass casualty attack- such as a group that massacres thousands of people suspected of switching their allegiance to the government- could affect the public attitude in a sense that they believe

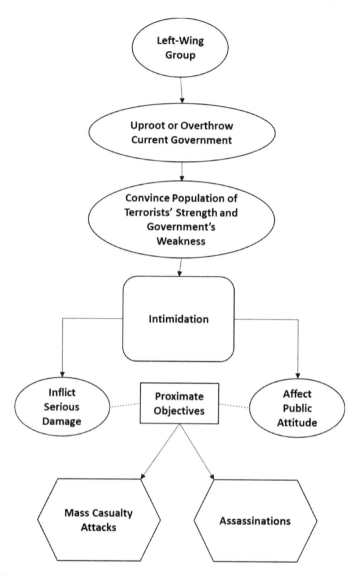

Fig. 2 Example of the terrorist decision-making framework applied to a group of one typology

that the most secure and safe option is to side with the terrorist organization. Both tactics lead to particular proximate objectives that contribute to the overall strategy of intimidation. Through these actions, the group hopes to fulfill the goals of their strategy and reach their desired end.

Figure 2 shows possible paths that could lead to a particular tactic and strategy. When incorporating influencing factors, capabilities, and other restraints, which will be discussed at length below, the motives for accomplishing the group's ultimate goals and proximate objectives may change. The left-wing organization, in Fig. 2, may refrain from mass-casualties if it is worried about its outside constituency, for example. Thus, the model is intended to help develop the most likely strategies and tactics based on the organization's motivations along with numerous other variables specific to the particular terror group.

While restraints and other influencing factors will be discussed in the following sections, it is important to note that the specific uses of CBW can affect the operational and tactical motivation of a group based on their typology. For example, the organizations most likely to inflict mass casualties using CBW are religiously motivated or right-wing groups [66, 110, 111]. Other politically motivated organizations, as well as those with separatist goals and ideological ends, are restrained by both environmental and strategic factors of mass casualty attacks. Jonathan Tucker summarizes why other politically motivated terrorists have not sought CBW in the past, particularly because of the unfamiliarity with relevant technologies, moral constraints, concern that indiscriminate casualties could alienate current or future supporters, and fear that a mass-casualty attack could bring down on the terrorists' heads the full repressive power of the affected government [111]. Single-issue, retaliatory groups are also less likely to use CBW on a large scale. When analyzing retaliatory strikes on industrial chemical or biological facilities, none of the recorded incidents had the intent or inadvertent result of causing mass casualties [78]. The only exception to reactionary groups are organizations opposing U.S. foreign or military policy, such as al-Qaeda or ISIS. These groups have had the intention of eradicating U.S. forces from their homeland. However, their overall motivation stretches beyond this particular intent into a group with a politically, and more so religiously motivated ideology.

Yet, CBW use is not limited to indiscriminate killing. As previously indicated, other tactics of CBW can be more discriminate, including assassinations and area denial to name but a few. Separatist organizations, for example, may not want to alienate supporters through mass casualty attacks, but could be motivated to use CBW to discriminately target symbolic government figures or entities [112]. Similarly, just because right-wing and religious groups are deemed more likely to use CBW in mass casualty attacks does not necessarily limit their use of CBW for those purposes. Rather, the same groups could have varying motivations to use CBW discriminately for other operational or tactical purposes such as propagandizing their cause or putting their organization in the spotlight [113]. For example, the Minnesota Patriots Council, a right-wing terror group prevalent in the U.S. in the 1990s, sought BW for assassination purposes in order to create a blow against the federal government [114]. Thus, while strategic motivation and typology play a major role in the threat of CBW terrorism, the operational and tactical motivations of terrorist organizations, along with the various uses of CBW, can also influence a group's decision to pursue or refrain from using CBW.

In order to capture the level of motivation for terrorist organizations' strategies, operations, and tactics, this study will measure the strength of motivation for each group. For example, intimidation is most frequently used when terrorist organizations wish to overthrow a government in power or gain social control over a given population, while the provocation strategy is often used in pursuit of regime change and territorial change [115]. Similarly, as just mentioned, right-wing and apocalyptic groups are more likely to pursue tactics that kill mass amounts of people indiscriminately due to a lack of constraints. These differences indicate that each group has varying levels of motivation according to their goals, plans of action, and tactics. Therefore, each group will be assessed in terms of their level of motivation for each strategic, operational, and tactical motivation. The measurement will be as follows: 0 indicating no motivation, 1 indicating slight or partial motivation, 2 indicating high or strong motivation.

3.2 Capability

As previously indicated, there are several tactics in which a CBW could be used. The question remains, however, is if the terrorist organization is capable of using a CBW in order to achieve their proximate objectives or even contribute to the more encompassing strategy. Therefore, it is necessary to include capability within the analytical framework. Capability, as defined by DHS, is the adversary's ability to attack with a particular attack method [116]. More descriptively, capability is the discrete abilities and physical items that need to be brought together to execute an action. Within discrete abilities are factors such as explicit and tacit knowledge and also the ability to operate weapons that are more or less complex. The physical items that are considered for capability include: time, money, accessibility, and covertness. Each of these factors contribute to the group's overall capability, and ultimately, the threat of a terrorist attack with CBW.

Before a terrorist can develop or use a CBW they need to acquire the necessary know-how, the explicit and tacit knowledge. For example, when analyzing the development of Soviet biological weapons and the subsequent proliferation threat posed by scientists from a Kazakh bioweapons facility, bioweapons expert Kathleen Vogel found that in order to develop or replicate a militarily useful biological weapon, tacit knowledge is a critical component [117]. She further contends that in addition to "explicit knowledge," such as recipes for producing and processing biological agents, would-be bioterrorists would require a great deal of "tacit knowledge" that cannot be written down but must be acquired through hands-on experience in the lab [118]. Similarly, when understanding the influence of tacit knowledge on companies, groups, or even terrorist organization, tacit knowledge, to include the presence of information and hands-on demonstration, can impact the group's ability to successfully deploy and adopt a new technology [119]. While the barrier to acquire and learn from explicit knowledge has significantly contracted due to globalization and the internet, the necessary requirements of tacit knowledge remain a hindrance to weapon efficiency and effectiveness.

How can one then measure the tacit knowledge required for a CBW, especially when using supposedly less complex frugal technology? Several researchers have proposed various methods to measure tactic knowledge, but many of them are theoretical, require conducting psychological and empirical tests, or involve interviews on individuals and organizations alike [120, 121]. Since the subject of the study is terrorist organizations, and interviewing or testing them for their tactic knowledge is difficult, a more accessible approach is necessary. Alexeis Garcia-Perez and Amit Mitra use a measurement that is more applicable to terror organizations [122]. They measure tactic knowledge using three variables. The first is tactic knowledge stocks, which is an individuals' education, experience, and abilities within an organization. When dealing with terrorists, analyzing intelligence reports on the experience, education, and abilities of recruits and key members can assist in understanding tacit knowledge stocks. The second variable is tacit knowledge flows, which are the streams of knowledge that may be assimilated over time and developed into stocks of knowledge. Since it is difficult to fully identify the flows of knowledge within an organization, this study analyzes the length of time an experienced person or someone with a high knowledge stock has been in an organization that is capable of transferring knowledge flows to other members. The third variable is tacit knowledge enablers which include technologies, any sort of personal or professional proximity between organizational participants, and links between organizational participants and external organizations and networks. Connection to members of the frugal science community, whether they be humanitarian aid workers, instructors, or the scientists themselves can be a measurement of tacit knowledge enablers.

Each variable can be measured on a scale of 0–2. 0 indicates that the recruit or member has no knowledge or experience, meaning they cannot transfer knowledge flows, and also have no contact or proximity to the frugal science community. 1 can be measured by signifying a member has some degree (a degree level lower than that needed to become a professional in the appropriate chemical and biological fields) or experience (1 year or less) in the field of study, less than a year in the organization, and close proximity to known frugal science communities and recipients. 2 identifies individuals with higher levels of education (professional degree in the necessary chemical or biological fields) and experience (over 1 year) in the pertinent field, over a year of existence within the organization, and direct contact with frugal science communities, researchers, or recipients.

Explicit knowledge is perhaps easier to measure than tacit knowledge. Explicit, or codified, knowledge is seen as information found in journal articles, scientific textbooks, websites, databases, and other written sources [123]. This measurement is binary, 0 meaning the group has no access to such materials and 1 meaning the group or individual has access to written sources. The measure of explicit knowledge, in combination with the measurements for tacit knowledge, will help solve the issue of assuming that groups will automatically be able to exploit emerging technologies if they were to somehow acquire them. Together, these two measurements can bring forward a better understanding of the information available to terrorist organizations and their ability to understand, interpret, and carry out that information based on their skills, experience, and tacit knowledge.

Another important factor is the complexity of the technology, where the production and dissemination of such weapons is far more difficult than the public has been led to believe [124]. Former deputy director of the State Department's Office of Counter-Terrorism, Larry Johnson, stated, "Producing these types of weapons requires infrastructure and expertise more sophisticated than a lab coat and a garage. Besides being tough to produce, these weapons also are difficult to use [125]." For example, when the UN investigated the chemical attacks in Syria in 2015, experts noted that special technical expertise and equipment would be needed in various steps of the weaponization process [126]. Not only is the equipment needed for such weapons complex, but effective production of CBW requires a facility the size of a research lab with corresponding infrastructure [127]. Both biological and chemical weapons labs require sufficient power grids and generators to keep refrigerators, incubators, and other technological equipment running. Therefore, in order to successfully develop and employ CBW, terrorist organizations need to overcome the complexity barrier.

When measuring complexity, two variables are to be considered. The first variable is the level of expertise required to operate the technology. Simply put, in order to operate and understand the science involved or the equipment used, how much education and experience is needed? For example, a collaboration between Harvard University, MIT, and Northwestern University tested the success of their simple, cheap BioBit kits in the Chicago Public School System for kids in K-12 [128]. Their study demonstrated that students and teachers were able to perform the experiments in the kits with the same success as trained synthetic biology researchers. On the other hand, certain studies have demonstrated that even basic experimentation is difficult to grasp for amateurs with no background when using unfamiliar equipment such as a pipette for disseminating samples [129]. Even highly motivated groups, such as Aum Shinrikyo, who invested millions of dollars and years of work into their program, had trouble effectively utilizing or creating significantly substantive products form their extensive scientific laboratory that included a centrifuge, fermenters, DNA/RNA synthesizer, incubator, and other equipment. These various examples demonstrate that the successful use of CB equipment heavily depends on the sophistication of the technology, which translates to the education and expertise needed in order to operate and use it. To measure this variable, this study uses a range of 0–2. 0 indicates that no education or experience of the personnel is needed to operate the equipment. 1 specifies that a rudimentary education, such as high school or college is needed or less than a year of experience. 2 indicates that a professional degree (in the appropriate chemical or biological fields) or 1 or more years of experience is required to operate and understand the equipment.

The second variable in complexity is the necessary infrastructure or facilities needed to create CBW. As previously indicated, groups such as Aum Shinrikyo had a 200 m2 laboratory to facilitate all of its equipment. On the other side of the spectrum is frugal science, in which a main component is being able to actually do science experiments and tests outside of the normal university research laboratory. Some frugal developers have indicated that they are inspired to create such technology for those in areas that have no infrastructure, roads, or electricity [22]. Thus, the variable that needs measured is the infrastructure and/or facilities that are needed to create a CBW or CBW program. This measurement will depend on the technology and equipment obtained or used by the group. If the organization plans on using equipment similar to that of Aum Shinrikyo or a state-run CB program, then the measurement for the indicator will be high and marked at 2. Equipment or technology that only requires a room or individual's home, as was the plan for terrorists such as Larry Wayne Harris before his arrest [130], then the measurement is 1. If hardly any facility or infrastructure is required, even in remote, rural areas of the world, then the measurement is 0.

Time can influence the decision to pursue CBW as well. Brian Jackson perfectly sums up the major factors dissuading groups from pursuing CBW as timing and effort. He states, "Most individuals drawn to terrorism want to take direct action rather than use slower, legitimate mechanisms to advance their political or religious agendas. Initiation of a multi-month to several-year research program to perfect a chemical weapon is incompatible with a group which may disintegrate unless it begins its operations immediately [119]."

Time can be measured using two variables: longevity of the terrorist organization and the length of time needed to create a CBW. Studies provide varying results on the longevity of terror organizations, with some claiming only 10% of groups survive past one year [131] and others pointing out that 50% of groups on average do not make it past their first year [132]. Another study indicated that 50% of groups remain active for at least four years, on average [133]. The longevity of the group is important because groups surviving longer than a year, or even four or more, are perhaps more likely to dedicate time and resources into a CBW that could take several months to develop. On the other hand, a group in its infancy with only minimal prospects of surviving in the future may attempt to develop short-term, quick, rudimentary CBW in order to stay relevant or survive. Similar to a small business owner who lacks the time to investigate new techniques or the leisure to reflect on how the technology might change his or her business plan, a terrorist group under pressure of pursuit will also have a serious disincentive to seek out or adopt a new technology such as those needed for a CBW [134]. Thus, time, or longevity, for terrorist organizations is measured by 0 (under a year old), 1 (1–4 years old), and 2 (over 4 years old).

As was just touched on, the time it takes to develop a CBW needs consideration. This in part is determined by the tactic and strategy chosen by the group. An organization wanting to assassinate a handful of people will need less of an agent or pathogen than a group that is acquiring thousands of kilograms or tons of material for a catastrophic attack. In most cases, creating and storing that much material will take significantly longer than acquiring or making a small amount for an assassination. Similarly, the time taken to obtain a usable weapon can depend on if the group created the agent from scratch or somehow purchased or captured the material. Therefore, the time needed to create or obtain the agents or pathogens for the desired goal, strategy, and tactic is also important. Time can be measured on a scale of 0–2. 0 indicates that the time required is less than 6 months. For weapons taking 6 months to a year to create, the measurement is 1. For CBW that take longer than a year to fully create and assemble, the measurement is 2.

Money is also a potential restraint. Although certain chemical and biological agents and precursors can be ubiquitous and cheap, obtaining the materials for most

CBW can be expensive [135]. Yet, an enticing characteristic of frugal science is low cost of materials and equipment. Therefore, the price of the weapon or tactic can vary greatly. Analyses indicate, for example, that average cost of terrorist attacks in Europe in the past twenty years was around USD 10,000 [136]. That number is significantly different than the USD 30 million Aum Shinrikyo spent on chemical weapon research and equipment [137]. It is also significantly larger than the cheap materials—97 cents for a Foldscope and 20 cents for a Paperfuge—being developed within the frugal sciences. Of course, how the terrorist group obtains the weapon matters. Organizations that receive supplies from state sponsors may have less of a financial burden when acquiring weapons than do organizations without any outside support.

Additionally, the financial assets of the group will indicate how much or how little the group can spend on weapons or attacks. Groups such as Hezbollah and the Taliban who have a yearly estimated income of USD 1.1 billion and USD 800 million, respectively, will be able to spend more than groups with more limited financial resources [138]. Thus, the appropriate measurement for money will include both cost of weapon/attack and the group's known income. Known income is described as the financial assets that are known to authorities, particularly because the true number is disguised by the illicit and underground methods terrorist organizations use to raise or receive funds. The known income of the terrorist organization will be on a scale of 0–6 in USD as follows:

0:	Less than 1,000
1:	1,001–10,000
2:	10,001–100,000
3:	100,001–1,000,000
4:	1,000,001–10,000,000
5:	10,000,001–100,000,000
6:	100,000,001 and above

Since the variation of weapons/attacks is so diverse, the measurement of the cost of a single attack and the weapons needed will be on a scale of 0–3 in USD as demonstrated below:

0:	0–100
1:	101–1,000
2:	1,001–10,000
3:	10,001 and above

Final considerations for terrorist organizations to consider when weighing the option of a CBW attack include their ability to get access to specialized chemical precursors or virulent microbial strains and creating an organizational structure capable of resisting infiltration or early detection by law enforcement [91]. The agents and equipment necessary for a CBW are not always readily accessible. Indeed, dual-use technologies and global use of toxic industrial chemicals and microbiological agents decrease the accessibility and capacity barriers, but these materials and agents still require sophisticated technology if the group wants to create a deployable weapon. International treaties, import and export controls, and other law enforcement mechanisms inhibit the trade of this technology, along with certain materials, chemicals, and agents through intensive regulation, making them difficult to access. Hence, in order to measure the accessibility of equipment, technology, or even the pathogens and agents, the study will use a binary indicator: 0 meaning there are no controls, limits, or laws prohibiting the importing, buying, or selling of such material. 1 indicates that there are mechanisms in place that hinder the buying, selling or importing of the material.

The organizations also need to remain covert so that their production and pursuit of such weapons go undetected. Infiltration by law enforcement or outsiders, or even betrayed informants can unveil the production and plots of chemical or biological terrorism. Since the covertness of an organization is difficult to measure, this paper uses the indicator of tolerance by governments. Tolerance is important because the motivation to destroy groups or the laws in place to protect them can contribute to a group's covertness. For example, Aum Shinrikyo was able to act as a legitimate organization under the Japanese Religious Corporation Law, enabling them to set up businesses, agencies, and fundraisers involving the public and the state [139]. The group was then able to carry out its terrorist objectives without taking extreme covert precautions. On the other hand, groups in Italy in the 1970s, such as the Red Brigades, had to worry about tenant and documentation laws, forcing them to become a more underground, clandestine organization [140]. Contemporary groups such as al-Qaeda or ISIS must also take cautionary clandestine measures in order to evade international watchdogs and coalitions attempting to destroy them. Thus, government or international tolerance to organizations plays a major role in the covertness of a group. Since each country's national laws differ, and are at times at odds with international law, measuring tolerance in that respect is insufficient. Instead, the indicator used is countries fighting against terrorist organizations. The scale for this measurement is 0–2. 0 indicates that no government or international coalition is countering the group. If there is one government- particularly the country in which the group resides- opposing the organization through military, financial, or other counterterror operations, the measurement is 1. If there is more than one country, and even more so a coalition of governments opposing the group with similar mechanisms, the measurement is 2.

3.3 Other Influencing Factors

An additional component of motivation in the equation Threat = $M * C$ is group characteristics and traits. While motivation is indeed an important factor, group characteristics and patterns of behavior also contribute to a terrorist's propensity to employ CBW weapons. The leading study that provides characteristics of likely CBW terrorists is Jonathan Tucker's Toxic Terror: Assessing Terrorist Use of Chemical and Biological Weapons [91]. Tucker's comprehensive work on case studies of CBW terrorism identified eight attributes of group characteristics or patterns of behavior that can help identify a group's proclivity to use CBW, which are analyzed below [141].

First, groups that employ greater levels of violence over time may have a higher propensity to pursue CBW. This characteristic indicates that terrorists might perceive conventional tactics to no longer be effective, or that a more lethal and dramatic form of violence is needed [141]. In order to fully grasp the levels of violence of a terrorist organization, two measurements are required: frequency of attacks and lethality of attacks. For instance, studies have shown that groups can be deadlier because of an increased frequency in attacks, not the severity of attacks [142]. Alternatively, a group's surge in violence could be attributed to increasing the number of fatalities per attack (i.e., "big attacks" or attacks that kill over twenty-one people account for 50% of total fatalities, while only comprise of just 3.5% of total attacks) [143]. Therefore, the escalatory patterns of violence can be in terms of frequency or severity. The average number of attacks and fatalities will be over a six-month period so as to ensure a better estimate as opposed to a single month of recordings. If there is an increase in attacks or average fatalities per attack, the measurement is 1. If there is no increase in frequency or severity in attacks, the measurement is 0.

Second, those that are more willing to take risks or innovate in their tactics or weapons could pursue CBW as well. An in-depth study on terrorist weapon innovation and tactics found that the characteristics of a group most likely to pursue or adopt new technologies is any group, "which is tapped into new technology options, open and hungry for new ideas, willing to take risks, not afraid to fail, and driven by its environment to pursue novelty [119]." More explicitly, a workshop and study sponsored by the Defense Threat Reduction Agency found that innovation pertaining to weapons of mass effect, to include chemical or biological weapons, is more likely to occur when groups have safe havens and external sources of support and finances, intend to overcome security measures or revitalize support with more effective and larger attacks, have leaders with technical knowledge, motivation, and charisma, and are larger, resource rich organizations with intentions of escalating conflict [144].

To adequately measure innovation, and hence a characteristic of a group's propensity to use CBW, three variables need evaluation. First, has the group been creative in their use of violence by using new tactics or weapons? ISIS, for example, surprised U.S. and Iraqi forces by demonstrating their ability to take advantage of modern technology such as drones to drop bombs and attack targets [145]. Thus, if groups have changed or altered their tactics or use of weapons, this could demonstrate their ability or motivation to innovate. The measurement is binary. 0 indicates the group has not innovated or used new technology or tactics, while 1 designates that the group has used new or innovate attacks or weaponry against its targets.

The second variable is also binary, measuring if the group has a leader, or leaders, driven by a self-perception as being inventive, innovative, or some sort of expert in a field or technology. Ramzi Yousef, the 1993 World Trade Center bomber, was partially driven to carry out ever more daring and destructive attacks to fulfill his self-perception as a "genius," a "professional terrorist," and an "explosives expert [146]." Thus groups with leaders who are driven by innovation, invention, or technology are marked as 1, while organizations without such leaders are designated 0.

The last variable for innovation is a willingness to take risks experimenting with unfamiliar and dangerous weapons. Terrorists who have tested or experimented with chemical agents or biological pathogens, such as Aum Shinrikyo, al-Qaeda, and ISIS to list but a few, could be seen as more willing to use CBW because they overcome the associated psychological and physical risks of dealing with such unfamiliar material. Therefore, if the group has worked with unusual or dangerous weapons, the measurement is 1, while those who have refrained from such experimentation receives a 0.

Third, people who maintain paranoid and grandiose personality traits tend to be involved in CBW attacks. Although there is a large debate pertaining to a terrorist's mind, psychiatrist Jerrold Post proposes the argument that terrorists disavow their intense feelings of inadequacy, self-hatred, and rage and project them onto others by blaming their misfortune on individual enemies, a despised minority group, or society as a whole [147]. This particular trait holds true in over half of Tucker's case studies, whether it was associated with leaders of groups such as the Rajneeshee cult or was reinforced by members of a group such as the Minnesota Patriots Council. Groups with leaders or members demonstrating paranoid or grandiose personality traits will be measured with 1 and those that do not demonstrate such traits are given the value of 0.

Five of the validated cases of CBW terrorism in Tucker's study involved a small group of two to five people or a militant subgroup within a larger organization. This "small group" trait is explained in the sense that normative constraints of a larger group may not apply to smaller groups. Further, small terrorist cells or socially deranged groups might be more prone to violence in order to remain relevant or perhaps because they maintained the violent tendencies of the larger, original organization [148]. To measure the small group trait, this study uses a range of the size of the organization. 0 indicates a lone-wolf or individual terrorist. 1 is used to measure a group with less than 10 individuals. Organizations with 11–100 members is given a value of 2, while groups with 101–1000 members is measured as 3. Terrorist organizations with more than 1000 members is marked with the value of 4.

The fifth characteristic pertains to groups that do not have a larger outside constituency. This trait will be further analyzed under weapon and tactic characteristics. This characteristic is given a binary measurement, 0 indicating no outside constituency and 1 meaning the group does have a larger outside constituency.

The sixth characteristic pertains to leadership. Tucker specifically states that a charismatic leader who enjoys unquestioned respect and authority and is psychologically inclined to extreme violence can influence the members of a terrorist group to engage in behaviors that they would not normally consider [149]. This characteristic also uses a binary measurement, with 0 designating that the group does not have a charismatic leader and 1 indicating that the organization does have a charismatic leader.

The last two characteristics involve the outlooks and ideologies of terrorist organizations. Groups in desperate situations, fearing an existential threat, whether real or perceived, come to feel they have nothing left to lose by employing every means at their disposal to smite their hated enemies [150]. These organizations under hostile situations may trigger extreme violence as a response of defensive aggression. Terrorists with an existential threat, whether real or perceived, are measured with an indicator of 1, while groups without such threats are measured as 0. The last characteristic includes terrorists with an apocalyptic ideology. To apocalyptics, the goal of bringing about God's Kingdom is more important than anyone or anything existing here and now [151]. Therefore, these groups are perhaps more willing to use CBW to bring about the final cataclysmic battle, or Armageddon, to achieve their end goal. If the organization has an apocalyptic ideology, the measurement is 1, while 0 indicates that their typology is not apocalyptic.

To begin, these eight characteristics can be used as warning signs that particular terrorists' groups, irrespective of ideologies, might be inclined to use and employ CBW [92]. A report from the Congressional Research Service has noted and furthered Tucker's findings, explaining that the two common characteristics among all reported cases were the lack of an outside constituency and a sense of paranoia/grandiosity [152]. Thus, when determining the threat of CBW terrorism, these factors are to be strongly considered.

3.4 Restraints and Inclinations

Just as there are group indicators of an organization's propensity to pursue CB terrorism, there are also characteristics of CBW themselves that could constrain or motivate a group to use them within their tactic or strategy. For example, there are several potential beneficial factors of using such weapons. CBW could be seen as tactically effective. Ultimately, does the action taken result in what the group wants, when they want it? How one measures the tactical effectiveness of a weapon or attack is more complex. The answer depends on the objective of the group. If the proximate objective of a terrorist organization is to inflict serious damage, then the group is tactically effective if they inflict damage on the targeted population. The Global Terrorism Index, for example, measures the impact of terrorism by calculating, weighing, and analyzing four factors: the number of incidents, fatalities, injuries, and property damage by an organization [153]. By this measurement, if a group increases the number of incidents, deaths, injuries, and property damage, they will be considered a more "impactful" terrorist organization.

However, tactical effectiveness can depend on the group's perception and goals. For example, Aum Shinrikyo, a terrorist organization with apocalyptic tendencies, killed twelve people and injured thousands in a subway attack in Tokyo, Japan in 1995 [154]. While the attack affected thousands of lives and cost the country billions of dollars to clean up the incident [155], the group failed to kill their targets on a mass scale and bring about the apocalypse. Thus, tactical effectiveness can change based on the group's goals and perceptions. These perceptions, however, are more important in the calculus before an attack rather than after it. Regardless if the attack resulted in the goals of the organization, it was the group's initial belief that the weapon or attack could have or would have achieved their ultimate desire, prompting them to realize the utility of their attack method. Since the analytical framework aims to determine the threat of a CBW attack instead of the actual consequences, it is important to understand if the terrorist organization recognizes the utility of CBWs as being tactically effective or not.

When measuring this indicator, it is difficult to determine if the group deems CBW to be tactically effective based on pure speculation without any concrete statements or evidence. As a result, the measurement for tactical effectiveness is best represented by any statements the group has made regarding utility or intent of CBW. For example, al-Qaeda has demonstrated in religious fatwas the utility of such weapons in creating mass casualties against the United States and the West. In Shaykh Nasir bin Hamid al-Fahd's, "A Treatise on the Legal Status of Using Weapons of Mass Destruction Against Infidels," he states, "Thus the situation in this regard is that if those engaged in jihad establish that the evil of the infidels can be repelled only by attacking them at night with weapons of mass destruction, they may be used even if they annihilate all the infidels [156, 157]." This indicates that the group deems WMDs, to include both biological and chemical weapons, as tactically effective to inflict mass casualties against its target. This indicator then takes a binary measurement, 1 indicating that the group has stated the utility of using CBW as tactically effective and 0 meaning the group has not demonstrated any intent on using CBW to achieve their goals or objectives.

Continually, terrorists may deem CBW to be effective if they aim to achieve some sort of psychological consequence. In fact, arguably one of the biggest advantages of using CBW is the tremendous psychological impact they can have on multiple audiences, whether they be the targeted enemy or their supporters [92]. The invisible, odorless, tasteless, silent, and insidious effects of CBW create deep human anxieties and can instill a qualitatively different kind of terror [158]. In comparison to a conventional weapon attack, a CBW attack that killed fewer people than perhaps a bomb or gun is commonly thought to have a disproportionate psychological impact [158]. Therefore, terrorists may select CBW due to its potentially large psychological manifestations.

It would be impetuous to assume that terrorist organizations automatically think about the psychological effectiveness of a CBW as compared to a conventional one, or that the intent of using a CBW stems from the psychological characteristics of such an attack. Terrorists groups such as al-Qaeda have in the past explicitly stated their intended reason for attempting to acquire CBW for reasons such as deterrence or provocation [159, 160], but to discuss the psychological effect of a CBW has yet to be seen. Indeed, particular analyses indicate that al-Qaeda leadership agreed to continue to refer to CBRN agents in their statements in order to sow terror and fear in the minds of the enemies [161], but without directly stating the intent or reason for developing CBW is, at least in partial, psychological, it is difficult to speculate that terrorists' intent for a CBW attack is grounded in the psychological effectiveness of the weapon. Therefore, in order to determine if the intent of using CBW stems from the psychological effectiveness of the weapon, the framework uses a binary measurement: 0 indicating the group has not stated the psychological utility of a CBW and 1, the group has stated the psychological utility of a CBW.

The same psychological effects seen as beneficial to terrorists can also be a limiting factor. As previously indicated, one of the group characteristics that could lead an organization to use CBW is their lack of an outside constituency. Yet, if the group does have a constituency outside of themselves, CBW could potentially harm the organization's image and overall cause. The mental and emotional distress created by CBW can instill fear and influence supporters to morally condemn any such use. Terrorist organizations are likely to consider these repercussions from sympathizers and supporters in their overall strategy or tactic [135, 162, 163]. If they believe that their constituencies draw a moral line to the use of CBW and would be less inclined to support or join the organization, then a terrorist group may reconsider pursuing such weapons. In measuring this factor, the study will determine if the group is constrained by an outside constituency (1) or if they don't have to worry about psychological blowbacks due to their lack of an outside constituency (0).

Further, moral lines could be drawn by governments which could potentially thwart support from a state sponsor, or worse, provoke a determined response to destroy the group [91]. This factor uses several variables revolving around state sponsorship and governments countering or targeting the organization. First, it is important to understand if the group has a state sponsor or supporter (1) or if they do not (0). This helps indicate if the group will consider repercussions from state sponsors or if they have no reason to be concerned. The second variable—type of state sponsor—is dependent on the first. If the organization has a sponsor(s), they can either be an active supporter—one of which is a state that actively provides weapons, funds, and safe havens to the group, indicating their lack of determination to dismantle or dissolve the organization [164] or a passive supporter—one who does not have the resources, training, or ability to counter or effectively target the terrorists within their state. Thus, the type of state sponsorship is indicated as being an active supporter (1) or a state incapable of destroying the terrorist group (0).

The next two measurements stem from the type of supporter and ultimately determine if the terror group is to be worried about some sort of international response to a CBW attack. If the sponsor is actively aiding the terrorist group, the level of pressure by outside governments can assist in understanding if the sponsors are more or less likely to thwart support for the terrorist group. Outside governments can enforce sanctions, name and shame state sponsorship, or even resort to military action to try and influence states to cease their support to terrorists [164]. Thus, if states are actively assisting a terrorist group but are not pressured by outside forces through the mechanisms listed, then they are designated as 0. If they are being pressured through sanctions, shaming, or military use or threats, then the measurement is 1.

Continually, determination by outside forces to destroy or target terrorist groups can be measured by the support given to passive sponsors incapable of fully destroying the organization. If the government does not receive any assistance-increasing intelligence capacity, military support, police training, financial assistance, weapons shipments- then the measurement is 0. If the state is given such support from a single government, the measurement is 1. If several states or a coalition of states is assisting the government in need, then the measurement is 2.

On an internal note, groups themselves could also possess a similar psychological deterrent to pursuing CBW. Fear of contamination or mishaps when developing a CBW could deter groups from pursuing the weapons program. Dying a slow, painful death from an infectious disease or chemical is perhaps more terrifying than a quick explosion of a suicide vest, making the effort to obtain CBW less attractive. When measuring this particular psychological effect, the study uses the same variable in helping determine terrorist innovation, the willingness of groups to experiment with new or unfamiliar materials or weapons such as chemical agents or biological pathogens. If the group has experimented with such materials, the group will be given a measurement of 1. If the group has not tested or used unfamiliar weapons or materials, the measurement is 0.

Another consideration is the efficiency of a CBW compared to conventional weapons. If conventional methods for reaching end objectives are working, or they do not see any strategic benefit for pursuing CBW, then organizations are typically dissuaded from any such program [162]. A concrete example is al-Qaeda's hesitancy to use WMDs in their attack on the World Trade Center in 2001. Prior to 9/11, al-Qaeda had publicly stated their ambition to develop weapons of mass destruction and use them against the United States, going so far as to create research and training camps dedicated to the cause. Yet, after analyzing the organization's decision to refrain from using such weapons, al-Qaeda believed that airplanes offered the best means of attacking the targets they intended to destroy [165]. To the group, conventional mechanism proved more efficient than unconventional methods of attack.

Ultimately, there is no single variable in the measurement of conventional weapons versus unconventional weapons. Rather, the best way to analyze the efficiency of a conventional weapon, such as using guns or a bomb, within a group's strategy, operation, or tactic, is to use the same assessment and factors that are used to analyze CBW. In fact, it is these factors, from motivation to capability to influencing characteristics, that could lead terrorists to choose either a conventional or CBW. It all boils down to the motivation of the group, their capabilities, and the influencing factors. In the assessment, if after all of the factors are analyzed and the group decides not to pursue or use CBW, then perhaps the organization deemed conventional methods to be more efficient, effective, and in accordance to their motivations and goals. Thus, to measure the efficiency of conventional weapons versus CBW is to use the CBW threat assessment provided.

4 A Prototypical Case Study

Now that an analytical framework for assessing the threat of CBW terrorism has been proposed, it is critical to place the threat into context so that intelligence and law enforcement agencies can look for certain types of groups, technologies, and environments that can increase the threat of CBW terrorism. In order to elucidate the effects of frugal science on the CBW threat, this paper extracts evidence from al-Qaeda's attempt at developing CBW in the 1990s and early 2000s, how and why it failed, and the possible outcomes that could have emerged had frugal technologies been used.

4.1 Motivation

In the 1990s and early 2000s, al-Qaeda demonstrated the first portion of the threat equation, motivation. Although al-Qaeda ultimately decided to use planes rather than CBW in their attacks on the World Trade Center in 2001, they still maintained a strong motivation for pursuing CBW programs. Stating in a 1998 interview, bin Laden declared, "Acquiring WMD for the defense of Muslims is a religious duty [76]." Bin Laden not only called for Muslims to acquire such weapons but received religious justification from Saudi Islamic scholar Shaykh Nasir bin Hamid al-Fahd who iterated in his fatwa, "A Treatise on the Legal Status of Using Weapons of Mass Destruction Against Infidels" that, "…if those engaged in jihad establish that the evil of the infidels can be repelled only by attacking them at night with weapons of mass destruction, they may be used even if they annihilate all the infidels [166]."

Public statements, religious justifications, and declarations from senior leadership clearly demonstrate the group's intent on developing weapons of mass destruction. Why though, would they try to develop and use CBW? al-Qaeda's typology, and thus strategic motivation, has been religious, but more so of a political-religious group than an apocalyptic organization. As described by the U.S. State Department, al-Qaeda's overarching goals have been to expel U.S. and Western forces from Muslim nations, restore the pan-Islamic caliphate, and impose Islamic rule [167]. As a religious group with political desires, al-Qaeda wished to carry out attacks with extremely high fatalities, coinciding with the assertion that religious terrorists are most likely to use CBW for mass casualty attacks [66, 111, 168].

Originally, the use of CBW was for the operational objective of deterrence. In discussions within bin Laden's inner circle, members frequently asked,

> Who will protect the Arab Mujahideen in their last abode on the face of the earth? How are they to be protected? Who is going to protect the people, the states, the wealth and the Islam of Central Asia, who have scarcely escaped the assault of the 'Red Satan', only to face a more sinister attack from Washington and Tel Aviv? [169]

These concerns motivated al-Qaeda to pursue WMDs as a deterrent against a massive offensive strike as bin Laden stated, "We have chemical and nuclear weapons as a deterrent and if America used them against us we reserve the right to use them [159]."

Yet, al-Qaeda's ultimate operational motivation for chemical or biological weapons has been more on the offensive front. Osama bin Ladin has signaled a specific purpose for using WMD in al-Qaeda's quest to destroy the global status quo and to create conditions more conducive to the overthrow of apostate regimes throughout the Islamic world [165]. His main operational objective was attrition, hoping to use these weapons to inflict such serious costs on the United States that they would eventually withdrawal their forces from the Middle East. Justification for this strategy was evident when he defamed U.S. soldiers as "paper tigers" [170] with low morale, further pointing to U.S. withdrawals from Lebanon in 1983 after Hezbollah bombed the Marine barracks and U.S. embassy there and the "Blackhawk Down" incident in Somalia in 1993 [171].

Furthermore, al-Qaeda has been driven by two prominent tactical motivations, provocation and gaining support. A senior military commander for al-Qaeda, Sayf al Adl, claimed that al Qaeda wanted to provoke the United States into attacking areas of the Islamic world associated with the organization and its affiliates [172]. Doing so would not only build the organization's credibility to the outside world but could also spark an unequivocal response by the West, ultimately igniting an increase in support for their cause and a call to arms.

Through a brief analysis, it is clear that al-Qaeda maintained several tactical, operational, and strategic motivations for potentially using CBW. With fervent religious tendencies, beliefs, and goals associated with their political ends, al-Qaeda upheld a "2-strong motivation" measurement for the religious strategic motivation. As it is difficult to totally separate the group's political incentives from their overarching goals, al-Qaeda receives a "1-slight motivation" measurement for political motivation. All other strategic motivations will receive a measurement of "0-no motivation." Each of the operational and tactical motivations can also be measured based on the explanations above, but in order to move forward, it is acceptable to say that al-Qaeda did possess the motivation for acquiring and using CBW.

4.2 Influencing Characteristics

Not only did al-Qaeda maintain the motivation to pursue CBW, but they also demonstrated several characteristics that increased their propensity to employ CBW. To begin, in demonstrating the group's increased level of violence, al-Qaeda leader, Osama bin Laden promised to "escalate the killing and fighting against you (Americans) [160]." This 2007 statement was realized years before, as the lethality of al-Qaeda's attacks increased due to the bombings on U.S. embassies in Tanzania and Kenya in 1998 and the 9/11 attacks on U.S. soil, giving them a measurement of 1 [165, 170].

The group also receives an indicator of 1 for all three variables pertaining to innovation in weapons and tactics. al-Qaeda's use of weaponized planes in the 9/11 attacks is a leading example of not only the group's weapon innovation, but also the creation of an entirely new tactic involving plane hijackings. The second variable—groups with a leader or members who are innovative and seen as "experts"—was also evident within al-Qaeda. The group's leader, Osama bin Laden, was not necessarily a technological expert or inventor, but several members of his inner circle were, including: Mubarak al-Duri, Abu Rida Mohammed Bayazid, and Abu Walid al-Masri [173–175]. These individuals were highly qualified scientists who frequently discussed chemical and biological attacks, programs, and possibilities with bin Laden. Furthermore, one of the heads of the organization and future leader of al-Qaeda, Ayman Zawahiri who holds a Master's degree in surgery, brought his scientific capabilities to the group and personally oversaw and managed the biological weapons development [165]. al-Qaeda has also shown its propensity to experiment with new types of weapons and materials, the third variable for measuring innovation. In an eyewitness account, Ahmad Rassam claimed that he had witnessed—in one of the multiple CBW laboratories and training camps—an experiment in which cyanide was used to gas a dog [176]. Thus, al-Qaeda is known to have been an innovate terrorist organization according to the study's measurements.

Continually, bin Laden demonstrated grandiose and paranoid personality traits defined by Jonathan Tucker and Jerold Post. In his "Letter to America," bin Laden exemplifies his ambitious and excessively grand plans for the Muslim world while also placing the blame of all misfortunes on the United States and the West [177]. This iconic letter is a primary reason al-Qaeda's grandiose and personality characteristic is indicated with a 1. In regard to the small group trait, al-Qaeda is measured with 3 for 101–1000 members. While the number of fighters in bin Laden-supported camps from 1996–9/11 attacks is estimated between 10,000–20,000, only a few hundred were indoctrinated as actual al-Qaeda members, as the 9/11 Commission Report exemplifies [178].

While some religious organizations are only concerned in pleasing their deity or higher power, al-Qaeda had an outside constituency to consider. In a letter sent by al-Zawahiri to Iraqi jihadist leader Abu Mus 'ab al-Zarqawi on July 9, 2005, al-Zawahiri explained,

> If we look at the two short-term goals, which are removing the Americans and establishing an Islamic amirate in Iraq, or a caliphate if possible, then, we will see that the strongest weapon which the mujahedeen enjoy - after the help and granting of success by God - is popular support from the Muslim masses in Iraq, and the surrounding Muslim countries [179].

Thus, while al-Qaeda has been a religiously fanatic group, they have appealed to an outside constituency, which equates to a measurement of 1 for this particular factor.

This sixth characteristic of the framework, which al-Qaeda also possessed, is having a charismatic leader. When discussing the leadership of Osama bin Laden, Joby Warrick explained that young men from several countries across the world came to Khartoum, Sudan to train in al-Qaeda camps. Some believed in Islamic purity while others sought blood and excitement. No matter the stark differences,

Osama drew them together with charisma, provided them with meaning, and united them against a common enemy, the United States [180]. Hence, al-Qaeda receives a 1 for this characteristic.

The last two characteristics involve defensive aggression, in which al-Qaeda receives a 1, and apocalyptic ideology, in which they receive a 0. When analyzing why Osama Bin Laden declared war on the United States in 1996, a multitude of reasons are associated with the perceived existential threat that the U.S. put on Muslims, including: the U.S. presence in Arabia, the U.S. presence in any Muslim state, U.S. support for Israel, Western influence on Islam, and the U.S. taking advantage of Muslim nation's resources [181]. Therefore, al-Qaeda's actions can be partially viewed as a "defensive jihad" to defeat a rival system portrayed as an existential threat to Islam [182]. Regarding the last characteristic, al-Qaeda was not necessarily an apocalyptic group that sought total destruction of the entire world. Rather, the overarching goals of the group have been to expel U.S. and Western forces from Muslim nations, restore the pan-Islamic caliphate, and impose Islamic rule [183]. Total apocalyptic destruction would prevent the group from attaining those goals.

Before moving forward, it is important to briefly touch on the other constraints or inclinations that al-Qaeda faced when pursuing CBW. As previously mentioned, al-Qaeda explicitly stated the tactical effectiveness of using CBW in their overall strategy, which gives them a 1 for tactical effectiveness. However, the group never mentioned any specific psychological effect or utility of CBW, especially compared to conventional weapons, so their measurement for psychological effectiveness is 0.

Since al-Qaeda was, and still is, a global organization not confined by state boundaries, it was susceptible to support or confrontation with several governments. When measuring state sponsorship, however, it is evident that al-Qaeda had support from a few countries. Iran, for example, admitted to having allowed al-Qaeda members travel secretly throughout the Middle East [184]. The 9/11 Commission also indicated that the Taliban government in Afghanistan directly supported the group before 9/11 and that Saudi Arabia and several other Gulf countries indirectly may have perhaps turned a blind-eye to al-Qaeda fundraising activities or even that charities with significant Saudi government sponsorship diverted funds to al-Qaeda [185]. These facts demonstrate that al-Qaeda did have some forms of state support, providing them with a measurement of 1 for the respective factor as well as a 1 for the sponsor having been an active supporter.

al-Qaeda was also susceptible to international coalitions fighting against them throughout the years, giving the variable for outside pressure a measurement of 1. The United States, NATO, and the United Nations, among several other countries, have been taking diplomatic, economic, and military action against al-Qaeda since the 1990s [167]. Despite these international efforts, the group still pursued CBW programs, but in the end, came up short as will be described in detail below.

4.3 al-Qaeda's CBW Programs: With and Without Frugal Science

With a breadth of motivations, coupled with an array of group characteristics and traits that could increase their propensity to use CBW, why did al-Qaeda not use CBW? One explanation is that al-Qaeda did not have the capabilities to create what they viewed as an effective CBW. Their goals and motivations required them to develop a weapon that could produce mass casualties, and according to analyses, the use of crude CBW was not sufficient to what would only amount to a pin prick to the United States [186]. Therefore, it is necessary to analyze the disconnect between the adamant will to develop CBW and the capabilities that prevented them from doing so. Using the analytical framework, this study will demonstrate the difficulties in creating CBW- for al-Qaeda's purpose of creating mass casualties- and how frugal science could either foster improved capabilities or have little effect on the overall threat.

al-Qaeda's calculus of the potential consequences of deploying a CBW led them to develop several chemical and biological production facilities. Ayman Zawahiri recruited a Pakistani governmental biologist to develop a biological program in Kandahar, Afghanistan [187], while bin Laden established a facility in Khost, Afghanistan [165, 188] as well as in Charassib, south of Kabul [189, 190]. A toxin and explosives laboratory was also created at Darunta base in the Afghan city of Jalalabad [191, 192]. Even al-Qaeda affiliate Ansar al-Islam developed a CBW facility in northern Iraq, where the group received money and assistance from al-Qaeda to test cyanide and ricin on animals [191].

Although al-Qaeda had several facilities and laboratories sprinkled throughout the Middle East, they internally struggled with the technical hurdles of developing a deployable CBW. In order to successfully carry out a CBW attack- in the form of a true WMD, not a crude weapon- terrorists must take four vital steps: secure a culture of a suitable pathogen or quantity of a toxin, develop a combination of the pathogen or toxin and the substrate in which it is suspended or dissolved, obtain a necessary container to safely store and transport the formulations, and apply an efficient mechanism to disperse the pathogen or toxin over or onto the population target [193]. When analyzing reports and studies of al-Qaeda's CBW programs, the group failed to make it past even the first stage. For example, according to the WMD Commission Report, although al-Qaeda successfully acquired several biological agents as early as 1999, the equipment and expertise enabled only a basic, limited production of Agent "X" [191]. Regarding CW capabilities, analysts suggested that al-Qaeda was able to produce small quantities of toxic chemicals and pesticides, were familiar with the production of common chemical agents, but were doubtful that the group could conduct attacks with advanced chemical agents potentially capable of causing thousands of casualties or deaths [192].

Part of the reason al-Qaeda could not develop more than crude agents or toxins was their lack of expertise. Referencing al-Qaeda's BW program, an assessment by the U.S. Department of State indicated that, "Terrorist development of a more advanced biological weapon capability would likely require direct assistance from disenfranchised technicians or scientists formerly affiliated with a state program [194]." This assessment corresponds to other analyses of the actual "experts" that were in charge of some of the group's CBW programs. Rauf Ahmed, for example, who was appointed by Zawahiri as the head of the biological and anthrax programs in Kandahar, Afghanistan, was hardly the ideal candidate for helping al-Qaeda achieve its biological weapons ambitions. Intelligence experts noted that, "He could potentially do a great deal of harm because of his knowledge and skills," but since his doctorate in microbiology specialized in food production, he "…lacked the specific knowledge and training al-Qaeda needed most," which slowed his progress considerably [195].

Another problem encountered by the group was their rudimentary and insufficient explicit knowledge and instructions on how to create anything beyond crude CBW capabilities. In analyzing the books, manuals, and web pages on CBW production proliferated by al-Qaeda, technical experts unveiled the amateurish instructions adequate only for the production of small quantities of crude agents that were not suitable for mass-casualty terrorism [196]. The instructions for ricin, mustard gas, and the botulinum toxin were either incomplete, insufficient in creating an actual agent, or failed to indicate the difficulty in successfully producing the agent. Thus, the al-Qaeda instructions, which were predominantly taken from open source, available U.S. biology books and studies, primarily dealt with the history and previous use of CB agents and toxins rather than providing the necessary information for creating such agents.

Further investigation into al-Qaeda's CBW program also demonstrates that the group did not have access to the necessary technical equipment used for producing CB agents and toxins. Indeed, the group had gloves, masks, beakers, and even dual-use medical equipment that could be used to create biological agents, but overall lacked the technical equipment needed to produce significant amounts and lethal dosages of the agents, as well as the technology and equipment needed to disseminate any sort of weaponized agent or toxin [190, 197, 198]. As a result, al-Qaeda did not have the expertise, knowledge, equipment, or technical capabilities to produce the CBW desired for mass-casualty attacks.

The conclusiveness of the inability of al-Qaeda to develop significant CBW capabilities is evident across government, intelligence, military, and analytical reports. It can be speculated, then, that al-Qaeda deemed conventional weapons more suitable for their goals because (a) the group lacked the capabilities to produce CBW and (b) conventional weapons were the only means available to effectively inflict mass casualties. Yet, the calculus and threat could have been different had the group had access to frugal science. It is not to say that the group would not have encountered any difficulties. On the contrary, al-Qaeda would still have had particular troubles with or without frugal science, which will be discussed in detail below. However, frugal science could have helped the group overcome certain technical and logistical obstacles that would not have been successful otherwise.

To begin, al-Qaeda would have been able to more easily access the technology and equipment of frugal science than the typical laboratory materials needed for major CBW programs. Instead of relying on the illicit procurement of state-of-the-art laboratory technology, which is often monitored and controlled by the OPCW, BWC, and other internationally recognized export control mechanisms, al-Qaeda could have acquired the necessary frugal science technology through legitimate avenues such as humanitarian aid to war-torn regions or as experimentalists and biologists seeking frugal tools in remote areas. As a result, al-Qaeda would potentially be able to utilize the necessary equipment, enabling them to experiment, test, work with, and grow accustomed to the agents and toxins.

Due to the classified information regarding the exact technology that was in the hands of al-Qaeda at the time, it is difficult to deduce the exact level of experimentation they were able to conduct. However, it has been indicated that the technology was insufficient to create anything beyond crude or basic agents or toxins. With the developments in frugal technology, such as microfluidics or chemistry kits, al-Qaeda may have had a better chance to develop more advanced weapons. A primitive feature of microfluidics is the thousands of chemical reactions that can occur on a single chip. This enables scientists to test, experiment, and figure out what sort of reaction, chemicals, and quantities are needed to get their desired product, and it can all be tested in a matter of minutes [199]. Thus, al-Qaeda could have worked on developing a virulent strain or lethal agent through the rapid, constant experimentation with frugal tools.

Frugal science could not only have helped al-Qaeda better understand the chemicals and toxins they were working with, but it could have also created significant amounts of the product through mass-scale and commercialized production. Using cheap materials or paper-based assays, the organization could have either bought enough equipment to develop more of the needed agent or toxin, or they could have attempted to produce more assays through ink jet or 3d printing. This could have allowed them to accumulate more of the chemicals or toxins needed for a weapon with mass-casualty capabilities.

Furthermore, al-Qaeda would not have been as confounded by the complexity of the frugal technology as with normal laboratory equipment. A key aspect of frugal technology, as mentioned above, are the manuals, instructions, and even hands-on instructions on how to operate the equipment to ensure that people all over the world can test and develop their own scientific experiments. As a result, al-Qaeda may have had a better understanding, through both explicit and tacit knowledge, of the technology and how to use it for their own purposes—creating sufficient CB agents and toxins for a deployable weapon.

When applying the analytical framework, al-Qaeda's capabilities improve when using frugal science. The legitimate uses of frugal technology—combined with the relatively new field of frugal science capable of being disseminated to people across the world—alter the accessibility measurement for al-Qaeda. Since these tools do not have controls or laws in place that limit their proliferation, the indicator for accessibility is 0, which differs from the original indicator of export-controlled lab equipment, 1.

Depending on al-Qaeda's methodology for acquiring the technology, they could have direct contact with frugal scientists who provide hands-on experience on how to use the equipment. Just as clinics and people in impoverished areas receive training on how to use the equipment, terrorists' direct contact with outside sources can change the measurement of tacit knowledge enablers from 0 to 2, increasing the overall threat. Additionally, the group would have access to the explicit information on how to operate the frugal technology through online databases and DIY instruction manuals provided to experimentalists and new users. This will also increase the group's score of explicit knowledge on how to operate the equipment from 0 to 1, indicating that they have access to written documents or instructions.

More importantly, the complexity measurement can change from the indicator 2-professional degree or over one year of experience needed to operate the technology—to either 0 or 1. There is no doubt that microfluidics can be complex and can create technical barriers to new users. However, part of the idea behind frugal microfluidics is to create simpler, cheaper technology for new biologists, chemists, and experimentalists. The drive to lower the complexity level of such equipment has motivated frugal developers to teach high school [200] and even elementary level school children how to use microfluidic LOC technology [191]. Since the gamut of frugal science that could be used to create CBW ranges from the Foldscope and Paperfuge, which can be operated without any education or experience (0), to microfluidic devices that can be operated with either a professional degree and more than one year of experience (2) or operated by students with rudimentary degrees (1), the overall complexity score for the frugal science equipment will be the average, 1.

The other variable for complexity—the facility and/or infrastructure needed to operate the equipment—also changes due to frugal science. Since the goal of frugal science is to provide science equipment to anyone, anywhere, especially those in rural, impoverished areas with little to no infrastructure, the equipment necessitates far less infrastructure and facility requirements than that of a university or state-run laboratory. Developments of microfluidic-based computers are also improving, which could provide al-Qaeda with a computer that is essentially a high-throughput chemistry and biology laboratory [201]. Thus, the required facilities and infrastructure needed for frugal science changes the score from 2 to 1—indicating only a basic room or home is necessary to operate the equipment.

Money has also been an issue with al-Qaeda's CBW programs. Zawahiri's anthrax scientist, Rauf Ahmed, frequently complained about financial issues. Ahmed's money demands may have led to a falling-out with Zawahiri who appeared to have decided to explore other options for obtaining bacteria and lab equipment [26]. Yet, with frugal technology, the cost of such equipment is far less than that used in state-run or university laboratories. The cost of a CBW or program using frugal science would be significantly less than the hundreds of millions spent on state-level CBW programs, such as the 100–200 million USD for Iraq's state program [202] or millions spent by Aum Shinrikyo [203]. With the speculation that al-Qaeda would purchase frugal technology for their CBW program, but would also need to purchase or somehow acquire chemicals or toxins capable of inflicting mass casualties, the cost of the weapon and attack will be measured as 2, indicating it will cost the group between 1001 and 10,000 USD to successfully acquire CBW capabilities. This lowers the original measurement of 3, which indicates that the weapon or attack would cost more than 10,000 USD.

5 Operational Challenges of Frugal Science

Before succumbing to technological determinism, it is crucial to note that frugal science, while having the potential to significantly influence several capability indicators in the analytical framework, falls well short of being able to increase the overall capabilities of the terrorist organization. Frugal equipment is intended to be less complex, easy to use, accessible, and cheap, but reality holds that the terrorist group would still need both the tacit knowledge and expertise to create chemical and biological agents and toxins for a weapon that can inflict mass casualties. Frugal technology can help groups experiment and test the materials they are working with, but, with only rudimentary knowledge of all stages necessary in developing a tactically effective CBW, the group is unlikely to increase their overall capability.

To further explain this analysis, take the shortcomings of frugal science in experimenting with and developing toxins or agents necessary for a CBW. As previously mentioned, a recent study demonstrated that when high school students and teachers were given frugal BioBit kits to conduct biology experiments, the kids were able to perform the experiments with the same success as trained synthetic biology researchers [50]. On the other hand, certain studies have demonstrated that even basic experimentation is difficult to grasp for amateurs with no background when using unfamiliar equipment such as a pipette for disseminating samples [190]. Given that a terrorist group such as al-Qaeda acquired frugal technology that is easier to use, such as the BioBit kit, they could then conduct biological experiments with cheaper, accessible technology. However, that does not correlate to gaining tacit or even explicit knowledge on working with, for example, the botulinum toxin—in which the group only possessed amateurish instructions on how to successfully produce the complex toxin that can be difficult to master. Access to frugal science does not improve the indicators for a group's tacit knowledge stocks or flows when it comes to weaponized materials. With or without frugal technology, al-Qaeda would still need the expertise and experience of working with chemical or biological agents and toxins needed for a CBW.

Further, even if al-Qaeda's tacit knowledge enabler measurement improved because of their potential direct contact with members of the frugal science community, there is still a large discrepancy between the tacit knowledge gained on the technology versus actually working with CBW grade materials. For these reasons, it is difficult to see how frugal science could improve the overall tacit knowledge of a terrorist organization outside of the hands-on experience of using the technology themselves. The explicit knowledge indicator can be viewed in the same light as tactic knowledge. Access to DIY documents and instructions on how to operate frugal equipment does not necessarily translate into gaining instructions on dealing with advanced CBW material. Explicit knowledge on frugal science can help overcome the obstacle of knowing how to operate equipment that can be used for such weapons, but it still does not correlate to coming to grips with the scientific technicalities of creating a mass casualty CBW.

Lastly, experimentation with agents and toxins using frugal science does not equate to overcoming the weaponization process. Foldscopes, Paperfuges, and microfluidic technology have an array of applications, but, as of now, weaponizing CB grade material is not one of them. As Jonathan Tucker points out, the dissemination of BW agents poses even greater technical hurdles than developing a highly virulent strain of a bacteria. Tucker states,

> Although aerosol delivery is potentially the most lethal way of delivering a biological attack, it involves major technical hurdles that most terrorists would be unlikely to overcome... terrorists would therefore have to develop or acquire a sophisticated delivery system capable of generating an aerosol cloud with the necessary particle size range and a high enough agent concentration to cover a broad area [204].

Chemical agents are no easier in weaponizing or disseminating. Not only have a majority of reports indicated that al-Qaeda has not been able to successfully weaponize CB agents and toxins [205], but Aum Shinrikyo, the terrorist organization with one of the most extensive CBW programs to date, even failed to produce effective weaponization of their chemical weapons. When examining the Aum Shinrikyo Tokyo subway attack in 1995, the group failed to carry out a devastating chemical attack because of their crude delivery system and low-grade sarin [128].

6 Future Threat Assessment

While keeping the challenges still present even with frugal technologies in mind, let us take brief look at how this threat could change in the future and how it might affect different national security environments. These environments include virtual, mega city, terrorist group, peer competitor, failing/failed state, and border/perimeter security, and we will look at the present situation and into the future 5 years and 10–15 years.

Firstly, frugal technology as it pertains to CBW does not currently and will not in the future affect the virtual environment simply by the nature of the disparate technologies. Presently, in 2020, misuse of frugal technology is ranked as low risk in all the other environments. In the peer competitor and failing/failed state environments this low level is due to their access to conventional laboratory equipment. These environments do not need and would likely not benefit from frugal technology. In terms of border/perimeter security and mega cities, there must be someone to create and want to use CBW who would benefit from frugal technology and currently they are not there. Terrorist groups could use it but the barriers to CBW are not just that lack of accessibly technology. As previously described, tacit knowledge and willingness to use are both significant barriers.

In 2025, the risks in all environments remain what they are in 2020. Five years will see further development of frugal technology but because of the lag as people work on finding alternative uses for the technologies the risk does not increase in this time frame.

In 2035, the risk from peer competitors, failing/failed states, and border/perimeter security does not increase. However, in mega cities and from terrorist groups the risk

Table 4 Risk of frugal technology begin used to create chemical or biological weapons in different environments. Blue is no possibility, green is low, yellow is medium, and red is high likelihood

Environments	2020 (Present)	2025 (5 Years)	2035 (10-15 Years)
Virtual	Blue	Blue	Blue
Mega City	Green	Green	Yellow
Terrorist Group	Green	Green	Yellow
Peer Competitor	Green	Green	Green
Failing/Failed State	Green	Green	Green
Border/Perimeter Security	Green	Green	Green

goes up. The biggest risk is the combination of these two environments with terrorist groups attacking a mega city. In 10–15 years, frugal technology could advance far enough and will have been available for long enough for groups to experiment with it and potentially develop techniques for how to use these technologies to create CBW. The reason that the overlap of these two environments is important is the risk comes from both the use of CBW in dense areas and from the fear and potential panic induced by CBW. The risk level in the different environments is highlighted in Table 4.

7 Lessons Learned and Recommendations

In conclusion, while frugal science can alter the indicators of technological complexity, accessibility, the cost of the weapon and attack, and potentially as a tacit knowledge enabler, it nonetheless fails to improve other central technical hurdles relating to a group's overall capabilities. This analysis further supports views arguing that more than just new technology is needed to create a CBW, as chemical experts note, "Making ineffective biological weapons is easy, making effective biological weapons is not easy [129]." This is evident in al-Qaeda's case study. The assessment using the analytical framework reinforces CBW terrorism skeptics' point of view, such as those attempting to debunk the several "myths" of how synthetic biology correlates to an increased use and capability by terrorist organizations. When countering the myths- some of which imply that the material, informational aspects of synthetic biology will make it easier for anybody to exploit this technology to do harm, or that producing a pathogenic organism equates to producing a weapon of mass destruction- the authors argue that such weapons still require specialist expertise and equipment, which are all available in academic laboratories but not necessarily easily accessible to an amateur working at home. The same authors point out that biological strains cannot be randomly created, but require the difficult understanding of stability, virulence, transmissibility, and other characteristics of agents [206], refuting the assumption that producing a pathogenic organism is parallel to producing a weapon of mass destruction. Each of these points were clear in al-Qaeda's attempt in creating a CBW capable of inflicting mass casualties, with or without frugal science.

Yet, the scope of the framework is not limited to a single case study, let alone one specific technology. On the contrary, the analytical framework is capable of incorporating both low-tech discoveries and high-tech innovations. Just as frugal science—a low-tech development—demonstrated the shortcomings of increasing the CBW terrorist threat, it is arguable that emerging high-tech instruments can pose even more technological problems for nefarious end-users. For example, CRISPR, a new gene-editing technique, has emerged at the forefront of synthetic biological weapons concerns due to its touted ease of use and diffusion [207]. Despite its potential for dual-use purposes, experts indicate that creating a mass-casualty biological weapon requires more than mere access to a pathogen, a particular technique, or a piece of biotech equipment [208]. Furthermore, the technological complexity and explicit and tacit knowledge issues that frugal science could have potentially alleviated do not necessarily apply to more advanced technology such as CRISPR. In fact, this gene-editing technique that has been a major concern for policy makers is actually quite complex, leaving many advanced scientists and biologists with an entire gamut of problems related to mastering CRISPR such as off-target and reproducibility challenges. Therefore, compared to low-tech innovations, high-tech developments like CRISPR often pose more advanced technological hurdles for would-be terrorists to overcome.

In some case over regulating can cause more deaths, higher cost, and instability, than under-regulation. For example, in the first half of 2007, there were a rash of chlorine attacks in Iraq [209] that resulted in the US placing restrictions on the importation of chlorine into the country. In September of 2007 there was an outbreak of Cholera. Cholera is transmitted through contaminated food or water resulting from poor sanitation [210]. In this case, poor sanitation was partially caused by a lack of available chlorine. The outbreak of cholera affected more than 4000 people and caused 24 deaths [211]. Whether this is less damaging than the restricted chlorine would have been if used as a weapon is an open question.

Apart from the initial case study's conclusions, there are two main takeaways from the overall analysis on frugal science, emerging technologies, and the CBW threat equation. The first is that emerging technologies such as frugal science are not to be ignored. On the contrary, the above assessment demonstrates how frugal science can improve the capabilities of terrorist organizations, if only by minimal increments. Those who downplay the expertise of terrorist organizations also need to be wary of the types of people terrorists recruit. While it is true that groups often recruit anyone to fill in the ranks or carry out operations, evidence also suggests that, "over time, successful terrorist groups engage in "talent spotting" and eventually recruit more educated and professional individuals with specific expertise to adapt to changing opportunities and increased pressures from a securitized environment

[212]." With groups such as Aum Shinrikyo, al-Qaeda, and ISIS having demonstrated their commitment to recruit disgruntled scientists and individuals with experienced backgrounds, the tacit knowledge implication could potentially be reduced through a combination of expert recruits and frugal technology. The trends of increased research, applicability, and proliferation of frugal science in recent years further attests to the need of monitoring by the intelligence and law enforcement communities on frugal technological developments and flows.

The second takeaway involves the utility of the analytical framework provided by this study. CBW expert Kathleen Vogel assesses various models of analysis, indicating that new models need to incorporate a combination of both social and technical factors- what she calls sociotechnical analysis [213]. She specifies that material and technical aspects of analysis (explicit knowledge, accessibility, economic drivers, material end products, etc.) in combination with social aspects of using such technology (tacit knowledge, social and material conditions required for the technology, troubleshooting efforts and challenges of producing desired products) are necessary for analyzing the threat of CBW terrorism with respect to emerging technologies. The analytical framework in this study attempts to do just that by determining the motivation and capabilities of terrorist organizations, and assessing how emerging technologies contribute to the overall threat equation, not only for low-tech innovations but for high-tech developments as well. Just because frugal science, at the moment, did not succeed in significantly increasing the overall threat of CBW terrorism does not mean that the framework is impractical. Rather, the intricacies of the framework reveal the numerous factors that are incorporated in the threat equation, and in turn are to be overcome by terrorists seeking to deploy a tactically effective CBW. The case of frugal science and al-Qaeda is just one such demonstration of the utility of the framework and how it can be used and improved in future analyses.

References

1. United States (2015) The national security strategy of the United States of America. [Washington]: President of the U.S. http://nssarchive.us/wp-content/uploads/2015/02/2015.pdf (Accessed April 30, 2018)
2. Humanitarian Assistance (2018) The organisation for economic co-operation and development (OECD) http://www.oecd.org/dac/stats/humanitarian-assistance.htm (Accessed April 2, 2018)
3. Glossary of Humanitarian Terms (2018) The World Health Organization http://www.who.int/hac/about/reliefweb-aug2008.pdf (Accessed April 2, 2018)
4. Bollyky TJ (2015) New, cheap, and improved
5. Whitesides GM (2012) The frugal way. The Economist-The World in 2011
6. Pandika M (2017) A conversation with Manu Prakash. ACS Publications
7. Zeschky MB, Winterhalter S, Gassmann O (2014) From cost to frugal and reverse innovation: Mapping the field and implications for global competitiveness. Res Technol Manag 57(4):20–27
8. Martinez AW, Phillips ST, Whitesides GM, Carrilho E (2009) Diagnostics for the developing world: microfluidic paper-based analytical devices. ACS Publications

9. Shazam for Mosquitoes (2018) Ed Yong, the Atlantic https://www.theatlantic.com/science/archive/2017/03/shazam-mosquitoes-cellphone-citizen-science/521505/ (Accessed April 2, 2018)
10. Martinez AW, Phillips ST, Butte MJ, Whitesides GM (2007) Patterned paper as a platform for inexpensive, low-volume, portable bioassays. Angew Chem Int Ed 46(8):1318–1320
11. Chin CD, Linder V, Sia SK (2007) Lab-on-a-chip devices for global health: past studies and future opportunities. Lab Chip 7(1):41–57
12. Frugal Science and Global Health (2018) Prakash Lab, Stanford http://web.stanford.edu/group/prakash-lab/cgi-bin/labsite/research/frugal-science-and-global-health/ (Accessed April 2, 2018)
13. Khiabani PS, Soeriyadi AH, Reece PJ, Justin Gooding J (2016) Paper-Based Sensor for Monitoring Sun Exposure. ACS Sensors 1(6):775–780
14. Switz NA, D'Ambrosio MV, Fletcher DA (2014) Low-cost mobile phone microscopy with a reversed mobile phone camera lens. PloS one 9(5):e95330
15. Cybulski JS, Clements J, Prakash M (2014) Foldscope: origami-based paper microscope. PloS one 9(6):e98781
16. Byagathvalli G, Pomerantz A, Sinha S, Standeven J, Bhamla MS (2019) A 3D-printed hand-powered centrifuge for molecular biology. PLoS Biol 17(5):e3000251
17. Byagathvalli G, Sinha S, Zhang Y, Styczynski MP, Standeven J, Bhamla MS (2020) ElectroPen: an ultra-low–cost, electricity-free, portable electroporator. PLoS Biol 18(1):e3000589
18. Sinha S, Irani UD, Manchaiah V, Bhamla MS (2020) LoCHAid: an ultra-low-cost hearing aid for age-related hearing loss. PloS one 15(9):e0238922
19. United States (2015) The national security strategy of the United States of America. [Washington]: President of the U.S.
20. Chandy L, Seidel B, Zhang C (2016) Aid effectiveness in fragile states: how bad is it and how can it improve?. Brookings Institute. https://www.brookings.edu/research/aid-effectiveness-in-fragile-states/
21. George Whitesides, The frugal way. In: The economist, science (November 2011)
22. Kris Newby, Inspired by a Whirligig Toy, Stanford Bioengineers Develop a 20-cent, Hand-powered blood centrifuge. In: Stanford News, January 10, 2017, https://news.stanford.edu/2017/01/10/whirligig-toy-bioengineers-develop-20-cent-hand-powered-blood-centrifuge/
23. Whitesides GM (2006) The origins and future of microfluidics. Nature 442(July 2006):368–373
24. Whitesides GM (2006) The origins and future of microfluidics. Nature 442(July 2006):368
25. Martinez AW et al (February 2007) Patterned paper as a platform for inexpensive, low-volume, portable bioassays. Angew Chem 46(8):1318–1320
26. Lisowski P, Zarzycki PK (2013) Microfluidic paper-based analytical devices (lPADs) and micro total analysis systems (lTAS): development, applications and future trends. Chromatographia 76:1201–1214
27. Grifantini K (2009) 10 Breakthrough Technologies. In: MIT technology review, February 24, 2009, http://www2.technologyreview.com/news/412187/tr10-paper-diagnostics/
28. Prakash M (2008) Microfluidic bubble logic (PhD diss., MIT, September 2008)
29. Liu S, Su W, Ding X (2016) A review on microfluidic paper-based analytical devices for glucose detectio. Sensors 16(12)
30. Kangas MJ et al (March 2017) Colorimetric sensor arrays for the detection and identification of chemical weapons and explosives. Crit Rev Anal Chem 47(2)(March 2017):138–153
31. Streets AM, Huang Y (2013) Chip in a lab: microfluidics for next generation life science research. Biomicrofluidics 7(1)(January 2013)
32. Adams A (April 2014) Inspired by a music box, Stanford bioengineer creates $5 chemistry kit. Stanford engineering: technology and society, April 8, 2014, https://engineering.stanford.edu/magazine/article/inspired-music-box-stanford-bioengineer-creates-5-chemistry-set
33. Rosenberg T (2014) Playing with toys and saving lives. In: The New York Times, January 29, 2014, https://opinionator.blogs.nytimes.com/2014/01/29/playing-with-toys-and-saving-lives/

34. http://www.teklalabs.org/about/
35. European Commission, Affordable High-Tech for Humanitarian Aid, https://ec.europa.eu/research/eic/index.cfm?pg=prizes_aid
36. Sher M et al (2017) Paper-based Analytical Devices for Clinical Diagnosis: Recent Advancements in the Fabrication Techniques and Sensing Mechanisms. Expert Rev Mol Diagn 17(4):351–366
37. Yamada K (2017) Toward practical application of paper-based microfluidics for medical diagnostics: State-of-the-Art and challenges. Lab on a Chip Issue 7
38. Akyazi T, Basabe-Desmonts L, Benito-Lopez F (February 2018) Review on microfluidic paper-based analytical devices towards commercialization. Anal Chim Acta 1001:1–17
39. Mitchell M (April 2018) Research team validates first-of-its-kind portable diagnostic technology at refugee camp in Northwestern Kenya. University of Toronto: global lens, our community, breaking research, April 25, 2018, https://www.utoronto.ca/news/u-t-s-lab-chip-delivers-critical-immunity-data-vulnerable-populations
40. Origins, from Foldscope instruments, www.foldscope.com/what-we-do
41. Made in Singapore lab-on-a-chip device to transform field testing for avian flu virus, Agency for science, technology and research, May 29, 2012, https://www.a-star.edu.sg/News-and-Events/News/Press-Releases/ID/1645
42. New biochip can detect multiple avian diseases using one sample, Today online, June 16, 2015, https://www.todayonline.com/daily-focus/science/new-biochip-can-detect-multiple-avian-diseases-using-one-sample
43. www.teklalabs.org/about
44. Reardon S (September 2013) Frugal science gets DIY science to world's poorest. NewScientist 219(2933)(September 2013):20–21
45. Frugal science: Manu Prakash, 125 Stanford Stories No. 70, http://125.stanford.edu/frugal-science/
46. Tarnoff C (2015) U.S. agency for international development (USAID): background, operations, and issues. Congressional Research Service (July 2015), pp 16
47. Tarnoff and Lawson, pp 29
48. Tarnoff and Lawson, pp 6
49. Tarnoff and Lawson, pp 14
50. Carey B (2015) Just add water: Stanford engineers develop a computer that operates on water droplets. Stanford News, June 8, 2015, https://news.stanford.edu/news/2015/june/computer-water-drops-060815.html
51. Temiz Y (January 2015) Lab-on-a-chip devices: how to close and plug the lab? Microelectron Eng 132:156–175
52. Martinez AW, Phillips ST, Whitesides GM (December 2008) Three-dimensional microfluidic devices fabricated in layered paper and tape. PNAS 105(50) (December 2008):19606–19611
53. U.S. Department of the Treasury (2010) U.S. department of the treasury: protecting charitable giving frequently asked questions (June 2010), https://www.treasury.gov/resource-center/terrorist-illicit-finance/Documents/Treasury%20Charity%20FAQs%206-4-2010%20FINAL.pdf
54. U.S. Department of the Treasury (2010) U.S. department of the treasury: protecting charitable giving frequently asked questions (June 2010), https://www.treasury.gov/resource-center/terrorist-illicit-finance/Documents/Treasury%20Charity%20FAQs%206-4-2010%20FINAL.pdf, pp. 7
55. Israel Ministry of Foreign Affairs (2016) Behind the headlines: Hamas exploitation of world vision in Gaza to support terrorism. Israel ministry of foreign affairs, August 4, 2016, http://mfa.gov.il/MFA/ForeignPolicy/Issues/Pages/Behind-the-Headlines-Hamas-exploitation-of-World-Vision-in-Gaza-to-support-terrorism-4-August-2016.aspx
56. Chang M (March 2016) Does providing aid in war torn zones do more harm than good?" Foreign policy in focus, March 7, 2016, https://fpif.org/providing-aid-war-zones-harm-good/
57. National Research Council (2010) Review of the department of homeland security's approach to risk analysis. The National Academies Press (2010); U.S. Department of Homeland Security, DHS risk Lexicon (September 2010)

58. U.S. Department of Homeland Security, DHS risk Lexicon (September 2010) pp 10
59. U.S. Department of Homeland Security, DHS risk Lexicon (September 2010) pp 36
60. U.S. Department of Homeland Security, DHS Risk Lexicon," (September 2010) pp 19
61. Department of Defense, Dictionary of military and associated terms (August 2018) pp 232
62. Tucker JB (2000) toxic terror: assessing terrorist use of chemical and biological weapons. MIT Press, Cambridge, MA, p 10
63. Yarger HH (2015) Strategic theory for the 21st century: the little book on big strategy. Strategic Studies Institute (February 2006); Major Barbara P. Benson, "The U.S. counterterrorism strategy: addressing radical ideologies," pp 6
64. Hudson RA (1999) The sociology and psychology of terrorism: who becomes a terrorist and why?", Federal research division library of congress (September 1999) pp 14
65. Rapoport DC (2004) The four waves of modern terrorism. In: In: Cronin AK, Ludes JM (eds) Attacking terrorism: elements of a grand strategy (Georgetown Univ. Press, Washington, D.C., 2004)
66. Hoffman B (1998) Defining terrorism. In: Hoffman B (ed) Inside terrorism (Columbia Univ. Press, New York, 1998)
67. Walter Laquer No End to War (2004) Terrorism in the 21st century. The Continuum International Publishing Group Inc., New York, NY
68. Kydd AH, Walter BF (2006) The strategies of terrorism. In: International security 31 (Summer 2006) pp 52
69. Ackerman GA et al (2014) Anatomizing chemical and biological non-state adversaries identifying the adversary, final report (National consortium for the study of terrorism and responses to terrorism, College Park, MD, 2014), pp 21
70. Rapoport DC (2004) The four waves of modern terrorism. In: Cronin AK, Ludes JM (eds) Attacking terrorism: elements of a grand strategy (Georgetown Univ. Press, Washington, D.C., 2004) pp 56
71. Hoffman B (1998) Defining terrorism. In: Hoffman B (ed) Inside terrorism (Columbia Univ. Press, New York, 1998) pp 26
72. Rapoport DC (2004) The four waves of modern terrorism. In: Cronin AK, Ludes JM (eds) Attacking terrorism: elements of a grand strategy (Georgetown Univ. Press, Washington, D.C., 2004) pp 53
73. Inkeles I (2014) Irredentism and american withdrawal. In: Harvard International Review (July 2014)
74. Rapoport DC (2004) The four waves of modern terrorism. In: Cronin AK, Ludes JM (eds) Attacking terrorism: elements of a grand strategy (Georgetown Univ. Press, Washington, D.C., 2004) pp 64
75. Charles D (2009) Ferguson, WMD terrorism. Combating weapons of mass destruction: the future of international nonproliferation policy (Athens. Georgia University Press, GA, p 29
76. Yusufzai R (1999) Osama bin Laden's interview: conversation with terror. In: Time (January 1999)
77. The CIA on Bin Laden, Foreign Report No. 2510 (August 1998)
78. Kosal M (2006) Terrorism targeting industrial chemical facilities: strategic motivations and the implications for U.S. security. Stud Conflict Terror 29(7):41–73
79. Meulenbelt SE, Nieuwenhuizen MS (2015) Non-state actors' pursuit of CBRN weapons: from motivation to potential humanitarian consequences. Inte Rev Red Cross 97(899):839
80. Ackerman et al. Anatomizing chemical and biological non-state adversaries identifying the adversary, Final Report, pp 21
81. Ferguson CD et al (2005) The four faces of nuclear terrorism (Routledge Taylor and Francis Group, New York NY, 2005), pp 20
82. Hudson E (1984) Corporations strengthen security in answer to terrorism. New York Times, November, 1984, https://www.nytimes.com/1984/11/11/nyregion/corporations-strengthen-security-in-answer-to-terrorism.html
83. Hanley R (1984) Ohio suspects tied to 10 bomb blasts. New York Times, November 9, 1984, https://www.nytimes.com/1984/11/09/us/ohio-suspects-tied-to-10-bomb-blasts.html

84. Ackerman et al. Anatomizing chemical and biological non-state adversaries identifying the adversary, Final Report, pp 21
85. Ferguson CD et al. The four faces of nuclear terrorism (Routledge Taylor and Francis Group, New York NY, 2005) pp 20
86. Kydd A, Walter B (2002) Sabotaging the peace: the politics of extremist violence. Int Organ 56(2)(Spring 2002):263–296
87. Per Baltzer Overgaard (September 1994) The scale of terrorist attacks as a signal of resources. J Conflict Resolut 38(3):452–478
88. Lapan HE, Sandler T (August 1993) Terrorism and signaling. Eur J Polit Econ 9(3):383–398
89. Robert A (2005) Pape, Dying to win: the strategic logic of suicide terrorism. Random House Inc., New York
90. Price EH Jr (1977) The strategy and tactics of revolutionary terrorism. Comp Stud Sci Hist 19(1)(January 1977):52–66
91. Tucker JB (2000) Toxic terror: assessing terrorist use of chemical and biological weapons. MIT Press, Cambridge, MA
92. Ackerman et al. Anatomizing chemical and biological non-state adversaries identifying the adversary, Final Report
93. Gurr N, Cole B (2000) The new face of terrorism: threats from weapons of mass destruction. I.B. Tauris, London
94. Tucker JB (2000) Toxic terror: assessing terrorist use of chemical and biological weapons (Cambridge. MIT Press, MA, p 268)
95. Kydd AW, Walter BF (2006) The strategies of terrorism. Int Sec 31(Summer 2006):51
96. Post JM (2002) Differentiating the threat of chemical and biological terrorism: motivations and constraints. Peace Confl J Peace Psychol 8(3):187–200
97. Roberts B (2000) Hype or reality: the "new terrorism" and mass casualty attacks (The Chemical and Biological Arms Control Institute, Alexandria, VA, 2000)
98. Kydd AH, Walter BF (2006) The strategies of terrorism. Int Sec 31(Summer 2006):59
99. Gurr N, Cole B (2000) The new face of terrorism: threats from weapons of mass destruction (London, I.B. Tauris, 2000) pp 88
100. Kydd AH, Walter BF (2006) The strategies of terrorism. Int Sec 31(Summer 2006) pp 51
101. Gurr N, Cole B (2000) The new face of terrorism: threats from weapons of mass destruction (London, I.B. Tauris, 2000) pp 89
102. Fromkin D (July 1975) The strategy of terrorism. Foreign Aff 53(4)(July 1975):683–698
103. Stedman SJ (Fall 1997) Spoiler problems in peace processes. Int Sec 22(2)(Fall 1997):5–53
104. Tucker JB (Autumn 2001) What's new about the new terrorism and how dangerous is it? Terror Polit Viol 13(3)(Autumn 2001):1–14
105. Crenshaw M (June 2000) The psychology of terrorism: an agenda for the 21st century. Polit Psychol 21(2):405–420
106. Crenshaw M (July 1981) The causes of terrorism. Comp Polit 13(4):386
107. Price EH Jr (1977) The strategy and tactics of revolutionary terrorism. Comp Studi Sci Hist 19(1)(January 1977):56
108. Pape RA (2005) Dying to win: the strategic logic of suicide terrorism (Random House, Inc., New York, 2005) pp 27
109. Crenshaw M (July 1981) The causes of terrorism. Comp Polit 13(4):389
110. Chemical, biological, radiological, and nuclear terrorism: the threat according to the current unclassified literature (Center for Counterproliferation Research: National Defense University, Washington, D.C., 31 May 2002) pp 6
111. Tucker JB (2000) Toxic terror: assessing terrorist use of chemical and biological weapons (MIT Press, MA, Cambridge, p 266)
112. Post JM (2002) Differentiating the threat of chemical and biological terrorism: motivations and constraints. Peace Confl J Peace Psychol 8(3):193
113. Post JM (2002) Differentiating the threat of chemical and biological terrorism: motivations and constraints. Peace Confl J Peace Psychol 8(3):193

114. Tucker JB, Pate J (1991) The minnesota patriots council (1991). In: Tucker JB (ed) Toxic terror: assessing terrorist use of chemical and biological weapons (MIT Press, Cambridge, MA, 2000)
115. Kydd AH, Walter BF (2006) The strategies of terrorism. Int Sec 31(Summer 2006)
116. U.S. Department of Homeland Security, DHS risk Lexicon, pp 9
117. Vogel K (October 2006) Bioweapons proliferation: where science studies and public policy collide. Soc Stud Sci 36(5):659–690
118. Vogel K (2006) Bioweapons proliferation: where science studies and public policy collide. Soc Stud Sci 36(5)(October 2006)
119. Jackson BA (2001) Technology acquisition by terrorist groups: threat assessment informed by lessons from private sector technology adoption. RAND Corporation (2001) pp 25
120. Richards D, Bush PA (2000) Measuring, formalising and modelling tacit knowledge (2000)
121. Horvath JA et al (1998) Tacit knowledge in military leadership: some research products and their applications to leadership development. United States army research institute for the behavioral and social sciences, Technical Report 1081 (May 1998)
122. Garcia-Perez A, Mitra A (2007) Tacit knowledge elicitation and measurement in research organizations: a methodological approach. Elec J Know Manage 5(4):373–386
123. Vogel KM (September 2013) The need for greater multidisciplinary, sociotechnical analysis: the bioweapons case. Center for the Study of Intelli 57(3)
124. Bennett D (January 2007) Terrorists and unconventional weapons: is the threat real? Low Intensity Conflict and Law Enforcement 12(1):20–50
125. Testimony by Larry Jonson before the National Security, International Affairs, and Criminal justice subcommittee of the house government reform and oversight committee. In: The CBW conventions bulletin, No. 42 (October 2, 1998):35
126. UN Security Council, Letter dated 24 august 2016 from the secretary-general addressed to the President of the security council
127. Hummel S (2016) The islamic state and WMD: assessing the future threat. Combatting Terror Center Sentinel 9(1) (January 2016)
128. Harvard University (2018) BioBits: teaching synthetic biology to K-12 students. Science Daily, August 1, 2018, https://www.sciencedaily.com/releases/2018/08/180801160050.htm.
129. Jefferson C Dr (2013) The growth of amateur biology: a dual use government challenge. Biochemical security 2030 project (November 2013) pp 4
130. Stern JE, Larry Wayne Harris (1998), In: Tucker JB (ed)Toxic terror: assessing terrorist use of chemical and biological weapons (MIT Press, Cambridge, MA, 2000)
131. David Rapoport quoted in Bruce Hoffman, Defining terrorism. In: Hoffman B (ed) Inside terrorism (Columbia Univ. Press, New York, 1998), pp 170
132. Phillips BJ (2017) Do 90 percent of terrorist groups last less than a year? Updating the conventional wisdom. Terrorism and Political Violence (September 2017)
133. Vittori J (November 2009) All struggles must end: the longevity of terrorist groups. Contemporary Sec Pol 30(3)(November 2009):444–466
134. Jackson BA (2001) Technology acquisition by terrorist groups: threat assessment informed by lessons from private sector technology adoption. RAND Corporation (2001) pp 20
135. Forest JJF (2012) Framework for analyzing the future threat of WMD terrorism. J Strateg Sec 5(2)(Winter 2012):51–68
136. Temple-Raston D (2014) How much does a terror attack cost? a lot less than you'd think. In: NPR, June 25, 2014, https://www.npr.org/sections/parallels/2014/06/25/325240653/how-much-does-a-terrorist-attack-cost-a-lot-less-than-you-think
137. Responding to Chemical Attacks, in Council on Foreign Relations (2006), https://www.cfr.org/backgrounder/responding-chemical-attacks
138. Zehorai I (2018) The richest terror organizations in the world. In: Forbes, January 24, 2018, https://www.forbes.com/sites/forbesinternational/2018/01/24/the-richest-terror-organizations-in-the-world/
139. United States Congress (1995) Senate government affairs permanent subcommittee on investigations. Global proliferation of weapons of mass destruction: a case study on the Aum Shinrikyo (October 1995)

140. Drake CJM (1998) Terrorists' target selection (Palgrave MacMillan UK, London, UK, 1998) pp 56
141. Tucker JB (2000) Toxic terror: assessing terrorist use of chemical and biological weapons (MIT Press, MA, Cambridge, p 255)
142. Clauset A, Gleditsch KS (2012) The developmental dynamics of terrorist organizations. PLoS One 7(November 2012)
143. Andy M et al (2014) Terrorist attacks escalate in frequency and fatalities preceding highly lethal attacks. PLoS One 9(4)
144. Hafez MM, Rasmussen M (2012) Terrorist innovations in weapons of mass effect, phase II, Center on Contemporary Conflict, 3(January 2012)
145. Warrick J (2017) Use of weaponized drones by ISIS spurs terrorism fears. In: The Washington Post, Februay 21, 2017, https://www.washingtonpost.com/world/national-security/use-of-weaponized-drones-by-isis-spurs-terrorism-fears/2017/02/21/9d83d51e-f382-11e6-8d72-263470bf0401_story.html?utm_term=.f4e118e3349c
146. Tucker JB (2000) Toxic terror: assessing terrorist use of chemical and biological weapons (MIT Press, MA, Cambridge, p 256)
147. Post JM (1990) Terrorist psycho-logic: terrorist behavior as a product of psychological forces. In: Reich W (ed) Origins of terrorism: psychologies, ideologies, theologies, states of mind (The Woodrow Wilson Center Press, Washington, D.C., 1990) pp 25–40
148. Sprinzak E (1998) From theory to practice: developing early warning indicators for terrorism. U.S. Institute of Peace, Washington, D.C.
149. Tucker JB (2000) Toxic terror: assessing terrorist use of chemical and biological weapons (MIT Press, MA, Cambridge, p 260)
150. Sprinzak E (2000) On not overstating the problem. In: Hype or reality?: the "new terrorism" and mass casualty attacks (The Chemical and Biological Arms Control Institute, Alexandria, VA, 2000)
151. Flannery FL (2016) Understanding apocalyptic terrorism: countering the radical mindset. Routledge, New York, NY
152. Bowman S (2002) Weapons of mass destruction: the terrorist threat. In: CRS Report for Congress (March 7, 2002)
153. Institute for Economics and Peace, Global terrorism index 2017: measuring and understanding the impact of terrorism (2017) pp 108
154. Tu AT (Autumn 1999) Aum Shinrikyo's chemical and biological weapons. Archiv Toxicol Kine Xenobiotic Metab 7(3)(Autmn 1999):49
155. Nehorayoff AA, Benjamin A, Smith DS (Spring 2016) Aum Shinrikyo's nuclear and chemical weapons development efforts. J Strateg Sec 9(1)(Spring 2016)35–48
156. Paz R (2005) Global jihad and WMD: between martyrdom and mass destruction. In: Fradkin H, Haqqani H, Brown E (eds) Current trends in islamist ideology (Hudson Institute, Washington D.C., 2005) p 82
157. Salama S, Hansell L (November 2005) Does intent equal capability? Al-Qaeda and weapons of mass destruction. Nonproliferation Rev 12(3):627–628
158. Tucker JB, Sands A (July 1999) An unlikely threat. Bullet At Sci 55(4):49
159. Mir H (2001) Osama claims he has nukes: if US uses N-arms it will get same response. Osama bin laden interview with Hamid Mir, Nov. 10, 2001, <www.dawn.com/2001/11/10/top1.htm>.
160. Blanchard CM (2007) Al Qaeda: statements and evolving ideology. CRS Rep Cong (July 2007) pp 5
161. Salama S, Hansell L (November 2005) Does intent equal capability? Al-Qaeda and weapons of mass destruction. Nonproliferation Rev 12(3):626
162. Bale JM, Ackerman G (2004) Recommendations on the development of methodologies and attributes for assessing terrorist threats of WMD terrorism. Center for nonproliferation studies
163. Meulenbelt SE, Nieuwenhuizen MS (2015) Non-state actors' pursuit of CBRN weapons: from motivation to potential humanitarian consequences. International Rev Red Cross 97(899) (2015)

164. Byman DL (2005) Confronting passive sponsors of terrorism. The Saban Center for Middle East Policy at the Brookings Institution, No. 4 (February 2005)
165. Mowatt-Larssen R (2010) Al Qaeda weapons of mass destruction threat: hype or reality? Belfer center for science and international affairs (January 2010)
166. Scheuer M (2004) Imperial hubris: why the west is losing the war on terror (Dulles: Brassey's, 2004), pp 156
167. U.S. Department of State (2001) Global patterns of terrorism. April 30, 2001, https://www.state.gov/j/ct/rls/crt/2000/2450.htm
168. Chemical, biological, radiological, and nuclear terrorism: the threat according to the current unclassified literature. pp 6
169. Book: the story of the Arab Afghans," *Asharq Alawsat*, Dec. 8, 2004, <http://aawsat.com/english/news.asp?section=8&bookid=2&secid=3>; Nick Fielding, "bin Laden's dirty bomb quest exposed," The Times Online, Dec. 19, 2004
170. Yusufzai R (1999) Osama bin Laden's interview: conversation with terror. In: Time (January 1999) pp 5
171. Usama bin Ladin: American Soldiers Are Paper Tigers *Middle East Quarterly* 5, No. 4 (September 1998), https://www.meforum.org/articles/other/usama-bin-ladin-american-soldiers-are-paper-tige
172. Byman DL (2015) Comparing al-Qaeda and ISIS: different goals, sifferent targets, *Brookings,* April 29, 2015, https://www.brookings.edu/testimonies/comparing-al-qaeda-and-isis-different-goals-different-targets/
173. Windrem R, Al-Qaida timeline: plots and attacks, NBC News, http://www.nbcnews.com/id/4677978/ns/world_news-hunt_for_al_qaida/t/al-qaida-timeline-plots-attacks/#.W6t3y2hKjIU
174. National Consortium for the Study of Terrorism and Responses to Terrorism (START) (2018) Global terrorism database [al-Qaida between 1992–1999], Retrieved from https://www.start.umd.edu/gtd
175. Kahn H, Ross B (2006) U.S. strike killed al qaeda bomb maker, ABC News, January 18, 2006, http://abcnews.go.com/WNT/Investigation/story?id=1517986
176. Yusufzai R (1999) Osama bin Laden's interview: conversation with terror. In: Time (January 1999) pp 21
177. Salama S, Hansell L (2005) Does intent equal capability? Al-Qaeda and weapons of mass destruction. Nonproliferation Rev 12(3) (November 2005)
178. Wright L (2002) The man behind Bin Laden, The New Yorker, September 16, 2002, http://www.newyorker.com/archive/2002/09/16/020916fa_fact2?currentPage=21
179. Hess P (2002) Al Qaida may have chemical weapons. United Press International, Aug. 19, 2002
180. Full text: Bin Laden's 'letter to america', The Guardian, November 24, 2002, https://www.theguardian.com/world/2002/nov/24/theobserver
181. 9/11 Commission report: the official report of the 9/11 commission and related publications," : U.S. G.P.O., Washington, D.C. (2004) pp 67
182. Letter from al-Zawahiri to al-Zarqawi, Global Security, 2005, https://www.globalsecurity.org/security/library/report/2005/zawahiri-zarqawi-letter_9jul2005.htm
183. Warrick J (2016) Black flags: the rise of ISIS (Anchor Books, a Division of the Public Random House, New York, 2016)
184. Warrick O (2016) Black flags: the rise of ISIS (Anchor Books, a Division of the Public Random House, New York, 2016)
185. Simon S (2003) The new terrorism: securing the nation against a Messianic Foe, Brookings, January 1, 2003, https://www.brookings.edu/articles/the-new-terrorism-securing-the-nation-against-a-messianic-foe/
186. Linge MK (2018) Iranian official: we protected al-Qaeda terrorists before 9/11," New York Post, June 9, 2018, https://nypost.com/2018/06/09/iran-admits-it-protected-al-qaeda-terrorists-before-9-11/

187. "9/11 Commission Report: The official report of the 9/11 commission and related publications, pp 171
188. North Atlantic Treaty Organization, "Countering Terrorism," July 17, 2018, https://www.nato.int/cps/ua/natohq/topics_77646.htm.; "The U.S. War in Afghanistan," *Council on Foreign Relations,* 2018, https://www.cfr.org/timeline/us-war-afghanistan
189. Yusufzai R (1999) Osama bin Laden's interview: conversation with terror. In: Time (January 1999) pp 6
190. Warrick J (2006) Suspect and a setback in Al-Qaeda anthrax case: scientist with ties to group goes free, Washington Post, October 31, 2006, http://www.washingtonpost.com/wpdyn/content/article/2006/10/30/AR2006103001250_pf.html
191. Salama S, Hansell L (November 2005) Does intent equal capability? Al-Qaeda and weapons of mass sestruction. Nonproliferation Rev 12(3):624
192. McWethy J (1999) bin Laden Set to Strike Again? ABC News, June 16, 1999
193. Afghan alliance—UBL trying to make chemical weapons, Parwan Payam-e-Mojahed, Dec. 23, 1999
194. Shanzer J (2003) Ansar al-Islam: Iraq's al-Qaeda connection, The Washington Institute, January 5, 2003, https://www.washingtoninstitute.org/policy-analysis/view/ansar-al-islam-iraqs-al-qaeda-connection
195. Pilch R, Zilinskas R (eds) Encyclopedia of bioterrorism sefense (Wiley-Liss, Hoboken, NJ, 2005) p 76
196. Commission on the intelligence capabilities of the United States regarding weapons of mass destruction, March 31, 2005, pp 269, https://fas.org/irp/offdocs/wmd_report.pdf
197. Commission on the intelligence capabilities of the United States regarding weapons of mass destruction, March 31, 2005, pp 270, https://fas.org/irp/offdocs/wmd_report.pdf
198. U.S. Department of State, Chapter 7- The global challenge of WMD terrorism," In: Country Report on Terrorism (2005) pp 179, https://www.state.gov/documents/organization/65477.pdf
199. Salama S, Hansell L (November 2005) Does intent equal capability? Al-Qaeda and weapons of mass destruction. Nonproliferation Rev 12(3):633
200. Gordon MR (2002) A nation challenged: weapons; U.S. says it found qaeda lab being Built to produce anthrax," *NY Times,* March 23, 2002, https://www.nytimes.com/2002/03/23/world/nation-challenged-weapons-us-says-it-found-qaeda-lab-being-built-produce-anthrax.html
201. Commission on the intelligence capabilities of the United States regarding weapons of mass destruction. March 31, 2005, pp 270, https://fas.org/irp/offdocs/wmd_report.pdf
202. Hemling M et al (2014) Microfluidics for high school chemistry students. J Chem Educ 91(1):112–115
203. Melvin AT (2016) A hands-on approach to teaching k-12 students about microfluidic devices (work in progress). American Society for Engineering Education 123rd Annual Conference and Exposition (2016)
204. Koblentz G, Pathogens as weapons: the international security implications of biological warfare. Int Sec 28(3)(Winter 2003/2004):84–122
205. Reader I (2000) Religious violence in contemporary Japan: the case of Aum Shinrikyo. University of Hawaii Press, Honolulu, p 148
206. Tucker JB (2000) Toxic terror: assessing terrorist use of chemical and biological weapons. MIT Press, Cambridge, MA, p 8
207. Salama S, Hansell L (November 2005) Does intent equal capability? Al-Qaeda and weapons of mass destruction. Nonproliferation Rev 12(3):618
208. Tucker JB (2000) Toxic terror: assessing terrorist use of chemical and biological weapons. MIT Press, Cambridge, MA, p 6
209. Ryan Cross, Synthetic biology could enable bioweapons development, Chemical and Engineering News June 19, 2018, https://cen.acs.org/biological-chemistry/synthetic-biology/Synthetic-biology-enable-bioweapons-development/96/i26
210. Jefferson C, Lentzos F, Marris C (2014) Synthetic biology and biosecurity: challenging the myths (August 2014) pp 10

211. Vogel KM, Ouagrham-Gormley SB (2018) Anticipating emerging biotechnology threats: a case study of CRISPR. Politics and life sciences, pp 1–17.
212. Vogel KM, Ouagrham-Gormley SB (2018) Anticipating emerging biotechnology threats: a case study of CRISPR. Politics and Life Sciences, pp 11
213. Reuters Staff "U.S. Says Iraq Chlorine Bomb Factory Was Al Qaeda's". Reuters.com. https://www.reuters.com/article/us-iraq-chemicals-qaeda/u-s-says-iraq-chlorine-bomb-factory-was-al-qaedas-idUSPAR44485120070224 (Accessed December 13, 2017)
214. Center for Disease Control "Cholera - Vibrio cholerae infection." CDC.gov. https://www.cdc.gov/cholera/general/index.html (Accessed December 13, 2017)
215. WHO. "Cholera in Iraq." WHO.int. http://www.who.int/csr/don/2008_09_10a/en/ (Accessed December 13, 2017)
216. Mia Bloom, Constructing expertise: terrorist recruitment and "talent spotting" in the PIRA, Al Qaeda, and ISIS, (October 2016)
217. Vogel, The need for greater multidisciplinary, Sociotechnical Analysis: The Bioweapons Case, pp 3

Military Aid and Innovation

Rana O. Shabb

Abstract Can military aid to developing countries trigger innovation in the recipient economy? This question emanates from a puzzle in the literature and policymakers' inclination to make aid more effective. Studies focused on military expenditure in the developed world show a positive relationship between military expenditure and innovation. Conversely, studies centered on military expenditure in developing countries often note the unintended, negative consequences of such expenditure. Borrowing from literature on innovation that examines diffusion channels from the military to the national economy, this research seeks to identify a similar process in developing countries. Using a congruence test on a least-likely case, this study finds that military aid—effectively a military expenditure subsidy—can indeed trigger innovation in a recipient economy. In Jordan, this is reflected by the emergence of an innovative domestic arms industry after its peace agreement with Israel and a major influx of U.S. military aid. Further, by dividing military aid into different sub-types and tracing and comparing their different effects, this study shows that military aid can lead to the emergence of new economic sectors when it supports the domestic government's industrial vision and local economic priorities.

1 Introduction

Can military aid to developing countries trigger innovation in the recipient economy? Foreign aid is a tool of foreign policy and will continue to be dispatched, especially as the main security concerns of the US—namely terrorism—continue. The U.S. gives a significant amount of this assistance in the form of military aid to strategic allies to combat terrorism and bolster allies' capabilities in the Middle East and elsewhere. Consequently, the question of whether military aid can be better spent to further long-term innovation, economic growth, and development in addition to the immediate security priorities is relevant to academics and policymakers alike. By design, the

---

R. O. Shabb (✉)
Georgia Institute of Technology, Atlanta, Georgia
e-mail: rshabb3@gatech.edu

explanatory variable in this study—military aid—is a factor that can be manipulated by policymakers. Therefore, better understating how military aid can help trigger innovation in recipient economies can lead to relevant policy recommendations as leaders find ways to increase aid efficiency and long-term economic development as a means to fulfill U.S. security concerns and global stability.

The question of military aid effectiveness in triggering innovative economic sectors arises from a puzzle in the current literature: military expenditure is generally portrayed as having positive ramifications—including innovation—in the developed world but is believed to have negative ramifications in the developing world. The main fault line in previous research is between the rich industrialized world and developing nations. The literature on innovation suggests that military spending in the developed world can help foster innovation and long-term sustainable economic growth by triggering several distinct mechanisms through military Research and Development (R&D) spending, defense technology spinoff, and/or military procurement. Conversely, military expenditure and military aid—which can be viewed as a subsidy for military expenditure—are portrayed generally as negative forces in the development and foreign aid literature. This latter body of work often highlights the negative and unintended ramifications of military aid, such as the undermining of democratic rule and human rights in recipient countries. This research tries to bridge these two diverging trends in the literature to better understand a thus far overlooked innovation mechanism in the developing world as triggered by military aid. Could military aid, which boosts domestic military spending, help trigger innovation in developing nations—emulating the generally positive relationship shown in industrialized economies?

Motivated by this gap in the literature, this research attempts to answer these questions: Is the developing world different? Can military aid trigger innovation in recipient economies? Under what circumstances can military aid help lead to long-term positive effects in the economy? Do different types of military aid trigger different types of innovation mechanisms, if at all? To do this, I borrow from a spillover mechanism framework derived from research on developed countries and apply it to military aid in Jordan—a least likely case. Using this framework, I initially hypothesize that different types of military aid will lead to different innovation outcomes in the recipient country's economy, and I trace each type of military aid to better understand its effects on innovation and the potential causal mechanisms at play. In particular, I hypothesize that military aid focused on training, the proliferation of US technical know-how, and scientific skill development will most likely lead to innovation as opposed to military aid focused on financial transfers. Categorizing military aid in this way allows for a more discriminating analysis on the effectiveness of military aid and also allows for the identification of new variables and conditions inductively that interact with military aid—either hindering or catalyzing its success in bringing about innovation.

Based on this analysis, I find that military aid can indeed help trigger innovation in recipient economies. However, other important variables interact with military aid to either help advance or hinder its success. Military aid, taken alone, has admittedly limited explanatory power in terms of triggering innovation. Nevertheless, military aid can amplify local science and technology (S&T) and industrial priorities, irrespective of its sub-type, as long as there is an alignment with local priorities. Following from this, further work is needed to better understand how domestic S&T and industrial policy affect how military aid translates into innovation. Better understanding how domestic policies interact with military aid can help donor countries better identify prospects for where their aid (either financial or skill transfer) can have secondhand positive effects in the innovation economy, or whether there will be missed opportunities.

2 Foreign Aid as a National Security Policy Tool

In 1949, President Harry Truman called for the sharing of U.S. technical knowledge, scientific advances, capital investment, and skill with "underdeveloped areas" to help propel their economic growth in the hopes that they would catch up with the industrialized world [1]. Since the end of World War II, this perspective has manifested itself as foreign aid. Improving the lot of the "free people of the world" [2] serves not only an altruistic objective but is also a crucial tool of U.S. foreign policy. Foreign aid is used to achieve humanitarian goals, further commercial interests, and most importantly advance national security objectives [3, p. 3].

Starting with the Marshall plan and throughout the Cold War, U.S. foreign aid was viewed as a way to curb communist expansion. With the collapse of the Soviet Union in the early 1990s, there was a sharp decrease in the foreign aid budget reflecting the lack of urgency and clear security threat to the United States. Nevertheless, foreign aid at an all-time low in the 1990s (1997 was the lowest year at right under $20 billion), persisted and focused on furthering Middle East peace and helping countries democratize among other objectives [3, p. 16]. However, in the decades after the September 11, 2001 terrorist attacks foreign aid reached a new high. With a revived pressing security threat, foreign aid was ramped up as a tool to combat terrorism and bolster allies. In the wake of this change, assistance to strategic partners in counter-terrorism efforts and funds to rebuild Iraq and Afghanistan were increased to help quell this emerging threat. For example, in 2015, U.S. foreign assistance was $48.57 billion, almost double what it was in 1997. Driving the resurgence of U.S. assistance in the past decades are the Bush [4], Obama [5], and Trump [6] national security strategies, which both highlight the terrorist threat as prime national security objective and global development, prosperity, and poverty reduction as a means to achieving a safer world. Therefore, foreign aid has acted as one of the main mediums by which to achieve both these goals in developing countries, which are also U.S. allies.

A significant subset of U.S. foreign aid is of a military nature and is on an upward trajectory since 2001. In 2015, 35% of all aid was distributed in the form of military assistance to strategic partners (in comparison to only 16% for humanitarian activities, 43% for bilateral economic assistance, and 6% to support multilateral institutions.) [3]. Military aid is targeted at strengthening allies' militaries and strengthening partner capacity for countering national security threats. Development assistance programs, on the other hand, are aimed at fostering shared economic growth and social stability in developing countries. This latter type of aid focused on agriculture, trade, health, protecting the environment, etc., tends to be managed by U.S. Agency for International Development (USAID) [3, p. 16]. Military aid amounted to over $15 billion in 2015 [7]—of this amount, $8 billion were managed by the U.S. Department of Defense (DOD) [7]. Matching overall trends of aid, the level of military aid has followed a similar pattern with security assistance steadily increasing since 2001 [7].

Since then, almost all the top recipients of U.S. military aid have been developing countries. Table 1 lists the top recipients from 2005 until 2016. There is an obvious overlap between signatories of peace with Israel (Egypt and Jordan) and allies involved in counter-terrorism efforts and U.S. security assistance. Israel, Egypt, Jordan, Iraq, Afghanistan, Pakistan all feature heavily in Table 1. All are developing countries with the exception of Israel. Given the U.S.'s long term security concerns, be it either counter-terrorism efforts in the Middle East, Afghanistan and Pakistan, or counter-narcotics programs, the U.S. has an interest in fostering

Table 1 Top 10 recipients of U.S. military foreign aid by year [8]

Rank	2005	2006	2007	2008	2009	2010
1	Israel	Iraq	Iraq	Afghanistan	Afghanistan	Afghanistan
2	Egypt	Israel	Afghanistan	Iraq	Israel	Israel
3	Iraq	Afghanistan	Israel	Israel	Egypt	Iraq
4	Afghanistan	Egypt	Egypt	Egypt	Iraq	Egypt
5	Pakistan	Pakistan	Pakistan	Pakistan	Pakistan	Pakistan
6	Jordan	Russia	Sudan	Jordan	Jordan	Jordan
7	Russia	Colombia	Colombia	Colombia	Colombia	Colombia
8	Colombia	Jordan	Jordan	Russia	Russia	Mexico
9	Sudan	Sudan	Russia	Sudan	Kazakhstan	Russia
10	Poland	Philippines	Philippines	Liberia	Mexico	Poland
Rank	2011	2012	2013	2014	2015	2016
1	Afghanistan	Afghanistan	Afghanistan	Afghanistan	Afghanistan	Iraq
2	Israel	Israel	Israel	Israel	Israel	Israel
3	Egypt	Egypt	Egypt	Jordan	Egypt	Afghanistan
4	Iraq	Iraq	Jordan	Pakistan	Iraq	Egypt
5	Pakistan	Jordan	Somalia	Lebanon	Jordan	Jordan
6	Jordan	Somalia	Iraq	Somalia	Pakistan	Pakistan
7	Colombia	Russia	Lebanon	Bangladesh	Lebanon	Philippines
8	Russia	Colombia	Colombia	Colombia	Philippines	Kenya
9	Kazakhstan	Pakistan	Mexico	Philippines	Tunisia	Ukraine
10	Mexico	Kazakhstan	Yemen	Mexico	Colombia	Colombia

long-term sustainable development in these countries as a durable strategy for peace and stability.

As these aid trends can be expected to continue given national security priorities, is there a way that military aid which is dispersed with immediate security concerns have a positive long-term effect on economic development, which is itself another security policy goal? Given the existing trends of foreign military aid and some of the negative consequences that emerge from the development and military aid literature discussed below, the question that emerges is: is there a better way to invest these funds? Can military aid have positive long-term effects especially in the realm of the goals of global development like innovation and economic growth?

3 Military Expenditure and Innovation

In addressing the question of can military aid to developing countries trigger innovation in the domestic economy, several bodies of literature are relevant to help answer this question. Though different perspectives help hone in on the issue, they also delineate a puzzle: why is military expenditure in the developed industrialized world associated with positive second hand effects in the economy, whereas in the developing world this relationship tends to be portrayed as negative? Can policymakers learn from the industrialized world in order to better select or design military aid interventions, so that they can have positive secondhand effects in the recipient country's economy? This question is important and remains unaddressed in the literature. In fact, the literature on innovation generally focuses on the developed world, mostly the U.S. [9], and other successful cases like Israel, Taiwan, and Ireland [10]. In stark contrast to this, the literature on development and military aid tends to focus on negative externalities such as regional arms races [11], the undermining of human rights and democratic institutions [12], increased probabilities of coups [13], etc. From this puzzle emerge several questions: under what circumstances can military aid have positive secondhand effects in the civilian economy? What would be the process? Can different types of military aid lead to different types of externalities? Are some military aid interventions more desirable than others?

3.1 Innovation and the Developed World

The literature on innovation and military expenditure is useful to get at potential causal mechanisms and processes that could then be applied to the developing world. It is important to highlight that this body of work largely focuses on industrialized developed nations—particularly the U.S.—and for the most part paints a positive relationship between military expenditure and innovation (however measured) [9]. Breznitz's examines three case studies of now developed economies: Ireland, Israel, and Taiwan. He argues that innovation requires the state to actively step into solve the market failure of R&D—private investors tend to underinvest because of high uncertainty in emerging markets—and connect local industry with international markets (as local demand is not enough to spur such innovation) [10, p. 191]. Despite the parsimony in his overarching theory, in his discussion of the Israeli case, he argues that the military in Israel and its security concerns played an important role in the initial demand for highly qualified labor in order to create an independent and local arms industry. He states that Israel's competitive edge and innovative sectors originate in the defense sector. The state provided the R&D funds and facilitated know-how transfer from the defense sector to the civilian one. Specifically, the origins of the successful Information and Technology (IT) sector in Israel can be traced back to the defense apparatus and state bureaucracy's pioneering role in developing computing [10, p. 47].

Partially echoing this point, Taylor's work on the politics of innovation posits a theory of creative insecurity. To explain why countries innovate and why we see different rates of innovation across countries (measured by patent data), Taylor theorizes that each country balances domestic and external security concerns; this balance influences its rate of innovation [14, p. 5]. Those countries that innovate tend to be driven by security concerns because these security threats help citizens accept the cost and risky endeavor of trying to become more competitive and innovative [14, p. 5]. Specifically, external threats to a nation's military can increase the relative cost of technological stagnation. This makes innovation more appealing because it can create an economy that is more competitive internationally. Domestically, threats can help rally support for technological advancement from the public [15, p. 114]. Subsequently, a local high-tech sector can provide the foundation for a domestic defense industry, making a country less dependent on importing weapons [14, p. 15]. Though Taylor focuses on external security threats as an important motivator, he looks at innovation as a whole and does not comment on the direction of innovation—be it from the military to the civilian sector or vice versa. Similarly, he does not distinguish between external and internal security threats, it is unclear how terrorism, for example, might affect state behavior when it comes to innovation.

Breznitz's work on Israel illustrates how security concerns can trigger innovation. According to him, it is Israel's security concerns that originally triggered its R&D spending and technological advancement in military defense industry, which eventually led to innovation in the private sector, specifically in the IT sector [10, p. 46]. It is now accepted that the U.S. and Israel are strong strategic allies. However, this was not always the case. In its first two decades of existence (since 1948), Israel's biggest ally was France. Most of Israel's equipment including fighter jets and ships were purchased from France. However, in 1967 during the Six Day War, French President Charles de Gaulle declared France's alliance with the Arab States, condemned Israel's pre-emptive strike against Egypt, and instilled an arms embargo on the Middle East, which hurt Israel primarily [16]. Overnight, Israel was no longer able to buy crucial weapon systems. In the wake of this experience, Israel decided to break its dependence on foreign powers for military platforms. It shifted large amounts of spending into military R&D and high-technology defense industry. In addition to creating the skill and R&D capacity, this new shift in policy and spending helped create more demand for scientists and engineers in Israel. This in part helped pave the way for innovative industries in the Israeli economy.

The literature on innovation suggests that security threats and the military have a positive effect on civilian innovation. How does this relate to recipients of military aid, which are in large part developing countries? Further, recipients of military aid are not a randomly selected group. Top recipients of U.S. bilateral military aid receive it because they are strategic allies in combatting terrorism, fighting drugs, or maintaining regional stability. In other words, they face a high level of internal and/or external security threat that is also of concern to the U.S. Thus, in applying the theory of creative insecurity, this subset of countries (though generally lower income than what has been discussed previously) are better positioned to innovate than other developing countries with lower security threats.

3.2 Military Expenditure and Innovation

The literature that attempts to explain innovation is broad. We can distill from it, that security concerns and the military might have a role to play in innovation. But how? The subset of literature that focuses on the military specifically and innovation is more useful in helping derive causal mechanisms as to how innovation might move from one realm to another. However, the work here almost exclusively focuses on the U.S. and the developed world [17]. Nevertheless, the major takeaways from this perspective reinforce the argument that military procurement promotes the development of new technology and industry. The military as a state-based organization with strategic vision sponsors and consumes emerging technologies that can lead to spillovers effects in the civilian economy and the emergence of new high tech and knowledge intensive industrial sectors [18]. A demonstrative example is Fordism—standardizing mass production to increase efficiency and productivity. This mode of production originated in the nineteenth century in the U.S. military arms industry and was later adopted by the private sector [19]. In addition to procurement, however, there are other channels by which innovation can diffuse from the military to the civilian economy.

Mowery highlights three such channels which will prove useful to better understanding the casual mechanism between military aid and innovation in developing countries. The first mechanism he identifies is through defense-related R&D. Military R&D can support the creation of new bodies of engineering and scientific knowledge that can lead to innovation in the economy. Mowery illustrates this relationship with defense-related spending during the Cold War that supported university research, which in turn served as a significant springboard for innovation. In the U.S., the Department of Defense (DOD) represented a lion share of overall federal spending on R&D during the postwar period. During this period, this funding mostly supported private firms and universities as opposed to national laboratories ("The Cold War University") [9, p. 1229]. This public funding directly addresses the market failure whereby private firms tend to underinvest in R&D [20]. By funding these activities,

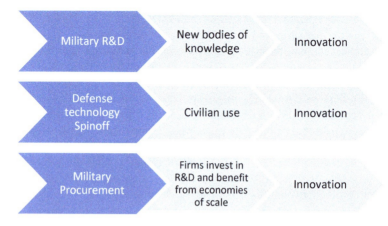

Fig. 1 Summary of spillover mechanisms from military expenditure to innovation [23]

the military helped create a knowledge base from which civilian innovation emanated. Second, the military can contribute to innovation via the channel of "spinoff." This is when technologies developed by the military originally suited for defense purposes find application in the civilian realm [9, p. 1236]. Commonly cited examples to illustrate this are the internet and semiconductors, which began in the military but triggered a large number of subsequent innovations and new economic sectors [21].

Finally, the third mechanism is that of procurement. Defense spending can also spur demand for new technologies; to meet this demand, private firms might be incentivized to increase their own R&D spending to help secure large government contracts and could also benefit from economies of scale to become more efficient at manufacturing their product [22]. Figure 1 summarizes Mowery's three mechanisms. This framework is rooted in and derived from the experience of the industrialized world. However, could this framework be applicable to developing countries? Could military aid, catalyze these processes in recipient countries?

For recipients of military aid, it seems that two of these mechanism by which military expenditure translates into innovation is most likely. Because of stages of development, developing countries are less likely to engage in "reinventing the wheel" and are less likely to develop cutting edge local indigenous defense technologies. Looking at the top 100 arms producing companies in the world over the past ten years, the top recipients of military aid—with the exception of Israel—do not feature on this list [24]. This shows that in these countries, the defense industry is not particularly competitive. For example, Egypt does have an old defense industry and Jordan a relatively newer one [25]. Nevertheless, it is unlikely to see technology spinoffs from the military to the civilian sector. If anything, technology transfer might be more likely to come from abroad. Hence, defense technology spinoff from the military to the private sector, can be eliminated as a mechanism for positive second-hand effects, at least in the near future. Similarly, the military procurement channel is a less likely channel for innovation when it comes to military aid recipients. For the most part military procurement with assistance funds tends to be redirected to firms in the US rather than in the recipient country. Defense systems acquired under the Foreign Military Financing (FMF) Program are generally imported. Therefore, in developing nations the last two channels are less applicable. Nevertheless, by indirect means, insofar as military aid frees local funds to invest more in their local R&D capacity or local procurement these positive spillover channels might be encouraged.

In a more direct way however, it seems that military aid in the form of training, capacity building, and skill transfer can increase the military's ability in a technical field, which could serve as a basis for innovation and the creation of new industry. Thus, based on this preliminary analysis, it seems that military aid focused on skill transfer will more likely lead to innovation than military aid focused on financial transfer. Given the available channels triggered by military aid, it seems that the most direct way to spur innovation is through increasing human capacity and creating a knowledge base (emulating R&D spending) that can serve as a springboard for further innovation in the recipient economy. The case study presented in this research will seek to explore this initial hypothesis by tracing the effects of two different subtypes of military aid in one recipient economy.

3.3 Military Expenditure in the Developing World

Military aid is a subsidy to military expenditure. Nevertheless, in the developing world context, the topic of military expenditure is controversial and is often portrayed as the "guns" versus "butter" debate [26]. This debate was ignited in the 1970 by UN-sponsored research on economic growth in developing countries and military expenditures [27]. Mainly, in direct contrast to the innovation literature discussed above, it views defense spending (guns) as a zero-sum game at the expense of social programs (butter) [28]. Despite several decades of research, there is still no consensus to this broader research question. In her historical summary on the issue, Neuman lumps in military assistance with procurement and local defense industry. However, this categorization is not entirely correct, as military aid can be considered a donation from a foreign country for a specific purpose (defense). Therefore, equating military assistance with procurement misrepresents how developing country governments might be allocating their government spending. Conversely, military assistance can free up funds of the host country that can be reallocated to social programs. From this perspective military assistance is a subsidy of defense spending that can increase the amount local governments can spend on butter. Nevertheless, more recent research specifically focused on aid by Collier and Hoeffler highlights the negative unintended consequences of aid. They argue, because aid is fungible, it ends up subsidizing defense spending. This in turn triggers a regional arms race, which has no positive impact on peace and stability [29].

Further, beyond the economics of developing nations, more recent literature has focused on the negative consequences of military aid specifically in the form of undermining democratic institutions and in some instances supporting human rights abusers [12]. Additionally, undermining the most basic motivation of military aid, which is immediate stability and security, Savage and Caverley argue that military aid—particularly in the form of training military personnel—results in the increased likelihood of coups. Strengthening human capital in the military is less fungible than other forms of military assistances that can be diverted to "coup-proofing." This increases the balance of power in favor of the military vis-à-vis the regime and leads to an increased propensity for military coups [13].

There are also perspectives that see military aid/military spending as potentially beneficial. In a first instance, skills gained from learning to operate and maintain equipment can be transferred to the civilian sphere. Increased security and stability, which some assume to be a byproduct of military aid/expenditure, is necessary for economic development [26]. Also, from a military spending perspective, specifically focused on the a domestic defense industry there are more positive linkages that echo what was discussed in the previous sections such as spinoff: the transfer of technology from the military to the civilian realm [26]. However, many of the top recipients of military aid (see Table 1) do not have competitive defense industries. Thus, the original question posed remains unanswered. Under what circumstances can military aid have positive effects on innovation? Do different types of military aid lead to different secondhand effects?

The discussion above highlights a puzzle. Military expenditure in the developed, industrialized world seems to contribute somehow to innovation, whereas military expenditure, and specifically military aid in the developing world is associated with negative secondhand effects in the recipient economy. Notwithstanding, military aid is different than military expenditure, because in a way it circumvents the guns versus butter debate. Military aid does not divert local government spending away from social expenditure. Therefore, this might be a less controversial way to increase R&D capabilities in the military. From the several bodies of literature examined here, countries receiving military aid should be more prone to industrialize and innovate in their domestic economies than others because they are, to begin with, a select group facing acute security concerns. Therefore, a competitive economy is also one of their aims in order to help increase both their economic and military capabilities. Further it would seem that military aid that furthers skill acquisition and capacity building in the military—emulating the benefits of R&D spending—is more likely to lead to the creation of new industries in the economy as opposed to aid that focuses on acquiring weapons systems designed and manufactured abroad. Therefore, depending on the type of military aid, secondary effects in the domestic economy could vary. I hypothesize that aid focused on human capacity and skill transfer is more likely to create a knowledgebase that can serve as a springboard for innovation in developing countries.

4 Measurement and Case Selection

To better understand how military aid could result in innovation and new knowledge intensive economic sectors in developing countries, I conduct a focused and structured within case analysis to better understand the potential causal mechanisms at play and to determine under what circumstances foreign military aid might lead to innovation. I superpose Mowery's framework on one least likely case—Jordan, where I track different types of military aid and assess their secondhand effects on innovation. This case study approach allows for several advantages compared with other methods. Even within the developed world, measuring innovation is challenging and the causal mechanism by which military expenditure leads to innovation is complex and not well understood [9, p. 1253]. The case study approach, as explained by George and Bennett, helps explore complex causality and complex interaction effects [30, p. 10]. Further, the case study approach helps with conceptual validity [30, p. 76]. For example, many large n studies exploring innovation use patents as a measure of innovation. However, this measure is narrow and would exclude many developing countries, which are arguably experiencing innovation—but not at the patent level. Innovation could take the form of new industries, new products, and increased productivity in the economy all of which are plausible measures of innovation [31] and occur to varying extents in developing countries. Given that the causal mechanisms behind innovation are not well understood in the significantly more developed literature on innovation in developed nations, a case study to better understand this causal mechanism in developing nations seems necessary. Even the mechanisms that are adopted as a framework to structure this study are not fully understood, as acknowledges by Mowery. Because of the nature of the causality being explored and the potential issues of conceptual validity, a case study helps better explain the complex causality in developing nations and understand what other interactive variables might be at play. Better grasping how the causality works will allow for more relevant generalization pertaining to military aid and innovation.

To this end, a universe of cases is selected. Looking at the time period after September 11, 2011 is most relevant because in this phase, military aid increases to pre-1990 levels and is motivated by similar U.S. national security concerns (see earlier discussion). Using official data from the United States Agency for International Development (USAID) from 2005 to 2016 Table 1 presented earlier in shows the top ten recipients of U.S. military assistance for the past 12 years. The table shows that Israel, Egypt, Jordan, Iraq, Afghanistan are the top recipients of U.S. aid. Among the top recipients, Israel is the only country considered to be developed. To see how different types of military aid might contribute to innovation in the economy this research will focus on developing economies to understand how such a process might unfold.

Looking at the universe of cases, Jordan presents a good least likely case. Jordan is a developing country, which consistently features in the top ten recipients and has not experienced a major war or civil strife over the 2001–2016 period. More importantly, Jordan signed a peace treaty with Israel on October 26, 1994, which eliminated a major security threat and enhanced stability for Jordan. Simultaneously, while bringing increased security to Jordan, this treaty also ushered in a significant influx of foreign aid—including military [32]. Applying Taylor's theory of creative insecurity coupled with Breznitz's analysis of Israel's innovation success and the role of external security threats, it would seem that Jordan's diminished external security threat would reduce Jordan's incentive to innovate. Interestingly, this reduction in external threat is coupled with increased military aid to Jordan providing a fitting natural experiment. Therefore, in the face of supposed reduced incentives to innovate, tracing military aid's effect in the Jordanian economy is relevant. If military aid helped trigger innovation under these least-likely circumstances, than we can generalize that military aid can be more effective in triggering innovation in countries that face more severe external security threats. Further, are different types of military aid in Jordan leading to different kinds of innovation effects in the local economy? I superpose Mowery's three suggested mechanisms on different types of military aid to help trace these effects and identify potentially relevant previously overlooked variables.

4.1 Independent Variable: Military Aid

This section operationalizes the main variables to explore the following hypothesis: military aid that furthers skill acquisition and capacity building in the military is more likely to lead to the creation of new industries in the domestic economy. To test the hypothesis, the independent variable is defined as military aid/assistance. The U.S. provides military assistance to allies in order to purchase military equipment and train their personnel. The immediate goal for U.S. policy is strengthening allies in their fight against common national security threats. However, this is an aggregate number. Military aid can be of several types. USAID disaggregates military aid/assistance in several categories listed in Annex 1. Most studies focused on military aid have not disaggregated this variable. However, this is important in addressing our hypothesis. Some forms of aid like the International Military Education & Training (IMET) Program, Cooperative Threat Reduction Program (CTR), and the CBRN Preparedness Program (CP2), are more directly focused on training military personnel and strengthening their capacity and transferring a skill-set in certain technical areas, whereas, Foreign Military Financing (FMF) tends to focus on cash or credit for procurement.

However, these categories are not clear-cut, because FMF, might have indirectly imbedded in it a skill-transfer and R&D strengthening component. One example of this is the U.S.-Israel agreement concerning the Development of Night Targeting System (NTS) for Cobra Aircraft [33]. This is a FMF procurement treaty with Israel from 1987. The treaty is focused on acquiring a specific capability within both militaries. The U.S. Department of the Navy (USN) and Israel's Ministry of Defense share the common goal of developing and acquiring a defense NTS for its Cobra helicopters. The government of Israel had been working on this capability via Israel Aircraft Industries Ltd. (IAI), a state-owned aerospace manufacturer. However, this cooperative effort would build upon IAI's achievements by jointly developing, integrating and producing a NTS and adding improved technologies and a laser designator. The U.S. will acquire 80 NTS and Israel 40. This memorandum of understanding (MoU) is mutually beneficial beyond the acquisition of the NTS capability for both parties. For the U.S., it will gain exposure to the emerging technology and has guaranteed itself a second NTS production source in the US. As for Israel, even though it has provided the seed idea and knowledge, the costs of developing, integrating, and producing the NTS capability are shared. This not only grants it financial benefits (in terms of economies of scale and some form of R&D), but also exposure to how other institutions like the USN work. Further, cooperation over developing the product will enable more sharing of technical knowledge. Therefore, some of the FMF projects might include some skill transfer elements that might not be apparent at face value. Given these at times blurry boundaries, an in-depth case study will help parse the difference and keep to the validity of what is being measured.

Nevertheless, the independent variable of military aid can be broadly categorized as two main subtypes: FMF and non-FMF. FMF for the most part (despite some exceptions like the Cobra NTS example above) will be characterized as low-skill transfer because the main focus is acquiring weapons rather than transferring human capacity and technical knowhow to foreign militaries. In contrast, other types of military aid are more deliberately focused on training and increasing human capacity. These non-FMF programs—including the CTR, IMET, and CP2—can be characterized as high-skill transfer programs as they aim to create a technical know-how in the recipient foreign military.

4.2 Dependent Variable: Innovation

Innovation is defined as "the discovery, introduction, or development of new technology, or the adaptation of established technology to a new use or to a new physical or social environment. Innovation occurs throughout the technical evolution of an invention. It includes the technological changes introduced from first prototype to the establishment of a globally competitive industry" [15, p. 118]. In order to measure innovation in developing countries that receive military aid, new sectors or products in the economy will serve as a measure of innovation. Focusing on patents or scholarly publications, for example, will probably miss the mark for many developing countries.

4.3 Controls

Because so many other factors might be at play, the military aid independent variable will probably interact with other variables to achieve various outcomes. Some of these potential variables can be absorption capacity, domestic institutions, type of threat (internal or external), type of bureaucracy, etc. For example, in countries with overall higher levels of education (or absorption capacity) it might be easier for human capital to seep from the military to the civilian realm. Therefore, in this context, military aid with a high skill-level transfer will be more likely to lead to innovation than in a place with low absorption capacity. Because so many variables are at play and military aid is likely not the sole driving factor, in depth cases could be a better way to test this relationship. Further, case studies—rather than a statistical approach—will allow to better tease out the causal mechanism by which military aid could lead to innovation in the recipient economy and identify new variables that affect the success of military aid. Looking at one case allows to hold the environment constant and focus on the different subtypes of military aid.

5 Military Aid and Innovation

5.1 Foreign Military Financing Effects

Using Mowery's framework, this section traces the effects of the FMF military aid subtype in the Jordanian economy. This will later be compared to the effects of the non-FMF military aid to test the initial probe that non-FMF military aid is more likely to lead to innovation than FMF.

FMF represents the largest bulk of aid to Jordan and many other recipient countries (see Fig. 3). FMF is credit given to a foreign government for the procurement of defense articles and defense services [34]. Using Mowery's mechanism of procurement, one could expect that the increased ability to spend on military weapon systems domestically via military aid might lead to increased efficiencies and new products and technologies by private firms in order to meet government needs and demand. This mechanism can be observed in Israel, whereby the development of its competitive local arms industry has been subsidized by U.S. FMF. This has been the case since 1984, when Israel was given permission to spend a portion of its U.S. FMF domestically on Israeli manufactured arms [35]. This is known as Off-Shore Procurement (OSP). In a MOU reached in 2007, the U.S. and Israeli governments agreed to a $30 billion aid package over 10 years (from 2009 to 2018) [36]. In this agreement, Israel was allowed to spend up to 26.3% of its FMF on locally manufactured equipment [37]. This amounts to a subsidy of close to $8 billion over ten years of U.S. funds to be spent in the local Israeli economy. While this might seem like an attractive way for developing countries receiving FMF to spur innovation in the local domestic economy, this channel is only available to Israel. No other country receiving FMF is allowed to spend these funds on domestic procurement [35].

Therefore, given the restriction on how FMF can be spent (with the exception of Israel), U.S. military aid does not directly trigger the innovation mechanism ignited by procurement. Jordan, like others, is obligated to spend its military aid funds in the U.S. As a result, the indigenous arms industry does not directly benefit from this aid.

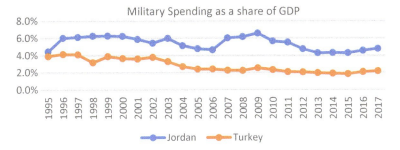

Fig. 2 Jordan and Turkey military spending as a share of GDP [41]

However, in a less direct manner, this FMF might free up local Jordanian government expenditure that can be more readily spent domestically, be it on military personnel, military R&D, or local arms procurement.

Most notably, in the case of Jordan, FMF has allowed Jordan to retain elevated levels of military spending over the past decades. Though FMF cannot be spent in the domestic Jordanian economy to trigger procurement or R&D channels for innovation directly, it indirectly supports the Jordanian defense budget and allows it to remain considerably high compared to its neighbors. For example, in the past decade, Jordan's military expenditure as a percent of GDP hovered around 5% in comparison to 2% for Turkey (Fig. 2). Aided by this massive inflow of FMF, the fungibility of these funds has helped Jordan sustain military spending at a relative constant and support its indigenous defense industry post 1994 [38, p. 142]. Since 2001, Jordan has been able to maintain its military expenditure at over 4% of GDP, and hitting over 6% for a couple years [39]. As part of its military spending, Jordan purposefully established the King Abdullah II Design and Development Bureau (KADDB) in 1999 to kick off an indigenous arms sector after signing peace with Israel in 1994. This bureau is nested within the Jordan Armed Forces (JAF), but its board of director reports directly to the King of Jordan, through the Chairman of the Joint Chiefs of Staff [38, p. 141]. Despite being funded from the defense budget, the main goal, however, was economic development. The KADDB intended to trigger the development of a scientific industrial base to help the development of domestic industries and technology. The hope was that this industrial park would create backward and forward linkages into the civilian economy [38, p. 131]. The KADDB's explicit mission statement is to "provide innovative solutions and exploit advanced technologies to serve National Security" and "to enhance independence and increase competitiveness through the improvement of local production capabilities and human competency." [40]

In tandem, the KADDB Investment Group (KIG) was designated as its commercial and investment arm. This group's aim is to help grow business in the defense industries and establish Jordan as a manufacturer and partner of choice in the region. So production is not only meant to serve the JAF, but also for export [42]. However, explicitly stated, the role of the KADBB is to strengthen Jordan's economy, industrial development, and innovation. KIG emphasizes the role of transferring "know-how" to Jordan via its joint ventures with international companies, establishing a competitive industry base, and retaining high level human capital in Jordan. Therefore, the Kingdom has clearly tied military spending to economic development and innovation, at least in theory.

As such, a closer look at this industrial park shows that Jordan, using military spending, has been able to establish new innovative high tech industries and products. For example, the KADDB, has launched a slew of new land system products to serve the JAF as well as for export. For example, the Desert Iris, is a Special Forces vehicle that is light weight and an all-terrain vehicle that can serve as an agile, multi-mission, and light patrol vehicle [43]. It was designed, developed, and manufactured by KADDB in partnership (through a joint venture) with two UK companies Jankel Group and SHP Motorsports [44]. Technologies that were based on the JAF's requirements, gained some traction internationally. This light weight jeep, which serves well for counter-terrorism border and internal security has found markets in other countries such as Saudi Arabia and the UAE. It was also used by the United Nations in some peacekeeping missions [45].

Looking at KADDB's range of new products and industries, this domestic arms industry has been able to achieve increased competency and produce more sophisticated products. This ranges from assembling less sophisticated weapons with a local component production and in some instances has been tacking on R&D improvements to locally produced arms. As such, Jordan has been able to successfully transfer technology from abroad to its local industry, arguably, more successfully than the qualified industrial zones (QIZ). Further, KADDB, makes it a deliberate point to partner with civilian entities as a way to ensure that technology and knowledge is also flowing from the arms industry into the civilian economy [46, p. 143].

In its quest for talent, KADDB has partnered with Jordanian Universities and foreign partners to help transfer technical know-how and create competency in emerging technology fields. KADDB established these partnerships with the hope that the JAF's knowledge needs can be met. For example, in 2003, the Prince Faisal Information Technology Center (PFITC) was launched as a collaboration between KADDB and Yarmouk University in Amman Jordan. This center offers technical training for engineers but also master programs in needed fields such as in Computer Engineering – Embedded Systems, wireless communication, and electrical power. Therefore, the KADDB seems to be investing in skills and human capital to satisfy its own demand for skilled labor and keep its industrial efforts successful [47].

Though FMF cannot be directly spent in the domestic Jordanian economy to trigger procurement or R&D channels for innovation, it indirectly supports the Jordanian defense budget and allows it to remain considerably high compared to its regional neighbors. Turkey for example, which receives less foreign aid than Jordan, from 2001 to 2016 military expenditure as a percent of GDP ranged from 2.2 to 3.7%. In comparison, Jordan's expenditure for the same time period ranged from 4.3 to 6.6% (See Fig. 2) [48]. Because of this fungibility, more can be spent on increasing local R&D capacity and the procurement of weapons locally (like the Desert Iris discussed above), which is the main goal of the KADDB. However, it is hard to determine how reliant the survival of this executive initiative is on foreign aid. Disaggregated data on Jordan military spending is not available [49]. Similarly, KADDB spending is also obscure. They do not disclose their budget. Therefore, it is not clear what is spent on R&D and how much is earned from exports.

Therefore, it is difficult to disentangle whether it is domestically generated funds or foreign aid that is behind this effort to increase local R&D capacity and knowledge intensive sectors.

It is challenging to gauge how much domestically generated funds going into the domestic arms sector and increasing local R&D capacity is reliant on the U.S.'s military subsidy to Jordan – namely in the form of FMF. In other words, the question is: does an increase in FMF result in an increase in domestic spending on local R&D and procurement in Jordan's domestic arms industry. With the data available, it is reasonable to deduce that that the U.S. FMF package to Jordan, broadly speaking, helps keep its military budget at a significant level, which in turn funds the R&D, innovation, and procurement efforts at KADBB. However, SIPRI does not have disaggregated data on military spending for Jordan [49]. Similarly, the JAD and KADDB itself do not provide disaggregate data of how military spending is allocated or in terms of arms sales, personnel, procurement, or R&D [46]. Therefore, it is not possible to correlate levels of U.S. aid with changes in military spending (domestic procurement and R&D spending) to see how closely connected they are. Nevertheless, irrespective of the direct source of funds, it is clear that the absence of FMF would significantly undermine the military's capacity to spend and invest in what it prioritizes, including the KADDB and other knowledge-intensive innovative efforts. This is evident in the aggressive efforts Jordan engages into sustain these levels of aid [50]. Short of this aid, Jordan would have to levy heavier taxes or divest from other government programs, which could upset local citizens. Therefore, because of its fungibility, FMF has been able to contribute to Jordanian's efforts to invest in R&D and spur new knowledge intensive economic sectors.

Finally, by tracing the effects of FMF military aid, I find that counter to expectations FMF military aid seems to have supported innovation in the Jordanian economy. Going against the creative insecurity prediction, Jordan develops a new local arms industry despite a reduced external threat environment after the peace agreement with Israel. Further, because of the fungibility of FMF funds, Jordan is able to leverage this subsidy of its military spending towards targeted innovation goals under the KADBB umbrella and mission.

5.2 The Evolution of Military Aid in Jordan

Foreign military aid is increasingly being criticized for its negative secondhand effects (such as undermining human rights as discussed in the literature review) and low effectiveness even in fulfilling its primary purpose, which is stabilizing fragile states [51]. Strong and authoritative voices within the military are having to defend the continued disbursement of military aid in the form of FMF and Foreign

Military Sales (FMS) in the face of these accusations. Of note, in a briefing to the Senate Arms Services committee, then US CENTCOM Commander General Joseph L. Votel acknowledged this criticism and warned against doing away with military aid because of human rights abuses and political oppression:

> In recent years we have seen an increase in restrictions placed on assistance provided to partner nations, limiting their ability to acquire U.S. equipment based on human rights and/or political oppression of minority groups. While these are significant challenges that must be addressed, the use of FMF and FMS as a mechanism to achieve changes in behavior has questionable effectiveness and can have unintended consequences. We need to carefully balance these concerns against our desired outcomes for U.S. security assistance programs – both DoD and State-funded – to build and shape partner nations' capability, interoperability, and self-reliance in support of broader U.S. foreign policy. We should avoid using the programs as a lever of influence or denial to our own detriment. [52]

This quote highlights the dedication to pursuing military aid despite potentially negative unintended consequences in other realms and the public debate surrounding military aid. For example, in the cases of Egypt and Bahrain FMF and FMS were temporarily suspended and or linked to improvement in human rights and progress towards democracy [35, p. 25]. In Egypt, after several months of Sisi's rise to power in October 2013, the Obama administration suspended delivery of F-16s and M1A1 tanks to Egypt for over a year, until they showed signs of progress towards democracy [35, p. 25].

Accompanying this skepticism from the public surrounding FMF and FMS, there is a proliferation of other types of military aid that are more focused on transferring skill and training to increase allied nations' capacity to respond to specific threats [53]. Before 2011, non-FMF military aid which focuses on training amounted to less than 10% of foreign aid to Jordan. However, after the civil war in Syria, which started in 2011, this percentage increases (as shown in Fig. 3). Specifically, after the 2013 chemical attacks in Syria, different types of aid dealing with chemical and biological threats proliferated. In 2001, there were only two types of aid: FMF and IMET. However in 2015, Jordan was receiving military aid under nine different categories, including the CTR bio engagement program. Arguably, these programs are more targeted on increasing an ally's military capacity in specific prioritized fields in direct response to U.S. national security goals. One of these programs is the Cooperative Threat Reduction Program focused on bio engagement.

5.3 Non-foreign Military Financing Aid Effects

This section traces the effects of the non-FMF military aid subtype (particularly the CTR Bio Engagement Program) in the Jordanian economy to test the initial probe that non-FMF military aid is more likely to lead to innovation than is FMF military aid.

The original Cooperative Threat Reduction (CTR) Program was known as the "Nunn-Lugar Amendment" to the Arms Export Control Act. It was established in

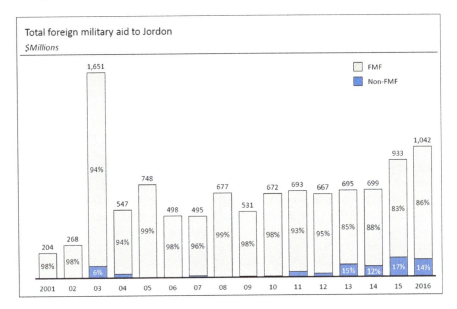

Fig. 3 Total foreign military aid to Jordan: FMF and non-FMF [54]

1991 with the intent of dealing with the Soviet nuclear, chemical, and biological weapons threat [55]. However in the past two decades, this program has expanded to other geographies where the DOD seeks to curtail the spread of and control the use of nuclear, chemical, biological, and other weapons. The program has moved from an emergency response to the collapse of the Soviet Union to a more preventative effort whereby the main focus is to keep CBRN weapons away from terrorist groups and rogue nations [56]. DOD classifies its CTR programs in several categories including strategic offensive arms elimination, chemical weapons destruction, global nuclear security, cooperative biological engagement, and proliferation prevention [56, p. 10].

In 2014, via the Defense Authorization Act of 2014, CTR efforts were expanded to countries in the Middle East and North Africa [57]. This is was in response to international efforts of disposing of chemical weapons in Syria and regime change in Libya and Iraq. The Cooperative Biological Engagement (CBE) program, which began as efforts to dismantle Soviet biological weapons, has transitioned to a program focused on pushing "best practices" in promoting security and safety in biological laboratories with pathogens and establishing bio-surveillance to help detect and prevent WMD terrorism. The main goal fits in the larger post 9/11 approach to counter the threat of state and non-state actors obtaining biological materials that could lead to a biological weapon [56, p. 37].

Countering bio threats is a priority for the U.S. Preventing non-state actors, particularly terrorist organizations, from acquiring tools and expertise to launch a bio attack is key [58, p. 8]. Therefore, the U.S. has focused on the proliferation of science technology and know-how in scientific communities around the world to better counter this threat via its CTR Bioengagment program. This threat is particularly acute when it comes to border security. Because of the use of chemical weapons in Syria in 2013 and the movement of people across the borders into neighboring countries such as Lebanon and Jordan, military aid to Jordan has soared and in addition to FMF now focuses on several activities connected with bioengagement, proliferation prevention, CBRN Preparedness Program (CP2), etc. Though the efficacy of these programs is hard to measure, they are fulfilling a US security concern in highly vulnerable areas—Syria's neighboring countries. Syria is a failing state with an ongoing civil war since 2011. It is harboring transnational terrorist groups such as ISIS. Therefore, a bio threat emanating from within Syria to neighboring countries is particularly acute. Despite the challenges in evaluating the bioengagement program, having existing relationships with national labs, universities, the Ministry of Health, and the science and technology community in countries surrounding Syria is crucial for an effective response. Helping to reduce this threat are other programs such as the CBRN Preparedness Program and the proliferation prevention and border security programs. Therefore from the U.S. perspective, continuing such programs which aim to build local capacity (potentially at the expense of FMF) is key to help counter the elusive and difficult-to-predict bio threat emanating from Syria. Since the use of chemical weapons in Syria in 2013, military aid in Jordan focused on training and increasing local capabilities via targeted programs has tripled – increasing from 5% of total military aid in 2012 to 17% of total military aid in 2015. This highlights US commitment to these types of programs to counter potential CBRN threats in Jordan.

Thus, the chemical weapon use in Syria by ISIS and the Syrian regime has brought to the fore the importance of containing CBRN threats, particularly in neighboring countries such as Jordan and Lebanon [59]. In addition to chemical weapons use in Syria, bioterrorism and Syrian refugees crossing the borders into Jordan carrying unknown infections are all concerns addressed by the CBE program [58, p. 5].

In Jordan, the CBE program focuses on promoting biosafety and biosecurity (BS&S) and bio surveillance (BSV) to confront biological threats—mitigating the potential of outbreaks of pathogens of major security concerns where there are weak capabilities in BS&S and BSV. The major concern is that increasingly non-state actors have increased asymmetric threats to the U.S. and its allies when it comes to biological threats, because of movement of people and the diffusion of biological expertise [60]. The CBE programs work with partner countries to further research and increase local capacity for improved early detection and rapidly reporting outbreaks of disease. Additionally, bio engagement programs focus on engaging with the scientists and scientific community for upgrading response mechanisms to a potential threat. The program helped international efforts to counter Ebola, for example [58, p. 8]. In Jordan, these efforts focused on increasing the capacity of the Jordan University of Science and Technology's (JUST) in detecting and reporting pathogens. They have a Biorisk Management and Genomics Training Divisions at the Princess Haya Biotechnology Center. Further, this CTR bio engagement intervention works with laboratory staff to help assure that they can safely perform lab practices and detect certain diseases [60, p. 20]. Additionally, work in Jordan included bringing together different agencies whose work overlaps when it comes to countering bio threats: the Jordan Armed Forces, Ministry of Interior, and Ministry of Health. This effort aimed at improving interagency communication. Training material focused on emergency operations and crisis communication [60, p. 24].

Already, there is concern about measuring the success of such a program. The CBE is dealing with biological threats which are by nature unpredictable. So measuring prevention on such an elusive target is difficult and developing metrics for partner's capabilities and the personal and institutional relationships established are challenging [56, p. 15]. However, the point of this exercise is not to measure how effective the CBE program is in countering bio threats but rather whether it is helping trigger a mechanism for innovation. Using Mowery's framework, this type of technical engagement, which focuses on transferring knowhow and creating capacity in the local scientific community, could in theory have ripple effects of triggering innovation via increased capacity in the local economy.

While the CBE program focused on increasing domestic scientific and research capacity it did not engage with the already successful local pharmaceutical industry [61]. All activities and trainings focused on government agencies, the military, and universities. Excluding the private sector from such an activity severs the potential bridge towards innovation and cooperation with the private sector. Building on the literature of regional innovation systems, the role of networks is extremely important in helping transfer ideas, technical knowledge, as well as tacit knowledge [62]. While the CBE effort might help create a pocket of excellence within the public sector to respond to a biohazard, there are limited channels for creating new industries, new products, or increasing efficiencies with the private sector. The CBE program sidelined the private pharmaceutical industry, which has advanced labs certified by the U.S. There seems to be a missing link to the private sector, whereby both could benefit from such a program and increase shared knowledge when it comes to lab safety and security. This type of missed connection could have helped the CBE programs' work reverberate further in the domestic economy.

However, it seems that this skill transfer is not resonating as far as it could, because Jordan might not be prioritizing its pharmaceutical sector in its S&T and Industrial policy. In stark contrast, the KADBB's mission was to increase science technology and engineering capabilities to spur a competitive domestic arms industry. In that policy space, there is a deliberate goal to partner with outside organizations via joint ventures to transfer technology and know-how to Jordan and then partner with the private sector to help trigger new products and industries. As a result of this, Jordan successfully started a domestic arms industry and new products. In the cases of FMF, we see U.S. military aid freeing up local resources that are invested in Jordan's industrial policy priorities. However, in the case of the CTR Bio Engagement Program, the U.S. is supplying skills where there might not necessarily be a strong demand on the Jordanian side– or at least a demand that fits or resonates with their domestic industrial policy. Prior to CBE initiation in 2015, the pharmaceutical industry already suffered from a disconnect with local universities and public policy. Therefore, because of the mismatch of priorities between U.S. security objectives and Jordan's S&T and industrial policy we see that the provision of training and engagement with the scientific community seems to have been a lost opportunity for potential partnerships and innovation via the private sector.

Countering the initial probe, tracing the effects of the non-FMF CBE military aid program in Jordan, which focuses on training, technical skill transfer, and building local capacity for bio terrorist threats, reveals that there is a major hurdle to triggering innovation – unlike the FMF scenario. In this case, the U.S. sponsored military aid program did not enhance a local Jordanian economic priority or industrial policy. The intervention created a pocket of excellence within the government and public sector. Explicit links to potential industries (pharmaceutical) or the private sector were not pursued and these actors were excluded from the trainings and the meetings. Therefore, it seems that the Jordanian government's commitment to an industrial strategy and leveraging financial resources and/or technical knowhow like in the KADBB case is a necessary condition to see innovation flourish, which is lacking in the CBE case. Therefore, tracing these two types of aid in one country shows that the local government's industrial and S&T policy is an important factor that can help military aid catalyze innovation in the local economies.

6 Conclusions and Ways Forward

Tracing the secondhand effects of military aid in the case of Jordan helps demonstrate that military aid can help trigger innovation in the recipient economy. Based on predictions of creative insecurity theory, it would appear that Jordan, amongst the universe of cases, is a least-likely case for innovation because of its peace treaty with Israel. However, I find that after a reduction of its external security threat and influx of military aid a new innovative high-tech domestic arms industry emerges. Therefore, countries with persisting external security threats should be better positioned to see innovation triggered by military aid in their economy. Further, to better understand the mechanisms at play, I trace the effects of two different types of aid—FMF which is characterized by financial and low-skill transfer and non-FMF which is characterized by high-skill transfer and focuses on training and increasing technical knowhow of foreign militaries. By following these two types of military aid through the Jordanian economy, I find that against initial expectations, military aid focused on high-skill transfer does not necessarily lead to innovation whereas military aid focused on low-skill and financial transfer did, because of certain underlying conditioning factors.

The Jordanian case demonstrates that military aid alone in recipient countries does not necessarily trigger innovation. We see important intervening variables that help or impede the translation of foreign military aid into innovation. Even though FMF is categorized as a low skill transfer, given its subsidizing effect, it is triggering innovation in the domestic economy as measured by new knowledge intensive industries and products. An illustrative example is the Desert Iris—a new Jordanian product—being exported to other countries with comparable terrain and similar border patrolling concerns. On the other hand, foreign military aid focused on skill transfer of technical know-how seems to have created isolated pockets of efficiency within the government. Though, there seems to be potential for boarder synergies for example between the CBE program and the vibrant Jordanian pharmaceutical industry, the aid and training intervention is not capitalizing on this potential. The private sector is largely absent from the CBE trainings and discussions. Even though the CBE has partnered with local universities to create know-how, the next step of engaging the private sector is missing. In stark contrast to this, the KADBB projects – indirectly subsidized by FMF—deliberately seek to engage companies from the private sector to trigger and sustain innovation in the domestic economy.

The major disconnect seems to emanate from a mismatch between US security concerns and the recipient country's priorities in terms of S&T policy and strategic priorities for economic development. Therefore, local S&T policy and strategic priorities for economic development emerge as important interactive variables that affect how Mowery's mechanisms of spinoff, procurement, and R&D play out in the recipient developing economies. When the recipient country has the liberty of investing its own domestic resources it will chose to invest those where its priorities are. For example, King Abdullah of Jordan was dedicated to creating a domestic arms industry via the KADDB initiative. This body, which is embedded in the military, invests in local R&D capacity and partners with local universities to generate the supply of skill necessary to produce high-tech locally-manufactured weapon systems that can meet the JAF demands, but that can also be competitive enough for export. However, in contrast to the initial hypothesis, aid focused on skill transfer—as shown via the CBE program—does not seem to necessarily result in innovation in the domestic economy. The main reason is that creating a local defense industry was an executive priority. There was commitment and local buy in for that project.

In contrast, the CBE program reflects a strategic priority for the U.S. Jordan seems to recognize this need, but this U.S. objective does not necessarily amplify a domestic industrial priority for Jordan. Because Jordan has a successful pharmaceutical industry which exports to the region and the U.S., there is the potential for cooperation and added synergies there. However, the private sector was not privy to the training or training materials offered by the CBE program. Their laboratories, which are competitive, some of which are even certified by the U.S., were not engaged in this endeavor. This could reflect the lack of public support the pharmaceutical industry receives in comparison to the defense industry.

Finally, as military aid will continue to be dispatched in large sums to achieve stability and security in fragile environments, policymakers can seek to magnify the secondhand innovation effects of military aid by being cognizant of the domestic S&T and industrial policies of recipient nations and factoring them into the decision making and design processes of military aid disbursement. Additionally, future research should consider the role of domestic S&T and industrial policy when it comes to understanding how military aid can trigger innovation, or whether there will be missed opportunities because of a disconnect between U.S. national strategic objectives and local priorities.

References

1. Truman Inaugural Address, January 20, 1949 (2017) Trumanlibrary.Org. Accessed 5 Dec 2017. https://www.trumanlibrary.org/whistlestop/5
2. Truman Inaugural Address, January 20, 194 (2017) Trumanlibrary.Org. Accessed 5 Dec 2017. https://www.trumanlibrary.org/whistlestop/5
3. Tarnoff C, Lawson ML (2016) Foreign aid: an introduction to US programs and policy. Library of Congress Washington DC Congressional Research Service. https://fas.org/sgp/crs/row/R40213.pdf
4. National Security Strategy (2002). Nssarchive. Accessed 6 Dec 2017. http://nssarchive.us/wp-content/uploads/2015/02/2015.pdf
5. National Security Strategy (2015). Nssarchive. Accessed 6 Dec 6 2017. http://nssarchive.us/wp-content/uploads/2015/02/2015.pdf
6. National Security Strategy (2017) The white house.org. Accessed 26 May 2020. https://www.whitehouse.gov/wp-content/uploads/2017/12/NSS-Final-12-18-2017-0905.pdf
7. US Foreign aid, Foreign Aid Explorer. Retrieved 30 Nov 2020, https://explorer.usaid.gov/aid-trends.html
8. Data accessed from Foreign Aid Explorer: The official record of U.S. foreign aid. https://explorer.usaid.gov/aid-trends.html
9. Mowery DC (2010) Military R&D and innovation. In: Handbook of the economics of innovation, vol 2, pp 1219–1256
10. Breznitz D (2007) Innovation and the state: political choice and strategies for growth in Israel, Taiwan, and Ireland. Yale University Press
11. Collier P, Hoeffler A, Söderbom M (2008) Post-conflict risks. J Peace Res 45(4):461–478. https://doi.org/10.1177/0022343308091356
12. Powers E (2008) Greed, guns and grist: US military assistance and arms transfers to Developing Countries. NDL Rev 84:383
13. Savage JD, Caverley JD (2017) When human capital threatens the Capitol: Foreign aid in the form of military training and coups. J Peace Res 54(4):542–557
14. Taylor MZ (2016) The politics of innovation: why some countries are better than others at science and technology, vol 92, no 6. Oxford University Press
15. Taylor MZ (2012) Toward an international relations theory of national innovation rates. Secur Stud 21(1):113–152. https://doi.org/10.1080/09636412.2012.650596
16. Bass GJ (2010) Opinion | When Israel and France broke up. The New York Times, 31 Mar 2010, sec. Opinion. https://www.nytimes.com/2010/04/01/opinion/01bass.html
17. Mowery DC (2010) Military R&D and innovation. In: Handbook of the economics of innovation, vol 2, pp 1219–1256. Snyder J (1989) The ideology of the offensive: Military decision making and the disasters of 1914, vol 2. Cornell University Press. Smith MR (Ed) (1985) Military enterprise and technological change: perspectives on the American experience. MIT Press; Rosen SP (1994) Winning the next war: innovation and the modern military. Cornell University Press; Schmid J (2017) The diffusion of military technology. Defence and Peace Economics
18. Mani K (2011) Military entrepreneurs: patterns in Latin America. Latin Am Polit Soc 53(3):25–55, p 28
19. Smith MR (Ed) (1985) Military enterprise and technological change: perspectives on the American experience. MIT Press
20. Arrow K (1962) Economic welfare and the allocation of resources for invention. In: The rate and direction of inventive activity: economic and social factors. Princeton University Press, pp 609–626. Nelson RR (1959) The simple economics of basic scientific research. J Polit Econ 67(3):297–306
21. Schmid J (2017) The diffusion of military technology. Defence and Peace Economics, pp 1–19, p 3
22. Lichtenberg FR (1984) The relationship between federal contract R&D and company R&D. Am Econ Rev 74(2):73–78

23. Figure 11.1 created based on the three mechanisms provided by Mowery DC (2010) Military R&D and innovation. In Handbook of the economics of innovation, vol 2, pp 1219–1256, p 1229
24. Source: SIPRI arms industry database. Retrieved Dec 2017
25. Amara J (2008) Military industrialization and economic development: Jordan's defense industry. Rev Fin Econ 17(2):130–145; Marshall S (2013) Jordan's military-industrial complex and the Middle East's New Model Army. Middle East Rep 267:42–45; Paul J (1983) The Egyptian arms industry. Merip Rep 112:26–28
26. Neuman SG (1994) Arms transfers, military assistance, and defense industries: socioeconomic burden or opportunity? Ann Am Acad Polit Soc Sci 535(1):91–109
27. Benoit E (1973) Defense and economic growth in developing countries
28. United Nations, Department for Disarmament Affairs (1983) Economic and social consequences of the arms race and of military expenditures. United Nations, New York, p 23
29. Collier P, Anke H (2007) Unintended consequences: does aid promote arms races? Oxf Bull Econ Stat 69(1):1–27, p 29
30. George AL, Andrew B (2005) Case studies and theory development in the social sciences. MIT Press
31. Taylor
32. Schenker D (2014) Twenty years of Israeli-Jordanian peace: a brief assessment. The Washington Institute for Near East Policy, 23 Oct 2014
33. U.S.-Israel Memorandum of Understanding Concerning Development of Night Targeting System (NTS) for Cobra Aircraft (1987) Accessed 1 Nov 2017. http://www.jewishvirtuallibrary.org/u-s-israel-memorandum-of-understanding-concerning-development-of-night-targeting-system-nts-for-cobra-aircraft-august-1987
34. Definition of Foreign aid retrieved from the Foreign Aid Explorer: The Official Record if U.S. Foreign Aid. Also in Annex 1
35. Clayton T (2017) Arms sales in the Middle East: trends and analytical perspectives for U.S. policy. The Congressional Research Service, 11 Oct 2017. https://fas.org/sgp/crs/mideast/R44984.pdf
36. United States-Israel Memorandum of Understanding, Signed by then U.S. Under Secretary of State R. Nicholas Burns and Israeli Ministry of Foreign Affairs Director General Aaron Abramovich, 16 Aug 2007
37. Sharp JM (2018) U.S. foreign aid to Israel. Congressional Research Service
38. Amara J (2008) Military industrialization and economic development: Jordan's defense industry. Rev Fin Econ 17(2):130–145
39. Source: SIPRI Arms Industry Database, retrieved Mar 2017
40. KADDB website, vision and mission statement. http://www.kaddb.com/en-us/ABOUT-US/VISION-MISSION
41. Source: SIPRI Military Expenditure Database 2018. https://www.sipri.org/databases/milex
42. KADDB Investment Group, Vision Statement. http://www.kaddbinvest.com/ABOUTUS
43. KADDB military vehicles. http://www.kaddb.com/en-us/KADDBs-PORTFOLIO/LAND-SYSTEMS
44. Jordan eyes expansion of domestic defense industry, National Defense Industrial Association, 2005. https://www.thefreelibrary.com/Jordan+eyes±expansion±of±domestic+defense+industry-a0132162761
45. Jordan eyes expansion of domestic defense industry, National Defense Industrial Association, 2005. https://www.thefreelibrary.com/Jordan+eyes+expansion+of+domestic+defense+industry-a0132162761
46. Amara J (2008) Military industrialization and economic development: Jordan's defense industry. Rev Fin Econ 17(2):130–145
47. Prince Faisal Information Technology Center. http://hijjawi.yu.edu.jo/en/prince-faisal-information-technology-center
48. Sipri, military expenditure as a percentage of GDP for Jordan and Turkey

49. Sipri does not disaggregate data on Jordan military spending https://www.sipri.org/databases/milex/frequently-asked-questions#10-do-you-have
50. New U.S.-Jordan Memorandum of Understanding on Bilateral Foreign Assistance to Jordan, U.S. Embassy in Jordan, February 14, 2018, retrieved Nov 30, 2020. https://jo.usembassy.gov/new-u-s-jordan-memorandum-understanding-bilateral-foreign-assistance-jordan-2/, Fishman B, Al-Omari G (2018) The Jordan exception in U.S. Foreign Assistance, The Washington Institute, 2 Mar 2018, retrieved Nov 30, 2020. https://www.washingtoninstitute.org/policy-analysis/view/the-jordan-exception-in-u.s.-foreign-assistance
51. Karlin M (2017) Why military assistance programs disappoint: minor tools can't solve major problems. Foreign Aff 96:111. Washington Institute discussion on aid efficiency
52. Statement of General Joseph L. Votel, Commander, U.S. Central Command, Before the Senate Armed Services Committee, 9 Mar 2017, at https://www.armed-services.senate.gov/imo/media/doc/Votel_03-09-17.pdf
53. Foreign Aid Explorer: The official record of U.S. foreign aid, U.S. Agency for International Development (USAID)
54. Data used from Foreign Aid Explorer: The official record of U.S. foreign aid, U.S. Agency for International Development (USAID)
55. Security Assistance and Cooperation: Shared Responsibility of the Departments of State and Defense. https://fas.org/sgp/crs/natsec/R44444.pdf
56. Nikitin MB, Woolf AF (2014) The evolution of cooperative threat reduction: issues for congress. https://fas.org/sgp/crs/nuke/R43143.pdf
57. National Defense Authorization Act For Fiscal Year 2014, Public Law 113–66—26 Dec 2013. https://www.congress.gov/113/plaws/publ66/PLAW-113publ66.pdf
58. Berger KM (2013) Future opportunities for bioengagement in the MENA region. The NPS Institutional Archive, Calhoun. https://calhoun.nps.edu/bitstream/handle/10945/37105/AAAS%20Future%20MENA%20Bioengagement%20102513%20with%20GP%20table.pdf?sequence=1&isAllowed=y
59. Statement of Mr. Peter Verga performing the duties of assistant secretary of defense for homeland defense and global security before the house armed services committee emerging threats and capabilities subcommittee 23 Mar 2017. http://docs.house.gov/meetings/AS/AS26/20170323/105748/HHRG-115-AS26-Wstate-VergaP-20170323.pdf
60. Cooperative Biological Engagement Program, Fiscal Year 2015, Annual Accomplishments, DTRA. http://www.dtra.mil/Portals/61/Documents/Missions/CBEP%20FY15%20Annual%20Accomplishments.pdf?ver=2016-09-16-150152-690
61. Al-Wazaify M, Albsoul-Younes A (2005) Pharmacy in Jordan. Am J Health-Syst Pharm 62(23):2548–2551
62. Simmie J (2005) Innovation and space: a critical review of the literature. Reg Stud 39:789–804; Gertler M (2003) Tacit knowledge and the economic geography of context, or the undefinable tacitness of being (there). J Econ Geogr 3:75–99

The Impact of Displaced Persons on National Security

Alaina Totten

Abstract Conflict causes a large portion of the world's existing and measured human displacement. In turn, displacement of individuals can also promote conflict. Through challenging economic and social stability, migration of individuals creates a disruption in which host nations or regions must accommodate and support the incoming individuals. The feedback loop analysis is expanded by considering a secondary cause of displacement—climate-induced disasters. Currently, individuals are being displaced at unprecedented rates due to both unstable political environments and changing climate conditions. I propose that internally displaced persons can stress nations, which contributes to increased likelihood of civil and external strife. Applying probit regression analysis, I explore this relationship between displacement and conflict. With data on internal displacement, militarized interstate disputes, and common trade control variables, this novel analysis adds to the existing displacement-conflict relationship literature by separately analyzing climate vs conflict-induced displacement and the respective impacts on militarized interstate disputes. There is a positive impact of disaster displacement on future conflict, especially when both nations in a pair experience disaster displacement. Results also suggest that contiguity, distance between nations, and political stability play important roles for conflict. This analysis is motivated with discussion on the channels of impact from displacement to conflict as well as the significance for United States national security.

1 Introduction

Displacement of populations is a challenge that results from a multitude of reasons. Political and religious reasons are likely the most well-known causes for forced migration, but a rising concern is the displacement of individuals due to climate problems [1]. More can be learned about these displacement scenarios through separating the causes of displacement and then comparing the impacts created by these

A. Totten (✉)
Georgia Institute of Technology, Atlanta, Georgia

movements. While certain challenges of displacement are universal, other generalizations may not be appropriate. The needs, goals, and intent to return home may vary based on the reason for displacement. For host countries, migration regulations are a political challenge that requires considerations of both humanitarian concern and domestic safety. Further understanding of the types, requirements, and threats of displaced persons must be explored for the sake of policy improvement and national security.

Conflict causes much of the world's existing displacement. At the same time, displacement can also promote conflict. Through challenging economic and social stability, migration of individuals creates a disruption in which the host nation or region attempts to accommodate and potentially financially support the incoming individuals [2]. Other than the cause of migration, an important distinction to consider is if these individuals left the borders of their home country. At a general level, refugees are those who migrated across the border, and internally displaced persons (IDPs) are those who relocated within their home country. UNESCO recognizes the growth in the population of these internally displaced persons [1]. There is a fundamental difference between these two migration decisions. Emigration involves greater challenges for rehousing, assimilation, and citizenship. Additionally, access to some forms of humanitarian aid or international protections differ based on "refugee" status, and these may not be afforded to internally displaced persons [1]. These challenges could potentially deter an individual from leaving until all other options have been considered. For this reason, it is useful to recognize that there may be major distinctions between IDPs and refugees. To fill a gap in the literature, I focus specifically on internal displacement and external conflict. I draw comparisons and ideologies from the external displacement literature which analyzes refugees and conflict at both the domestic and international levels. With the recognition that there are fundamental differences between internally and externally displaced persons, this project proceeds in two parts. First, I discuss the existing literature on the relationship between migration and conflict and show the importance of this connection. Second, I perform an analysis of internal migration through the channels of conflict and climate and their respective impacts on future new conflicts.

2 Background

To motivate and explain the relationship between migration and conflict, I present the following table to set up the discussion of existing literature. Migration and conflict occur both within a state and between states. Civil and international conflicts could have similar causes, such as competition for resources or political differences, but the effects will likely vary greatly with respect to magnitude and international impact. These differences suggest a need to separately analyze each of the four quadrants of Fig. 1. I focus on a few exemplar papers to inform and guide my analysis.

To start with the upper-left quadrant, Fearon and Laitin (2011) study the internal migration impact on internal conflict. They note that 31% of ethnic civil wars

		Conflict	
		Internal	External
Migration	Internal	Fearon and Laitin (2011)	
	External	Salehyan and Gleditsch (2006)	Salehyan (2008) Reuveny (2007)

Fig. 1 Literature by focus

analyzed were started because of recent migration from other parts of the country. They deem the indigenous individuals the "sons of the soil." These groups felt threatened by the incoming displaced persons and the conflicts followed [3].

An example of the first quadrant is Syria, which has been experiencing difficulties with their water resource for a long time. They have had rapid increases in population in conjunction with prolonged and repeated droughts. The limited access and mismanagement of water has forced much of the population toward the cities, which lack the infrastructure to support these population changes [4]. The displacement of individuals caused by the water crisis and subsequent agricultural crisis resulted in "urban unemployment and economic dislocations and social unrest", which in turn, contributed to the civil war [5].

Moving in a counter-clockwise rotation, the second quadrant shows how external migration can result in internal strife. Salehyan and Gleditsch (2006) claim that internal conflict is not solely a result of internal matters. Relations with surrounding nations and other external variables can contribute to civil wars. For instance, they argue that relationships develop outside state lines. Individuals who often interact with neighboring nations through social scenarios, various externalities of domestic policies, and "external intervention and peacekeeping on conflict patterns and outcomes" have influence over civil disputes but may not be captured in a standard analysis. Salehyan and Gleditsch (2006) use this argument to support the idea that both internal and external conflicts may be impacted by external migration patterns [6].

In the case of external migration, refugees are costly for the host nations. In quadrant 3, Salehyan (2008) discusses potential negative externalities connected to refugees such as negative impact on GDP, use of humanitarian assistance, and bringing increased competition for jobs and resources within the host country. Other concerns mentioned include public health problems with the spread of disease, social concerns cited as "'demographic' externalit[ies]", and safety problems resulting from "organized armed conflict" [7]. These, and other, challenges create stress on the host nation as they try to find the appropriate balance between helping the persons of concern and protecting their residents. By imposing new cultural and economic dynamics through a reallocation of resources, external migration leads to external conflict between these neighboring nations [7].

The last paper I include in this simplified literature review is Reuveny (2007). This paper pulls in the thread of climate change. Consider two nations impacted by some climate-related disaster: rich and poor. The author argues that while the rich nation will be able to plan for and protect from various types of climate change issues, the poor nations will face higher risk. For instance, the rich nation could build a retaining wall for areas that are below sea level. The poor nations, unable to protect and prevent these challenges will face more devastating results relative to the rich nations. This will lead to external migration of individuals and then, potentially, conflict for the host nation [8].

The relationships between internal and external with respect to both migration and conflict are not disjoint. These cannot always be distinguished, and the direction of the causal impact is often not separable. The literature is displayed in this way to simplify and clarify a few distinctions. From this analysis, I argue that there is room for extension, specifically in the upper right quadrant which looks at internal migration on external conflict. This relationship may not be immediately obvious, but it is worth exploring, nonetheless.

Previous literature has explored some of the challenges presented by refugees that can lead to conflict. While these do not perfectly parallel for the internally displaced persons, the mechanisms should still be recognized as potential concerns. The following causal factors are from Salehyan and Gleditcsh's (2006) study on the spread of civil war. First, migration leads to the "'importation' of combatants, arms, and ideologies from neighboring states." If an individual is fleeing from a dangerous situation, there is a possibility that they have already obtained weapons for protection. Taking these weapons across borders and then sharing and or selling them creates weapons proliferation. The second cause of conflict spread results in the sharing of resources and ideas between these neighboring groups. The "social networks" of rebel groups extend with the movement of people. These networks also allow for increased proliferation of weapons as well as sentiment. Third, the changing ethnic balance of a country allows for frustrations among the host citizens. A nation such as Sudan, which in 2001 hosted 307,000 refugees, may not be largely impacted by this element of conflict because their 2001 refugee population to total population was 1:104 [6]. Alternatively, consider Jordan where refugees and work migrants comprised 30.6% of the 2015 population [9]. In these types of scenarios, majority populations can be threatened by the changing demographic of their nation, and minority populations can be made even weaker by rising populations of other demographics. Citizens can feel threatened by these changes and become frustrated with the refugees and their governments who allow the open borders. Fourth and finally, resources are made scarcer by the increased populations. Economic competition for goods and services becomes greater, driving prices higher. Similarly, competition for work changes the labor force equilibrium. Refugees may be willing to accept jobs for low pay, forcing out existing citizens who demand higher wages [6].

The literature on climate and conflict is not confined to the displacement arena. Burke, Hsiang, and Miguel (2015) show that climate variation over time leads to conflicts which range from assault and murder, to riots and civil wars [10]. The mechanisms through which climate change lead to these forms of conflict are continually being studied, and in my paper, I focus on displacement as this key driver. The changing climate represents a growing concern for levels of displacement: "The climate refugee crisis will surpass all known refugee crises in terms of the number of people affected" [11], particularly as environmental shocks force migration as individuals seek better living conditions or simply seek survival [12]. These challenges result in both local and international migration, and the differences of a nation's wealth will greatly affect levels of destruction.

Though the term "climate refugee" or "environmental refugee" is commonplace, there is some dispute over the accuracy of this terminology. For the purposes of the military community, I will preserve the term "refugee" for individuals who are politically persecuted and have migrated outside of their own country. To encompass all individuals, internally and externally displaced, I use the "displaced persons" terminology.

3 Relevance

Because of the placement of many major cities along coastlines, the infrastructure and housing in these locations will be particularly threatened. Some estimates suggest that by 2050, approximately 200 million individuals will become displaced due to climate related changes [13]. Rising sea levels impact small islands and coastal nations such as Bangladesh. Similarly, Tuvalu has initiated migration conversations with New Zealand in preparation for potential rising sea levels [13]. But other climate related events pose threats as well, such as droughts. Sub-Saharan African nations have faced draughts and seen migration shifts from rural to urban cities [14]. This pattern equated to about 5 million individuals displaced from 1960 to 2000 [15]. An example of a more recent contributor to mass environmental migration in Africa is the changing resource of Lake Chad. This lake is utilized as a water resource for multiple nations including Niger, Nigeria, Chad, and Cameroon [16]. Rainfall variability, poor infrastructure and irrigation technology, information gaps, and a growing population have resulted in decreased water levels. Lack of water and its inevitable impact on food sources has forced individuals to relocate. As of March 2019, there were an estimated 2.5 million internally displaced persons from the four nations surrounding Lake Chad [17]. Other important impacts include disruptions in trade and the economy [16].

I propose that climate displacement offers a unique group of migrants and should be separately analyzed in research. These individuals are not fleeing conflict or escaping discrimination. Their homes are uninhabitable for a different reason: climate-related disasters. The literature discusses displacement through both long-term and short-term climate effects. Long-term climate changes including rising sea levels and temperatures will affect competition for limited resources [13]. Short-term ecological variability, such as periods of heavy rainfall followed by periods of droughts leads to dramatic fluctuations in the growth of the developing nations and economic inconsistency. Periods of slow down are accompanied by "higher risks of conflict as work opportunities are reduced, making recruitment into rebel groups much easier" [13].

While countless reasons and ranges of migration are plausible, I seek to empirically separate two distinct causes of displacement and distinguish the differential impacts of these causes on international conflict. Economic and social migration are excluded from this study because they do not qualify as 'forced' migration and are not expected to occur in masse. Economic migrants leave in search of improved living conditions but can return to their homes. Salehyan (2005) considers the possible channels through which migration could lead to conflict. He proposes that environmentally-displaced persons are less likely to evoke conflict than those who migrate due to political reasons. Though the climate channel still leads to "inter-ethnic tensions," he supports the differing impacts of these individuals on instability [18]. I challenge this assumption with empirical estimation.

In 2016, the UNHCR recorded that "10.3 million people were newly displaced by conflict or persecution" [19]. This statistic specifically excludes individuals displaced by climate related incidents. The current stock of forcibly displaced persons as of 2016 was 65.6 million individuals. This number includes refugees and asylum-seekers as well as internally displaced persons [20]. In many cases, refugees are seeking asylum or safety from the threatening state or non-state actors. However, not all incoming migrants are harmless. In the case of the 2015 Paris Attacks, three of the terrorists had posed as Syrian refugees by using fake passports [21]. The Brussels attacks can also be attributed some faux Syrian refugees entering Europe through the Balkan route [22]. In 2013, the Boston Marathon bombings in the United States were performed by two brothers who sought political asylum in the United States when they were children [23]. These and other examples can be noted as terrorist-like attacks initiated by displaced persons. While these threats are uncommon, the anecdotal evidence provides serious challenges for governments attempting to structure immigration policy.

For the individuals seeking escape and without harmful intent, the terrorist attacks present "real risk from over-caution on the part of host governments" [24]. On January 27, 2017, President Trump's Executive Order, *Protecting the Nation from Foreign Terrorist Entry into the United States*, issued a temporary ban for migrants from Iran, Iraq, Libya, Somalia, Sudan, Syria, and Yemen, an indefinite suspension of Syrian refugees, and a cap of 50,000 refugees for fiscal year 2017 [25]. Though the threat posed by migrants is very low, the Executive Order cites terrorism and national protection as the reason for refugee policy changes. Policies such as this pose a difficulty to non-threatening displaced persons.

Perhaps these host governments are not exercising 'over-caution.' Threats of migrants extend past terrorist events. In a few instances "armed and unarmed troopers" have entered areas under the guise of refugees [24]. Occasionally, "refugee camps often serve as a double purpose as sanctuaries for militant groups" [7]. Consider a nonviolent refugee who enters a host country and faces life in a very poor-quality refugee camp. This individual is likely to live in "crowded and unsanitary... conditions ripe for infectious disease" [7]. For these individuals, joining a group with militant or insurgent objectives may offer an improved living situation and perhaps a "sense of purpose" [7]. Host governments recognize these potential threats and may change their policies on open borders.

Existing research shows that refugees are linked to weapon proliferation through trafficking of small arms and thus can sometimes be blamed for expanding civil conflicts into international disputes [26]. Through a lagged count of refugees in a probit model, Salehyan (2008) shows that there is evidence to support the claim that the existence of 100,000 refugees in the initiator or from the target country will result in a 2.3% increase in the probability of militarized interstate disputes. Combining refugees with existing civil wars in either country will increase this probability [7].

The issue has been recognized as a factor in defense planning. A 2018 Department of Defense report states that "global climate change will have wide-ranging implications for U.S. national security interests over the foreseeable future because it will aggravate existing problems-such as poverty, social tensions, environmental degradation, ineffectual leadership, and weak political institutions-that threaten domestic stability in a number of countries" [27].

4 Data

The necessary data for my analysis is a compilation of three main sources—conflict, displacement, and a set of standard trade control variables for country analysis. The conflict data for this analysis comes from the Correlates of War (CoW) website. Data is at the dispute level and includes information such as participants, start and end of the dispute, and number of fatalities. Note that Figs. 2 through 4 may have missing

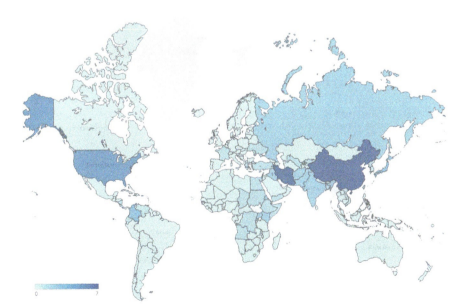

Fig. 2 Conflict count by Country 2009–2010

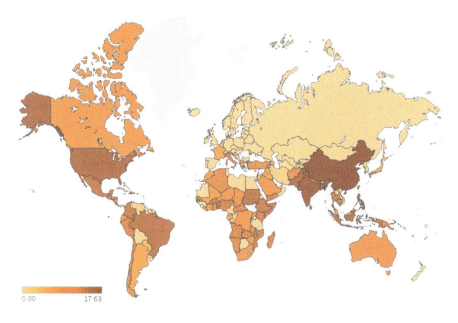

Fig. 3 Total transformed displaced by Country 2008–2009

data, and therefore, some countries may not appear on the maps. Figure 2 provides an indication of the spread of conflicts by country included in this data. Displacement data originates from the Internal Displacement Monitoring Centre. This dataset has country-year observations with information on how many individuals were internally displaced by disaster or by conflict. Figure 3 shows the transformed value of total displacement for the two years by country. Lastly, control variables come from the World Bank. This data has the required information including if the country-pair is contiguous, if they share a common language, and the distance between the countries (in terms of kilometer-distance between selected major cities). Other country-level controls include GDP per Capita and a measure of political stability. The overlap with respect to years between these multiple data sources is limited. The CoW data begins in the 1800's and ends in 2010. The displacement data spans from 2008 to 2015. The displacement variables are lagged one period to show the causal impact on future conflict. Because of this, I use displacement data from 2008 to 2009 and conflict data for 2009–2010. I match this information to the appropriate country-pair trade information.

I assume that if there is no new conflict listed in the CoW database, then there is no new conflict in that country-pair during that year. I assume that displacement is zero for any unreported information for a given country-year. This assumption should be explored in future research. Table 1 explains each of the relevant variables in the empirical models.

Table 1 Variable Explanations

Variables	
Displacement in i (j)	For country-pair ij, the number of individuals displaced by denoted cause in country i
Distance	Kilometers between major cities of the two nations
Contiguous	Whether the countries share a common border
Common language	If the countries share a common official language
GDP per capita	Constant 2010 USD
Political stability	Political stability and absence of violence/terrorism measure from World Bank
Disaster interaction	Disaster-displaced persons from both countries interacted

5 The Model

I begin with a standard regression model that looks at the impact of displacement on the conflict indicator variable. I include three variables which are commonly used in Economic theory to analyze country-pair relationships: distance between nations, whether the countries are contiguous, and if they share a common official language [28]. To gain further understanding, I also include GDP per Capita and a measure of political stability as calculated by the World Bank. For robustness analysis, some equations include a set of interaction variables between the displacement information and the three country-pair trade variables. These have particular importance in the conflict analysis because displacement can influence conflict through these various channels. For instance, contiguous countries are likely to be most readily accessible for displaced persons to access; neighboring nations may be more likely to share cultures, religions, and ideologies; common languages allow the growth of social networks which supports Salehyan and Gleditcsh's (2006) causal channels for conflict ignition [29]. Lastly, some models in the disaster displacement analysis include an additional control which interacts the values of simultaneous disaster-displacement in each country of the pair. In the model, i and j indicate the countries, and t indicates the year.

$$Conflict_{ijt} = \beta_0 + \beta_1 Displaced_{i,t-1} + \beta_2 Distance_{ijt} + \beta_3 Contiguous_{ijt} + \beta_3 CommonLanguage_{ijt} + \gamma' X_{ijt} + e_{ijt}$$

An additional manipulation of this analysis is used to help deal with the large number of zeroes and large magnitude of the displacement information. Log transformation can help deal with these large magnitudes. However, due to the presence of numerous zeros in the data, I instead use an inverse hyperbolic sine transformation. This preforms a similar transformation while allowing for zeros in the data.

$$y_{\text{IHS}} = \ln\left(y_i + (y_i^2 + 1)^{\frac{1}{2}}\right)$$

I use this transformation only on displacement, distance, GDP per capita, and political stability as the remaining variables are indicator variables. I run multiple regressions, some with transformed variables and others as standard values, some with and without the interaction control variables. I begin with an analysis which sums both types of displacement and subsequently discuss the models which separate the source cause of displacement. The summary statistics of the model variables are provided in Table 2.

Table 2 Summary statistics

Variable	Observations	Mean	Std. Dev.	Min.	Max.
Conflict	76,080	0.001	0.029	0	1
Year	76,080	2009.5	0.5	2009	2010
Lagged conflict displaced	38,041	27,310.860	222,762.700	0	3,000,000
Lagged disaster displaced	76,080	121,912.900	1,070,576.000	0	18,700,000
% Conflict displaced	31,798	0.001	0.003	0	0.034
% Disaster displaced	63,595	0.001	0.004	0	0.030
% Displaced	31,798	0.002	0.005	0	0.034
Distance (km between major cities)	76,050	8140.770	4576.676	1.7236	19,951.16
Contiguous	76,050	0.014	0.119	0	1
Common official language	76,050	0.161	0.368	0	1
GDP per capita (2010 $)	62,230	13,316.570	18,887.800	230.05	104,965.3
Political stability	64,766	−0.071	1.016	−3.3149	1.461

6 Results

I present the results of a collection of probit regressions, which are useful in the case that the dependent variable is an indicator. In this case, the dependent variable takes on the value of 1 if there is a new dispute between country-pair, ij, in year t, and 0 otherwise. The sample size is reduced when including conflict-displacement due to lack of data for the first year of analysis. This results in a sample size of 31,556 which decreases to 31,200 when removing the United States. For the disaster-displaced analysis, the full sample size includes 62,916 observations at the country-pair level, but the United States is removed for specific models to more fully understand how the US drives global relations. Without the US, there are 62,205 observations. Each country-pair indicates two observations as every included country occurs as both an i and a j country in the data. Each displacement variable, both stand-alone and interacted with other terms, is lagged one year. "Reason for displacement" is separated by table to compare across the results. Robust standard errors are reported in parentheses and statistically significant results are indicated with bold lettering and stars which indicate the level of significance. All models are probit regressions, and all results reported are the marginal effects.

Table 2 shows the impact of total internal displacement on conflict by simply adding conflict displacement and climate displacement. In Table 2, each instance of displacement, distance, GDP per capita, and political stability are transformed using the Inverse Hyperbolic Sine transformation discussed previously. Models 1 and 2 include the full sample, then I remove the United States for Models 3 and 4 to show how the US may be driving results. Removing the US removes any significance found in this version of the model. Results are insignificant for combined displacement throughout each variation of the regression (Table 3).

Table 3 Combined results

Variables	(1)	(2)	(3)	(4)
Displacement in i	2.68e−07	5.71e−06	−1.46e−06	1.29e−05
	(3.14e−06)	(2.00e−05)	(1.75e−06)	(1.45e−05)
Distance	**−8.41e−05***	−7.35e−05	−4.62e−05	−3.88e−05
	(4.88e−05)	(4.81e−05)	(4.07e−05)	(3.47e−05)
Contiguous	0.00222	**0.00406***	0.00170	0.00251
	(0.00136)	(0.00238)	(0.00123)	(0.00173)
Common language	0.000170	8.75e−05	2.48e−05	3.37e−05
	(0.000166)	(0.000118)	(3.30e−05)	(4.31e−05)
GDP per capita	−5.78e−06	−6.57e−06	−1.11e−05	−1.04e−05
	(1.97e−05)	(1.80e−05)	(8.48e−06)	(8.26e−06)
Political stability	**−8.67e−05***	−7.40e−05	−4.28e−05	−3.92e−05
	(4.84e−05)	(4.74e−05)	(3.38e−05)	(3.19e−05)
Controls	(No)	(Yes)	(No)	(Yes)
Include USA	(Yes)	(Yes)	(No)	(No)
IHS Transformation	(Yes)	(Yes)	(Yes)	(Yes)
Observations	31,556	31,556	31,200	31,200

Robust standard errors in parentheses
***$p < 0.01$, Significant at the 99% level; **$p < 0.05$, Significant at the 95% level; *$p < 0.1$, Significant at the 90% level

Table 3 indicates the conflict-displacement analysis. There is no direct significant impact of the number of individuals displaced by conflict in year $t - 1$ on new conflicts in year t. Models 1 through 4 include the US, the remaining models omit the US. Distance is significant only when US is not included. Because of the United States' unique geography and involvement in affairs far from its borders, this nation does skew the findings for the distance measure. The occasional significance of distance and contiguity here provide further evidence for Salehyan and Gleditcsh's (2006) theory regarding the positive impact of social networks on external conflicts [6] (Table 4).

Table 4 Conflict-displacement on conflict

Variables	(1)	(2)	(3)	(4)	(5)	(6)	(7)
Displacement in i	4.53e−11	−8.02e−11	1.09e−06	2.37e−05	−3.23e−16	−2.05e−06	3.54e−05
	(5.85e−11)	(1.47e−10)	(6.36e−06)	(6.22e−05)	(0)	(3.77e−06)	(3.83e−05)
Distance	**−2.07e−08****	−1.49e−08	**−8.43e−05***	−7.63e−05	−3.48e−13	−4.57e−05	−3.84e−05
	(1.00e−08)	(1.72e−08)	(4.88e−05)	(4.84e−05)	(0)	(4.08e−05)	(3.47e−05)
Contiguous	0.00315	0.00155	**0.00225***	**0.00319***	1.35e−08	0.00158	0.00202
	(0.00344)	(0.00309)	(0.00135)	(0.00170)	(9.19e−08)	(0.00115)	(0.00128)
Common language	0.000133	4.46e−05	0.000170	0.000103	1.19e−10	2.48e−05	1.95e−05
	(0.000186)	(0.000113)	(0.000167)	(0.000139)	(8.61e−10)	(3.26e−05)	(3.14e−05)
GDP per capita	8.39e−10	4.85e−10	−5.82e−06	−7.48e−06	−2.13e−15	−1.10e−05	−1.09e−05
	(1.95e−09)	(1.45e−09)	(2.01e−05)	(1.85e−05)	(0)	(8.37e−06)	(7.84e−06)
Political stability	−4.70e−05	−2.68e−05	−8.49e−05	−7.61e−05	−1.83e−10	−4.08e−05	−3.52e−05
	(4.44e−05)	(4.92e−05)	(5.32e−05)	(5.21e−05)	(1.35e−09)	(3.42e−05)	(3.02e−05)
Controls	(No)	(Yes)	(No)	(Yes)	(No)	(No)	(Yes)
Include USA	(Yes)	(Yes)	(Yes)	(Yes)	(No)	(No)	(No)
IHS transformation	(No)	(No)	(Yes)	(Yes)	(No)	(Yes)	(Yes)
Observations	31,556	31,556	31,556	31,556	31,200	31,200	31,200

Robust standard errors in parentheses
*** $p < 0.01$, Significant at the 99% level; ** $p < 0.05$, Significant at the 95% level; * $p < 0.1$, Significant at the 90% level

Lastly, Table 4 analyzes the impact of disaster-displacement on new militarized interstate disputes. Models 1–6 include the US and Models 7 and 8 omit the US observations. Notable in this analysis is that there does exist some significance for the disaster displacement variable. Both with and without a disaster interaction variable, Models 1 and 2 show a small, positive, and significant impact of disaster displacement on future conflict. The magnitude is very small, and the significance disappears once controls are added. An added variable in this table is the Displacement Interaction variable. This variable is the multiplicative interaction between disaster-displaced persons from country i and country j. This variable is, of course, correlated with the disaster-displacement variable, and it could potentially be diminishing the significance of that variable. Models 4 through 8 include the interaction term and change the coefficient of country i's displacement variable to negative. This suggests that disaster displacement can increase the probability of conflict, especially when both countries are experiencing disaster displacement. Removing the US reduces the significance of this impact, indicating that the US is involved in disproportionately more conflicts where both countries experience high levels of disaster displacement. Inclusion of the US causes GDP per capita to have a significant and positive impact on the probability of conflict. Omitting the US, however, eliminates this significance and decreases the coefficient. This indicates that the US is an unusually wealthy nation compared to other conflict-prone nations. Note that the last four models use the Inverse Hyperbolic Sine transformation. Omitting the stability indices and GDP per capita variables create more significant disaster-displacement impacts. These results are not reported because they do not accurately reflect the true causality of conflict without these two independent variables (Table 5).

Table 5 Disaster-displacement on conflict

Variables	(1)	(2)	(3)	(4)	(5)	(6)	(7)	(8)
Displacement in i	2.44e−11**	2.07e−11**	1.17e−11	−1.18e−11	−2.82e−06	−5.88e−05	−1.64e−06	−3.26e−05
	(0)	(0)	(0)	(0)	(6.47e−06)	(3.95e−05)	(4.61e−06)	(3.04e−05)
Distance	−1.19e−08	−1.12e−08	−1.29e−08*	−1.35e−08*	−5.32e−05**	−7.04e−05**	−4.64e−05*	−5.79e−05**
	(7.79e−09)	(8.04e−09)	(7.40e−09)	(7.23e−09)	(2.67e−05)	(2.93e−05)	(2.43e−05)	(2.70e−05)
Contiguous	0.00921**	0.00953	0.00801	0.00746	0.00623**	0.00406*	0.00609**	0.00331
	(0.00421)				(0.00271)	(0.00235)	(0.00289)	(0.00208)
Common language	4.11e−05	4.63e−05	5.52e−05	5.55e−05	4.10e−05	3.23e−05	−4.28e−06	1.11e−05
	(6.37e−05)		(7.04e−05)		(6.03e−05)	(6.23e−05)	(3.00e−05)	(4.42e−05)
GDP per capita	4.21e−09**	4.24e−09**	3.88e−09**	3.74e−09*	5.13e−05*	4.15e−05	2.80e−05	2.59e−05
	(1.94e−09)	(1.91e−09)	(1.97e−09)	(1.91e−09)	(2.77e−05)	(2.63e−05)	(2.14e−05)	(2.17e−05)
Political stability	−0.00012***	−0.00012***	−0.00011***	−0.00011***	−0.00014***	−0.00012***	−0.00011**	−0.00011**
	(3.90e−05)	(3.83e−05)	(4.13e−05)	(4.08e−05)	(4.52e−05)	(4.65e−05)	(4.24e−05)	(4.42e−05)
Disaster interaction		3.39e−18		4.12e−18*	1.58e−06**	1.30e−06**	6.77e−07*	5.86e−07
		(0)		(0)	(6.59e−07)	(5.81e−07)	(4.00e−07)	(3.66e−07)
Controls	(No)	(No)	(Yes)	(Yes)	(No)	(Yes)	(No)	(Yes)
Include USA	(Yes)	(Yes)	(Yes)	(Yes)	(Yes)	(Yes)	(No)	(No)
IHS transformation	(No)	(No)	(No)	(No)	(Yes)	(Yes)	(Yes)	(Yes)
Observations	62,916	62,916	62,916	62,916	62,916	62,916	62,205	62,205

Robust standard errors in parentheses
***$p < 0.01$, Significant at the 99% level; **$p < 0.05$, Significant at the 95% level; *$p < 0.1$, Significant at the 90% level

7 Importance for National Security

> Climate change, in both scale and potential impact, is a strategically-significant security risk that will affect our most basic resources, from food to water to energy. National and international security communities, including militaries and intelligence agencies, understand these risks, and have already taken meaningful actions to address them. However, progress in comprehensively preventing, preparing for, adapting to, and mitigating these risks will require that policy-makers, thought leaders and publics take them seriously. -The Center for Climate and Security [30]

Given the consistent and persistent changes to our environment, the United States military must be aware and prepare for a range of disruptions. Protecting our citizens does not always look like traditional warfare. In fact, responsibilities include natural disaster relief efforts and humanitarian assistance (HA/DR), such as rescue efforts and supply delivery. In 2017 alone, the United States experienced weather-related damages of $306 billion [31]. To name a few of the larger disasters, Hurricane Harvey, Hurricane Maria, Hurricane Irma, the California wildfires, and subsequent landslides. Other billion-dollar disasters include hailstorms, flooding, tornados, draughts, and the southeast freeze. These events are an indication of the diversity, and a result of the span, of our country. Displacement due to these and other environmental disasters poses risks to our security.

Another significant challenge that environmental strain creates for our country is the harm for existing military bases. The primary concern for the US military is the "safety and suitability of our infrastructure" which is used for deployments, training, and living. "The DoD maintains over 500 installations across the globe with thousands of associated individual sites." Survey analysis shows each branch of the military has had sites impacted by "flooding, extreme temperatures, drought, wildfire or wind events" [32]. Thus far, operational restrictions have only occurred in limited instances such as the 2003 Langley Air Force Base in the path of Hurricane Isabel [32]. Some domestic bases have experienced flooding and 128 military bases are currently threatened by rising sea levels, including some domestic bases such as USN's Kings Bay Base in Georgia [33].

A 2015 DoD report identified the following four pillars for their planning: "Humanitarian disaster relief; Security cooperation; Building partner capacity; and Sharing best practices for mitigation of installation vulnerabilities" [34]. These areas of focus of the Geographic Combatant Commands (GCCs) show that the responsibilities of the US military forces extends beyond protecting and serving domestic interests; our efforts extend to our allies and a larger humanitarian need for assistance. In fact, the DoD has recognized "climate change as a 'threat multiplier' because it has the potential to exacerbate many of the challenges we are dealing with today—from infectious disease to terrorism" [35]. Displacement operates as a mechanism through which climate change intensifies these challenges.

Figure 5 shows the risk level posed for a variety of environments with respect to security concerns. The risk of refugees and environmental challenges does not impact the virtual environment and this realm can be ignored. Megacities are likely to grow

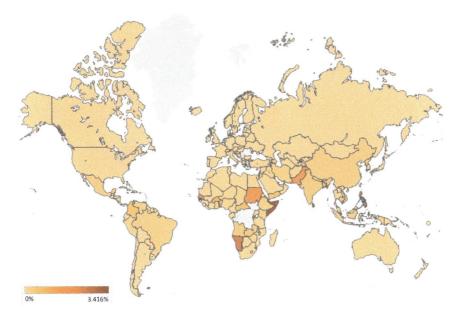

Fig. 4 Percent displaced 2009

over time and the threat of a changing environment will increase with the growth of these structures. Terrorist groups are already taking advantage of displaced persons and could potentially develop their strategies over time to increase these risks by 2035. China has the largest number of disaster-displaced persons in my analysis but looking at percentage of population displaced, Somalia has the highest percent displaced with 3.4% displaced in 2009 all from conflict. Percent displaced can be seen in Fig. 4. In the same year, the Philippines exhibits the highest disaster displacement with 3% of its population displaced. However, the political and economic relationships between the United States and its peer competitors, such as China or Russia, are unlikely to be swayed by internal displacement or environmental challenges. The final two environments posed in Fig. 5, Failing States and Border Security are both immediate concerns for the United States. Increasing environmental distress is likely to add further complexity to these areas over time and displacement could become a more serious risk by 2035.

8 Conclusions

"There still is no consensus as to the implications of climate change or other such pressures for human security .... For the most part, scholars have relied upon anecdotal case-studies ... [in which] authors deliberately select cases that best fit their

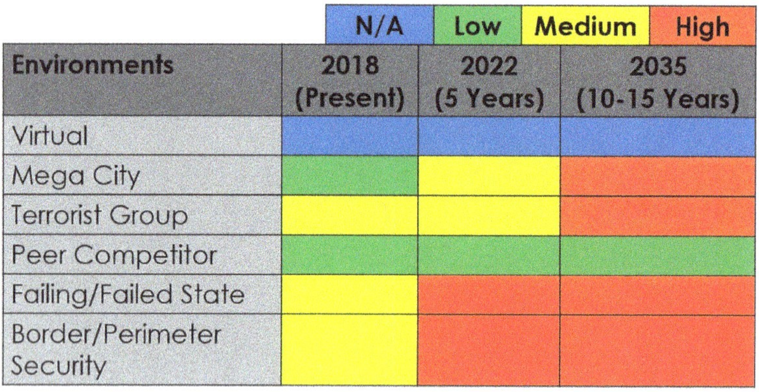

Environments	2018 (Present)	2022 (5 Years)	2035 (10-15 Years)
Virtual	N/A	N/A	N/A
Mega City	Low	Medium	High
Terrorist Group	Medium	Medium	High
Peer Competitor	Low	Low	Low
Failing/Failed State	Medium	High	High
Border/Perimeter Security	Medium	High	High

Fig. 5 Threat assessment in different environments

theory while ignoring other possible causes of the same phenomena." [18] My empirical analysis contributes to this gap by building on the displacement-conflict literature and bringing in the component of climate change to address the distinction between source of displacement and impact on future conflict.

An initial look at my findings would suggest that disaster-displacement influences future conflict more than conflict-displacement does. However, it is important to note that there may be some endogeneity issues with the conflict-dispute analysis. For instance, if a dispute begins between countries i and j in year t, this may result in conflict-displaced persons in that same year. My study focuses solely on the impact of displacement in year t on new conflicts in year $t + 1$. The estimates in Table 2 could therefore be biased downward because of the model structure, meaning that internally displaced persons resulting from conflict may not directly create new conflicts in the following year because we would not expect to see a simultaneous second international conflict within the same country-pair. However, these individuals may still have an important impact on militarized interstate disputes through severity or differing timelines, which are not captured in my analysis.

The relationship between disaster-displaced persons and conflict, though not consistent through each model, is likely to be freer from endogeneity than the conflict-displacement variable. This expectation arises from the idea that conflict cannot create natural disasters and the causal relationship should only have one direction. It is, however, possible that there may be some failure to correctly identify the impact based on the timing of events. For example, the one-year lag may be too short or too long to accurately identify the causal link from disaster-displacement to militarized interstate dispute. Previous literature suggests that longer durations of climate change result in stronger impacts on conflict. Future research should look at longer time spans to further test the impact of environmental displacement on conflict [36]. Given these potential limitations, I still find a positive and significant impact shown in the disaster-displaced analysis (directly, or when interacted with the other country's displacement) which indicates that more internally displaced persons due to disasters will increase the likelihood of conflict. With the oncoming increase in frequency of climate-change induced natural disasters, further research should be done to continue to test this relationship.

Throughout the various analyses, distance and contiguity maintain high levels of significance, which indicate a robust, causal relationship of these variables on conflict. Contiguity allows for ease of trade, of both legal and illegal goods; sharing of ideas and networks; and competition for local resources or in local markets. These three aspects of contiguity can be used to either build or harm international relations. De Groot (2011) uses African nations to show that the "ethnolinguistic" compatibility of nations leads to conflict spillover between contiguous nations. To measure this index, he looks at language and other cultural aspects [37].

The incidents of disputes between contiguous nations suggest an important connection to the spread of communities, frustrations, and ultimately weaponry, which can result in conflict. Specifically, these frustrations might build from a lack of resources or poor standard of living, especially for displaced persons. New communities and networks allow for grassroots movements and opportunities for uprising. Frustrations and communities of internally displaced persons can lead to the acquisition of weaponry. "The proliferation of such weapons is a central factor in the 'militarization' of refugee and internally displaced person (IDP) camps, exacerbating already difficult situations, and ultimately contributing to national and even regional instability." [38] Given this perspective and the results from my empirical analysis, displacement is an indicator of distress within a nation, regardless of whether the IDPs result from conflict or natural disasters. This distress builds through communication amongst networks and can lead to militarized interstate disputes. Although the causal mechanism is not clearly defined as resulting from the displacement, the linkage mechanism does exist and is much stronger for contiguous nations.

From the perspective of United States domestic security, this is good news. In 2008, the United States had about 2 million individuals internally displaced, all of whom originated from disasters. While this could influence external conflict, distance from and contiguity to our partner nations would provide a more statistically significant and larger magnitude of impact. Geographically, the United States is somewhat unique in that it only has two contiguous nations and does not have many other close neighbors. This allows for diminished impact of the distance variable as a typical distance between the United States to another nation will be much larger than the average distance for a country in the Eastern hemisphere. With only two contiguous neighbors, our ability to structure political relationships varies greatly from a country such as Pakistan which has four contiguous nations, all of whom have unique relationships with their surrounding nations.

As a country which is heavily involved in international security, the United States should recognize that these disputes between other nations are influenced by internal distress as well as international factors such as distance from other countries. Certain challenges faced when working to improve international relations abroad cannot be changed, such as contiguity and distance. But working toward improvements of the more minor causal channels could make a large difference. Ensuring that displaced persons have a path to recovery and safe temporary living conditions might be one potential preventative measure to lessen the likelihood of future conflict.

Further research should consider intensity changes in conflicts, ability of displaced persons to return to their homes, and duration of absence in the cases in which return is possible. Improved data as well as longer durations for analysis would greatly add to this study. Analysis by disaster type could indicate differences in the impacts of events such as a hurricane versus changing sea levels. A final recommendation for future work would look only at specific regions of the world rather than all possible country pairs. For instance, comparing only contiguous nations may provide a more accurate analysis of the impact of displaced persons on future conflict.

References

1. Displaced Person/Displacement. United Nations Educational, Scientific and Cultural Organization (2018) Unesco.Org. Accessed 3 May 2018. http://www.unesco.org/new/en/social-and-human-sciences/themes/international-migration/glossary/displaced-person-displacement/
2. UN Agency Launches Appeal to Fund Aid Efforts in Crisis-Struck South Sudan (2018) Refugees and migrants. Accessed 3 May 2018. https://refugeesmigrants.un.org/un-agency-launches-appeal-fund-aid-efforts-crisis-struck-south-sudan
3. Fearon JD, Laitin DD (2011) Sons of the soil, migrants, and civil war. World Dev 39(2):199–211
4. Femia F, Werrell C (2012) Syria: climate change, drought and social unrest. The Center for Climate & Security. Accessed 27 Mar 2018. https://climateandsecurity.org/2012/02/29/syria-climate-change-drought-and-social-unrest/
5. Gleick PH (2014) Water, drought, climate change, and conflict in Syria. Weather Clim Soc 6(3):331–340
6. Salehyan I, Gleditsch KS (2006) Refugees and the spread of civil war. Int Organ 60(2):335–366
7. Salehyan I (2008) The externalities of civil strife: refugees as a source of international conflict. Am J Polit Sci 52:787–801. https://doi.org/10.1111/j.1540-5907.2008.00343.x
8. Reuveny R (2007) Climate change-induced migration and violent conflict. Polit Geogr 26(6):656–673
9. Is Jordan hiding how many palestinians are in the Country? (2018) Ynetnews.Com. Accessed 3 May 2018. https://www.ynetnews.com/articles/0,7340,L-4751617,00.html
10. Burke M, Hsiang SM, Miguel E (2015) Climate and conflict. Annu Rev Econ 7(1):577–617
11. Biermann F, Boas I (2010) Preparing for a warmer world: towards a global governance system to protect climate refugees. Glob Environ Polit 10(1):60–88
12. Warner K, Ehrhart C, Sherbinin AD, Adamo S, Chai-Onn T (2009) In search of shelter: mapping the effects of climate change on human migration and displacement. In: In search of shelter: mapping the effects of climate change on human migration and displacement
13. Stern NH et al (2006) Stern review: the economics of climate change. Cambridge University Press, Cambridge, UK
14. Barrios S, Bertinelli L, Strobl E (2006) Climatic change and rural–urban migration: the case of sub-Saharan Africa. J Urban Econ 60(3):357–371
15. Marchiori L, Maystadt J-F, Schumacher I (2012) The impact of weather anomalies on migration in sub-Saharan Africa. J Environ Econ Manage 63(3):355–374
16. Lake Chad Basin Commission (2016) The Lake Chad development and climate resilience action plan
17. International Organization for Migration (IOM) (2019) Within and beyond borders: tracking displacement in the Lake Chad Basin
18. Salehyan I (2005) Refugees, climate change, and instability. In: Paper, "Human Security and Climate Change" conference, Asker, Norway, pp 1–10
19. Global Trends: Forced Displacement in 2016 (2017) Unhcr.Org. Accessed 15 Dec 2017. http://www.unhcr.org/dach/wp-content/uploads/sites/27/2017/06/GlobalTrends2016.pdf

20. Global Trends: Forced Displacement in 2016 (2017)
21. Koran L (2016) Will refugees bring Europe's terror woes to US homeland? CNN. Accessed 9 Nov 2017. http://www.cnn.com/2016/09/15/politics/syrian-refugees-isis-screenings/index.html
22. Majority of Paris & Brussels Attackers Infiltrated EU Posing As Refugees—Hungarian Intelligence (2016) RT International. Accessed 9 Nov 2017. https://www.rt.com/news/361399-terrorists-refugees-hungary-intelligence/
23. Levenson E (2017) How many fatal terror attacks have refugees carried out in the US? None. CNN. Accessed 9 Nov 2017. http://www.cnn.com/2017/01/29/us/refugee-terrorism-trnd/index.html
24. Sheffer G (2005) Diasporas, terrorism, and WMD. Int Stud Rev 7(1):160–162. https://doi.org/10.1111/j.1521-9488.2005.479_11.x
25. Executive Order: Protecting The Nation From Foreign Terrorist Entry into the United States (2017) Whitehouse.Gov. Accessed 9 Nov 2017. https://www.whitehouse.gov/the-press-office/2017/01/27/executive-order-protecting-nation-foreign-terrorist-entry-united-states
26. Mogire EO (2003) Refugees and the proliferation of illegal small arms and light weapons in Kenya. Moi University Press. https://vtechworks.lib.vt.edu/handle/10919/50836
27. National Security Implications of Climate-Related Risks and a Changing Climate (2018) Archive.Defense.Gov. Accessed 26 Mar 2018. http://archive.defense.gov/pubs/150724-congressional-report-on-national-implications-of-climate-change.pdf?source=govdelivery
28. Anderson JE, Van Wincoop E (2003) Gravity with gravitas: A solution to the border puzzle. Am Econ Rev 93(1):170–192
29. Salehyan I, Skrede Gleditsch K (2006)
30. About (2011) The center for climate & security. Accessed 27 Mar 2018. https://climateandsecurity.org/about/
31. Pierre-Louis K (2018) These billion-dollar natural disasters set a U.S. record in 2017. The New York Times Company. Accessed 26 Mar 2018. https://www.nytimes.com/2018/01/08/climate/2017-weather-disasters.html
32. Department of Defense Climate-Related Risk to DoD Infrastructure Initial Vulnerability Assessment Survey (SLVAS) Report (2018) Office of the under secretary of defense for acquisition, technology, and logistics. Accessed 26 Mar 2018. https://climateandsecurity.files.wordpress.com/2018/01/tab-b-slvas-report-1-24-2018.pdf
33. Bergengruen V (2018) Trump may doubt climate change, pentagon sees it as threat multiplier. Military.Com. Accessed 2 Apr 2018. https://www.military.com/daily-news/2017/06/02/trump-may-doubt-climate-change-pentagon-sees-it-looming-threat.html
34. DoD, U. S. (2015) National security implications of climate-related risks and a changing climate
35. Department of Defense 2014 Climate Change Adaptation Roadmap (2014) Office of the Assistant Secretary of Defense for Energy, Installations & Environment. Accessed 1 Apr 2018. https://climateandsecurity.files.wordpress.com/2018/01/tab-b-slvas-report-1-24-2018.pdf
36. Iyigun M, Nunn N, Qian N (2017) DP11760 winter is coming: the long-run effects of climate change on conflict, 1400–1900
37. De Groot OJ (2011) Culture, contiguity and conflict: on the measurement of ethnolinguistic effects in spatial spillovers. J Dev Stud. 47(3):436–454
38. Muggah R (ed) No refuge: the crisis of refugee militarization in Africa. Zed Books Ltd.

Data Driven Review of Health Security Adoption in 95 Countries

Judy Kruger

Abstract Disease surveillance continues to grow in importance as new and reoccurring infectious diseases emerge and reemerge at increasing rates. The World Health Organization adopted the International Health Regulations in 2005 with the aim to prevent, protect against, control, and provide a public health response to the international spread of biological diseases and other threats (including chemical, radiological, nuclear, or other threats). To measure a country's individual status and progress in building the necessary health security capacity, a Joint External Evaluation assessment from 95 countries completed from 2016 to 2019 are reviewed. Findings suggest that high and upper middle-income countries have established capacities to prevent, detect, and respond to biological, chemical, or radiological threats. Results show that low and lower-income countries are in the early stages of addressing priority areas. Continued funding is needed across low and lower-income countries in efforts to increase their surge capacities to respond to disruptions and contain outbreaks of high-threat diseases. The differences in health security are tied to adequate funding and contribute to health protection benefits. This chapter recognizes the importance of investment in multiple countries to develop health surveillance and response capabilities using complimentary public health approaches to address widespread disease concerns and suggests what additional resources may be needed.

1 Introduction

Emerging infections caused by pathogens in humans and animals pose special concerns due to their capacity to cause widespread disease in a pandemic. The covert dissemination of these unknown or novel biological agents contributes to severe illness and death when the disease spreads to multiple countries or geographical regions before the agent has been detected. It was the need for governance over

---

J. Kruger (✉)
Atlanta, GA, USA
e-mail: jkruger@emory.edu

© The Author(s), under exclusive license to Springer Nature Switzerland AG 2021
M. E. Kosal (ed.), *Proliferation of Weapons- and Dual-Use Technologies*,
Advanced Sciences and Technologies for Security Applications,
https://doi.org/10.1007/978-3-030-73655-2_13

infectious diseases that contributed to the development of the World Health Organization (WHO) in 1948 [28]. The international community has been concerned about disease containment through previous international health agreements dating back to 1981. The early International Health Regulations (IHR) focused on containing a few historically relevant diseases (e.g., cholera, plague, yellow fever, smallpox, typhus, and relapsing fever) and in 2003 following the Severe Acute Respiratory Syndrome (SARS) outbreak, several changes were made to the previous IHR [21]. Under the revised [10], the WHO Director-General was granted the authority to declare any natural, accidental, or deliberate event a public health emergency of international concern if it had the potential to pose a significant global threat. The revised [10] evoked a new approach to the old agreements and called for better disease surveillance and response tools [29]. The more stringent [10] regulations shifted the emphasis from international cooperation to containing public health threats when and where they occur. It also signified new obligations on countries to prepare for health crises and share information with the WHO to coordinate international public health response to the spread of disease [30]. IHR [10] is the most current version used by WHO and were agreed upon by 196 countries. These regulations require countries to develop appropriate surveillance and response capacities to address these widespread health concerns on an annual basis [19].

2 Background

Because adoption of IHR [10] can improve health security on a global scale through effective detection and response to a public health emergency, the purpose of this chapter is to review country adoption to predict future response to infectious diseases or other health events. This chapter reviews 95 countries' capacities to prevent, detect, and respond to biological, chemical, and radiological or nuclear threats. The 2009 H1N1 influenza pandemic was declared the first public health emergency of international concern by the WHO [12]. In recent years, newly emerging and reemerging infectious diseases, such as COVID-19, have affected millions of people worldwide and contributed to economic loss and political instability [26]. Diseases caused by emerging viruses are a major threat to global public health and emphasize the need to detect and respond to the globalization of emerging health threats. The WHO declared COVID-19 a global pandemic after the scale of the global impact had surpassed 19 countries in five WHO regions [26].

With the growing concern about the next pandemic flu or smallpox outbreak, it is important to identify countries that may need additional technical support to upgrade or add active surveillances. It is in societies' best interests to closely monitor for the uptick of emerging and reemerging diseases to prevent the potential for pathogens and viruses to be used for harmful instead of benevolent purposes. IHR [10] obligates countries to develop core functions (e.g., detect, assess, report, and respond to all public health threats) in near real-time in order to protect lives and livelihoods worldwide (Fig. 1) [27]. While there are countries capable of meeting these core func-

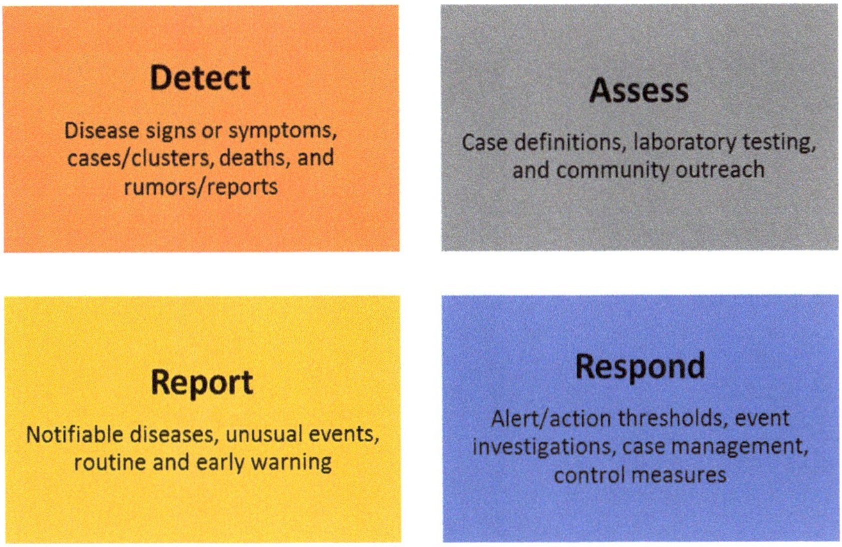

Detect
Disease signs or symptoms, cases/clusters, deaths, and rumors/reports

Assess
Case definitions, laboratory testing, and community outreach

Report
Notifiable diseases, unusual events, routine and early warning

Respond
Alert/action thresholds, event investigations, case management, control measures

Fig. 1 Illustration of the International Health Regulations [19] core functions

tions, many resource poor countries lack the capacity to achieve these demands on their own without financial and technical assistance. IHR [10] emphasizes reciprocal responsibility, and countries must also provide proof of their strength in outcome implementation using a standardized measure to detect, report, and contain public health threats.

Since widespread disease outbreaks contribute to significant economic loss and political instability, in 2014, a group of 44 countries and organizations, including the WHO, launched the Global Health Security Agenda (GHSA) with the purpose to accelerate the implementation of the IHR set in 2005 [24]. The GHSA is a multi-agency effort to promote global health security and future successes in global health and was created as an effort to proactively build countries' capacities to address these challenges and provide a long-term foundation for addressing new global pandemics. The development of public health infrastructure and expansion of countries' capacities to address health security issues is dependent upon efforts to leverage existing investments [4]. In 2017, GHSA was expanded to include additional countries and extended through 2024 to encourage countries to reach a standardized level of core function capacity to combat infectious diseases [7].

Improving global health can improve health in the U.S. and support national and global security interests by fostering political stability, diplomacy, and economic growth worldwide [16]. Therefore, disease surveillance plays an essential role in disease prevention, detection, control, and elimination. The GHSA provides a strategic framework to increase engagement. The premise is based on preventing avoidable outbreaks through early disease outbreak detection and rapid response to save lives. In countries that lack the ability to report an emerging infectious disease

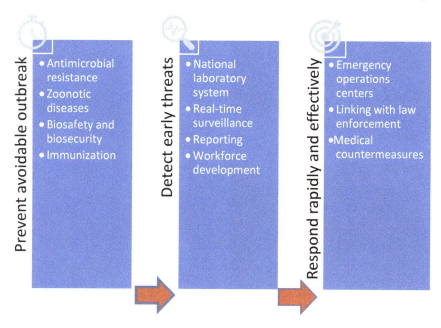

Fig. 2 Prevent, detect, respond framework with technical areas to increase global health security

outbreak before it affects populations everywhere, technical workgroups exist. WHO technical experts work collaboratively with countries to support technical capabilities towards reaching improved health security (Fig. 2) [30].

3 Relevance and Importance

Biosafety and biosecurity are essential pillars of the IHR [1]. Although GHSA and [10] align within the prevent, detect, and respond framework, there are different core capacity indicators. Katz and colleagues demonstrated the overlap for each of the GHSA and IHR objectives [15]. In order to help countries' make progress to accelerate compliance with [10], the WHO recognized the need to increase awareness of GHSA initiatives and increase commitment from the United States Government (USG) and other multi-sector non-governmental involvements (private sector, multi-lateral organizations, academic organizations, and non-governmental organizations). Promoting a cross-functional system that championed an "all-hazards" approach for disease surveillance and response from USG together with participating countries is essential for capacity building efforts in order to elevate global health security as a priority worldwide.

In accordance with IHR [10] Article 54.1, the 61st World Health Assembly (WHA) adopted the resolution requiring state parties and the WHO to report to the WHA on their progress [31]. The WHO developed a monitoring framework to provide technical guidance to assess the status of IHR compliance, facilitate reporting of state parties to the WHA, and provide countries and partners information as to where support was needed. In 2010, a more detailed guideline with a questionnaire was developed and sent to state parties to use for their annual self-assessment. Each year, countries report to the IHR Secretariat at the WHO, a summary is sent to the WHA, and the summary is made publicly available on the Web.

3.1 Cost of Disease Outbreaks

Widespread infectious disease outbreaks cost a population much more than morbidity and mortality. Disease outbreaks can cause economic instability to the economy [3]. A previous CDC Director, Dr. Tom Frieden, stated on Twitter on August 19, 2020 that investing in public health preparedness is far cheaper than the estimated cost of a pandemic. He then stated that the H1N1 (2009) pandemic cost taxpayers $45 billion dollars, the Ebola outbreak (2015) cost $55 billion dollars, and the COVID-19 pandemic (2020) may cost more than $8.8 trillion dollars. Global health security principles strive to minimize the magnitude of disruptive impacts from disease outbreaks by the establishment of a disease surveillance system and through coordination and collaboration in response. Therefore, support for global health security is the responsibility of many governments.

In the U.S. for the year 2019, biosecurity funding made up 12% of fiscal year (FY) funding ($1613.7 million), and federal funding for health security was supported by funds by the Department of Defense (DoD), Department of Homeland Security (DHS), and Department of Health and Human Services (HHS) [23]. Trends in federal civilian biosecurity program funding for fiscal years 2015–2019 (Fig. 1) have decreased over the past four years. Author Watson and colleagues analyzed federal funding amounts from FY2010 through funding for FY2019, using budget documents from prior years and noted a downward trend in budget allocates to civilian biodefense programs [23]. In FY2019, biosecurity funding was $50 million below ($-3\%$) less than the FY2018 budget of $14.24 billion. Also, both chemical security and radiological and nuclear security (represent 3% and 18% of the health security-related programs budget respectively) received decreased funding from prior years. Only one category (for pandemic influenza and emerging infectious disease programs) would receive a 11% increase above FY2018 estimates.

The U.S. government has taken the lead in promoting the implementation of GHSA. However, President Trump's budget proposed cuts to the biodefense appropriations, leading to concerns of the effectiveness of federal emergency preparedness and response programs. The GHSA investments for the biosafety and biosecurity elements examined were approximately 5% of the $350 million planned funds, which is a small amount compared to the 12% for the national laboratory system and the 10% for the workforce development [9] (Fig. 3).

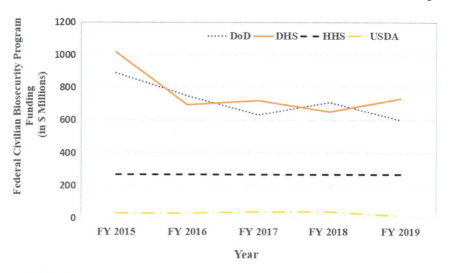

Fig. 3 Trends in federal civilian biosecurity program funding for Fiscal Years (FY) 2015–2019

3.1.1 How Biological Agents Are Classified

The Centers for Disease Control and Prevention (CDC) and U.S. Public Health Service developed a category system to classify high priority biological agents that pose a risk to national security [5]. This system allows primary providers and laboratories to classify bioterrorist organisms based on how easily the agent can be spread and the severity of illness (e.g., death) it causes. The agents are classified into three major categories: Category A, B, or C (Fig. 4). Category A organisms are considered high priority agents (such as smallpox), as they can be easily disseminated or transmitted from person to person and result in high mortality rates. They pose a risk to national security because of the potential for major public health impacts (public panic and social disruption), and therefore require special action for public health preparedness. Category B organisms are rare but considered the second priority because they are moderately easy to disseminate, result in moderate morbidity rates with low mortality rates and require specific enhancements of the CDC's diagnostic capacities and enhanced disease surveillance. Category C organisms are considered the third highest priority (including emerging pathogens) that could be engineered for mass dissemination in the future due to their availability, dispersion, ease of production, potential high morbidity and mortality rates, and major health impacts. These require ongoing research to improve disease detection, diagnosis, treatment, and prevention.

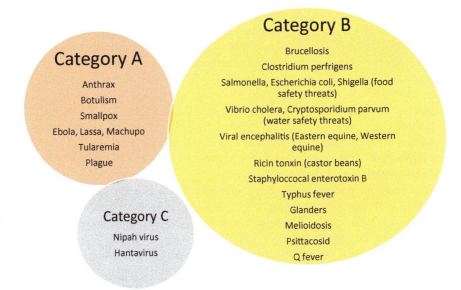

Fig. 4 Classification of biological agents

3.1.2 Disease Surveillance

Biological agents can be used as weapons of mass destruction. Many of the Category A to C high-priority agents require verification from a laboratory. Diagnostic testing can take time, and if there is a delay in diagnosis due to a country's lack of testing facilities or need to send specimens to nearby laboratories, the disease of concern can spread and infect many people in the interim. Typically, biological agents begin with flu-like symptoms, making initial diagnosis difficult, and the onset of symptoms is gradual. Biological agents take the form of disease-causing organisms or toxins produced by living organisms. Also, biological agents are commonly available in nature (e.g., Anthrax is commonly found in the soil) and easily available commercially in local communities (e.g., hospitals, veterinary, and diagnostic laboratories; university facilities; food production plants; and industries with contact with animals and animal products). Biological organisms that are visible or promulgated by public announcement (overt releases) are easier to address by medical and emergency response teams. This is because the organism can be rapidly identified so operational procedures can be put in place to reduce the spread and hinder the impact. Covert releases are those that are hidden or concealed (no prior warning) and usually present as an unusual illness of unknown origin in a geographic area. However, because the effects of a biological attack are not likely to be immediately visible, when terrorists use biological agents, people in the immediate area (e.g., first responders and medical providers) may not see the signs of a biological dispersant into the air.

Response to an unknown disease outbreak requires coordinated actions to detect an unusual event, investigate and contain the organism for laboratory identification, and coordination with interdisciplinary professionals. Infectious diseases can rapidly spread between humans, animals, and vectors, so a multi-sectoral biosafety and biosecurity disease surveillance system is needed. Disease surveillance systems can serve as an early warning system for public health emergencies and also provide information that can help define the epidemiology of health problems (e.g., information on person, place, and time), which could inform policy development and strategic planning. Often, a biological release would require healthcare professionals to recognize the disease occurrence presenting in a cluster of people, which would initiate a community-wide alert and response. For example, if smallpox was released, several patients would show up in emergency rooms with a rash-like illness [17]. A cluster of people with unexplained symptoms in a certain geographical area would trigger an alert to officials to communicate to the community to take protective actions (e.g., quarantine and immunization).

At the community level, disease surveillance is part of a systematic collection, analysis, and evaluation of health information from health professionals who report information on illnesses they see in their clinical practice [6]. Traditionally, healthcare providers report infectious disease information to local health authorities, who then report to centralized Ministries of Health. This approach has many advantages since there are standards in place to support a uniform reporting structure, which funnels information through an interconnected system that is triaged to those that need to know and is easily verifiable. The disadvantage is that sometimes there is missing information due to the fact that not all people have access to healthcare providers (e.g., they go to a pharmacist for medication or go to a traditional healer), and outbreaks may present with non-specific symptoms, leading to vague case definitions, which make it hard to detect clusters in geographical areas when they emerge (e.g., Avian Influenza). Through systems in place, the rapid recognition of emerging infectious diseases and early sharing of information through disease surveillance channels may lead to more rapid detection and official confirmations of disease outbreaks.

3.2 Indicators of the Health Security

Following a 2015 external piloted evaluation in Georgia, Uganda, Peru, Portugal, United Kingdom, and Vietnam, the WHO and CDC piloted the Joint External Evaluation instrument assessments and external reviews. These evaluative reviews validated the self-assessment status of countries and provided outcome evidence to the global community of their disease surveillance and response capacities. The pilot evaluation demonstrated it was possible to create a collaborative external evaluation to validate self-reported findings. Thus, the GHSA review committee recommended moving towards a combined approach of self-evaluations, peer reviews, and voluntary external evaluations. The 68th WHA (2015) resolution urged member states to support the recommendations of the review committee to move towards transparent, objective, and external evaluations. This led to the development of Joint External Evaluations (JEEs) [10].

3.2.1 Utility of the Joint External Evaluation Tool

The purpose of the JEE assessment was to utilize qualitative and quantitative measures in a tool to identify gaps and priority actions. The tool is arranged according to the core elements, and the broad categories of what is evaluated include: preventing and reducing the likelihood of outbreaks and other public health hazards and events; detecting threats early to save lives; and rapid, effective response requiring multisectoral, national, and international coordination and communication. It allowed evaluation across multiple areas (such as human, security, defense, and other hazards) using a numeric scoring system. The JEE tool is deemed useful to monitor and evaluate progress towards the objectives. In the future, it is expected that additional countries will undergo a JEE using a revised tool before 2024 [11].

3.2.2 Joint External Evaluation Process

The JEE framework was adopted to integrate multiple disease surveillance systems and response functions into a single framework. Globally, because information collected on Category A, B, and C diseases that have a large outbreak potential is lacking, challenges associated with a slow response to isolate and identify organisms and findings could be used to develop and implement a national action plan for health security one country at a time. A JEE is a comprehensive methodology applied by participating countries, WHO experts, and the External Evaluation Team using the JEE tool, which includes technical areas such as biosafety and biosecurity elements. The JEE tool has 19 elements, is designed to be customized for multiple priority diseases and allows for the inclusion of a single pathogen (such as Ebola virus) into the integrated disease surveillance system.

The JEE process is a peer-to-peer review and a collaborative effort between participating country experts and JEE team members. The first step in the JEE process is completing the self-evaluation as part of preparing for an external evaluation. Countries provide information on their capabilities based on the indicators and technical questions included in the JEE tool. The participating country may score their self-evaluation or propose a score during the onsite visit with the JEE team. The entire external evaluation, including the discussions around the score, in a collaborative manner with the JEE team members and country experts. The JEE tool can measure countries' individual status and progress in building the necessary capacities to prevent, detect, and respond to infectious disease threats through the JEE process.

The scoring system framework uses three distinct color-coded capability levels to be consistent across JEE measured countries. Capacity levels ranged from red, numerically coded with 1 (which refers to early or no capacity), to yellow, coded as 2 or 3 (which refers to intermediate or developed capacity), to green, coded as

4 or 5 (which refers to established or sustained capacity) for each technical area for visual representation. For each element, the three distinct color-coded capability level informs the development of the implementation plan and highlight gaps for donors and countries to prioritize for their own investments.

4 Results

In this chapter, data from an assessment using the joint external evaluation (JEE) tool in 95 countries was used to assess each country's capacity to prevent, detect, and rapidly respond to public health threats independently of whether they are naturally occurring, deliberate, or accidental. Findings from countries that conducted a JEE self-evaluation and completed external reviews between 2016 and 2019 were combined into this report to make recommendations. In-depth evaluations from each country's external evaluations were used to measure each country's baseline status in achieving GHSA targets that support full implementation of IHR [10]. The evaluations allow transparency and openness of data and information sharing through the public release of JEE summaries, which showcased individual countries' progress in building capacities.

4.1 Summary from Participating Countries

To assess baseline capacity among 95 participating countries, a rank order of performance capacity was used to implement the JEE assessment. Rankings for each country were calculated using the JEE tool by adding up the assessment findings. Countries with assessments that included the number of 1 (which refers to early or no capacity), 2 or 3 (which refers to intermediate capacity), and 4 or 5 (which refers to established or sustained capacity) were collated into tables and then averaged in Excel. The total combined score was ordered based on the highest average in the capacity levels (established, intermediate, early). Findings indicate that most of the top five ranking countries (Singapore, Australia, Japan, Republic of Korea, and United Arab Emirates) were developed countries (Table 1).

Table 1 also displays each country's ability to respond to, detect, and prevent all-hazards scenarios. Variables under each category were summed to get an average and then ranked by each countries' capability towards implementation of IHR [10] core capacity requirement and coded into three capacity levels from red (which refers to early or no capability), yellow (which refers to intermediate capability), to green (which refers to established or sustained capability). It is evident from this data that well-established countries are more likely to be able to respond to multiple hazards and are generally more prepared for biosecurity threats. The North America region is well established in the core function of response and detect and ranks as intermediate in the prevent function. Southeast Asia region countries are on average, at an early level of support for response and prevent functions, and intermediate for the detect function. The African region countries are, on average, at an early level of support for the response and prevent functions, and at an intermediate level for the detect function. The Western Pacific region countries are, on average, at an intermediate level of support for the response and detect functions and at an established level for the prevent function. The Europe and Central Asia region countries are at an intermediate level of support for the response, prevent, and detect functions. The East Mediterranean region countries are at an intermediate level of support for the response, prevent, and detect functions. This report suggests most countries are reactive and have established strong response systems as opposed to the detect and prevent functions.

Table 1 Regional ranking of countries by multi-hazard respond, detect and prevent ability

Region	Country	Respond	Detect	Prevent	Rank
North America	United States	Established	Established	Intermediate	9
South East Asia	Bangladesh	Early	Intermediate	Intermediate	46
South East Asia	Bhutan	Early	Intermediate	Early	58
South East Asia	Indonesia	Intermediate	Intermediate	Intermediate	24
South East Asia	Maldives	Early	Intermediate	Early	59
South East Asia	Myanmar	Early	Intermediate	Early	62
South East Asia	Sri Lanka	Intermediate	Intermediate	Early	29
South East Asia	Thailand	Intermediate	Intermediate	Established	16
South East Asia	Timor-Lester	Early	Intermediate	Early	78
African Region	Benin	Early	Intermediate	Early	74
African Region	Botswana	Early	Intermediate	Intermediate	65
African Region	Burkina Faso	Early	Intermediate	Early	79
African Region	Burundi	Early	Intermediate	Early	85
African Region	Cameroon	Early	Intermediate	Early	69
African Region	Central African Republic	Early	Early	Early	95
African Region	Chad	Early	Early	Early	92
African Region	Comoros	Early	Intermediate	Early	83
African Region	Republic of the Congo	Early	Early	Early	93
African Region	Cote d'Ivoire	Early	Intermediate	Intermediate	64
African Region	Democratic Republic of the Congo	Early	Intermediate	Early	76
African Region	Eritrea	Intermediate	Intermediate	Early	52

(continued)

Table 1 (continued)

Region	Country				
African Region	Ethiopia	Intermediate	Intermediate	Intermediate	44
African Region	Gabon	Early	Early	Early	94
African Region	Gambia	Early	Early	Early	84
African Region	Ghana	Early	Intermediate	Intermediate	60
African Region	Guinea	Early	Intermediate	Early	77
African Region	Guinea-Bissau	Early	Early	Early	87
African Region	Kenya	Intermediate	Intermediate	Intermediate	47
African Region	Kingdom of Eswatini	Early	Intermediate	Early	72
African Region	Lesotho	Early	Intermediate	Early	73
African Region	Liberia	Intermediate	Intermediate	Early	55
African Region	Madagascar	Early	Intermediate	Early	71
African Region	Malawi	Early	Intermediate	Early	86
African Region	Mali	Early	Intermediate	Early	75
African Region	Mauritania	Early	Intermediate	Intermediate	70
African Region	Mauritius	Intermediate	Intermediate	Intermediate	28
African Region	Mozambique	Intermediate	Intermediate	Intermediate	48
African Region	Namibia	Early	Intermediate	Intermediate	61
African Region	Niger	Early	Intermediate	Early	81
African Region	Nigeria	Early	Intermediate	Early	67
African Region	Rwanda	Intermediate	Intermediate	Intermediate	31
African Region	Sao Tome & Principe	Early	Early	Early	82
African Region	Senegal	Intermediate	Intermediate	Intermediate	53
African Region	Seychelles	Intermediate	Intermediate	Early	41
African Region	Sierra Leone	Intermediate	Intermediate	Early	57
African Region	South Africa	Intermediate	Intermediate	Intermediate	25
African Region	South Sudan	Early	Early	Early	91
African Region	Togo	Early	Intermediate	Early	80
African Region	Uganda	Intermediate	Intermediate	Intermediate	39
African Region	United Republic of Tanzania	Intermediate	Intermediate	Intermediate	51

(continued)

Table 1 (continued)

African Region	United Republic of Tanzania-Zanzibar	Early	Early	Early	90
African Region	Zambia	Early	Intermediate	Intermediate	54
African Region	Zimbabwe	Early	Intermediate	Early	66
Western Pacific	Australia	Established	Established	Established	2
Western Pacific	Cambodia	Intermediate	Intermediate	Intermediate	50
Western Pacific	Federated States of Micronesia	Intermediate	Intermediate	Early	34
Western Pacific	Japan	Established	Established	Established	3
Western Pacific	Laos	Intermediate	Intermediate	Early	45
Western Pacific	Mongolia	Intermediate	Intermediate	Intermediate	27
Western Pacific	New Zealand	Established	Established	Established	8
Western Pacific	Republic of Korea	Intermediate	Established	Established	4
Western Pacific	Philippines	Intermediate	Intermediate	Intermediate	43
Western Pacific	Singapore	Established	Established	Established	1
Western Pacific	Vietnam	Intermediate	Intermediate	Intermediate	32
Europe/Ctrl Asia	Albania	Intermediate	Intermediate	Intermediate	26
Europe/Ctrl Asia	Armenia	Established	Established	Established	7
Europe/Ctrl Asia	Belgium	Established	Established	Established	11
Europe/Ctrl Asia	Finland	Established	Established	Established	10
Europe/Ctrl Asia	Georgia	Intermediate	Intermediate	Intermediate	36
Europe/Ctrl Asia	Kyrgyzstan	Established	Intermediate	Established	15
Europe/Ctrl Asia	Latvia	Intermediate	Intermediate	Intermediate	20
Europe/Ctrl Asia	Lithuania	Intermediate	Intermediate	Intermediate	19
Europe/Ctrl Asia	Moldova	Intermediate	Intermediate	Intermediate	33
Europe/Ctrl Asia	N Macedonia	Intermediate	Intermediate	Intermediate	35
Europe/Ctrl Asia	Serbia	Intermediate	Intermediate	Intermediate	40

(continued)

Table 1 (continued)

Region	Country				
Europe/Ctrl Asia	Slovenia	Established	Intermediate	Intermediate	13
Europe/Ctrl Asia	Liechtenstein	Established	Established	Established	6
Europe/Ctrl Asia	Turkmenistan	Intermediate	Intermediate	Intermediate	23
E Mediterranean	Afghanistan	Intermediate	Intermediate	Early	68
E Mediterranean	Bahrain	Established	Established	Intermediate	14
E Mediterranean	Djibouti	Early	Early	Early	89
E Mediterranean	Iraq	Intermediate	Intermediate	Intermediate	56
E Mediterranean	Jordan	Intermediate	Intermediate	Intermediate	37
E Mediterranean	Kuwait	Established	Intermediate	Intermediate	18
E Mediterranean	Oman	Established	Intermediate	Intermediate	12
E Mediterranean	Lebanon	Intermediate	Intermediate	Intermediate	42
E Mediterranean	Libya	Early	Intermediate	Intermediate	63
E Mediterranean	Morocco	Established	Intermediate	Intermediate	21
E Mediterranean	Pakistan	Intermediate	Intermediate	Intermediate	49
E Mediterranean	Qatar	Intermediate	Intermediate	Intermediate	22
E Mediterranean	Saudi Arabia	Established	Intermediate	Intermediate	17
E Mediterranean	Somalia	Intermediate	Early	Early	88
E Mediterranean	Sudan	Intermediate	Intermediate	Intermediate	38
E Mediterranean	Tunisia	Intermediate	Intermediate	Intermediate	30
E Mediterranean	United Arab Emirates	Established	Established	Intermediate	5

4.2 Country Performance Capability Level by World Bank Income Level

An analytic table was created to evaluate country capacity by country income level (Table 2). Data came from two sources: the JEE and the World Bank income level. The JEE previously calculated capability levels (established, intermediate, or early) were collated with the World Bank income group levels for each country and were based on the 2019–2020-dollar value of the gross national product per capita values [25]. The World Bank Atlas uses the following categorizations for income group levels:

Table 2 Country performance capability levels by World Bank income classification

	High (≥$12,536)	Upper middle ($4,046 to $12,535)	Low middle ($1,036 to $4,045)	Low (≤$1,035)
All countries with established capabilities	United States Australia Japan New Zealand South Korea Singapore Belgium Finland Latvia Liechtenstein Lithuania Slovenia Bahrain Kuwait Oman Saudi Arabia UAE	Thailand Armenia	Kyrgyzstan Morocco	N/A
All countries with intermediate capabilities	Mauritius Seychelles North Macedonia Qatar	Indonesia Maldives Namibia South Africa Albania Georgia Serbia Turkmenistan Iraq Jordan Lebanon Libya Botswana	Bangladesh Bhutan Myanmar Sri Lanka Timor-Leste Cameroon Côte D'Ivoire Ghana Kenya Eswatini Mauritania Nigeria São Tomé & Principe Senegal Tanzania Zambia Cambodia Micronesia Laos Mongolia Philippines Vietnam Moldova Pakistan Tunisia Zimbabwe	Burkina Faso DRC Eritrea Ethiopia Guinea Liberia Madagascar Mali Mozambique Niger Rwanda Sierra Leone Togo Uganda Afghanistan Sudan

(continued)

Table 2 (continued)

	High (≥$12,536)	Upper middle ($4,046 to $12,535)	Low middle ($1,036 to $4,045)	Low (≤$1,035)
All countries with early capabilities	N/A	Gabon	Djibouti Lesotho Guinea-Bissau Comoros Benin Zanzibar	Somalia South Sudan Malawi Gambia CAR Chad Democratic Republic of the Congo Burundi

Note This table is based on the World Bank classification of the world's economies into groups: high, upper-middle, lower-middle, and low using 2019–2020 income levels. Established refers to sustained capability; intermediate refers to developed capability; early refers to limited or no capability

CAR Central African Republic, *DRC* Democratic Republic of the Congo, *UAE* United Arab Emirates

low-income countries ($1,035 or less), lower middle-income countries ($1,003 to $4,045), upper middle-income countries ($4,046 to $12,535), and high-income countries ($12,536 or more). These assignments are based on Gross National Income (GNI) per capita (current US$) using the World Bank Atlas method. The classification of countries is determined by two factors: (1) a country's GNI per capita, which can change with economic growth, inflation, exchange rates, and population, and (2) classification threshold (thresholds are adjusted for inflation annually). Revisions to national accounts methods and data can also influence GNI per capita.

The top tier countries consist of 20 countries with established performance capabilities (16 countries in the high-income status, two in the upper-middle income status, and two in the low-middle income status). The middle tier countries consisted of 60 countries with intermediate performance capabilities (five countries with high-income status, 13 countries with upper-middle income status, 26 countries with low-middle income status, and 16 countries with low-income status). The bottom tier countries consisted of 15 countries with early performance capabilities (one country in the upper-middle income group, six countries in the low-middle income group, and eight countries in the low-income group). The three-tiered matrix indicates that most countries are in the middle tier (intermediately prepared).

4.3 Country Performance Capability Level by Freedom in the World

An analytic table was created to evaluate country capacity by country freedom of the world level (Table 3). Data came from two sources: JEE and Freedom in the World rating summary status. The JEE previously calculated capability level (established, intermediate, early) was collated with the Freedom in the World data, which were used for each country and were based on 2020 Freedom in the World rankings [8]. Summaries of political rights and civil liberties were combined to create an aggregate score. Political rights were based on an aggregate polling of scores from a Political Rights score (0–40) and a Civil Liberty score (0–60). The total scores are equally weighted. The summary aggregate score represents a Universal Declaration of Human Rights, including: the right to vote freely in legitimate elections, the right to participate freely in the political process, the right to have representatives that are accountable to them, the right to exercise freedoms of expression and beliefs, the right to be able to freely assemble and associate, the right to have access to an established and equitable system of rule of law, the right to enjoy social and economic freedoms, the right to access to economic opportunity, and the right to hold private property.

Top tier countries consisted of 21 countries with established performance capabilities (11 countries were in the free status, six were partially free, and four were not free). The middle tier countries consisted of 58 countries with intermediate performance capabilities (10 countries were in the free status, 30 were partially free, and 18 were not free). The bottom tier consisted of 15 countries with early performance capabilities (six were partially free, and nine were not free). The three-tiered matrix indicates that most countries have made preparations to expand capabilities in an emergency.

The exact same countries identified as low or lower-middle income categories in the early capability function were also noted to be partially free or not free (Benin, Burundi, Comoros, Chad, CAR, Djibouti, Gambia, Guinea-Bissau, Lesotho, Malawi, Somalia, South Sudan, Republic of the Congo, and Zanzibar). Most countries were in the middle tier (intermediate capability).

Countries with programs that focus on prevention, preparedness, and response to large-scale acute chemical exposures of civilian populations, both intentional and accidental, were ranked by capability. By region, North America was at an established capability level and at an early level of support for chemical security. On average, countries in the Southeast Asia region were at an intermediate capability level and in an early level of support for chemical security. In the African region, most countries were at an intermediate capability level and at an early level of support for chemical security. Most countries in the West Pacific region were at an intermediate capability level and at an established level of support for chemical security. In the Europe and Central Asia region, most countries were at an established capability level and at an intermediate level of support for chemical security. In the Eastern Mediterranean region, most countries were at an intermediate capability level and at an intermediate

Table 3 Country performance capability levels by global freedom score status

	Free	Partially free	Not free
All countries with established capabilities	Belgium Finland Latvia Lithuania Slovenia Liechtenstein South Korea New Zealand Japan Australia United States	Morocco Kuwait Kyrgyzstan Armenia Singapore Thailand	UAE Saudi Arabia Oman Bahrain
All countries with intermediate capabilities	Tunisia Timor-Leste Micronesia Mongolia South Africa São Tomé & Principe Namibia Mauritius Ghana Botswana	Bhutan Indonesia Maldives Bangladesh Sri Lanka Burkina Faso Jordan Lebanon Pakistan Mali Mauritania Mozambique Niger Nigeria Senegal Seychelles Sierra Leone Philippines Zambia Serbia Moldova Togo Georgia Albania Côte d'Ivoire Madagascar Liberia Kenya Guinea Zimbabwe	Myanmar Sudan Qatar Libya Iraq Afghanistan Turkmenistan Vietnam Laos Cambodia Tanzania Uganda Rwanda Kingdom of Eswatini Ethiopia DRC Eritrea Cameroon

(continued)

Table 3 (continued)

	Free	Partially free	Not free
All countries with early capabilities	N/A	Malawi Lesotho Guinea-Bissau Gambia Comoros Benin	Somalia Djibouti South Sudan Gabon Republic of the Congo Chad CAR Burundi Zanzibar

Note Freedom in the World summary scores were categorized as free, partly free, or not free. Established refers to sustained capability; intermediate refers to developed capability; early refers to limited or no capability. North Macedonia is not included in this table

CAR Central African Republic, *DRC* Democratic Republic of the Congo, *UAE* United Arab Emirates

level of support for chemical security. The West Pacific region countries were at an intermediate capability level and reached an established level of support for chemical security. In the U.S., FY2019 funding for chemical security comprised of only 3% of the budget and has decreased by 2% since FY2018.

Countries with programs that focus on prevention, preparedness, and consequence management of radiological and nuclear terrorism and large-scale radiological accidents by capability. By region, we see that North America is at an established capability level for chemical security and at an intermediate level of support for radiation security. In the Southeast Asia region, most countries are at an intermediate capability level for chemical security and at an early level of support for radiation security. In the African region, most countries are at an intermediate capability level for chemical security and at an early level of support for radiation security. In the West Pacific region, on average, most countries are at an intermediate capability level for chemical security and at an intermediate level of support for radiation security. In the Europe and Central Asia region, most countries are an established capability level for chemical security and at an established level of support for radiation security. In the Eastern Mediterranean region, most countries are at an intermediate capability level for chemical security and at an intermediate level of support for radiation security. In summary, the Southeast Asia, Western Pacific, and Europe and Central Asia regions are better at preparing for radiological disasters than chemical security concerns. In the U.S., FY2019 18% of the budget was for radiological and nuclear security funding and has decreased by 6% since FY2018.

5 Discussion

Findings described in this chapter sought to assess [10] adoption through GHSA using the JEE tool to measure country-specific baseline capacity. Since 2016, there is strong political will to develop [10] capacities given that 95 countries have used the first external evaluation standardized tool to allow country programs to identify gaps. The hope is that countries will conduct subsequent evaluations within five years, with a second assessment to identify the progress made in achieving the targets and ensure that improvements in capacity are sustained. Transparency is an important element for attracting and directing resources to where they are needed most (e.g., highly vulnerable, low resource settings). In the future, content drawn and lessons learned from the tested JEE tool could include content from several multisectoral initiatives (such as survey, interview, and discussion-based instruments) or analysis of direct and indirect funding opportunities [2]. The UPMC Center for Health Security developed a synopsis of relevant frameworks to minimize biosafety and biosecurity risk, and the center suggests that ongoing investment is required to support the growing technical challenges and workforce needs in the twenty-first century [22].

The results of this report identified that more developed countries had greater capacities to respond to emerging and re-emerging diseases than the reduced capacities of low-income countries. Advocacy for a sustained political and financial commitment on the part of each country's government, in addition to updating laws, regulations, and standard operating procedures, may ensure optimal implementation of IHR [10] capacities. A budget line should be created for [10]. Funding allocated for IHR [10] core capacities may come from domestic and international sources in order to provide a stable, dedicated, and strong biodefense budget (includes biosecurity, chemical, and radiological security). To maintain a long-term investment in the GHSA initiative, a method to invite public and private investments to help prevent infectious disease threats from becoming global crises may be considered. Factors that may mediate country capacity to properly implement [10] capabilities include an existing biosecurity system and training network, a responsive public health workforce, an integrated national laboratory system, a strong economy, and the support of free political participation and civil liberties. To reach the goal of widespread adoption of IHR [10] and the building of resilient health systems, countries should strive to achieve all the attributes of its current capacity levels in order to reach an intermediate or demonstrated capacity.

Based on the results found, while some countries have made great strides in detecting and responding to priority diseases, some regions of the world (e.g., Southeast Asia and African Region) must strengthen existing capacities and develop action plans to address gaps in surveillance. Baseline information that monitors [10] implementation improves surveillance, early warning, and response system performance in the event of threat detections from biological organisms, food safety, and zoonotic events. These problems could be ameliorated with enhanced surveillance systems for a number of critical diseases in the human and animal health sectors and systems for detecting antimicrobial-resistant microbes. Countries may consider integrating surveillance efforts across human and animal health sectors with the inclusion of an early warning system to detect and monitor potential threat, and focused efforts to improve data quality, information management, and use.

This report identified that biosecurity capacity needs in low/lower income countries differ from needs of middle- and high-income countries. High income countries (i.e., Australia, South Korea, United States) are at a lower risk from biosecurity hazards compared to low/lower income countries that have low capacities to address biosecurity hazards. It is possible that low/lower income countries lack the necessary technical capacities to implement required laboratory capabilities, to ramp up their workforce in order to meet the testing demand, and to operate equipment to mitigate threats. Income appears to play a role in the African region and Eastern Mediterranean region countries, which more frequently were classified in the early capability category. The public health laboratory biosafety and biosecurity capacity relies on numerous interconnecting factors, such as the physical infrastructure and support systems, and workforce training and staffing. The WHO established biosecurity targets in the JEE as targets where a whole-of-government national biosafety and biosecurity system is in place. These targets are ones that ensure dangerous pathogens are identified, held, secured, and monitored according to best practices and that biological risk management training is conducted to reduce dual use research risks and deliberate use for benevolent and harmful purposes. They include educational outreach to ensure the safe transfer of biological agents. In addition, country-specific biosafety and biosecurity legislation or licensing for laboratories are in place as appropriate control measures. Random assessments or laboratory site visits may inform control measures, as national laboratory systems expand their laboratory capacities to test for chemical, radiation and nuclear deposits to determine where country capacities lie. Laboratories working with novel pathogens of pandemic potential should undergo exceptional external evaluations of safety and security [14].

Workforce issues help support capacity in the country and the effective implementation of IHR [10]. In the U.S. JEE report, the areas of improvement were development of a general oversight framework, creation of a mechanism to monitor laboratory staff competence and training at all laboratories, and revisions of procedural documentations [27]. Workforce issues such as few human resources, limited training programs, and the lack of a workforce strategy are indicative of countries with the highest risk. To achieve the laboratory diagnostic capacity for the WHO top ten causes of death in low-income countries, a well-integrated national laboratory system is needed [13]. Enhancing laboratory capacity and workforce capacity in both animal and public health sectors to prevent and detect human and animal disease outbreaks by further investing in laboratory capabilities and capacity can help expand a biosecurity system. Strengthening laboratory resources and training personnel, along with enhanced biosecurity and biosafety measures, will benefit countries' surveillance systems and increase communication to promote better health.

6 Conclusions and Recommendations

The evaluation of country metadata is not new, but this is the first time a comprehensive regional evaluation to identify overarching issues and priority actions has been conducted under IHR [10]. This report found that the use of existing data from joint external evaluations is a novel way to evaluate IHR implementation and can guide the development of an IHR action plan to help countries better prepare to respond to public health threats. Baseline findings from 95 countries identified the following overarching issues that need improvement to uphold global health security: multisectoral engagement, enhanced surveillance, enhanced laboratory capacity, and workforce. In countries where diminishing capacities were noted, new legislation to enable IHR implementation and coordination functions could be developed. USG agencies can work together to support countries, Ministries of Health, public health laboratories, and other public and private stakeholders to apply recommendations to accelerate progress towards a world that is secure from high-threat infectious diseases. There is a need for an increase in funding for biosecurity to address limitations and gaps in policy and downstream consequences resulting from infectious disease outbreaks. Next steps in this research could involve assessing the impact of dedicated donor funding to strengthen [10] implementation in highly vulnerable, low resource countries, and an evaluation of the cost of implementation.

There is a need to strengthen the capacity of and create resilient health systems in low/lower income countries, given the tremendous growth in international trade and travel over the last few decades and the increase in emerging disease threats. Recommendations to address the cross-cutting themes across many of the countries evaluated include promoting sustainable financing, strengthening legislation, and improving the coordination of human and animal laboratory capacity and multisectoral coordination.

- **The need for sustainable financing.** Government financing of both routine and emergency public health activities should be considered in order to sustain progress and IHR [10] core capacity achievements. The development of a strategy for sustainable government financing for essential public health functions, such as surveillance and response, would contribute to the sustainability of global health security.
- **The need for a legal framework to protect health security in relationship to pandemics.** There is a need to strengthen the legal basis for evidence-based policy, planning, and regulatory capacity in order to facilitate and institutionalize [10] implementation. The review or finalization of draft laws, policies, and procedures would improve the clarity of roles and responsibilities and ensure the consistency and continuity of established systems. Strengthened regulatory enforcement mechanisms, capacities, and practices could also enhance [10] implementation.
- **The need to build lab capacity that spans human, animal, agricultural, food, and environmental aspects to respond to novel diseases.** Opportunities exist for significantly enhanced multi-sectoral collaboration, information exchange, and

cross-disciplinary exchanges between human health and animal health. Mechanisms have been developed to foster intersectoral collaboration. Future efforts are needed to implement functional measures for multiple sectors to collaborate, coordinate, and communicate on preparedness and response to all public health emergencies.

- **The need to create strong coordination and collaboration among various stakeholders.** The adoption of a multisectoral approach with informal exchanges of information between coordinating bodies could increase the involvement of leadership with ongoing monitoring of the capacity of threats and IHR-related hazards. A coordinating body could secure against biosafety and biosecurity threats. A global interagency coordination group would have the authority to coordinate across departments, agencies, and country focal points to promote efficiency in the physical security of laboratory facilities that house pathogens, laboratory entry access, inventory monitoring, licensing policy, and storage and containment of biological agents. There is a need for formalized multisectoral coordination and capacity-building support to allow for more effective prevention, detection, and response to chemical risks and events and to formulate policies and plans for detection, assessment, and response to radiation emergencies.

Health security includes the protection from emerging and re-emerging infectious diseases and requires additional biosafety and biosecurity policies and practices supported by an appropriate legal framework [1]. A 2016 WHO report cited that the African region experiences 100 public health events a year, of which 80% are caused by infectious disease, and a smaller proportion is caused by dangerous pathogens such as Ebola [20]. Restricted access to storage areas of deactivated Category A, B, and C organisms would help to ensure the safe and secure storage of infectious materials and could also include records of access to and from storage spaces in addition to emergency response procedures [18].

References

1. Bakanidze L, Imnadze P, Perkins D (2010) Biosafety and biosecurity as essential pillars of international health security and cross-cutting elements of biological nonproliferation. BMC Public Health 10(Supp 1):S12. https://www.ncbi.nlm.nih.gov/pmc/articles/PMC3005572/pdf/1471-2458-10-S1-S12.pdf
2. Berger KM, DiEuliis D, Meyer C, Rao V (2018) Roadmap for biosecurity and biodefense policy in the United States. Gryphon Scientific, National Defense University, and Parsons
3. Cassell C, Bambery Z, Roy K, Meltzer MI, Zara A, Payne RL, Bunnell RE (2017) Relevance of global health security to the US export economy. Health Security 15(6):563–568
4. Centers for Disease Control and Prevention (2014) Global health security: vision and overarching target. US Department of Health and Human Services, Atlanta, GA. https://www.cdc.gov/globalhealth/security/pdf/ghs_overarching_target.pdf
5. Centers for Disease Control and Prevention. Bioterrorism Agents/Disease. Accessed Dec 2020. https://emergency.cdc.gov/agent/agentlist-category.asp
6. Centers for Disease Control and Prevention. Introduction to public health surveillance. Public Health 101 Series. Accessed Dec 2020. https://www.cdc.gov/publichealth101/surveillance.html
7. Congressional Research Service. The Global Health Security Agenda (GHSA): 2020–2024. March 16, 2020. https://crsreports.congress.gov
8. Freedom House (2020) Freedom in the world. Accessed Dec 2020. https://freedomhouse.org/countries/freedom-world/scores
9. Global Health Security Agenda Annual Report (2017) Advancing the global health security agenda: progress and early impact from U.S. investment. Accessed Dec 2020. https://www.cdc.gov/globalhealth/security/ghsareport/images/ghsa-report-2017.pdf
10. Global Capacities Alert and Response (GCR) (2016) IHR (2005) monitoring and evaluation framework joint external evaluation tool. https://www.who.int/ihr/publications/WHO_HSE_GCR_2016_2/en/
11. Global Capacities Alert and Response (GCR) (2018) IHR (2005) Monitoring and evaluation framework. Joint External Evaluation (JEE Tool).Second edition. https://www.who.int/ihr/publications/WHO_HSE_GCR_2018_2/en/
12. Gostin LO, Katz R (2016) The international health regulations: the governing framework for global health security. Millbank Quarterly 94(2):264–313
13. Ijaz K, Kasowski E, Arthus RR, Angulo FJ, Dowell SF (2012) International health regulations-what gets measured gets done. Emerg Infectious Diseases 18(7):1054–1057
14. Inglesby TV, Relman DA (2016) How likely is it that biological agents will be used deliberately to cause widespread harm? EMBO Rep 17(2):127–130
15. Katz R, Sorrell EM, Kornblet SA, Fischer JE (2014) Global health security agenda and the international health regulations: moving forward. Biosecur Bioterror 12(5):231–238
16. Khan AS, Lurie N (2014) Health security in 2014: building on preparedness knowledge for emerging health threats. The Lancet 384(9937):93–97
17. Landesman LY (2001) Public health management of disasters: the practice guide. American Public Health Association. ISBN: 0875530257
18. National Academies of Sciences, Engineering, and Medicine (2017) Global health and the future role of the United States. Washington, DC. The National Academies Press. https://doi.org/10.17226/24737
19. Nuttall I (2014) International health regulations (2005): Taking Stock. Bull World Health Organ 92(5):310
20. Regional Office for Africa, World Health Organization (2016) Report on the Status of EDPLN BSL-3 in Select Countries in the African Region. World Health Organization. https://www.afro.who.int/sites/default/files/2017-08/Report%20on%20the%20Status%20of%20EDPLN%20BSL-3%20in%20Select%20Countries%20in%20the%20African%20Region.pdf

21. The Stimson Center (2011) International health regulations 101. Stimson Global Health Security Policy Brief. Washington, DC. https://www.stimson.org/program/global-health-security/
22. UPMC Center for Health Security (2015) Synopsis of biological safety and security arrangements. https://www.centerforhealthsecurity.org/our-work/pubs_archive/pubs-pdfs/2015/SynopsisofBiologicalSafetyandSecurityArrangements-072115.pdf
23. Watson C, Watson M, Gastfriend D, Kirk ST (2018) Federal funding for health security in FY2019. Health Security 16(5):281–303
24. Wikipedia. Global health security agenda. Accessed Dec 2020. Wikipedia.org/wiki/global_health_security-agenda
25. World Bank (2020) New country classifications by income level: 2019–2020. Accessed December 2020. https://datahelpdesk.worldbank.org/knowledgebase/articles/906519-world-bank-country-and-lending-groups
26. World Health Organization. Statement on the Second Meeting of the International Health Regulations (2005) Emergency Committee regarding the Outbreak of Novel Coronavirus (2019-nCoV). January 30, 2020. Accessed Dec 2020. https://www.who.int/news/item/30-01-2020-statement-on-the-second-meeting-of-the-international-health-regulations-(2005)-emergency-committee-regarding-the-outbreak-of-novel-coronavirus-(2019-ncov)
27. World Health Organization (2017) Joint external evaluation of IHR core capacities of the United States of America. World Health Organization, Geneva. Accessed Dec 2020. https://apps.who.int/iris/handle/10665/254701
28. World Health Organization (2017) The International Health Regulations (IHR)—10 years of global public health security. Weekly Epidemiol Record 23(92):321–322
29. World Health Organization (2016) International Health Regulations (2005). Geneva. https://www.who.int/ihr/ihr/publications/9789241580496/en/
30. World Health Organization (2010) Protocol for assessing national surveillance and response capacities for the International Health Regulations (2005): A Guide for Assessment Teams. Dec 2010. Accessed December 2020. https://www.who.int/ihr/publications/who_hse_ihr_201007/en/
31. World Health Organization (2008) International Health Regulations (2005). 2nd ed. WHO, Geneva. https://www.who.int/ihr/9789241596664/en/

Analyzing the Threat, Vulnerability, and Consequences of Agroterrorism

Olufunke Adebola

Abstract Agroterrorism is a type of low-tech, high-impact biological, radiological, chemical, and, more recently, cyber terrorism targeted at the agriculture industry. With the abundance of information on developing biological weapons and the relative ease of accessing chemical agents, agroterrorism could be an attractive form of terrorism for separatist, religious, right-wing, and left-wing groups. The U.S. agricultural sector is a viable target for a terrorist attack because of the high economic, political, and social impact an attack can pose. This chapter finds that changes in human migration patterns could increase the risk of an agroterrorism attack in the United States. It also finds that the attention devoted to biological agroterrorism exposes the vulnerabilities of a potential radiological, chemical, and cyber agroterrorism attack.

1 Introduction

Agroterrorism is the "deliberate introduction of an animal or plant disease for the purpose of generating fear, causing economic losses, or undermining social stability." [1]. It is also defined as "the deliberate introduction, use, or threatened use, of a chemical, biological, radiological, nuclear, or explosive agent against one or more components of the food or agriculture sectors, with the goal of causing mortality and morbidity, generating fear, precipitating economic loss, or undermining sector stability and confidence in government." [2]. Agroterrorism can also be described as a global catastrophic biological risk (GCBRs). A global catastrophic risk is defined as "those events in which biological agents—whether naturally emerging or reemerging, deliberately created and released, or laboratory engineered and escaped—could lead to sudden, extraordinary, widespread disaster beyond the collective capability of national and international governments and the private sector to control." [3].

Historically, in warfare, the agriculture sector has been a target. For example, in the sixth century BCE, the Assyrians poisoned enemy wells with rye ergot [4].

O. Adebola (✉)
Georgia Institute of Technology, Atlanta, GA, USA
e-mail: oadebola3@gatech.edu

© The Author(s), under exclusive license to Springer Nature Switzerland AG 2021
M. E. Kosal (ed.), *Proliferation of Weapons- and Dual-Use Technologies*,
Advanced Sciences and Technologies for Security Applications,
https://doi.org/10.1007/978-3-030-73655-2_14

During World War II, the British manufactured and tested five million anthrax cattle cakes. The plan aimed at destroying German beef and dairy herds [5]. In 1970, it is suspected that members of the Ku Klux Klan introduced cyanide into the water supply to a cattle farm in Alabama, resulting in the death of thirty cattle [6]. In recent times, terrorists have considered the United States' agricultural sector a potential target in terror attacks. In 2002, the U.S. and allied forces discovered many al Qaeda training manuals encouraging the targeting of U.S. agriculture [7]. While there is no positively known imminent public threat to the United States' agriculture, a potential attack on this sector could have a high economic, political, and social impact. This study is motivated by a March 2017 audit report of the USDA Inspector General's Office found that the United States was not adequately prepared to respond to an attack on the agriculture infrastructure [8]. It is also motivated by a lack of comparative attention in scholarly literature and the policy world of a terrorist attack on one of the U.S. critical infrastructure. Research and policy on agroterrorism wane compared to those in other critical infrastructures such as the energy and financial sectors. The events following the Coronavirus (COVID-19) pandemic have exposed some of the vulnerabilities in the agricultural sector, particularly with the expansion of large-scale industrial farms. These farms, also known as 'factory-farms,' create the opportunity for viruses to spread and mutate [9]. In light of the pandemic, scholars have recommended the creation of resilient food systems that can recover and withstand disruptions [10]. The central research question in this chapter is "what is the risk of an agroterrorism attack in the United States?"

2 Analysis of the U.S. Agricultural Sector

The Homeland Security Presidential Directive 7 (HSPD-7) identifies the agricultural sector as a critical infrastructure element [11] of the U.S. because any disruption of the U.S. agricultural sector would have an impact on the local and national economy, on food security, and public health. For example, as one of the largest global food exporters, the United States' agricultural sector contributes up to about six percent of the country's annual GDP [12]. As of 2017, about 1.7 percent of Americans work in the agricultural sector [13].

In addition to this, food plays an essential role in global politics. Rothschild argues that the rise of the United States' as a global hegemon results from its role as the world's largest food exporter [14]. During the global food crisis of the 1970s, the U.S. role "as custodian of the bulk of the world's exportable grain" [15] helped the U.S. maintain its global political powers as many developed, developing, and the least-developed world looked to the U.S. for food, particularly grains. The United States has used food as a tool for foreign diplomacy since World War 1. During the War, Herbert Hoover, the Director of Food Administration, promoted the "Food Will Win the War" slogan as a strategy for victory. Hoover's effort aimed at boosting national food production to ensure that the U.S. allies in the war had access to food supplies [16].

2.1 Motivations for Agroterrorism

The realism and constructivism theories of international relations (I.R.) offer explanations for States' attraction to weaponize biological agents for agroterrorism attacks. Realism in I.R. assumes that because of the international system's anarchical nature, States in their desire for survival, prioritize security. To ensure their survival, States develop military force [17]. Therefore, it can be explained that the investment of the former Soviet Union and the American governments during the cold war was for self-preservation. However, the realist theory may not explain terror groups' interest in agroterrorism because of its State-Centrist approach in its unit of analysis. The realist school is primarily concerned with relations between States, particularly relations among great powers. Realists do not consider transnational actors such as terrorist groups [18]. On the other hand, constructivism argues that the existence of norms on the use of biological, nuclear, and chemical weapons compel States to deploy these weapons [19]. In other words, the reason States have not engaged in agroterrorism is because of the Chemical Weapons Convention (CWC) and the Biological Weapons Convention (BWC). However, because terrorist groups are not signatories to these conventions, the constructivist theory may not explain why terrorist groups have not deployed biological or chemical weapons in agroterrorism.

Agroterrorism could appeal to non-State actors such as groups opposed to the cultivation of genetically modified (G.M.) crops or animal rights activists [20]. "Opposition to the use of G.M. crops and animals has sometimes taken the form of vandalism and destruction, and it is quite possible that some activists will at some point turn to diseases as weapons to attack G.M. organisms. Radical animal rights groups may wish to attack animal agriculture to prevent corporations from profiting from animal suffering" [21].

Corporations, individuals, organized crime groups, and even national governments could attempt to manipulate the global agriculture market by introducing diseases in their competitors' agricultural products. For example, when a country reports a disease in agricultural exports, international trade for agricultural products is halted or reduced. A state competitor of an agricultural product could be motivated to attack its competitor's agricultural sector to become the primary trader of that product [22].

Narcotic traffickers, particularly drug cartels, could also be motivated to attack U.S. agriculture in retaliation. In 1989, the United Nations Drug Control Program (UNDCP) and the United States tested a fungus, *Pleospora papaveracea*, that kills poppies by attacking their roots. According to some researchers, "drug cartels could themselves acquire the technology and in revenge attacks use a form of agricultural terrorism against Britain or the U.S." [23]. In addition to this, disgruntled employees seeking revenge could motivate an attack [24].

2.2 Possibility of Accident

Given the definition of agroterrorism as intentional action, this chapter does not consider the possibility of unintentional accidental exposure of animals or plants to dangerous disease agents may occur as part of routine operations, testing, or experimentation. Accidental leakage could also follow natural disasters or structural incidents in storage facilities. Transportation of hazardous organisms may lead to unintentional leakage or exposure that may spread disease organisms. Biosafety has increasingly gained prominence following various high-profile incidents described later in the chapter. Biosafety has been integrated into standard practices set by the World Organization for Animal health (OIE) and the International Standards Organization [25], such as Quality Management Systems for laboratories, and this practice is strengthened by regulations and oversight of potentially toxic or hazardous biological and chemical agents. As awareness has increased on the risks biosafety incidents pose, laboratory accreditation has become one such regulatory enforcement mechanism.

Also, efforts to combat drug production are not considered agroterrorism. For example, in the mid-1980s, the U.S. declared war on drug production and trafficking and funded efforts to eradicate cocaine production in Colombia. One of the methods adopted to achieve this purpose was an aerial spraying of herbicides and pesticides on coca plantations [26]. This action is not considered an act of agroterrorism because it was not aimed at "generating fear, causing economic losses, or undermining social stability."

This chapter considers three forms of agroterrorism—the importation and introduction of foreign animal disease, the importation and introduction of foreign animal disease, and a cyber-attack on the agricultural sector.

2.3 Importation of Foreign Animal Diseases (FAD)

Foreign Animal Diseases (FAD) are described as "important transmissible disease of livestock or poultry believed to be absent from the United States and its territories" [27]. FAD agents have been attractive in biological warfare. This is because, unlike chemical agents, biological agents such as bacteria and viruses are not volatile, can be dispersed in small quantities with the ability to cause huge economic and human losses [28], can be stealthily dispersed to infect animals and humans, and can cause disease or death within a short period [29]. Agroterrorism, through the importation of FAD agents was a threat to the United States economy during the Cold War [30], and has continued with globalization resulting in an increase in trade, illegal importation of infected animals, and human movement [30]. For example, Asian long-horned beetles are suspected of arriving in the United States from Asia through eggs laid in wooden packing material. This pest could cause damage estimated in the billions of dollars to the U.S. fruit, lumber, and tourism industry [31].

The Public Health Security and Bioterrorism Preparedness and Response Act of 2002 mandates that the U.S. Secretary of Agriculture "by regulation establish and maintain a list of each biological agent and each toxin that the Secretary determines has the potential to pose a severe threat to animal or plant health, or animal or plant products [32]." The Act also mandates the Secretary of Agriculture to increase "the number of inspections under this section for the purpose of enabling the Secretary to inspect food offered for import at ports of entry into the United States [32]...". The Act's wordings suggest that the Act is more concerned with biological diseases appearing at the ports of entry while overlooking chemical and radiological agents that could be developed locally within the country [33]. Although the H.R. 1238: Securing our Agriculture and Food Act, (an amendment to the Public Health Security and Bioterrorism Preparedness and Response Act of 2002) includes wordings that suggest that domestic food products would be inspected, it is not clear the government agency that would perform this function.

The 2002 Act charges the Centers for Disease Control and Prevention and the U.S. Department of Agriculture to maintain a list of biological agents that pose the highest risks to U.S. agriculture. Of the twenty biological agents on the list, five of them have been ranked by as being of the highest threat based on six criteria including the disease knowledge, impact on animal health and welfare, impact on public health, impact on wider society, impact on trade, and control tools [34, 35].

In the U.S., foreign plant disease could be intentionally introduced into the U.S. by international travelers or through food, particularly fruits, vegetables, and spices shipped by mail from abroad [36]. The USDA maintains a list of nine biological plant toxins that could introduce diseases to the United States [37].

In the years following the September 2011 terror attack, it is reported that dozens of foreign insects and plant diseases entered the country undetected because of a shortage of workforce at the nation's border posts. According to the report, "hundreds of agricultural scientists responsible for stopping invasive species at the border were reassigned to anti-terrorism duties in the newly formed Homeland Security Department [36]." The economic cost of the invasion of foreign plant disease in the country is estimated at $120 billion [38], a price that is borne by the consumers, in the form of higher food costs, and the government in eradicating programs [36].

3 Animal Agents and Toxins

3.1 Foot and Mouth Disease

Foot and Mouth Disease (FMD), often regarded "as the most important transboundary animal disease in the world" [39], is a threat to the U.S. livestock industry [40]. FMD is a highly contagious viral disease predominant in Africa, Asia, South America, the Middle East, and Eastern Europe. The disease affects cloven-hoofed animals such as cattle, sheep, goats, antelope, deer, bison, and pigs. It is characterized by fever, lesions in the mouth and feet of the animals, and lameness. There is no universal vaccine for the disease [41].

The United States has been free of FMD since 1929. However, globalization, international trade, and human migration pose a risk of reintroducing the disease to countries that were previously free of these diseases [40]. The fast speed at which human and animal migration occurs and the slow rate of detecting disease at its early stages and preventing a significant disease outbreak magnifies this disease's risk. For example, the last outbreak of FMD in England occurred in 2001. Before that, the country had been FMD free since 1967. British authorities suspected that the disease was introduced into the country from infected meat used in animal feed. The meat had been brought into the country illegally from Asia or the Middle East. The disease also affected animals in France, the Netherlands, and Ireland [42].

There are also possible threats of this virus dispersal by state actors [43]. According to some reports, the Russian agricultural biological weapons program targeting animal and plant life codenamed *Ekology* [44], developed, produced, and tested the FMD virus from 1973 until 1992 [45]. During this period, the Soviets allegedly had about six agricultural research centers with 10,000 scientists and technicians developing these weapons [46]. One of the concerns about biological weapons in the former Soviet states is that some of these weapons have not been secured in modern biosafety containment laboratories since the collapse of the Soviet Union [47]. This could result in an accidental dispersal of the virus or the virus's potential getting in the hands of non-state actors like terrorist groups. Also, there are concerns that Russia could reactivate an offensive biological weapons program based on its existing infrastructure and expertise [48].

There are also concerns about the accidental release of the virus from laboratories producing the vaccines. In 2008, the Government Accountability Office (GAO) identified fourteen global instances, including one in the United States, where laboratories had unintentionally released the virus. In September 1978, there was an accidental release of the virus from the Plum Island Animal Disease Center of New York (PIADC). The virus had infected animals quarantined outside the laboratory. "An internal investigation concluded that the most probable routes of escape of the virus from containment were (1) faulty air balance of the incinerator area, (2) leakage through inadequately maintained air filter and vent systems, and (3) seepage of water under or through a construction barrier near the incinerator area. Animal care workers then most likely carried the disease back to the animal supply area on the island, where it infected clean animals being held for future work" [49].

FMD is traditionally controlled by restricting animals' movement suspected to have been exposed to the virus and culling the infected animals [50]. There are vaccines developed to mitigate the risk of an FMD outbreak. However, vaccination is difficult because the vaccine administered must match the virus's strain causing the outbreak. Therefore, vaccines may only be delivered after the disease outbreak. The United States participates in the North American FMD Vaccine Bank (NAFMDVB) with Mexico and Canada. Today, FMD vaccines are only manufactured in the NAFMDVB located in Plum Island Animal Disease Center (PIADC). There is no commercial manufacturing of the vaccine because of the provisions of 21 U.S.

Code § 113a that mandates the virus be held only at the PIADC. As a result, only the PIADC keeps FMD vaccines in the country. This law aims to prevent the accidental release of the virus. In a testimony to the U.S. House Committee on Agriculture, the Veterinarian for Cattle Empire testified that because of inadequate funding for the vaccine bank, "the amount of antigen in the North American FMD Vaccine Bank is far below what would be needed to provide vaccine for a single livestock dense state in the United States" [40]. Consequently, it has been suggested that the USDA might not be adequately prepared for an FMD outbreak [51].

A potential outbreak of FMD would have substantial economic impacts. Culling infected animals would result in potentially severe financial losses [52]. A study conducted at Kansas State University estimates that the costs associated with an FMD "outbreak in the Midwestern U.S. could result in a total of $188B in losses to the livestock and allied industries and up to $11B to the U.S. government" [53] from reduced beef and animal feed exports and tourism [54].

3.2 African Swine Fever

This is a viral disease in pigs that is caused by the African swine fever (ASF) virus. The disease was first identified in Kenya in 1921 [55]. The disease was contained to Africa until 1957, when it was identified in Portugal, and in subsequent years in Brazil, Italy, Russia, Dominican Republic, and Cuba. As of today, ASF has not been reported in the United States. However, because of the disease's high mortality rates, a potential outbreak could affect the $20 billion (U.S.) hog industry. There is no treatment or vaccine available for ASF [56].

3.3 Avian Influenza

This is a highly contagious viral zoonotic influenza disease: that is, it infects avian (birds) [57] and can be transmitted to humans with direct contact with infected birds. The natural reservoirs for the virus are wild birds, especially ducks and pigs [58].

The first case of A(H5N1) strain in poultry emerged in China in 1996. In 1997, the virus was identified in humans, killing six of the 18 infected people [59]. By 2003, the disease had spread into Mongolia, southern Russia, the Middle East, Europe, and Africa [60]. According to the Food and Agriculture Organization, it is widely estimated that at least 200 million domesticated birds (out of a total world population of 10 billion) have either died or been culled because of H5N1 [61]. The 2003 outbreak of the influenza H7N7 in the Netherlands resulted in the 89 human infections, including the death of a Dutch veterinarian [62]. In the spring of 2013, influenza A(H7N9) virus was first detected in humans in mainland China. Since then, there have been 1625 confirmed human infections resulting in 622 deaths [63].

There have been six recorded outbreaks of avian flu in humans since 1918. The first reports of probable avian flu (H1N1) resulted in 675,000 human mortality. During the second occurrence, the H3N2 virus resulted in 116,000 deaths in 1957. The H1N1 is blamed for 18,000 deaths in 2009 [64]. Since 2014, the United States has reported the following avian virus detections in 21 U.S. states: H5N2, H5N8, and H5N1. There were 15 States with outbreaks in domestic poultry or captive birds and six States with H5 detections in wild birds, only [65]. These outbreaks did not cause infections in humans. In 2016, the first reported case of avian influenza H7N2, a strain of influenza A virus in cats emerged in New York [66]. The virus was later identified in a "veterinarian who had prolonged close exposure to respiratory secretions of sick cats" [67]. In 2017, H7N9 avian influenza in two commercial flocks in Lincoln County, Tennessee, led to the culling of 73,500 birds [68].

According to the Food and Agricultural Organization (FAO), economic activities constitute the most important risk factor for the local and cross-border spread of the avian flu virus [69]. There are concerns that state actors could pose a threat by manipulating, modifying, and weaponizing the avian virus. In 2006, the British intelligence agency MI6 reported that North Korea was trying to weaponize the avian influenza virus [70]. However, it is not clear the extent to which North Korea has achieved its goal. Also, there are concerns about the proliferation of genome engineering research, publicly-available information about gene editing, and the relatively diminishing costs of reproducing the available results of previous research [71]. In 2013, a Dutch virologist Ron Fouchier published a journal article *Gain-of-function experiments on H7N9*, [72] that showed the detailed methodology of mutating the H5N1 strain of avian influenza into a highly infectious airborne human virus. The U.S. National Science Advisory Board for Biosecurity (NSABB) requested that the article's authors "not include the methodological and other details that could enable replication of the experiments by those who would seek to do harm" [73] out of concern that terrorists could reproduce these results [74].

A pandemic avian flu outbreak in the United States would have huge impacts on the economy. The 2014 and 2016 avian flu outbreaks in the country resulted in the deaths of millions of domesticated poultry in 15 states and $1–3.3 billion (U.S.) in costs to the U.S. economy [75], and about $930 million loss to the federal government [64]. Following the 2017 outbreak in Tennessee, countries in Africa, Asia, South America, and the European Union imposed restrictions on poultry imports from the United States [76].

3.4 Camelpox

This is a highly contagious viral skin disease that affects camels. The condition is caused by the camelpox virus (CMLV) found in every country with domesticated camels [77]. The camelpox virus is like the Variola virus (VARV) that causes smallpox [78]. In 1990, an Iraqi defector revealed that the country had researched weaponizing the camelpox virus at the Foot and Mouth Disease Vaccine plant (FMDV) in Al

Dawrah, Iraq [79]. The choice of including camelpox in Iraq's biological weapons program is because "it was near to smallpox" [79]. In a speech delivered at a U.N. Security Council meeting in 2003, former Secretary of State Colin Powell stated the U.S. concerns that "Saddam Hussein has investigated dozens of biological agents causing diseases such as gas-gangrene, plague, typhus, tetanus, cholera, complex, and hemorrhagic fever. And he also has the wherewithal to develop smallpox" [80]. According to the Nuclear Threat Initiative, the new government in Iraq does not seem interested in pursuing Saddam Hussein's biological weapons program and, as a result, no longer represents a biological weapons threat [81].

3.5 Rinderpest Virus

This is a highly contagious viral disease that affected ruminants and swine in Asia and Europe. The virus is believed to be the first biological weapon deployed in war. According to folklore, in the twelfth century, Genghis Khan, founder of the Mongol empire, deployed rinderpest infected cattle into enemy herds to infect their cattle and cut off their food supplies. In the twentieth century, Germany, the United Kingdom, the United States of America, Canada, and the Soviet Union included rinderpest in the biological weapons programs [82]. Although the disease was eradicated in 2011 [83], there are concerns that the availability of virus and blood samples in many countries could threaten the reintroduction of the disease [84].

4 Cyber Threats in the Agriculture

As the global population and the demand for food grows, the need to increase global food yield and supplies has made farmers turn to precision agriculture. Precision agriculture involves using "advanced information and measurement technologies to monitor agricultural output levels, capture detailed information on the progress of crop growth, and apply agricultural inputs more accurately [85]." Precision agriculture makes use of the GIS, GPS, internet, sensors transmitters, and data systems to optimize the activities along the agricultural value chain.

Some of the vulnerabilities contributing to precision agriculture include the outdated industrial control systems (ICS) used in the food industry. Examples of the ICS include SCADA systems, distributed control systems, and Programmable Logic Controllers [86]. These systems were not designed to be cyber secure but were designed to be self-contained and isolated, running on specially developed software and hardware. However, it is becoming more common to connect these systems to corporate networks to allow remote access capabilities. The ability to have remote access could attract hackers to gain remote access to the physical cyber system, the enterprise resource planning (ERP), and other vital systems in a farm or food production company [87].

While many farms are adopting precision agriculture technologies, many of the senior executives and board of directors lack an awareness of the risks, vulnerabilities, and consequences of a cyber-attack [88]. According to a survey conducted by the American Farm Bureau Federation, "eighty-seven percent of farmers do not have a response plan if a security breach occurred at a company holding their data [89]."

In 2016, the Federal Bureau of Investigation (FBI) report warned that "Food and Agriculture (F.A.) sector is increasingly vulnerable to cyber-attacks as farmers become more reliant on digitized data [90]". According to the report, cybercriminals could attack the sector with the intent to steal farm-level data in bulk, to carry out ransomware attacks, or attempt to destroy farm data. Cybercriminals could also hack into the food supply chains to disrupt food distribution and reduce food availability and panic buying in affected areas. For example, in 2017, Mondelēz International, an American based food and beverage company, resulted in its inability to ship and send invoices during the last four days of its second-quarter [91]. Cybercriminals could gain access to the programs that control the process of food irradiation, introduce dangerous amounts of chemicals resulting in widespread illness, and potentially, death [92].

5 International Stakeholders

A potential agroterrorism attack in a country could have a global impact because of global trade in food production and human migration patterns. In light of this, there are international organizations that monitor animal and plant diseases. These include the United Nations Food and Agricultural Organization (FAO), Office International des Epizooties/ Epizootics (OIE), and World Health Organization (WHO). These organizations work in collaboration to coordinate the "One World, One Health" concept. One of the aims of the idea is to monitor zoonotic diseases and pathogens that could be used in agroterrorism.

The organizations perform individual roles to achieve the "One World, One Health" goals. For example, the FAO develops toolkits that provide information and training on biosecurity, the OIE provides vaccination guidelines to countries and coordinates the global information system of animal diseases. Through this system, countries report animal disease outbreaks to the OIE. The WHO coordinates the International Health Regulations (IHR), a global surveillance system for public health emergencies including bioterrorism [93]. There are also tasks performed collaboratively by all three organizations. For example, the creation Crisis Management Centre—Animal Health (CMC-AH) to respond to transboundary animal diseases, and establishment of the Global Early Warning System (GLEWS) that provides real time, verified reports of human and animal diseases [94]. The GLEWS eliminates the multiple individual verification time taken by prior information systems by streamlining the process into a single verification process. Thus, making emergency response faster.

Despite the success in information sharing and disease surveillance, there are still challenges. For example, some countries still lack "formal mechanism for reporting local outbreaks to regional and international organizations, the failure of surveillance systems to gather disease outbreak data in standard formats [95]." Also, there are challenges with sharing of virus samples and sequence information. For example, there are still contentious issues regarding the sharing of virus genome data have been resolved. Some countries unwilling to share these data place strict prohibitions guiding international sharing or prohibit it entirely. One of the reasons is that there is a potential for profit and other benefits to be obtained from materials and vaccines produced from their isolates [95].

6 US Domestic Stakeholders

Four national institutions are concerned with the protection and regulation of the U.S. national agriculture. These include the U.S. Department of Agriculture (USDA), the Department of Health and Human Services (HHS), Food and Drug Administration (FDA), the Department of Homeland Security (DHS), and the Department of Defense (DoD). The Department of Health and Human Services, through its agency, the Centers for Disease Control and Prevention, works with APHIS in operating the FSAP. The agency also conducts research on zoonotic disease of public health importance, such as the Rift Valley disease. The FDA makes regulations to protect the nation against chemical, biological, radiological, and nuclear threats and emerging infectious diseases.

Through the Veterinary Services Foreign Animal Disease Diagnostic Laboratory (FADDL), the USDA coordinates the Plum Island Animal Disease Center of New York (PIADC) located at Plum Island, New York. The center serves as an international reference center for the FAO and OIE. The laboratory provides training to veterinarians on the identification and treatment of foreign animal diseases. It also maintains the North American Foot-and-Mouth Disease Vaccine Bank (NAFMVB), an international collaboration between the U.S., Canada, and Mexico. The USDA's Animal and Plant Health Inspection Service (APHIS) manages the Federal Select Agent Program (FSAP). The program "oversees the possession, use and transfer of biological select agents and toxins, which have the potential to pose a severe threat to public, animal or plant health or to animal or plant products [96]." The Agriculture Research Service (ARS) Foreign Animal Disease Research Unit (FADRU) branch of the USDA conducts scientific research on livestock transboundary animal diseases.

The DHS, through its Agricultural Defense Branch in the Chemical-Biological operates the Division Foreign Animal Disease (FAD) Vaccines and Diagnostics Countermeasures program. The program's goal is to develop vaccines for Foreign Animal Disease, particularly for FMD and African Swine Fever. The DHS Office of National Laboratories (ONL) also provides funds for the construction of a biosafety level-4 (ABSL-4-agriculture) facility- the National Bio- and AgroDefense Facility (NBAF). The facility will replace the PIADC upon completion. It will "serve as a national interagency and international resource, offering capabilities for research, veterinary countermeasure development, disease diagnosis, and training [34]. The H.R. 1238: Securing our Agriculture and Food Act 2017 tasks the Department of Homeland Security's Office of Health Affairs with defending the nation's food and agriculture against agroterrorism [97].

In a 1964 Memorandum of Understanding between the DoD and USDA, the "DoD agrees to assist the USDA in the event of biological contamination to the U.S. agricultural base [98]." During an agricultural emergency, the USDA may request assistance from the DoD in the form of military specialists or laboratory support to the Animal and Plant Health Inspection Service on a reimbursable basis in accordance with the Economy Act [99]. If the act of agroterrorism involving the use of chemical, biological, radiological, nuclear, or high yield explosive agents (CBRNE), the governor of a U.S. state could seek the assistance of the National Guard. The National Guard, through its Weapons of Mass Destruction Civil Support Teams (WMD-CST). The WMD-CST "has the ability to identify agents, assess consequences, advise on response measures, and assist with requests for state support [100]." An incident identified as being of national impact will activate a Joint Task force of other agencies in the DoD. The U.S. Northern Command (NORTHCOM) coordinates this task force. The NORTHCOM also collaborates with the CDC to contribute information to the National Biosurveillance Integration System (NBIS)-a real-time surveillance system on animal diseases.

The U.S. Army also operates the U.S. Army Medical Research Institute of Infectious Diseases, emerging infectious disease and zoonotic laboratory that carries out countermeasure R&D and disease surveillance [34].

Despite some of the successes recorded by these domestic institutions, some gaps are identified in their activities. For example, "in a time of war, the military may have other national defense priorities and obligations that prevent fulfilling responsibilities detailed in a Memoranda of Understanding to the U.S. Department of Agriculture, Animal and Plant Health Inspection Service (USDA/APHIS) as demonstrated by the military's inability to respond to the exotic Newcastle disease epidemic (C.A., NV, TX, and AZ; 2002–2003) due to Operation Iraqi Freedom and Operation Enduring Freedom deployments [100]."

One of the criticisms of the DoD in agroterrorism is the lack of a clear definition of the military's role in responding to disease outbreak [100]. The DoD's role has been thought to be "limited or engaged as an afterthought when civilian forces became overwhelmed [100]." It is assumed that if the military is deployed earlier on at the detection of a disease outbreak, a quicker resolution would be reached [100].

Also, funds for countermeasure activities operated by the HHS are mostly allocated to public health research, "and little if any of these funds support emerging and zoonotic disease research in livestock [34]." For example, in the FY2017 funding for biodefense and emerging infectious at an agency of the HHS, priority was given to "targeted to countermeasure development for public health activities, and little if any of these funds support emerging and zoonotic disease research in livestock [34]."

As discussed earlier, vaccine supplies at the NAFMDVB fall below the capacity needed in an FMD outbreak [51]. While it is expected that the NBAF would bridge this vaccine capacity gap, "funding to operationalize and stand up a robust vaccine and diagnostic countermeasure R&D program has not been allocated for this facility, nor has the funding been committed to equip and operate the facility [34]."

There are existing domestic laws and international regulatory instruments that apply to agroterrorism intending to limit the diversion or misuse of dual-use technologies for harming human food supplies. Since 2011, the United States has enacted several laws and national policies to address agroterrorism. These include The Public Health Security and Bioterrorism Preparedness and Response Act, the Homeland Security Act 2002 (amended by the H.R. 1238: Securing our Agriculture and Food Act of 2017), Homeland Security Presidential Directive 7 on protecting critical infrastructure, and the Homeland Security Presidential Directive 9 (HSPD-9) on the Defense of United States Agriculture and Food. In international law, there are no legislations on agroterrorism. However, the Biological Weapons Convention of 1972 prohibits the development, stockpiling, and production of biological weapons, including those against plants and animals.

7 Analysis

In analyzing the risk of an agroterrorism attack in the United States, the dependent variables used in this chapter are risk of intentional FAD attack, the risk of deliberate FPD attack, and a cyber-attack risk. The dependent variables are the adversary type-State actor or terror groups, the capabilities of the terror group measured by the skill or expertise needed to carry out an attack, access to chemical, biological, radiological or nuclear materials that can be used in an agroterrorism attack, countermeasures in place to respond to an attack, and the potential impact or consequences of an attack.

The chapter adopts the Department of Homeland Security (DHS) risk assessment measures. The DHS measures risk by multiplying threats by vulnerabilities and consequences [101]. In this chapter, risk is assessed as the multiplicative effect of the threat in the year that is considered, vulnerabilities in the environment, and the consequences of an agroterrorism attack. Threat is measured by the capability and intent to attack; in other words, the probability of an attack based on the prevailing skills and expertise in the year that is considered. Vulnerabilities are defined as the likelihood that the attack results in fatalities, injuries, property damage, or other consequence. The vulnerability is determined by the vulnerabilities in each of the environment that is considered. Consequences are determined by the drivers or modifiers in each year.

8 Discussion

In 2018, agroterrorism is ranked medium risk in the border/perimeter security environment because of the increases in international trade and human and animal migration due to state failure and climate change. As humans migrate due to conflict situations in many countries, they could import foreign animal and plant diseases from terror groups interested in agriculture. This risk also increases as international trade across the borders continues. A terror group could intentionally introduce a FAD or FPD into the country by trading infected livestock or plants. It is often difficult to detect disease without advanced clinical testing in the early stages of a disease. This risk is intensified because of the extensive animal movement patterns in the U.S. It is common practice to move animals across State lines between their birth and slaughter. There is the possibility that a sick animal infects other animals, increasing the risk of disease spread. However, human migration from failing or failed States increases the mega-city environment's risk because humans can illegally import plant and animal agents and toxins. Terrorist groups would find it attractive to attack the cyberinfrastructure of food supply chains to disrupt food distribution and cause food insecurity. Also, terrorist groups could contaminate large cities' food supplies because of the substantial potential impact an attack could have.

The peer competitor is ranked medium risk because of the existence of international norms that prohibit the "development, production, acquisition, transfer, stockpiling, and use of biological and toxin weapons [102]." These international norms reduce the risk of a State actor with access to these materials and capabilities deploying these materials in the act of agroterrorism. The virtual environment is also ranked medium risk because of open communities of scientific cooperation and data sharing that encourage the development of cybersecurity guidelines. The terrorist group is ranked high risk because based on rational choice considerations, terrorists will choose agroterrorism if it will align with their goals and has a high impact at relatively low cost compared to other alternatives. The relative ease of introducing livestock of plants and the potential damage could make biological agroterrorism attractive to terrorist groups. Also, the dual-use capabilities of chemical agents can make chemical agroterrorism attractive. For example, while chemical agents such as anhydrous ammonia, chlorine, and hydrogen cyanide are useful for legitimate purposes in industrial purposes, and as such, easily available, introducing these agents in the food supply can cause enormous damage.

In 2023, the risks in all environments increase as the advancement of current gene modification technologies may increase access to these technologies, especially by terrorist groups. With the abundance of easy-to-follow guidelines on gene modification, terrorist groups could create bioweapons such as pathogens that are pesticide resistant and other zoonotic diseases. The emergence of ISIS-type insurgents, due to continued instability in different parts of the world, would also lead to failing or total State failure would increase the terrorist group environment's risk. ISIS was known for recruiting and inspiring followers through social media and encouraged to conduct homegrown attacks. At significant risk, it could be exploiting human and animal migration to neighboring States, particularly the mega-cities, making them attractive targets for an agroterrorism attack. Also, as mega-cities become inundated with a continuous influx of people, city infrastructure, particularly water and sanitary facilities, could become stretched beyond capacity and resulting in cholera and typhoid diseases. When these diseases occur, chlorine can be useful for disinfecting healthcare facilities and drinking water but could also be introduced into food sources.

A weakened international order due to difficulty in enforcing penalties against State actors and their proxies that violate international norms increases the risks in the peer competitor and virtual environments. International norms operate on the principle of good faith that requires signatories to an international norm act under the stipulations of the norm [103]. For example, signatories to international norms are expected to be honest with the reporting of their chemical, biological, and radiological stockpiles. In other words, these norms have no actual power to force individual members to comply with their rules. As more rouge States flout international laws without penalty, it could encourage more States to disregard the regulations resulting in weakening the laws.

In 2035, the risks in all six environments is expected to be high. At this time, terrorist groups would have increased their cyberwarfare capabilities in the virtual environment, operated in the virtual space, and created vaccine-resistant bioengineered animal or plant pathogens. These pathogens can cause enormous plant and animal damage and wage psychological warfare on the citizens. The increased virtualization of currency and financial transactions will also increase the risks in the virtual environment. These currencies and financial transactions will enable nefarious activities while complicating tracking and attribution of responsibility.

As violent terrorist groups seize more territories in failed and failing States with ability to operate without regard to international norms, they could develop sites for creating chemical, biological and radiological weapons that could be used in an agroterrorism attack.

Advancements in transportation capabilities would enable the rapid mobilization of humans and animal migration. These migration patterns would further heighten the risk of transmissibility in the event of an agroterrorism attack, and increases the risk in the border and perimeter security environment. Also, drug cartels could infiltrate migrant crowds to carry out retaliatory attacks on U.S. agriculture.

The internal collapse of international order due to inability to enforce penalties against State actors and their proxies that violate international norms. This collapse may also be due to external forces arising from changing environments and currently, existing standards becoming irrelevant, all acting to increase the threat in the peer competitor environment (Fig. 1).

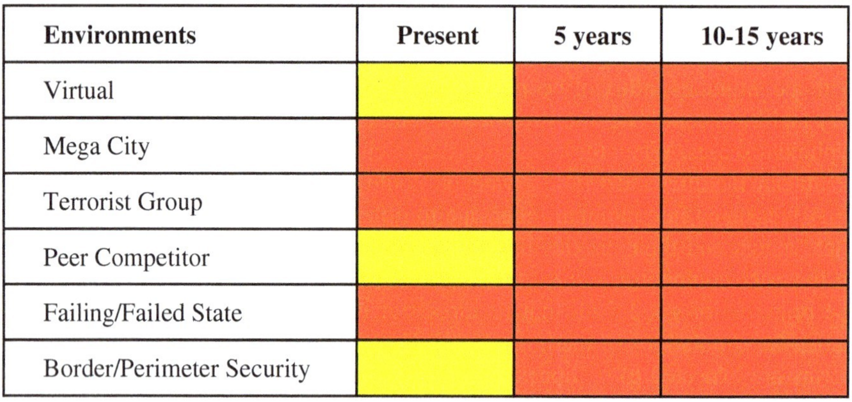

Environments	Present	5 years	10-15 years
Virtual			
Mega City			
Terrorist Group			
Peer Competitor			
Failing/Failed State			
Border/Perimeter Security			

Fig. 1 Agroterrorism threat analysis across different environments

9 Conclusion and Recommendations

Agroterrorism is a multifaceted challenge and would require a multipronged approach of national surveillance measures of zoonotic diseases. Combating agroterrorism would require a prompt deployment of human, animal, and environmental health systems to reduce an attack's impact.

This chapter finds that in agroterrorism literature, it appears that a lot more attention has been paid to the biological threat. This is also evident in the Bioterrorism Act of 2002, particularly the lists of agents compiled by the government agencies tasked with protecting the nation against attacks, namely the USDA and the CDC. Attention must be given to the other means of carrying out an agroterrorism attack such as the deployment of chemical, radiological, nuclear, explosive agents, and cyber warfare acts. Also, the Bioterrorism Act appears to focus on introducing foreign animal and plant diseases while ignoring the local development of these chemical, biological, and radiological agents. It is recommended that a broader approach to addressing agroterrorism such as including these other methods of agroterrorism are included in an amended version of the Bioterrorism Act.

Also, it is crucial to develop cybersecurity capabilities in the agricultural sector. As farmers continue to adopt precision agriculture, there is a need for rapid innovation in cybersecurity in the agricultural industry. This could be achieved through partnerships among various stakeholders such as the public sector, academia, private sector, and farmers.

It is recommended that the government decentralizes food traceability. Food traceability allows tracking food products' movement, including the ingredients used in making the products through each step of the supply chain, from production until it reaches the final consumer. As of 2020, all food traceability activities in the United States are coordinated by the U.S. Food and Drug Administration (FDA). The FDA regulations on food traceability require the food industry to keep records of each activity in the food supply chain "one-step-forward and one-step-back". However, according to the FDA, there are no harmonized systems of traceability that is followed because "these records often prove insufficient too effectively and rapidly link shipments of food through each point in the supply chain." [104]. Further complicating food traceability regulations' effectiveness is that the laws do not apply to farms and restaurants. It is recommended that the government decentralizes the information exchange process by allowing anyone to access real time information that traces the origin of the animal or food products to make the regulations more effective.

Finally, capabilities for the development, production, and deployment of countermeasures and vaccines must be ahead of disease agents' current risk profiles. Simulated drills that build the readiness of responders must be maintained to assure an adequate response. To achieve this, the government could partner with the private sector and educational research institutions on the one hand and private companies in ally nations on the other hand and speed up the completion of the National Bio- and AgroDefense Facility. However, this must be done with government oversight to prevent live viruses from getting into the hands of terrorist or other adversarial groups.

References

1. Monke J (2007) Congressional research service report for Congress, agroterrorism: threat and preparedness
2. The Industrial College of the Armed Forces (2010) Agribusiness industry. Fort McNair, Washington D.C.: National Defense University. Retrieved from https://es.ndu.edu/Portals/75/Documents/industry-study/reports/2010/icaf-is-report-agribusiness-2010.pdf
3. Schoch-Spana M, Cicero A, Adalja A, Gronvall G, Kirk Sell T, Meyer D et al (2017) Global catastrophic biological risks: Toward a working definition. Health Security 15(4):323–328. https://doi.org/10.1089/hs.2017.0038
4. Olsen D (2012) Agroterrorism: threats to America's economy and food supply. [Online] FBI: Law Enforcement Bulletin. Available at: https://leb.fbi.gov/articles/featured-articles/agroterrorism-threats-to-americas-economy-and-food-supply. Accessed 16 Jan 2018
5. Rossie G (2001) Real history, Churchill, Anthrax, and Bio-Terror. [Online] The Herald. Available at: https://www.fpp.co.uk/bookchapters/WSC/Bwar2.html. Accessed 16 Jan 2018
6. Cameron G, Pate J (2001) Covert biological weapons attacks against agricultural targets: assessing the impact the impact against U.S. Agriculture. BCSIA Discussion Paper 2001-9, ESDP Discussion Paper ESDP-2001-05, John F. Kennedy School of Government, Harvard University, August 2001
7. Agroterrorism: the threat to America's breadbasket: hearing before the Committee on Governmental Affairs United States Senate, 108th Cong. 1 (2003) (Opening Statement of Senator Collins)
8. United States Department of Agriculture (2017) Agroterrorism prevention, detection, and response, audit report 61701-0001-21. Washington D.C.: United States Department of Agriculture
9. Altieri M, Nicholls C (2020) Agroecology and the emergence of a post COVID-19 agriculture. Agric Hum Values 37(3):525–526
10. Kolodinsky J, Sitaker M, Chase L, Smith D, Wang W (2020) Food systems disruptions. J Agric Food Syst Community Dev 9(3):1–4
11. American Agriculture and Our National Security: Hearings before the Committee on Agriculture, House of Representatives, 114th Cong. 10 (2015) (Testimony of Tammy

Beckham) Homeland Security Presidential Directive 7: Critical Infrastructure Identification, Prioritization, and Protection
12. ERS USDA., Ag and Food Sectors and the Economy. (2017) ERS. Retrieved 23 April 2018, from https://www.ers.usda.gov/data-products/ag-and-food-statistics-charting-the-essentials/ag-and-food-sectors-and-the-economy/
13. World development indicators. The World Bank, Washington, DC
14. Rothschild E (1976) Food politics. Foreign Affairs 54(2):285–307. https://doi.org/10.2307/20039573
15. Central Intelligence Agency, Directorate of Intelligence: Office of Political Research (1974) Potential of trends in world population, food production and climate (OPR 401). Available at https://documents.theblackvault.com/documents/environment/potentialtrends.pdf. Accessed 26 Mar 2018
16. Burbach R, Flynn P (1975) NACLA's Latin America and empire report 9(7):12–17. https://doi.org/10.1080/10714839.1975.11724007
17. Waltz K (2010) Theory of international politics. Waveland Press, Long Grove, Ill
18. JJ Mearsheimer (2006) Conversations in international relations: interview with (Part II). Int Relat 20(2):231–243. https://doi.org/10.1177/0047117806063851
19. Price R (1997) The chemical weapons taboo. Cornell University Press, Ithaca
20. Parker HS (2002) Agricultural bioterrorism: a federal strategy to meet the threat. National Defense University, Washington DC. Institute for National Strategic Studies
21. Wheelis M, Casagrande R, Madden LV (2002) Biological attack on agriculture: low-tech, high-impact bioterrorism: because bioterrorist attack requires relatively little specialized expertise and technology, it is a serious threat to U.S. agriculture and can have very large economic repercussions. AIBS Bull 52(7):569–576
22. Wheelis M, Casagrande R, Madden LV (2002) Biological attack on agriculture: low-tech, high-impact bioterrorism: because bioterrorist attack requires relatively little specialized expertise and technology, it is a serious threat to U.S. agriculture and can have very large economic repercussions. AIBS Bull. Biosci 52(7):569–576. https://doi.org/10.1641/0006-3568(2002)052
23. Stone R (2000) Bioterrorism: experts call fungus threat poppycock. Science 290(5490):246a–2246. https://doi.org/10.1126/science.290.5490.246a
24. Schmitt GR (2007) Agroterrorism—why we're not ready: a look at the role of law enforcement. NIJ J 257:36–39
25. International Standards Organization (2005) General requirements for the competence of testing and calibration laboratories. Retrieved from 23 Apr 2018. https://www.iso.org/standard/39883.html
26. Dion ML, Russler C (2008) Eradication efforts, the state, displacement and poverty: explaining coca cultivation in Colombia during plan Colombia. J Latin Am Stud 40(3):399–421
27. United States Department of Agriculture Food Safety and Inspection Service (2015) Disposition/food safety: reportable and foreign animal diseases. United States Department of Agriculture Food Safety and Inspection Service, Washington, DC
28. Wheelis M, Casagrande R, Madden L (2002) Biological attack on agriculture: low-tech High-Impact bioterrorism. Bioscience 52(7):569. https://doi.org/10.1641/0006-3568(2002)052[0569:baoalt]2.0.co;2
29. Franz DR (1999) Foreign animal disease agents as weapons in biological warfare. Ann N Y Acad Sci 894(1):100–104
30. Whitby S, Rogers P (1997) Anti-crop biological warfare-implications of the Iraqi and U.S. programs. Defense Anal 13(3):303–317
31. Animal and Plant Health Inspection Service, U.S. Department of Agriculture (2016) Asian long horned beetle (*Anoplophora glabripennis*) USDA APHIS Factsheet, February 2016
32. Public Health Security and Bioterrorism Preparedness and Response Act of 2002
33. Kosal M, Anderson D (2004) An unaddressed issue of agricultural terrorism: a case study on feed security. J Anim Sci 82(11):3394–3400. https://doi.org/10.2527/2004.82113394x

34. Beckham T, Brake D, Fine J (2018) Strengthening one health through investments in agricultural preparedness. Health Secur 16(2). https://doi.org/10.1089/hs.2017.0069
35. O'Brien D, Scudamore J, Charlier J, Delavergne M (2016) DISCONTOOLS: a database to identify research gaps on vaccines, pharmaceuticals and diagnostics for the control of infectious diseases of animals. BMC Vet Res 13:1. https://doi.org/10.1186/s12917-016-0931-1
36. Cone T (2018) U.S. food supply threatened: Foreign insects, diseases got into U.S. post 9/11. msnbc.com. Retrieved from 21 Apr 2018. https://tinyurl.com/y7audjum
37. USDA APHIS, Select Agent and Toxin List (2015) USDA. Retrieved from 31 Mar 2018. https://tinyurl.com/y8mzgytp
38. Pimentel D, Zuniga R, Morrison D (2005) Update on the environmental and economic costs associated with alien-invasive species in the United States. Ecol Econ 52(3):273–288. https://doi.org/10.1016/j.ecolecon.2004.10.002
39. Roth J, Spickler A (2014). FMD vaccine surge capacity for emergency use in the United States. Center for Food Security and Public Health at Iowa State University, Ames. Retrieved from https://www.cfsph.iastate.edu/pdf/fmd-vaccine-surge-capacity-for-emergency-use-in-the-US
40. Foot and Mouth Disease Preparedness: Hearings before the Committee on Agriculture Subcommittee on Livestock and Foreign Agriculture, House of Representatives, 114th Cong. 32 (2016) (Testimony of Dave Sjeklocha)
41. Sobrino F, Domingo E (2001) Foot-and-mouth disease in Europe: FMD is economically the most important disease of farm animals. Its re-emergence in Europe is likely to have consequences beyond severe livestock production and trade alterations. EMBO Reports 2(6):459–461. https://doi.org/10.1093/embo-reports/kve122
42. Segarra A, Rawson J (2001) Foot and mouth disease: a threat to U.S. Agriculture. Washington D.C.: Library of Congress, Congressional Research Service
43. Wright A (2012) Stemming the flow: the red army anti-desertion campaign in Soviet Karelia (1919). Revol Russia 25(2):141–162. https://doi.org/10.1080/09546545.2012.729859
44. Zilinskas R (2016) The Soviet biological weapons program and its legacy in today's Russia. Center for the Study of Weapons of Mass Destruction, Washington, DC. Retrieved from https://wmdcenter.ndu.edu/Portals/68/Documents/occasional/cswmd/CSWMD_OccasionalPaper-11.pdf?ver=2016-07-18-144946-743
45. Alibek K, Handelman S (2000) Biohazard. Delta Trade Paperbacks, New York, NY
46. Alibek K (1999) The Soviet Union's anti-agricultural biological weapons. Ann N Y Acad Sci 894(1):18–19
47. U.S. General Accounting Office (2000) Effort to reduce former Soviet threat offers benefits, poses new risks. U.S. General Accounting Office, National Security and International Affairs Division, Washington, DC April 28
48. Cook MS, Woolf AF (2002, April) Preventing proliferation of biological weapons: U.S. assistance to the former Soviet states. Library of Congress Washington DC Congressional Research Service
49. Government Accountability Office (2008) High-containment biosafety laboratories: DHS lacks evidence to conclude that foot-and-mouth disease research can be done safely on the U.S. Mainland. Washington D.C.: Government Accountability Office. Retrieved from https://www.gpo.gov/fdsys/pkg/GAOREPORTS-GAO-08-821T/html/GAOREPORTS-GAO-08-821T.htm
50. Grubman MJ, Baxt B (2004) Foot-and-mouth disease. Clin Microbiol Rev 17(2):465–493. https://doi.org/10.1128/CMR.17.2.465-493.2004
51. Roth JA, Spickler AR (2014) FMD vaccine surge capacity for emergency use in the United States.
52. Artz J, White WR, Thomsen BV, Brown C (2010) Agricultural diseases on the move early in the third millennium. Vet Pathol 47(1):15–27
53. American Agriculture and Our National Security: Hearings before the Committee on Agriculture, House of Representatives, 114th Cong. 10 (2015) (Testimony of Tammy Beckham)

54. Segarra AE, Rawson JM (2001, April) Foot and mouth disease: a threat to U.S. agriculture. In Congressional research service report for Congress, pp 1–6
55. Arzt J, White WR, Thomsen BV, Brown CC (2010) Agricultural diseases on the move early in the third millennium. Vet Pathol 47(1):15–27
56. Rock DL (2017) Challenges for African swine fever vaccine development— "… perhaps the end of the beginning." Vet Microbiol 206:52–58
57. The virus is also reported in cats and related animals such as leopards and tigers, in ferrets and stone martens, and in dogs and pigs. Avian Flu (2018) FAO. Retrieved 30 March 2018, from https://www.fao.org/avianflu/en/background.html
58. Koch A, Zimmerman B (2007) Is the avian influenza virus a suitable agent for a biological weapon? Nuclear threat initiative. Retrieved from 30 Mar 2018. https://www.nti.org/analysis/articles/avian-virus-biological-weapon/
59. Webster RG, Govorkova EA (2006) H5N1 influenza—continuing evolution and spread. N Engl J Med 355(21):2174–2177
60. Kilpatrick AM, Chmura AA, Gibbons DW, Fleischer RC, Marra PP, Daszak P (2006) Predicting the global spread of H5N1 avian influenza. Proc Natl Acad Sci USA 103(51):19368–19373. https://doi.org/10.1073/pnas.0609227103
61. Avian Flu (2018) FAO. Retrieved from 30 Mar 2018. https://www.fao.org/avianflu/en/backgr ound.html
62. Hien TT et al (2004) Avian influenza a (H5N1) in 10 patients in Vietnam. N Engl J Med 350(12):1179–1188
63. FAO H7N9 situation update - Avian Influenza A(H7N9) virus - FAO Emergency Prevention System for Animal Health (EMPRES-AH) (2018) FAO.org. Retrieved from 30 Mar 2018. https://www.fao.org/ag/againfo/programmes/en/empres/H7N9/Situation_update.html
64. U.S. Government Accountability Office (GAO) (2017) AVIAN INFLUENZA: USDA has taken actions to reduce risks but needs a plan to evaluate its efforts. Washington D.C.: U.S. Government Accountability Office (GAO) Retrieved from https://www.gao.gov/assets/690/684086.pdf
65. H5 Viruses in the United States | Avian Influenza (Flu) (2017) CDC. Retrieved from 30 Mar 2018. https://www.cdc.gov/flu/avianflu/h5/index.htm
66. New York City Health, Health Department Investigation of H7N2 Influenza in Shelter Cats Confirms Risk to Humans is Low. (2016). NYC Health. Retrieved from 30 Mar 2018. https://www1.nyc.gov/site/doh/about/press/pr2016/pr107-16.page
67. Marinova-Petkova A, Laplante J, Jang Y, Lynch B, Zanders N, Rodriguez M, Jones J, Thor S, Hodges E, De La Cruz JA, Belser J (2017) Avian Influenza A (H7N2) virus in human exposed to sick cats, New York, USA, 2016. Emerg Infect Diseases 23(12):2046
68. United States Department of Agriculture Animal and Plant Health Inspection Service (2017) USDA confirms highly Pathogenic H7 Avian Influenza in a Commercial Flock in Lincoln County, Tennessee. Retrieved from https://www.aphis.usda.gov/aphis/newsroom/news/sa_by_date/sa-2017/hpai-tn
69. Food and Agriculture Organization of the United Nations. (2016) H5N8 highly pathogenic avian influenza (HPAI) of clade 2.3.4.4 detected through surveillance of wild migratory birds in the Tyva Republic, the Russian Federation – potential for international spread. FAO, Rome. Retrieved from https://www.fao.org/3/a-i6113e.pdf
70. NTI, North Korea (2017) Nti.org. Retrieved 30 March 2018, from https://www.nti.org/learn/countries/north-korea/biological/
71. Oxbridge Biotech, Roundtable Review: Colours of Biotechnology: Mutant flu – A Potential Weapon for Bioterrorism? (2014) Oxbridgebiotech.com. Retrieved from 30 Mar 2018. https://oxbridgebiotech.com/review/colours-of-biotechnology-mutant-flu-8211-a-potential-weapon-for-bioterrorism
72. Fouchier RAM et al (2013) Gain-of-function experiments on H7N9. Nature 500:150
73. Enserink M (2011) Grudgingly, virologists agree to redact details in sensitive flu papers. Science. Retrieved from 30 Mar 2018. https://www.sciencemag.org/news/2011/12/grudgingly-virologists-agree-redact-details-sensitive-flu-papers

74. Imperiale MJ, Casadevall A (2015) A new synthesis for dual use research of concern. PLoS Med 12(4):e1001813. https://doi.org/10.1371/journal.pmed.1001813
75. Sun L (2017) With bird flu surging, U.S. needs to do more to prevent a possible pandemic, GAO says. Washington Post. Retrieved from 30 March 2018. https://www.washingtonpost.com/news/to-your-health/wp/2017/05/11/with-bird-flu-surging-u-s-needs-to-do-more-to-prevent-possible-pandemic-gao-says/?utm_term=.c138f5ab6dd8
76. U.S. Government Accountability Office (2017) AVIAN INFLUENZA: USDA has taken actions to reduce risks but needs a plan to evaluate its efforts. Washington D.C.: U.S. Government Accountability Office. Retrieved from https://www.gao.gov/assets/690/684086.pdf
77. Duraffour S, Meyer H, Andrei G, Snoeck R (2011) Camelpox virus. Antiviral Res 92(2):167–186. https://doi.org/10.1016/j.antiviral.2011.09.003
78. Balamurugan V, Venkatesan G, Bhanuprakash V, Singh RK (2013) Camelpox, an emerging orthopox viral disease. Indian J Virol 24(3):295–305. https://doi.org/10.1007/s13337-013-0145-0
79. Duelfer C (2004) Comprehensive report of the special advisor to the DCI on Iraq's WMD. Central Intelligence Agency
80. Powell C (2003) Remarks to the United Nations Security Council. Presentation, U.N. Security Council, New York
81. NTI (2017) Iraq. Retrieved from 31 Mar 2018. https://www.nti.org/learn/countries/iraq/biological/
82. Millett P (2006) Anti-animal biological weapons programs. In Wheelis M, Rózsa L, Dando M (eds) Deadly cultures: biological weapons since 1945. Harvard University Press, Cambridge, pp 224–235
83. Roeder P, Mariner J, Kock R (2013) Rinderpest: the veterinary perspective on eradication. Philos Trans R Soc B: Biol Sci 368(1623):20120139. https://doi.org/10.1098/rstb.2012.0139
84. FAO (201) Post-rinderpest era but not "case closed". Food and Agriculture Organization of the United Nations. Retrieved from 31 Mar 2018. https://www.fao.org/in-action/post-rinderpest-era-but-not-case-closed/en/
85. Sonka S (2003, January) Forces driving the industrialization of agriculture: implications for the grain industry in the United States. In Presentation at USDA/ERS symposium on product differentiation and market segmentation in grains and oilseeds: implications for an industry in transition, pp 27–28
86. Food and Drug Administration (FDA), United States Department of Agriculture (USDA), and Department of Homeland Security (DHS) (2015) Food and agriculture sector-specific plan. Retrieved from https://www.fda.gov/downloads/Food/FoodDefense/FoodDefensePrograms/UCM483872.pdf
87. Weiss J (2016) Industrial Control Systems (ICS) cyber events—issues and concerns. In Food industry cybersecurity summit. Food Protection and Defense Institute, Washington, DC. Retrieved from https://foodprotection.umn.edu/sites/default/files/food_industry_cybersecurity_summit_meeting_report.pdf
88. Industrial Control Systems (ICS) Cyber Events—Issues and Concerns. In Food industry cybersecurity summit. Food Protection and Defense Institute, Washington, DC. Retrieved from https://foodprotection.umn.edu/sites/default/files/food_industry_cybersecurity_summit_meeting_report.pdf
89. Homeland Security Newswire (2015) Agriculture, farming, cyber-attacks. Homelandsecuritynewswire.com. Retrieved from 22 April 2018. https://www.homelandsecuritynewswire.com/dr20150220-u-s-farming-sector-increasingly-vulnerable-to-cyberattacks
90. Federal Bureau of Investigation and the U.S. Department of Agriculture (2016) Smart farming may increase cyber targeting against U.S. Food and Agriculture Sector. Retrieved from https://info.publicintelligence.net/FBI-SmartFarmHacking.pdf
91. Pisani B (2017) Cybersecurity stocks rally as global hackings start to impact corporate bottom lines. CNBC. Retrieved from 22 Apr 2018. https://www.cnbc.com/2017/07/07/cybersecurity-stocks-rally-on-mondelez-hacking.html

92. Markets/Food and Agriculture (2018) Fortalice. Retrieved from 21 Apr 2018. https://fortalicesolutions.com/markets/food-agriculture-cyber-security
93. Andrus JK, Aguilera X, Oliva O, Aldighieri S (2010) Global health security and the International Health Regulations. BMC Public Health 10(Suppl 1):S2. https://doi.org/10.1186/1471-2458-10-S1-S2
94. GLEWS—The Global Early Warning System. (2018) Glews.net. Retrieved from 24 Apr 2018. https://www.glews.net
95. Ankers P, Harris P (2018) Towards a safer world animal health and biosecurity. Retrieved from https://www.fao.org/fileadmin/templates/cpesap/C-RESAP_Info_package/Links/Module_5/tasw-animal_health_and_biosecurity_0.pdf
96. USDA Updates Select Agent Regulations. (2017) USDA APHIS. Retrieved from 22 Apr 2018. https://www.aphis.usda.gov/aphis/newsroom/stakeholder-info/sa_by_date/sa-2017/sa-01/select-agent-regulations
97. H.R. 1238: Securing our Agriculture and Food Act
98. Peterson ME (2002) Agroterrorism and foot-and-mouth disease: is the United States Prepared? USAF Counterproliferation Center.
99. "The Economy Act of 1932, as amended (31 USC 1535), authorizes an agency to place orders for goods and services with another government agency when the head of the ordering agency determines that it is in the best interest of the government and decides ordered goods or services cannot be provided as conveniently or cheaply by contract with commercial enterprise."
100. Force UA, Center C (2006) Agroterrorist attack: DoD roles and responsibilities.
101. of National Research Council (2010) Review of the Department of Homeland Security's Approach to Risk Analysis. The National Academies Press, Washington, DC. https://doi.org/10.17226/12972
102. Jenkins B (2017) The biological weapons convention at a crossroad. Brookings. Retrieved from 31 Mar 2018. https://www.brookings.edu/blog/order-from-chaos/2017/09/06/the-biological-weapons-convention-at-a-crossroad/
103. D'Amato A (1995) Good faith. Encycl Public Int Law 2:599–601
104. U.S. Food and Drug Administration (2020) Tracking and Tracing of Food. [Online] Available at: https://www.fda.gov/food/new-era-smarter-food-safety/tracking-and-tracing-food. Accessed 19 Nov 2020

CPSIA information can be obtained
at www.ICGtesting.com
Printed in the USA
LVHW061256120821
695142LV00002BA/14

9 783030 736545